RECONSTRUCTING UNDERGRADUATE EDUCATION

Using Learning Science to Design Effective Courses

RECONSTRUCTING UNDERGRADUATE EDUCATION

Using Learning Science to Design Effective Courses

Robert B. Innes
Peabody College of Vanderbilt University

LEA LAWRENCE ERLBAUM ASSOCIATES, PUBLISHERS
2004   Mahwah, New Jersey   London

Lawrence Erlbaum Associates, Inc., Publishers
10 Industrial Avenue
Mahwah, New Jersey 07430

Cover design by Kathryn Houghtaling Lacey

Library of Congress Cataloging-in-Publication Data

Innes, Robert B.
  Reconstructing undergraduate education : using learning science to design
effective courses / Robert B. Innes.
      p. cm.
  Includes bibliographical references and indexes.
  ISBN 0-8058-4841-X
  1. Education, Higher—Philosophy. 2. College teaching. I. Title.

LB2324.I55   2004
378.1'2—dc22   2004043330
                                                         CIP

Books published by Lawrence Erlbaum Associates are printed on acid-free paper,
and their bindings are chosen for strength and durability.

Printed in the United States of America
10 9 8 7 6 5 4 3 2 1

Contents

Preface

I am convinced that learning science has produced enough theoretical analysis, research support, and models for effective teaching to guide the reconstruction of undergraduate education. For the most part, however, these new perspectives have not affected teaching practices in higher education. This book is designed to introduce professors and administrators in higher education to the philosophical, theoretical, and research support for a call to use a constructivist perspective on learning to guide the reconstruction of undergraduate education.

My research for this book began with an effort to review the body of theory and research in learning science. I was beginning to redesign the course that I would eventually use as a case study for this book, and I was developing a set of teaching principles to share in workshops on university teaching. I found that the existing literature was targeted at K–12 educators and offered little direct guidance to professors in colleges and universities. There were few sources that systematically linked educational philosophy and learning theories to their implications for teaching practice. The literature on teaching practices did not connect teaching methods to their philosophical and theoretical roots. I did find a number of excellent philosophical and theoretical articles and books, but most of these sources were focused on exploring specific theoretical issues surrounding debates between the theoretical positions within constructivism. I did not find a single source that was designed for professors interested in using constructivist theory and learning science to develop a model for teaching their courses.

I am the kind of person who is not comfortable taking advice about how to do something without knowing *why* the practice is recommended. A friend who teaches statistics tells his students that statistics is not about memorizing formulas. If students really understand the principles being taught, they should be able to make up their own formulas. At the least, they should be able to recognize answers that do not make sense. In the area of teaching, I have a personal need to work through the process of establishing a well-aligned philosophical and theoretical perspective that provides a model for how learning might really be acquired and used. Without this foundation, I do not have the tools to make up my own formulas for teaching my courses. This book is designed for college and university professors who share my need to have clear answers to "why" questions about teaching and learning.

I admit that many participants in workshops on university teaching have been frustrated by my attempts to get them to explore philosophy and theory as well as "tips for teaching." I try to convince my colleagues that we should not accept a standard in our teaching that we would never accept in our scholarly work. Although I believe that theory must be grounded in successful practice, I am also committed to the principle that effective practice must be grounded in a well-articulated and well-aligned continuum of philosophy, theory, and research support. In our own disciplines, we push our students at every turn to answer "why" questions that demonstrate their understanding of the phenomena they are studying. We should apply the same standard to our own teaching.

OVERVIEW

This book summarizes the sources that I found most useful for developing my own set of teaching principles and course development process. It makes an argument for a particular perspective on learning, transactional constructivism, which is consistent with the philosophy of John Dewey and supported by current theory and research in learning science. Transactional constructivism (the "combined" approach) builds on the strengths of the two competing views of constructivism: psychological constructivism and the sociocultural perspective.

I begin the book with a short overview of the philosophical and theoretical underpinnings of the teaching model. A teaching model and a course development process are presented in the first chapter and then restated at the end of the book. A case study built around a course entitled "Understanding Organizations" is also introduced in chapter 1. This case study is used throughout the book as a practical example of how the philosophy and theories presented can be used to guide the development of a university course.

Like most constructivists, I acknowledge a debt to John Dewey for providing the philosophical foundation for this perspective. Chapter 2 presents a summary of Dewey's educational philosophy and connects Dewey's work to current theory and research in learning science. A chapter that examines psychological constructivism, one of the basic positions within the range of learning theories that take a constructivist perspective, follows the chapter on Dewey. Chapter 4 offers the next installment of the case study that uses the "Understanding Organizations" course to provide a concrete example of a course that is designed and taught from this perspective. Chapters 5 and 6 review two other basic constructivist perspectives—the sociocultural perspective and the transactional constructivist or combined perspective. Chapter 7 explores a specific issue that is critical to the success of models derived from a transactional constructivist perspective on learning: the quality of dialogue and disciplinary discourse in the classroom. Chapter 8 returns to the case study to explore specific issues related to the quality of classroom dialogue and its relationship to learning. The final chapter shifts the focus of the book to explore the broader issues related to education reform in higher education.

Although the realities of space limitations mean that many important authors are barely mentioned, I have done my best to focus on the theorists who are most prominently cited in the literature. This will help readers who want to participate in further conversations about teaching and learning. Many of the conversations that take place in colleges and universities assume a familiarity with the basic theorists. It is difficult to participate in these conversations without some familiarity with the basic positions of key theorists. I also slighted topics that are readily available elsewhere (e.g., the vast body of research on cognition and cognitive development, theorists in higher education such as Chickering, King and Kitchener, Baxter-Magolda). The book says very little about technology, although the use of technology has been important in my teaching. Part of this relates to issues of space and focus, but it also reflects my opinion that technology should always function in service of instructional design and should never lead it. Finally, I did not attempt to review the body of research on the brain that provides strong support for a constructivist view of learning.

ACKNOWLEDGMENTS

Much of my career has focused on the development of graduate and undergraduate programs at research universities. Although my academic appointments have been in Psychology and Human and Organizational Development, I have benefited from dialogue with education faculty from a number of departments at Peabody College of Vanderbilt University. I am especially indebted to the intellectual leadership that John Bransford, Jim Pellegrino, and Paul Cobb have provided for the college over the years. Although I could thank almost everyone at Peabody, I am especially indebted to Kevin Leander, Kay McClain, Michael McLendon, and Chris Iddings for offering ideas and assistance at key times when I was writing this book. I would also like to thank Terry Deal, the professor who developed the "Understanding Organizations" course and co-author of the textbook. He is a gifted teacher and valued friend. In my own teaching, I have benefited from participating on several teaching teams in courses in the Human and Organizational Development Program. I am especially grateful to my frequent teammates, Pat Arnold and Brian Griffith, who have served as an example and inspiration for my teaching. In addition, I would like to thank Joe Cunningham, the current chair of my department, who provides a supportive environment for research and teaching for our entire faculty.

Like many of you, but probably more than most, I feel fortunate to have been part of both my family of origin and the extended family that has evolved through marriage, committed relationships, and birth. My mother and father, who are both very interesting and very nice, can take credit for creating a large group of very interesting and very nice people who are a natural learning community. Most are committed "book people," and all are knowledgeable and interesting to talk to. With apologies to an equally interesting group of nieces and nephews (and readers who are bored by academy awards speeches), thanks for a lifetime of good conversations to Kathy and Roger, Kathy and Andy, Nancy and Bob, Chris and Abby, Tim and Christine, Laura and David, and Mel and Judy. Because I grew up in a learning community, it was natural for me to spend my professional career seeking them out and trying to create them for my students.

I would also like to thank my wife, Sharon, who I have always loved and always will. She is my closest friend and colleague and the "queen of the book people." She has supported me through my life and the process of writing this book. Finally, I would like to thank my children and their life partners: Michael and Lizzy and Robert and Michael—and most of all, my grandson, Owen.

Introduction

Constructivism is often presented as if it represents a single theory with clear implications for reforming teaching practice. There are, however, important differences among the various versions of constructivism. In addition, the application of learning theory to teaching practice is never straightforward. In preparing this book, I was faced with the task of pulling together a field that is still deeply divided about many important issues. I argue that a perspective is emerging that draws from the range of competing constructivist theories that can serve as a solid foundation for reforming undergraduate education.

Although I present an overarching case that includes specific teaching methods, I want to make it clear that constructivist perspectives on learning do not provide prescriptions for teaching practice or reject any particular method of instruction. Within the constructivist framework, the relationship between theory and practice is always transactional. For example, although lecturing and memorization, the frequent targets of strident criticism from constructivists, are greatly overused in higher education, it is a misuse of the theory to say that they should *never* be used. For example, it may be a waste of time to memorize isolated facts for a test, but it is not a waste of time to memorize a poem. Memorizing a poem is part of the process of understanding it.

It is not always what the professor does, but *when and how* he or she does it that distinguishes effective from ineffective methods. Constructivism is a lens for viewing learning that has profound implications for teaching. It is a learner-centered perspective. Whether learning is active or passive depends more on the attitude of the learner than the type of activity in which he or she is engaged. As scholars, our thirst for knowledge is based on its usefulness for our teaching, our research and scholarly work, and for the project of building our own lives. As teachers, we are constantly challenged to create what Schwartz and Bransford (1998) called "a time for telling" for our students. We are creating learning environments where students are motivated to listen to us, to each other, and through reading, to the words of great thinkers of the past and present because we have helped them connect these sources of knowledge to problems that are personally meaningful to them.

TERMINOLOGY

Although constructivist approaches to education date back at least to John Dewey and the progressive education movement, the current theories are relatively new. The literature that frames the debate between various constructivist perspectives frequently creates new vocabulary and changes the vocabulary it uses to describe different views of constructivism. The different perspectives within constructivism are often confused with each other and with other philosophical and theoretical positions that hold similar views on specific questions (e.g., postmodern and critical theory). This is important because the different positions within constructivism can have different implications for educational practice. It is not surprising that constructivism is widely misunderstood.

All the versions of constructivism agree that knowledge is actively constructed by people, either as individuals or in groups, rather than being *received* from a natural or supernatural source (or even a professor; Phillips, 1995). Beyond this, definitions of constructivism vary according to the various questions being debated within the constructivist movement. The most basic arena for debate is represented by a continuum from viewing learning as an act of individual construction to seeing learning as socially constructed. This continuum is anchored on one end by a position known as radical or psychological constructivism, which describes the construction of knowledge as a process that takes place in the mind of the individual. The other end of the continuum is occupied by a position known as social constructionism or the sociocultural position that sees "mind" as almost totally embedded in the social practices of the culture. Many definitions of constructivism use the vocabulary of internal mental operations (e.g., "how our minds create knowledge," "knowledge structures," "mental models" [Oliver, 2000, p. 5], "deeper conceptual understanding" [Fosnot, 1996, p. 30]). Yet even authors who use words that sound like they believe knowledge is constructed "in the head" have a range of views about how knowledge gets in the head. Many theorists extend the process of knowledge construction beyond the individual to the arena of social action.

Although this book explores these theories in detail, I would like to begin by establishing some basic guidelines for the terms I use to describe the different constructivist positions.

When I speak generally of the range of positions associated with these approaches, I use the term *constructivism*. This can be confusing because many authors use the term constructivism to indicate radical or psychological constructivism. If I want to emphasize that I am referring to the range of constructivist positions, I use the designation *constructivist and sociocultural* positions. If I refer specifically to theories that lean strongly in the direction of describing knowledge construction as occurring in an individual mind, I use the term *psychological constructivism*. If I refer to theories that lean strongly toward describing knowledge as socially constructed, I use the term *sociocultural*.

For the middle-of-the-road position occupied by John Dewey and several other learning scientists who combine psychological constructivist and the sociocultural perspectives, I use the terms *combined position* or *transactional constructivism*. Using the word *transactional* connects to Dewey's philosophical position (i.e., transactional realism). The combined position is a designation suggested by Paul Cobb, a leading theorist in mathematics education. Cobb and Yackel (1996) compared the psychological constructivist and social constructionist theories and concluded that both approaches could provide valuable insights about the learning process. They proposed what they called the emergent or combined perspective that utilizes the insights of both the psychological constructivist and sociocultural perspectives. Cobb's combined position is similar to Dewey's transactional constructivism in that it is nondualistic. It places the individual's constructive activities in a transactional relationship with the environment of social practices and the cultural context.

The placement of individual theories within these categories is problematic. My placement of theorists in the chapters that focus on different perspectives is more opportunistic than systematic. For example, I introduce Schank's "goal-based scenarios" and Bransford's "anchored instruction and situated cognition" in the chapter on psychological constructivist approaches, although both of these approaches address the cognitive and social aspects of learning. My decision to introduce them in the chapter on psychological constructivism gave me an opportunity to introduce the cognitive elements of these programs before I returned to the case study in the next chapter. Although Vygotsky is often cited as the "father of sociocultural perspectives," I categorize Vygotsky and most of the situated cognitive theorists as combined perspectives. However, I placed Lave and Wenger with the socioculturalists, even though they can be considered the "mothers of the situated cognitive perspective." I apologize to readers who are sensitive to the deeper implications of these labels.

I considered using the term *idea-focused social constructivism* or *idea-focused experiential education* to refer to the transactional or combined position, but the terms seemed too cumbersome. Using the term idea-focused social constructivism does have several advantages. The designation *idea-focused* is based on ideas presented by Prawat (1995) and Wong, Pugh, and the Dewey Ideas Group at Michigan State (2001). Throughout this book, I make a case that, because transactional constructivism combines the strongest features of the psychological constructivist and sociocultural positions, it provides the strongest foundation for reforming undergraduate education. I use the terms *combined* and *transactional* interchangeably. Although the word *combined* does a disservice to the reflexive/dynamic nature of the relationship between ideas and action in transactional constructivism, it is less cumbersome.

Regardless of the label used to designate the combined/transactional position, there are several reasons that it is important to maintain a focus on ideas. Most important, it makes it clear that I am advocating for a form of constructivism that focuses on providing students with the deep principles that are the foundation for productive disciplinary discourse. It also infers that I am rejecting forms of constructivism that are exclusively student centered. Progressive education was often referred to as experiential education. Because Dewey emphasized the importance of beginning with the students' concrete experience, some progressive educators misinterpreted this to mean that education should focus on experience rather than ideas and concepts. I believe it is especially important to disassociate transactional constructivism from these approaches. I share Prawat's (1995) concern that if we follow a liberal interpretation of Dewey's theory, "constructivist practice, . . . [modern constructivism] . . . is likely to go the way of other child-centered reforms" (p. 14) of the 1930s and 1960s. Students do not flourish if they are just left alone and "allowed to grow." Dewey (1934/1980) placed great importance on the word *idea*. He used the term *idea* to label the larger questions that motivate students to learn. Using the word *idea* indicates that I think it is important to distinguish deep principles from the isolated factual knowledge and concepts that become the focus of many traditional courses. In addition, focusing on developing ideas helps keep education focused on its primary objective, producing useful knowledge, rather than on the methods used to achieve that objective.

Because Dewey rejected the idea that students could really "know" things that they had no active role in constructing, it was and still is easy for some critics to jump from this basic assertion to the conclusion that Dewey was saying that students should disregard the wealth of knowledge that has been developed by scientists and scholars and create their own truth. Contrary to what his critics and some of his misguided supporters might think, Dewey did not reject "the wisdom of the ages" or the existing body of scientific knowledge in favor of whatever truth students construct from their own experience. Although Dewey believed that learning should *start* with the students' experience, he did not think it should *end* there. Dewey's approach to teaching asks the professor to start with the students' present knowledge and experience and then guide them through an active inquiry process that includes correcting misconceptions and connecting this knowledge to the existing body of knowledge.

This brief introduction to key terms does not begin to address the complex issues involved in defining the basic terms related to constructivism. Adopting a constructivist approach changes the definitions of all the major terms associated with teaching and learning. For example, the classic definition of learning as permanent behavior change is not acceptable to constructivists. The situation is further complicated by the fact that the three primary perspectives within constructivism each has a different definition of learning. Psychological constructivists tend to see learning in terms of increasingly efficient organization of cognitive structures. Efficient cognitive organization is reflected in flexible, adaptive, and expert behavior. Socioculturalists see learning as increasingly successful participation in a community of practice and the development of an identity as a member of a community of practice. Those holding a situated cognitive view (a combined position) describe learning as becoming attuned to the constraints and affordances present in an activity structure and becoming centrally involved in a community of practice (Greeno & the Middle School Mathematics Through Applications Project Group, 1998). The differences in the way these perspectives define learning are also reflected in their definitions of associated terms like *meaning, transfer, identity*, and *intelligence*. These definitions emerge and are clarified as these perspectives are introduced and discussed in future chapters.

Chapter 1

Overview of Constructivism

Constructivist views of learning include a range of theories that share the general perspective that knowledge is *constructed by* learners rather than *transmitted to* learners. Most of these theories trace their philosophical roots to John Dewey. This book explores the implications of constructivism and research in learning science for undergraduate education. It presents a model for undergraduate education, grounded in the educational philosophy of John Dewey and informed by theory and research in learning science.

The learning science revolution has had a broad impact on curriculum design and classroom teaching practices in primary and secondary education around the world. With notable exceptions, however, undergraduate education, especially at research universities in the United States, has been the least affected (Berger, 2002; Gardiner, 1994, 2000; Halpern & Hakel, 2003; National Center for Postsecondary Improvement, 2002; Stark & Lattuca, 1997). Yet there is evidence of growing interest in the implications of these theories for university teaching (Krockover, Shepardson, Eichinger, Nakhleh, & Adams, 2002; Marchese, 1997; Thompson, Licklider, & Jungst, 2003; Tien, Roth, & Kampmeier, 2002). In their report, *Reinventing Undergraduate Education: A Blueprint for America's Research Universities,* The Boyer Commission on Educating Undergraduates (1999) issued a call for reform in undergraduate education. Although the Boyer Report did not include either the philosophical or research base that supported their recommendations, their conclusions were clearly consistent with Dewey's philosophy and research in learning science.

This book introduces a range of constructivist positions and makes a case for a particular brand of constructivism—the combined or transactional constructivist approach. This approach draws from constructivist theories that focus on building internal cognitive structures as well as approaches that focus on the sociocultural context of learning. The combined position maintains the central roles of both ideas and social experience. A key feature of the combined position is that it proposes a transactional relationship between theory and practice. In this model, theory and practice inform each other through a recursive, iterative process that results in competent problem solving and well-formed abstractions that can be used to solve a class of problems in the future. Neither theory nor practice is privileged in this approach to teaching.

In this frame of reference, there are many ways to characterize the relationship between theory and practice (e.g., theoretical and practical understandings are recursive and transactional, theory and practice continually inform each other, conceptual and procedural knowledge reinforce each other to enhance problem-solving ability). These views of the relationship between theory and practice do not provide an obvious answer to the question of whether we should initiate a lesson by introducing theory or begin on the level of concrete experience. Traditional approaches to university teaching, which privilege theory over practice, usually start by presenting the theory. Constructivists usually begin on the level of experience (e.g., presenting students with a problem to solve, assessing the students' previous experience and present understanding related to the content).

COMPETING VIEWS OF EDUCATION

In their classic article "Development as the Aim of Education," Kohlberg and Mayer (1972) analyzed the basic positions that have framed the debate over educational reform over the last 100 years. They identified three streams of Western educational ideology: (a) *romanticism*—associated with Rousseau and other philosophers and educators who see the child as inherently good (for educators with this perspective, the emphasis is on allowing students to grow and develop unfettered by societal constraint); (b) *cultural transmission*—focused on passing along the knowledge, skills, and values developed by previous generations; and (c) *progressivism*—associated with the philosophy of John Dewey. Progressivism promotes development in students by presenting them with problems or conflicts they can solve through active engagement. Kohlberg and Mayer concluded that, of these three approaches, only progressivism "sees the acquisition of 'knowledge' as an active change in patterns of thinking brought about by experiential problem-solving situations" (p. 455).

Education performs two important and potentially conflicting societal functions: maintaining cultural continuity and helping a society adapt to change. In his classic work, *Democracy and Education*, John Dewey (1916) made the clearest case for the critical role education plays in a democratic society. Dewey's early work also provided one pole for a debate about how American education should be conducted. Dewey and his followers in the progressive education movement at the turn of the 20th century challenged the "essentialists," who saw curriculum development as defining "what every educated person should know" and the goal of education as transmitting an externally prescribed and structurally intact body of knowledge into the minds of students. Dewey (1938a) summarized his view of the opposing positions:

> The history of educational theory is marked by opposition between the idea that education is development from within and that it is formation from without; [for the essentialists] . . . The subject-matter of education consists of bodies of information and of skills that have been worked out in the past . . . the chief business of the school is to transmit them to the new generation. (p. 17)

Recent books by Hirsch (1987), *Cultural Literacy: What Every American Needs to Know*, and Ravich and Finn (1987), *What Do Our 17-Year-Olds Know?*, and a debate between Hirsch (1998) and one of his critics (Feinburg, 1998) demonstrate that the shape of the debate between these two positions has not changed substantially over the last 100 years.

The essentialists (both past and present) believe that scholars in the academic disciplines have the expertise to organize knowledge in the most effective way. Dewey did not dispute this assertion, but he did not share their belief that learners can use the preconstructed knowledge of experts and scholars to guide their own lives and solve their own problems. Dewey's theory of learning as reconstructing experience requires that learners take an active role in constructing their own knowledge.

WHY DEWEY?

When I make presentations about transactional constructivist models for undergraduate education, I am frequently asked some form of the question, "Why Dewey?" Although Dewey is back in fashion as a philosopher, many educators wonder why it is helpful to focus on the work of a philosopher whose work is now 50 to 100 years old. In or out of fashion, I have always found that Dewey's philosophy provides important insights for theory building. As successive generations of philosophers, constructivist theorists, and researchers occupy extreme positions, new combined positions similar to Dewey's continue to assert themselves and Dewey is rediscovered.

Dewey's efforts to change the goals and methods of education were an extension of his project to develop American pragmatism. One of the most distinctive features of Dewey's version of pragmatism was his attempt to reconstruct philosophy without the dualisms that characterized most of the work that preceded him (e.g., the physical world and the ideal world of forms, theory and practice, mind and experience). In each case, he positioned the focus of his analysis on the point of the dynamic transaction between the elements of the old dualisms. Following Dewey's rejection of the traditional dualisms of philosophy always leads me to educational theories that make more sense than any of the radical positions taken by whatever theories are occupying the educational "right" or "left" at any particular time.

John Dewey also takes a middle-of-the-road position (or, more accurately, an on-a-totally-different-road position) on the long-debated and poorly resolved question of what is real and how we can know what is real. This question is relevant to several of the issues explored in this book. The question of what is real and the nature of the relationship between the thing in itself and what we can know about it "in our heads" has occupied a significant portion of the energies of both philosophy and psychology over their disciplinary histories. In Dewey's philosophy, the individual mind and the real world still exist, but the action takes place in a transactional relationship that encompasses the person and the world. In effect this allows Dewey to free the mind from its location "in the head" and also avoids the conclusion that the mind is not in the head at all. Most important, it focuses our attention on understanding the nature of the transaction between ideas and social practices.

Every reader has his or her own preferences about how he or she would like to approach a topic. John Dewey and the constructivists recommend beginning with an unstructured problem situation that is likely to be relevant to the reader. Dewey's method is anchored in inquiry and always begins with a problem situation that is relevant to the learner. Dewey's approach toward the world is instrumental: finding problems and addressing them through inquiry and action. Most university courses begin by presenting students with the basic knowledge and theories of an academic discipline and then address how that knowledge can be applied to practice. This book asserts that, in the end, these two perspectives (theory and practice) must be interwoven in reflective practice. It presents the development of abstract conceptual knowledge and the ability to use that knowledge to recognize, define, and solve problems effectively as an iterative process. In the next section, I begin this process by presenting a problem: How would you redesign a traditional course in light of the constructivist perspective of learning?

THE "UNDERSTANDING ORGANIZATIONS" COURSE

I decided to build this book around a case study of a course called "Understanding Organizations," which I recently began teaching again after a 10-year break. This book alternates between concrete descriptions of the changes I made in this course over a 3-year period and presentations of philosophy, theory, and research. The iterative approach of cycling back and forth between my concrete experience in the classroom and theory and research on learning fits Dewey's approach to building useful knowledge and understanding.

I begin by asking you to compare the general descriptions and syllabi for a traditional version of the "Understanding Organizations" course and the current version of the course. I present the two versions of the course side by side to allow you to compare the general approaches and specific features of the two versions of the course.

This approach contrasts with the usual practice of presenting theory first and then using that theory to guide practice. There are many reasons that constructivists do not think it is possible to apply theory to practice. First of all, that phrase implies that the theories come first rather than being grounded in experience. Theories are tools for solving problems embedded in natural settings. If they do not work, we change them or throw them out. The idea of applying theory to practice also implies that the way a theory works in a real situation is unaffected by the social practices of the situation. The relationship that constructivists see between theory and practice is transactional; it involves constant interaction and dialogue between the theory and activity in the real setting. The practice of teaching takes place in a powerful social milieu that is difficult to change. In addition to designing an ideal constructivist course, professors interested in experimenting with this approach have to think about the process they will use to help themselves and their students make the transition from the traditional model to the constructivist model.

When we change the way we do things in the classroom, it disturbs a system that is working well on some level for both the students and professors. It is important to remember that we cannot change any system without causing a great deal of discomfort and resistance. This book does not take the problem of overcoming this resistance lightly. I believe there are many instances where the principles of good teaching and learning have to bend to the reality of the system. The trick is to move along a path that is taking us in a positive direction.

TWO VERSIONS OF THE "UNDERSTANDING ORGANIZATIONS" COURSE

If you are familiar with the literature on organizational behavior, group dynamics, and organizational leadership, you may have some idea how you would design a course to introduce this content to undergraduates. If you take some time to think about how you would approach this task, it makes the exercise of reviewing the syllabi for the two versions of the "Understanding Organizations" course more useful. This approach toward developing understanding by first placing the learner in an authentic problem situation fits the constructivist model. When I teach a course, my problem at this point in the process is to overcome the students' tendency—conditioned by years of schooling—to think of learning as a passive activity. Like most readers, I would resist stopping in the middle of the first chapter of a book to spend time thinking about how I would design a course I will not even have to teach. Nevertheless, taking time to explore your own approach enhances the usefulness of the exercise of reviewing the syllabi for the "Understanding Organizations" course. It would also be helpful to compare the two syllabi for the course with syllabi from your own courses.

The descriptions of the "Understanding Organizations" course that follow include two versions: a traditional one that I taught a number of years ago and the most recent one. Placing these two versions of the course in juxtaposition emulates a method used to introduce topics in many courses taught from a constructivist perspective. The contrasting cases method helps highlight the important differences between two models. In a science course, the professor might begin by asking a novice and a scientist to comment on what they see happening in an experiment. The students would be asked to compare the two explanations and generate hypotheses about why the novice and scientist see different aspects of the same situation. We would expect the scientist to describe the situation in terms of deep principles and the novice to describe surface characteristics. For this exercise, I would like readers to compare the two syllabi, note the differences, and generate their own ideas about why I might have made the changes I did.

OVERVIEW OF THE TRADITIONAL VERSION OF THE "UNDERSTANDING ORGANIZATIONS" COURSE

I first taught the "Understanding Organizations" course about 10 years ago. I did not have the opportunity to teach it again until 3 years ago. I do not actually have a copy of the syllabus I used when I first taught the course. The syllabus that follows is a fictionalized version of the course that I taught. Although, like many TV shows, the syllabus is "based on a true story," the course description has been altered to make the course more traditional than it really was and to draw a clearer contrast between the two approaches to teaching the same course. When I taught the course 10 years ago, I used an earlier edition of Daft's (2000) popular text, *Organizational Theory and Design*. The competitive environment and the issues facing organizations have changed in the last 10 years. I designed this fictional course with the current edition of Daft's book to make the topics parallel to the issues we address in the current course. The other readings listed in the syllabus are drawn from the current management literature and are also used in the current version of the course. In the original version of the course, all the students read the same articles. In the current version, different groups of students read different articles.

The original version of "Understanding Organizations" used a lecture and discussion group format. The professor delivered lectures to 80 students on Tuesdays, and four discussion groups of 20 students were conducted on Thursdays. The discussion groups were conducted by teaching assistants. The discussion groups gave students an opportunity to ask questions about the reading and lectures and to discuss the major issues in the course. Activities in discussion groups included case discussions, structured group experiences, and student presentations.

OVERVIEW OF THE MOST RECENT VERSION OF THE "UNDERSTANDING ORGANIZATIONS" COURSE

The current version of the "Understanding Organizations" course is built around a large simulation involving a fictional organization called 4Frames. Kamm, which experiences a number of problems throughout the semester. The basic case is presented in the beginning of the semester, and students receive addenda that fit the types of organizational problems under discussion throughout the semester. The 36 students in the class were organized into six consultation firms that analyzed the organization's problems and made presentations to get the organization to hire them to help address the problems. In each round of presentations, three groups competed for the organization's business.

Groups of students assumed different roles during each session: (a) *The clients* played the role of the characters from the 4Frames.Kamm case, (b) *the presenters* played the role of the consultants, (c) *the evaluators* used the evaluation criteria to evaluate the presentation or acted as group process observers and gave the student group feedback, and (d) *the experts* read articles from the current management literature related to the organization's problems and contributed to the discussion about the problems. Outside experts were often invited to comment on presentations.

Students in the course applied the theories presented in the course lectures, presentations, and readings to understanding four organizations: (a) The personal organization was an organization that the student had been involved with as an employee or a member. Students were asked to select the organization that had been the most meaningful to them. Each student wrote a paper in six installments about his or her personal organization. The Personal Organization Paper assignment is described in the syllabus.

(b) Each group selected a group organization in the community and studied it throughout the semester by interviewing managers, making observations in the organization, and conducting research. Each group made a presentation about its group organization at the end of the semester. (c) The consultation firms addressed problems from the 4Frames.Kamm case. Students were asked to compare and contrast the problems at 4Frames. Kamm with the problems in their personal and group organizations. (d) Scenes from the TV show *The West Wing* were also used as a comparative case. The students digitized and edited clips from the show and included them as comparative examples in their Power Point presentations.

The course did not have lectures in the traditional sense. Most of the topics were introduced in group presentations or discussions. I presented minilectures in response to issues that came up in the discussions or questions from students. I had six Power Point presentations that covered the core concepts from the course that I could use as support. I delivered one scheduled lecture on leadership near the end of the semester. My lectures were available through the class Web page if students wanted to refer to them as an aid in completing their assignments (see Appendix).

DESCRIPTIONS OF ASSIGNMENTS FOR LATEST VERSION OF HOD 1200 COURSE

Personal Organizational Assessment

One of the major assignments for this class is to select an organization that has played an important role in your own development. It may be an organization you presently belong to or one you have belonged to in the past. You will analyze this organization from the various perspectives presented in this course. You will develop your assessment throughout the semester in five separate assignments.

Section 1. This section of the paper has four parts: (a) *An introduction* that provides a one- to two-page description of the organization, including the name of the organization, its basic mission, size, formal organizational structure, key members of the organization, and their formal roles. This section should describe your role in the organization and how you became a member. If you are no longer a member of the organization, explain the reasons you left the organization. (b) The *concrete experience* section includes descriptions of three critical incidents that occurred during the time you were a member of the organization. You should pick crises that shaped the organization. Make sure that you select incidents that were important for the organization and not just for you personally. (c) Describe the *leadership style* of the person who serves as the primary leader of the organization. (d) The *reflection* section asks you to share the personal values that affected the way you viewed each of the critical incidents you describe, your personal reactions, your speculations about the values and emotional reactions of other key figures in the incidents, and the reasons they acted as they did. You will receive feedback on this section, but it will not be graded until the end of the semester. You will rewrite this section at the end of the semester using the information acquired during the semester. You will need to save the first version of this section and hand it in with your rewrite at the end of the semester. You will edit the critical incidents from this section and turn them in with each frame paper. You will receive your final grade for Section 1 at the end of the semester.

Sections 2 through 4 (Section 2—Structural Frame; Section 3—Human Resource Frame; Section 4—Political & Symbolic Frames). These sections will ask you to examine your organization from each of the four frames presented in the Bolman and Deal text and to analyze the performance of the organization's leader using the criteria suggested by Bolman and Deal and Gardner. Your grade on these three sections will depend on how well you link the events you describe to specific theories in the course. You should cite the page number of the theories you reference from the course texts. You will attach a new version of your three critical incidents to each of these sections of the paper. Edit the three incidents each time you write a new section of the paper, adding new details that relate to the new frame. Print the new material in bold print. You may rewrite these three sections of your paper. Your grade will be an average of the first version of the paper and the rewrite. Rewrites must be completed within 1 week of the date when your reader returns your paper.

Rewrite of Section 1 (Leadership) & Section 5 (Recommendations). This rewrite will synthesize the material presented in the first four sections of the analysis. Your major task in rewriting Section 1 of the paper is to use the leadership theories presented by Bolman and Deal and Gardner to analyze the effectiveness of your personal organization's leader. Your task in Section 5 is to develop a list of recommendations for ways to improve the organization. You should provide support for each recommendation from the organizational theories and research from the course. The rewrite of Sections 1 and 5 (Recommendations) may not be rewritten.

"Expert" Articles. For each of the four frames that we study in this course, members of designated groups will assume the role of experts on ways to solve the problem presented. Those designated as group members will be responsible for reading an article from the current management lit-

erature that presents a current theory or model for dealing with problems in the area covered by the frame. You will be exchanging expert report/question letters with another student in your group. The letter exchange will focus on two articles you read during the week that you are acting as an expert. All letters must be typed. Articles for each expert group will be available in a separate ClassPak available through Campus Copy. Be sure to purchase the correct ClassPak for your expert group. Hand in two copies of your expert report/question letter at the beginning of class on the due date. Give one copy to the professor and one copy to the student who will be answering your question.

Part 1—Your Expert Report/Question Letter. After you complete your article, write a description of the major points in the article and how you think it relates to the organizational problem presented. Relate the points in the article to specific theories from the readings for the frame. Be as specific as possible about the connections between the article and the class reading and the organizational problems being discussed for your frame. Then describe some aspect of the article that you find troubling or difficult to understand—a specific concept that you find difficult to interpret or fully comprehend. If you honestly think that you fully understand the points in the article, present your reader with a controversial issue raised in the article, state and support your own position on this issue, and ask your reader to respond with their own opinion. Please refer to specific passages in the article by putting page and paragraph numbers in parentheses. This will let your readers know exactly what concepts you want them to discuss. Make two copies of your question letter: one for the student who will be responding to your questions and one for the faculty member reading your work for this course.

Part 2—Your Response Letter. For the next class session, write a one- to two-page letter in response to the inquiry you received from a fellow group member. Please suggest possible answers to your classmate's question and raise any issues you believe are relevant to her or his question or the relevance of the article to the organization's problems. Make as many connections as possible to the theories in the course readings.

Policy on Grading

Each of the course requirements contribute the following proportions to your final grade:

Quizzes	20%
Personal Organizational Assessment	30% (6% each section)
Team Organizational Assessment & Presentation	15%
Final Exam	10%
"Expert" Article Report / Question Letter	12%
Answer Letter	3%
Team Frame Presentations	10% (5% each)

BRIEF OVERVIEW OF DEWEY AND CONSTRUCTIVIST LEARNING SCIENCE

I begin the task of developing a preliminary model for a combined constructivist approach to undergraduate education by presenting a few lists that summarize the basic principles of Dewey's philosophy and current theories in learning science. These lists are far from comprehensive, but they provide an overview of the basic principles that can be derived from the philosophy of Dewey and current theory and research in learning science.

Some Basic Principles of Education Drawn From the Work of John Dewey

These assumptions are derived from the extensive writing of John Dewey. What impresses me most about Dewey's work is not that it is a flawless guide to educational practice in the 21st century, but that even after 100 years it is remarkably consistent with the principles we have derived from current educational theory and research on human learning.

1. The fundamental goal of education is the growth and development of the learner.
2. Learning is grounded in the student's experience:
   - there is a transactional relationship between the person and his or her environment.
   - prior experience and beliefs play a central role in shaping perceptions.

- an experience can be defined as *educative* if it increases the learner's adaptive capacity (this is the criterion for labeling knowledge as useful or *inert*).
- the teacher functions as the architect of the educational environment rather than as the transmitter of knowledge.

3. Inquiry plays a central role in learning.
   - problematic situations addressed through inquiry lead to scientific intelligence.

4. Education should focus on understanding the structure of knowledge and the connections between knowledge and the learner's previous, present, and future experience.

5. Education should increase the learner's ability to take meaningful action informed by reflective thought.

6. Learning is always social and involves communication in a community of learners.

7. It is important to promote a sense of community and democratic social values.

The Boyer Commission Report

The Boyer Commission on Educating Undergraduates' (1999) Report, *Reinventing Undergraduate Education: A Blueprint for America's Research Universities,* outlined "Ten Ways to Change Undergraduate Education." Selected recommendations are listed next with a few short quotes from the report that clarify the meaning of the recommendations. When the summary of Dewey's principles is compared with the Boyer Commission's recommendations, it is clear that they are consistent:

1. Make research-based learning the standard.

   "Discovery guided by mentoring rather than transmission of information."

   "Traditional lecturing should not be the dominant mode of instruction."

   "Internships" [are highly recommended].

2. Construct an inquiry-based freshman year.

   "Freshman experience intellectually integrated."

   "Learning through collaborative efforts."

3. Build on the freshman experience.

   "Inquiry-based learning, collaborative experience, and writing and speaking expectations need to characterize the whole of the research university education."

4. Remove barriers to interdisciplinary education.
5. Link communication skills to coursework.
   "Writing and presentation skills across the curriculum."

SOME BASIC PRINCIPLES OF EDUCATION DRAWN FROM LEARNING SCIENCE

By definition, learning science is focused on exploring the implications of theory and research for practical learning situations. Theory and practice are related to each other recursively. Theory is not privileged over practice, nor is practice over theory. Several learning scientists and educators have attempted to distill the body of work in the field into a set of basic principles of teaching and learning. I would like to summarize these principles to provide an initial model for a constructivist perspective. These principles are drawn primarily from two sources. The first was an address given by Robert Glaser (1994) to the International Congress of Applied Psychology in 1994. Glaser is a leading researcher and pioneer in learning science. His speech defined the emerging principles in learning science for theory development and practical implementation. The second source, *How People Learn* by Bransford, Brown, and Cocking (1999), summarized the conclusions of the Committee on Developments in the Science of Learning organized by the National Research Council of the National Academy of Sciences. Taken together these sources represent a good cross-section of the authoritative sources in the field.

1. *The structure of knowledge affects its accessibility and usefulness.* The quality of knowledge (as defined by its usefulness for problem solving) is determined by how well structured it is. An efficiently structured conceptual system organized around deep principles facilitates the storage and retrieval of factual knowledge and the transfer of knowledge for use in dissimilar situations. Learning involves changes in the organization of cognitive structures. (This principle would be rejected by many constructivists with a socio-cultural perspective.)

2. *The acquisition of new knowledge is affected by how well it harmonizes with existing knowledge.* Learners almost always have preconceptions or everyday theories about the world and the way it works. New knowledge that conflicts with existing knowledge is more difficult to retain and more likely to be rejected. Accurate knowledge provides a foundation for future learning.

3. *Knowledge is connected to the context and conditions of its acquisition.* Learning environments that have important similarities with the settings, conditions, and procedures where knowledge will be used are more likely

to produce useful knowledge. Defining which elements are important is the focus of ongoing research in learning science. In any case, it is important for students to understand how knowledge will be used.

4. *Learning is enhanced if students acquire metacognitive skills that increase their ability to regulate their own learning.* Learning scientists have established the importance of metacognitive skills and other self-regulating mechanisms for enhancing learning, problem solving, and transfer. Teachers need to design specific ways to develop skills such as monitoring your own thinking, understanding what you do not understand, and understanding the dynamics of the social practices of a decision-making process as well as prompting students about when to use them. This goal is facilitated by creating arenas for students to make their thinking overt. Making thinking overt gives teachers an opportunity to evaluate, support, and shape their students' thinking.

5. *Useful knowledge involves developing the reasoning and problem-solving abilities associated with expertise.* Learning scientists have developed an understanding of how knowledge can be applied to effective problem solving by comparing the problem-solving strategies of experts and novices. Effective teaching helps students develop the specific skills associated with the effective problem identification and problem-solving strategies used by experts.

6. *Learning is fostered by supportive social practices in a community of learners.* Learning scientists have explored the dynamic relationship between learning and the social practices that either foster or inhibit it. Special attention has been paid to the patterns of communication that foster the development of symbolic thinking. Developing competent thinking skills and efficient conceptual frameworks is enhanced by social modeling and scaffolding within productive dialogues with teachers and fellow students. Dialogic interaction facilitates the internalization of knowledge and thinking skills.

These principles provide a convenient summary of the implications of learning science for education formulated by the leading figures in the field. There is a striking similarity between these principles derived from recent theory and research in learning science and the previous list of principles derived from Dewey's philosophy.

The Application of Constructivism to Teaching

Several models have been developed to guide the application of the basic principles of constructivism to teaching. Most of these methods could be described as a form of situated learning. After an extensive review of the literature, Herrington and Oliver (2000) developed a set of nine design elements associated with programs based on theories of situated learning and cognition. This list makes a good summary of features of programs designed through the lens of constructivist and situated cognitive theories: (a) provide authentic contexts that reflect the way knowledge will be used in real life, (b) provide authentic activities, (c) provide access to expert performances and the modeling of processes, (d) provide multiple roles and perspectives, (e) support collaborative construction of knowledge, (f) promote reflection to enable abstractions to be formed, (g) promote articulation to enable tacit knowledge to be made explicit, (h) provide coaching and scaffolding by the teacher at critical times, and (i) provide authentic assessment of learning within tasks.

A COMBINED CONSTRUCTIVIST APPROACH TO UNDERGRADUATE TEACHING

The list of basic principles that follows provides a vehicle for organizing the material presented throughout the remainder of the book. These principles provide an overarching structure that relates the specific topics reviewed to a broader conceptual framework. Referring back to the basic model throughout the book and adding important connections and details in each chapter organizes the book's content around central themes.

The following list of basic principles and steps for developing a course based on a combined constructivist model represents a summary of the work of learning scientists. It incorporates the ideas summarized earlier in this chapter as well as those presented in the following chapters. The notes under each point present some extension and clarification of the meaning of each principle. This list helps readers familiar with the literature on constructivist and sociocultural approaches to education to see a broad outline of the approach I am taking. The literature I present throughout the remainder of the book attempts to build support for the basic principles and approach to teaching presented next.

BASIC PRINCIPLES

1. *The fundamental goal of education is increasing learners' adaptive capacity.* Education should develop learners' adaptive capacities and increase their potential for future learning and growth. Education should be adaptive both on the level of the individual and that of communities and larger collectivities. Ultimately, it is not adaptive for an individual to gain in a way that does not contribute to the common good.

2. *Useful knowledge is embedded in an authentic and meaningful context.* An authentic context creates a narrative framework where knowledge can be indexed to link personal experience, concepts and ideas, and the context of application. Contexts should be authentic in three ways. They should: (a) be relevant to the students' interests and concerns (e.g., generating cases and problems from their own experience that can be connected to the content, reading a novel that explores an important aspect of the human condition), (b) be relevant to disciplinary discourse and methods of inquiry, and (c) have important similarities to contexts of application.

Authentic contexts help organize and connect experience to theory by containing the elements of a problem space within a unifying structure. They link (a) past, present, and future experience; and (b) primary and secondary experience (empirical and theoretical knowledge). In practice, this principle can be interpreted in many ways. Authentic contexts can be designed within field-based experiences, classroom simulations, or problem-based learning. Simulations should be designed to replicate the patterns of communication, decision making, and the cognitive demands required to solve problems in the environment of application.

According to Dewey, *an* idea stimulates anticipation and problem solving. *An* experience (an experience that is authentic and meaningful) creates a unity that defines the boundaries of the experience within a problem space (problematizes it) that involves the students intellectually and emotionally and stimulates goal-directed activity (i.e., creates a goal-directed systematic inquiry in a community of scholars).

3. *The quality of knowledge depends on how well structured it is.* To be useful for problem solving, knowledge must be efficiently organized and indexed to facilitate retrieval. Knowledge organizes perception, and much of it is tacit. Problems in access to knowledge are created by the fact that much of what experts know is tacit knowledge that is not consciously available. Expert knowledge is qualitatively different from the knowledge of novices. Developing expertise has more to do with the organization of knowledge than assembling a larger collection of facts. Therefore, the factoring assumption (the idea that complex skills and knowledge can be broken down into small pieces that are acquired individually and then reassembled into expert knowledge) is not a productive way to approach the development of expert knowledge.

4. *Useful knowledge is acquired through active knowledge construction during goal-directed inquiry, rather than through transmission.* It is important to present students with problems that personally engage them and give them the authority to address important questions and become actively involved in finding and generating knowledge. Professors should create learning communities where students can develop expertise. We should encourage own-

ership and voice in the learning process and design environments that discourage the passivity associated with educational methods that rely on transmission.

5. *Useful knowledge is socially constructed in learning communities.* The process of knowledge construction is embedded in social processes and mediated by socially produced cultural artifacts. Knowing is essentially a social rather than a solitary activity. Useful knowledge is developed by groups in goal-directed activity and is connected to past, present, and future experience (i.e., it is built on what we bring to a situation, embedded in the physical and social context of the current learning situation, and designed to be used in future problem-solving situations). The role of dialogue and productive disciplinary discourse is a central factor in understanding the development of productive learning communities.

6. *The acquisition of new knowledge is strongly affected by prior knowledge.* Learning almost always involves changing concepts rather than acquiring new ones. Prior knowledge (usually in the form of largely unconscious "everyday theories" learned through experience) influences what we notice and resists change. Everyday theories tend to be more powerful than scientific theories because they are connected to experience. Prior knowledge is especially resistant to change if it is not made explicit to the learner. Unless theoretical and scientific knowledge acquired in educational settings is explicitly contrasted with everyday knowledge, students will protect their worldview by sequestering their "school knowledge" to the school context.

7. *All knowledge is conditionalized and contextualized.* The fact that knowledge is embedded in the conditions and context of its acquisition makes it difficult to transfer knowledge to applications outside the school setting. Theories cannot be "applied" to practical situations. If the goal of education is to produce flexible, generalizable knowledge, the knowledge gained in one setting must be indexed to a range of situations where it can be applied. Students must also acquire the metacognitive thinking skills they need to adapt knowledge to new contexts and social practices.

The role of representational systems, problem representation, mental models, schemes, schemas, schemata, thematic organization packets, and so on is important for understanding issues of transfer and generalizability. There are alternate theories about how knowledge is organized and indexed to facilitate retrieval in a situation where it can be applied. It is also important to understand the difference between dynamic and static transfer and the instructional strategies that produce them. *Static transfer* refers to the students' efficiency in using knowledge acquired in one setting in another setting. *Dynamic transfer* refers to enhanced ability to acquire new knowledge in a new setting.

8. *Effective learning environments should involve students in productive disciplinary discourse that actively engages them in dialogue about important questions.* Learning, especially learning in universities, is always learning about something and is seen through a particular disciplinary lens. It is more productive to focus on understanding learning in specific domains than on general principles of learning. We expect students to acquire disciplinary methods of inquiry and to be able to engage in discourse that conforms to disciplinary norms (e.g., [a] using evidence in scholarly ways, [b] understanding methods of inquiry, and [c] understanding the standards for an acceptable, a good, and an excellent response). Acculturation to the social practices of the community of scholars is an important goal of education (e.g., we expect students in a history class to understand how historians establish criteria for historical evidence, methods of determining historical significance, and the limits of interpretive license).

9. *Combined constructivist approaches maintain a focus on ideas.* Idea-focused experiential approaches retain a focus on building and modifying knowledge structures (representations, abstractions, and mental models that are at least somewhat transferable) in an iterative process. Because humans have limited mental resources, our problem-solving capacities need to be supported (scaffolded) by abstractions and other mediating structures (e.g., representations, abstractions, mental models, cognitive structures, cultural artifacts, automatization, implicit knowledge, conceptual and procedural knowledge).

10. *Knowledge is constructed through a recursive, iterative process that fluctuates between empirical and theoretic knowledge* (i.e., from poorly formed abstractions and models to well-formed abstractions). Education is crafting knowledge structures in the context of artifacts and social practices.

11. *It is important to use multiple perspectives for addressing ill-structured problems.* Professors need to present students with several perspectives on the same problem. One way to stimulate thought about multiple perspectives is to elicit diverse expert opinions.

12. *Establishing a productive dialogue across boundaries (cultures, communities of practice, from experts to novices) is the most difficult challenge for constructivist approaches.* There are significant forces that make it difficult to foster open dialogue across cultural boundaries and communities of practice. Social practices, especially patterns and styles of communication, are strongly maintained to preserve the interests of dominant cultural groups. The success of combined constructivist approaches depends on being able to foster conversations that traverse these barriers.

13. *Learning involves the construction of identity.* Students enter our courses with identities that are interwoven with their positions in their so-

cial environment, their past experiences in schools, and the social capital they bring to the situation in the classroom. The fact that their identities are implicated with their funds of knowledge and ways of participating in the practices of schooling is a significant barrier to changing the way they function in the classroom (identity is developed in figured worlds and tied to roles students see themselves playing). Classrooms should create what Bakhtin called "spaces for authoring" new identities for students (to escape from "being ventriloquated by first one and then another authoritative voice"). Incorporating creativity and play and highlighting cultural contradictions can create authoring spaces for students if they are provided safe spaces for expression (e.g., Bakhtin's carnival).

14. *There is an inherent contradiction between the two goals for the ideal classroom discourse—promoting communication across cultural boundaries and creating productive disciplinary discourse.* This is particularly challenging because disciplinary discourse is shaped by the values of the dominant culture.

Steps in the Development of a Course Based on Constructivist Principles

Based on these principles, guidance from the learning science literature, and personal experience designing and teaching constructivist courses, I defined the following steps for developing a course based on the combined constructivist perspective:

1. *Predict the types of situations in which your students might predictably and profitably use the knowledge and skills they might acquire in the course.* Identify a set of problem situations where you imagine the knowledge and skills might improve the probability of adaptive solutions.

2. *Define the enduring understandings (big ideas and deep principles) you want students to acquire.* Many experiential educators believe students should dictate or play a key role in selecting learning goals and work with teachers to define performance criteria. Within limits, this is an important process, but I am taking the position that professors should establish the broad learning objectives of their courses.

3. *Problematize the content by "anchoring" it in an authentic context* (e.g., a problem situation, a research question, a strong narrative context connected to a personally relevant problem).

4. *Assess students' current understanding* (everyday theories). The first step in engaging students with the course content is to elicit the students' previous experience related to the content. Students should generate cases and problems from their own experience that connect to the authentic

context. We should spend time helping students generate personally relevant questions and systematically articulate their everyday theories.

The rest of the steps in the process are presented linearly, but it would be more accurate to present them as a circle or spiral. Through all these steps, professors need to provide students with the informational resources, technological resources, conceptual resources, communication training, and the methodological guidance they need.

5. *Scaffold the development of abstractions while students are involved in an active inquiry process using methods appropriate to the discipline.* Involving students in active problem solving defines the experience as authentic. The discipline's ways of observing, exploring, and discovering patterns in information as part of systematic inquiry ties the problem to disciplinary norms. The professor's role is to support links between the inquiry process and the development of useful representations, abstractions, and enduring understandings. The professor needs to facilitate abstraction in context (cognitive mediation to enhance the development of theoretical knowledge) by helping students link the course's enduring understandings (big ideas and deep principles) to problems in the context of activities and social practices. The professor's role is to foster *progressive model building* by helping students use preliminary abstractions and "classes of things" to recognize examples and concepts in unstructured problem situations.

6. *Provide resources for knowledge construction.* The primary role of the professor is to function as an architect of the educational environment rather than as a transmitter of knowledge. In addition to resources like research tools, readings, and simulations, the professor becomes an expert resource to facilitate problem solving.

7. *Provide students with training in effective communication, metacognitive thinking, and disciplinary norms for inquiring and discourse.* Most students are not equipped with the communication skills they need to perform successfully in cooperative learning environments. They need training in both basic communication and in the norms of productive disciplinary discourse. They may not understand the standards of evidence used in the discipline. It is helpful if they are provided with rubrics that capture the higher order thinking and standards of evidence we want them to exhibit. The content needs to include introducing students to new social practices (new communication structures) that redefine the roles of teachers and students.

8. *Involve students in collaborative learning* (create learning communities where students can develop expertise). For collaborative learning to successfully achieve course objectives, it is important to promote meaningful, transactional dialogue across boundaries of culture and communities of practice as well as promoting justifactory (why questions) and critical discourse (addressing issues of power and social justice). If students are going to learn from each other, their groups need to create "zones of proximal

development," where students learn from more competent students, and "instrumental development zones," where students bridge the gap between their individual knowledge and the total expertise distributed throughout the group.

9. *Communication* (transactional telling and scaffolding of knowledge construction). An important organizing principle of constructivist approaches to education is to create "times for telling," where students receive information from professors, reading, and experts at a time when they need this information to solve problems that are important to them. The professor plays an important role in the dynamic nesting of epistemic actions by scaffolding connections between concrete problem-solving experience and conceptual and procedural knowledge (e.g., semiotic mediation that links examples to concepts, orchestrating dialogic inquiry, "Just in time" lectures matched to the students' information needs).

10. *Create arenas for making knowledge visible.* Students in constructivist classrooms are involved in projects that produce significant products and are encouraged to make their knowledge visible through mechanisms like making presentations to the rest of the class. The professor's role in this stage is *fostering knowledge refinement* by helping students use the knowledge they have acquired to construct new knowledge (*building with*) and *fostering productive disciplinary engagement* around the issues raised by the presentation.

11. *Application.* In the application phase, students use knowledge to understand new situations. This is often used as an assessment of transfer. Students make and test predictions and receive feedback about how useful the concepts and ideas are for solving real-world problems.

CONCLUSION

This brief exploration of the range of positions associated with constructivism makes it clear that understanding these positions and using them to develop a theory of instruction is not a straightforward task. Although no way of teaching "really works," I believe that undergraduate education could be reconstructed to make useful learning more possible and more common and the teaching experience of university faculty more interesting and satisfying. Sorting through these theories is more manageable if we adopt an overarching philosophical framework. I think that John Dewey's philosophy provides an excellent foundation for understanding these perspectives and selecting which ones are best equipped to guide our teaching. The next chapter presents an overview of the aspects of Dewey's philosophy that provide the context for understanding the constructivist positions that it inspired.

APPENDIX

Human & Organizational Development 1200-01:
Understanding Organizations
"Traditional" Version

Readings:

1. Daft, Richard (2000) *Organizational Theory and Design* (7th Edition) Cincinnati, OH: South-Western Thompson Learning
2. *ClassPak: HOD 1200 (Sec 1) (fall, 2002)* Available from Campus Copy

Overview of Course

All of us live with both the limitations and support of organizations for most of our lives. The quality of organizational life and the ability of organizations to perform their functions effectively are major factors affecting the quality of our lives. You have experienced many organizations, both as employees and as customers that fell along a continuum from very effective and satisfying to painfully inept and damaging. This course is designed to help you understand the basic characteristics of organizations and the range of theories of organizational design and effectiveness. This course is designed to help you understand modern manufacturing and service organizations and the competitive pressures they confront in today's globalized economy.

Human & Organizational Development 1200-01:
Understanding Organizations
Latest Version

Readings:

1. Bolman, Lee G. & Deal, Terrance E. (2003) *Reframing Organizations* (3rd Edition) San Francisco: Jossey-Bass
2. Gardner, Howard (1995) *Leading Minds.* New York: Basic Books
3. *ClassPak: HOD 1200 (Sec 1) (fall, 2003)* Available from Campus Copy

Overview of Course

All of us live with both the limitations and support of organizations for most of our lives. The quality of organizational life and the ability of organizations to perform their functions effectively are major factors affecting the quality of our lives. We all have belonged to and helped lead many other organizations that fell along a continuum from very effective and satisfying to painfully inept and damaging. One of the most important objectives of this course is to help you to deal successfully with organizational life and acquire the skills and understanding you need to improve the organizations in your life. This course is designed to help you understand organizations on both the theoretical and practical levels. During the course you will learn a general framework for understanding the different aspects of organizational life (the four frames) and be introduced to a range of theories about organizations and how to improve them.

Syllabus—Page 2—Traditional Version

August 29—Introduction: Review Syllabus, objectives, assignments.

September 3—Lecture: Introduction to Organizational Theory
Reading: Daft, Ch. 1, Organizations and organizational theory, pp. 1–46

September 5—Discussion Groups—Introduction to Cases

September 10—Lecture: Strategic Planning & Structural Design
Reading: Daft, Ch. 2, Organizational purpose & structural design, pp. 47–76.

September 12—Discussion Groups—Workshop on Strategic Planning
Reading: Daft, Ch. 2 Workbook & Cases, pp. 76–83.

September 17—Lecture: Organizational Structure
Readings: (1) Daft, Ch. 3, Fundamentals of organizational structure, pp. 127–158.
(2) Wang, Linking Organizational Context with structure: A preliminary investigation of the information processing view, ClassPak, pp. 1–15

Syllabus—Page 2—Latest Version

August 29—Introduction: Review Syllabus, objectives, explanation of methods, review assignments, form teams, set schedule, pick personal organization.

September 3—Introduction to West Wing—Reading: (1) B&D, pp. 3–34—Overview of Organizational Theory & Introduction, (2) Gardner, pp. 3–40.

September 5—Workshop: Editing tapes and making presentations (Computer Lab), Introduction to Structural Frame Case (West Wing Video). **Note: Group 2 needs to schedule a planning meeting outside class time.**

September 10—Workshop on communications (Argyris' Model I & II). Standards for grading Personal Organization papers.—Reading: B&D, pp. 81–97; 142–158

Assignment due: **Draft of Section 1 of Personal Organization Paper**

September 12—QUIZ # 1—INTRODUCTION & STRUCTURAL FRAME Reading: (1) Gardner, pp. 41–65 (The Leader's Stories), (2) B & D, Structural Frame pp. 37–80. After Quiz—Group 2—lab, Group 4 & 6–planning meetings. Groups 1, 3, 5 meetings to select group organization to study in the community.

September 17—Groups 2 Presenters (Structural Frame Consulting Firm), Group 5—Clients (4Frames.Kamm), Group 3—Evaluators, Group 1 & 3A Experts, Group 4 work meeting, Group 6—computer lab. **Reading**: Gardner, pp. 132–145 (Alfred P. Sloan) and pp. 148–163 (George Marshall). *Assignments due:* **Groups 1 & 3A—Expert reports—structural frame. (See description of assignments)**

Syllabus—Page 3—Traditional Version

September 19—Discussion Groups—Workshop—Developing an Organizational Design

September 24—Organizational Design Presentations (Large Group)

September 26—Discussion groups: Self-managed Work Teams
Reading—Stewart & Barrick "Team structure and performance" Class-Pak, pp. 16–29.

October 1—Discussion Groups—Organizing Teams for Organizational Presentations

October 3—Lecture: Assessing the External environment
Reading: Daft, Ch 4, The external Environment, pp. 129–163.

October 8—Lecture: Interorganizational Relationships
Reading: Daft, Ch. 5, Interorganizational and Strategic Partnerships relationships, pp. 165–196.

October 10—Discussion Groups: Cases on Organizational Competition, Partnerships, Mergers, and Take-Overs.

Syllabus—Page 3—Latest Version

September 19—Groups 4 Presenters, Group 5—Clients, Group 2—Evaluators, 3B—Group process observation, Group 1 & 3A Experts, Group 6—work meeting.

Assignments due: **Answer letters on the structural frame.**

September 24—Groups 6 Presenters, Group 5—Clients, Group 3 Evaluators, Group 1 & 3A Experts, Groups 2 & 4—meeting to select outside organization—return for last 20 minutes of the class for Introduction to Human resources Frame.

Assignments due: **Section 2 of Personal Organization Paper—Structural Frame. Note: Group 3 needs to schedule a planning meeting outside class.**

September 26—**QUIZ #2—HUMAN RESOURCE FRAME**

After Quiz: Group 3 lab, Group 5—planning, Groups 2, 4, 6—workshop—

Group 1—outside organization Communications II. Reading: B&D, pp. 101–14; Gardner, pp. 182–202 (Eleanor Roosevelt).

The Class Meetings for the next 3 class sessions follow the pattern established with the presentations on the Structural Frame. The class sessions on October 1st, 3rd & 8th focus on the Human Resource Frame.

October 10—**QUIZ #3—POLITICAL & SYMBOLIC FRAMES**

After Quiz: Group 6 lab, Group 4 planning mtg., Groups 1, 3, 5—Workshop Communication II, Group 2—Outside organization. **Reading:** Bolman & Deal, pp. 161–211; pp. 215–262

Syllabus—Page 4—Traditional Version

October 15—Lecture: Manufacturing and Service Technologies

Reading: (1) Daft, Ch. 6, Manufacturing and service technologies, pp. 199–237, (2) Devarj, Hollingworth & Schroeder "Generic manufacturing strategies" ClassPak, pp. 30–53.

October 17—MIDTERM EXAMINATION

OCTOBER 19–22—FALL BREAK

October 24—Discussion Groups: Organizing Group Organizational Analysis Project—Workshop on gathering information on Corporations.

October 29—Lecture: Information Technology & Knowledge Management

Reading: Daft, Ch. 7, Information technology & knowledge management pp. 239–275, Ch. 11, Decision-making processes, pp. 398–439.

October 31—Outside Speaker (Large Group)—Derwood Kirby—Vice President for IT RDG International (The role of technology and information in corporate decision-making)

November 5—Lecture: Organizational Size, Life Cycle Control

Reading: Daft, Ch. 8, Organizational size, life cycle & control, pp. 279–311.

November 7—Discussion Groups—Managing Information in Different Types of Organizations.

Syllabus—Page 4—Latest Version

The Class Meetings for the next 2 class sessions follow the pattern established with the presentations on the previous frames. The class sessions on October 15, 17, & 24 focus on the Political & Symbolic Frames.

OCTOBER 19–22—FALL BREAK

October 29—QUIZ ON LEADERSHIP

Reading: (1) Bolman & Deal, pp. 365–380, Gardner, pp. 285–306.

After quiz: Group 1 planning meeting, Groups 2–6 meet on outside organizations.

Note: Group 1 needs to schedule a lab outside of class time.

October 31—Leadership Lecture

Assignments due: **Section 4 of Personal Organization Paper—Political & Symbolic Frame. Note: Group 5 needs to schedule a planning meeting outside class time.**

November 5—Leadership Lecture

November 7—Groups 1—Presenters, Group 4—Clients, Group 6—Evaluators, Groups 2 & 6B Experts, Group 5 in Computer Lab, Group 3 planning meeting.

Assignments due: **Groups 2 & 6B—Expert reports on Leadership**

November 12—Groups 5 Presenters, Group 4—Clients, 6—Evaluators, Groups 2 & 6B Experts, Group 3 in Computer Lab, Group 1—Group Organization Presentation Workday. *Assignments due:* **Answer letters on Leadership**

Syllabus—Page 5—Traditional Version

November 12—Lecture: Organizational Culture.

Reading: (1) Daft, Ch. 9, Organizational culture, pp. 313–325; (2) Cornelissen & Harris "The corporate identity metaphor" ClassPak, pp. 54–74.

November 14—Corporate Culture—Assessing the Culture of Group Cases

November 19—Lecture: Ethical Issues in Business

Reading: (1) Daft, Ch 9, Ethical values, pp. 326–348, (2) Di Norcia, V. & Tigner, J. "Mixed motives and ethical decisions in business" ClassPak, pp. 75–89.

November 21—Case Study on Workforce Diversity

Reading: Schnieder & Northcraft "Three social dilemmas of workforce diversity in organizations" ClassPak, pp. 90–106.

NOVEMBER 23–DECEMBER 1—THANKSGIVING BREAK

December 3—Lecture: Innovation & Change

Reading: Daft, Ch. 10, Innovation and change, pp. 351–396.

December 5—Workshop on Change Management

December 10—Lecture: Conflict, Power, and Politics

Reading: (1) Daft, Ch. 12, Conflict, power, and politics, pp. 441–479; (2) Brett, Northcraft, & Pinkley "Stairways to heaven: An interlocking self-regulation model of negotiation" *Assignment due:* **Personal Organizational Paper**

December 12—Group Organization Presentations

December 19—FINAL EXAMINATION—3 PM

Syllabus—Page 5—Latest Version

November 14—Groups 3 Presenters, Group 4—Clients, Group 5, 6A—Evaluators, Groups 2 & 6B Experts, Group 2—Group Organization Presentation Workday

November 19—Group 1—Group Organization Presentation
Groups 2 & 3—Group Organization Presentation Workday

November 21—Group 2—Group Organization Presentation
Group 3 & 4—Group Organization Presentation Workday.
Assignments due: **Personal Organization Papers—Groups 5 & 6**

NOVEMBER 23–DECEMBER 1—THANKSGIVING BREAK

December 3—Group 3—Group Organization Presentation,
Groups 4 & 5 Group Organization Presentation Workday.

December 5—Group 4—Group Organization Presentation, Groups 5 & 6—Group Organization Presentation Workday. *Assignments due:* **Personal Organization Papers—Groups 1 & 2**

December 10—Group 5—Group Organization Presentation—Groups 6—Group Organization Presentation Workday

December 12—Group 6—Group Organization Presentation
Assignments due: **Personal Organization Papers—Groups 3 & 4**

December 19—FINAL EXAMINATION—3 PM (In computer Lab)

December 14—ALTERNATE EXAMINATION—12 NOON (In computer lab)

Chapter 2

John Dewey and the Foundations of Constructivism

Philosophy may seem far removed from the practical day-to-day decisions that have to be made to design, revise, and deliver a university course. Yet the frequently quoted statement (attributed to Kurt Lewin, James Maxwell, and Poincaré, among others) that "there is nothing more practical than a good theory" is equally true of a good philosophy. Few specific questions about teaching can be answered directly by research. Theory provides a broader set of principles for organizing learning experiences, but philosophy provides the broadest criteria for making judgments about competing theories. Without a clear philosophical framework, teachers often find themselves at sea without a compass. Truly competent teaching demands constant reflection about how well philosophy, theory, research, and effective practice are aligned.

Dewey's work is especially useful as a guide for navigating the range of constructivist theories that are explored in this book. I make the case that Dewey's position represents a middle ground between the two basic forms of constructivism described in chapter 3 (psychological constructivism) and chapter 5 (sociocultural perspectives). Dewey's philosophy directs us to types of constructivism that grant legitimacy to established bodies of knowledge and strike a balance between student-centered and idea-focused approaches. It specifically rejects some of the conclusions that many critics and some supporters have drawn from constructivist theory (e.g., students' commonsense theories cannot be challenged by scientific research, no statement can be judged to be truer than any other; T. L. Simpson, 2002). This chapter provides a foundation for the judgments I make in subsequent chapters about the implications of Dewey's philosophy for teaching.

For Dewey, the aim of education was to increase the adaptive capacity of learners. Dewey saw knowledge in the context of experience, as constructed not received, as something stable but not eternal, as a living product of inquiry within a problem-solving process. Knowledge is produced when people solve problems together. It is not transmitted directly from teachers to learners. Knowledge and meaning, therefore, are socially constructed through cooperative inquiry. Inquiry can lead to "warranted assertions" that function as *true* within certain contexts.

Dewey's naturalized worldview and concept of experience provided a foundation for his form of American pragmatism (transactional realism). This basic orientation placed inquiry and problem solving as the core processes for successful adaptation (which, for Dewey, is the measure of growth, the definition of intelligence, and the goal of education). Dewey's views about the nature of knowledge and the content of the curriculum and his educational philosophy and its implications for teaching and learning are logical extensions of this basic philosophical orientation.

THE NATURE OF KNOWLEDGE AND THE CONTENT OF THE CURRICULUM

Gaining knowledge is generally accepted as a primary goal of most university departments, but few departments outside of philosophy actually wrestle with the question of what knowledge really is. Instead university departments usually focus all of their attention on addressing questions about what students should know to be thought of as legitimate members of their discipline. Conversations about the nature of knowledge are considered to be too academic even for academics. Within the framework of Dewey's philosophy and the various constructivist theories in learning science, the question assumes more practical significance, and the answers ultimately refocus the curriculum and alter the conduct of the classroom.

Dewey often frustrated questioners who asked him to define the goal of education by simply saying, "growth." If his answer had been "increased adaptive capacity," it would have been equally dissatisfying to people who really wanted to know, "Exactly, what do the students learn in this class?" Dewey's philosophy led him away from setting educational goals in terms of content. The contextual nature of his worldview subordinated content to the problem and the situation. The curriculum development process does not begin by defining what students should know. The first step is to ask what types of problems students are likely to confront in the future and what enduring understandings they will need to solve these problems.

The most common criticism of the educational programs in Dewey's progressive schools of the 1920s and 1930s was that the curriculum lacked content. Lack of content is still the most frequent criticism of constructivist approaches to teaching. This criticism reflects the fundamental difference in the way constructivists and essentialists define the nature of knowledge. It is easy to misinterpret Dewey's refusal to produce a list of things people should know to mean that students should not acquire content from the existing body of knowledge. Dewey has been characterized as focusing on process rather than content (Glassman, 2002). It is more accurate to say that Dewey contextualized content within inquiry/problem-solving processes. This orientation privileges acquiring the logic of inquiry over memorizing scientific facts, but it positions *warranted assertions* (Dewey's term for the current body of scientific knowledge) as important tools for problem solving. Prawat (2002) challenged Glassman's (2002) assertion that Dewey placed process over product by citing several examples of Dewey's emphasis on students acquiring important ideas related to disciplinary knowledge. My position in this debate is that Dewey's method of helping students acquire important content (big ideas and deep principles that can facilitate effective problem solving) was to embed content in meaningful problems—to challenge students with problems that can be addressed using important ideas. What makes the ideas important is their usefulness. What qualifies content as a "big idea and deep principle" is its usefulness across a range of contexts.

It is more difficult to articulate the objectives of a curriculum that avoids defining its goals in terms of specific memorized facts. It is also more expensive and time consuming to evaluate how well these objectives have been met. For Dewey (1938b), logical forms emerge within the problem-solving process (i.e., within inquiry). Dewey's logic of practice structures, but does not isolate, the objective from the subjective aspects of experience (Alexander, 2002). Meanings and the activities from which they are gleaned, as well as the being of the knower, are intertwined (Rosenthal, 2002).

Habits of the Mind and Heart

Dewey might have answered the "Exactly what do they learn in this class?" question by saying "adaptive habits of the mind and heart." Dewey used the word *habits* to describe the flexible adaptive behaviors (skills/knowledge packages) acquired through inquiry that allow learners to effectively and successfully encounter similar problems in the future. Habits are adaptive if they help students solve important problems. The facts students learn have to fit into these processes or they will be inaccessible for problem solving in the future. Habits are the complex behavioral, cognitive, and affective repertoires that characterize expertise. For Dewey (1916), they provide learners with tools for "the economical and effective control of the environment" (p. 48, MW9:53).

Dewey used the word *habit* in a different way than we would typically use it today. He was not referring to a conditioned response or a mindless routine, but a broader repertoire of adaptive behaviors that contain knowledge, skill, and art. They are not thoughtless, but they are largely implicit. They are skills that we use when we are confronted with problems that we know how to solve without inquiry. They are learned ways of approaching and solving problems (Dewey, 1922).

Dewey's use of the word *habits* may confuse modern readers who associate habits with simple conditioned responses. This inference is more what Dewey wanted to avoid than what he wanted to achieve. Habits in Dewey's frame of reference are *habits of the mind and heart.* They are learned ways of using objects from the environment and our own attitudes, knowledge, and skills for mastering the environment. Dewey, in fact, rejected learning that resulted in rigid habits rather than flexible and artistic behaviors to encounter new situations in the same class of problems.

If we think of habits as the ideas/knowledge/skill/subjective experience skills sets that define expertise, a primary issue relates to the degree of consciousness and accessibility of these habits. Dewey (1916) recognized two categories of knowledge: (a) practical knowledge that is embedded in the knower's habits (i.e., in the activity of doing), and (b) generalizable "scientific" knowledge. Abstract knowledge has the advantage of being portable from one situation to another—if the learner recognizes important similarities and retrieves the appropriate habit. The learner has to be able to reintegrate the knowledge into a real-world context. "A meaning detached from a given experience cannot remain hanging in the air. It must acquire local habitation" (Dewey, 1916, p. 227, MW9:235).

The assertion that inquiry is a group activity and knowledge is socially constructed is a basic principle that Dewey shares with the current constructivists. Dewey saw inquiry as an activity engaged in by groups rather than individuals and all logical structures as arising from the process of inquiry (Schutz, 2001). To engage in cooperative inquiry, a group must share a critical mass of "shared habits." Shared habits are important because they provide the glue that holds work teams, communities, and cultures together and allows them to engage in cooperative activity (Schutz). In situations where it is important to promote cooperative activity across cultural barriers, it is critical to develop specific interventions to build a core of shared habits that facilitate communication and joint action.

In Dewey's theory of communication, meanings are carried primarily by language, but not totally contained within language. The heart of language is communication between people. For Dewey (1925/1958), "To fail to understand is to fail to come to agreement in action, to misunderstand is to set up action at cross purposes. Meaning is not indeed a psychic experience; it is primarily a property of [cooperative] behavior" (p. 141, LW1:141). In other words, meanings are not entirely in the head—they are connected to experience and action.

In his later writings, Dewey made it clear that reflective meaning is informed by "the nonreflective web of experience" in which it is embedded. Although it may be technically true that Dewey saw meaning as contained within language (Garrison, 1994a), much of the *meaning* of reflective cognitive structures (in the everyday sense of the word) depends on their connections to what Dewey (1934/1980) called "ideas involving emotional response and imaginative projection" (p. 341, LW8:342). He went on to clarify the implication of this insight for teaching:

> Human beings are not normally divided into two parts, the one emotional, the other coldly intellectual—the one matter of fact, the other imaginative. The split does, indeed often get established, but it is always because of false methods of education. Natively and normally, the personality works as a whole. There is no integration of character and mind unless there is fusion of the intellectual and the emotional, of meaning and value, of fact and imaginative running beyond fact into the realm of desired possibilities. (LW8:342)

Garrison (1994a) also pointed out that Dewey's philosophy differs from that of other pragmatists in its version of realism. Dewey believed that inquiry could achieve more than simply developing a coherent body of knowledge—it can "make sense" of the world and give the learner tools for solving problems in the environment of the actor and the world. All meanings are fixed by their consequences. We find Dewey's version of truth (the warranted assertion) through participation in the social practices of a community of scholars (inquiry). Garrison (1994a) pointed out that for Dewey:

> all meanings—cognitive, aesthetic, and moral—are made. They are sociolinguistically constructed between two selves participating in a shared undertaking. Meaning is objective, having external and real reference. It is the making of something intersubjectively stable and fixed, for a time, between two actors. We are concerned with knowledge. These are the meanings that connect and are the product of inquiry controlled by the labor and tools of scientific workers. (p. 11)

The world we inquire about is real, but it does not exist (is not meaningful) as fixed eternal structures prior to inquiry. We do not receive a truth or invent it in our individual heads; we construct truth with other people. Garrison cited a passage from a letter to Arthur Bentley, with whom Dewey wrote his final book, *Knowing and the Known* (Dewey & Bentley, 1949):

> If I ever get the needed strength, I want to write on knowing as the behaving in which linguistic artifacts transact business with physical artifacts, tools, implements, apparatus, both kinds of planning for the purpose and rendering inquiry . . . an experimental transaction. (Letter from Dewey to Bentley, December 8, 1945)

This quote connects Dewey with activity theorists like Vygotsky, who emphasize the role of mediating structures in human meaning-making activity. For Dewey, the structure of reality is not eternal; it is made meaningful by inquiry. The structures that are the object of our inquiry are the products of nature, which includes the actions of people. They are not permanent, but they are stable enough for us to inquire about them and use the results of that inquiry to take action and solve practical problems. This is a difficult concept because it never denies the existence of a real world, but restricts our experienced reality to things that have been made meaningful.

For Dewey, then, the specific content of the curriculum was secondary because knowledge was judged by its usefulness and had no independent status:

> The problem for progressive education is: What is the place and meaning of subject matter and of organization *within* experience? Now we have the problem of discovering the connection which actually exists *within* experience between the achievements of the past and the issues of the present. We have the problem of ascertaining how acquaintance with the past may be translated into a potent instrumentality for dealing with the future. We may reject knowledge of the past as the *end* of education and thereby only emphasize its importance as *means*. (Dewey, 1938a, pp. 20, 23, LW:13.8 & 13.9)

So Dewey would not have us ask whether this piece of literature or that fact is "what every educated person should know." Rather, he asks whether it would enrich the lives of our students in the world they do and will inhabit. This does not mean that the content students get in their professional and vocational courses is more important than the things they learn in a poetry class because it is "more practical." That is not the way that Dewey and the proponents of learning science use the word *useful*. To quote William Carlos Williams (1962),

> It is difficult to get the news from poems
> Yet men die miserably every day from lack
> Of what is found there.

This directs us to the distinction between inert knowledge and useful knowledge. The value of traditional knowledge is not judged by its privileged place in the canon, but by its usefulness for solving problems in the future. Dewey would reject the idea that an educational program could be evaluated by measuring the total amount of material memorized by the students: He would want to know how much useful knowledge was acquired. The following quote demonstrates how closely Dewey's (1938a) concept of useful knowledge presaged the position taken by today's learning scientists:

> Almost everyone has had occasion to look back upon his school days and wonder what has become of the knowledge he was supposed to have amassed during his years of schooling, and why is it that the technical skills he acquired have to be learned over again in changed form in order to stand him in good stead. Indeed, he is lucky who does not find that in order to make progress, in order to go ahead intellectually, he does not have to unlearn much of what he learned in school. These questions cannot be disposed of by saying that the subjects were not actually learned, for they were learned at least sufficiently to enable a pupil to pass examinations in them. One trouble is that the subject matter in question was learned in isolation; it was put, as it were, in a watertight compartment. When the question is asked, then, what has become of it, where has it gone to, the right answer is that it is still there in the special compartment in which it was originally stowed away. If exactly the same conditions recurred as those under which it was acquired, it would also recur and be available. But it was segregated when it was acquired and hence is so disconnected from the rest of experience that it is not available under the actual conditions of life. It is contrary to the laws of experience that learning of this kind, no matter how thoroughly ingrained at the time, should give genuine preparation. (pp. 47–48; LW:13.28)

Dewey goes on to state that if the students' encounters with education leave them with negative feelings about learning and they avoid learning experiences in the future, the results of education can actually reduce their adaptive capacity to solve future problems. The most important criticism of education may not be that people learn too little while they are in school, but that they stop learning when they leave.

Dewey recognized that both the internal structure of knowledge and its connections to classes of problems were essential to the development of useful knowledge. The orientation toward learning to learn rather than storing knowledge is facilitated by focusing on what Brown and Campione (1996) called "big ideas and deep principles." Constructivists believe learning involves much deeper cognitive processes than memorizing material. Learning involves restructuring or creating an integrated system of relationships (i.e., creating or modifying schema in a way that has powerful effects on what is noticed and learned from then on; Bransford, Franks, Vye, & Sherwood, 1989). If students acquire deep principles in several domains, they can transfer their learning to less similar situations governed by the same principles (Lin et al., 1995). Learning scientists recommend that the present focus on the breadth of factual coverage be replaced by in-depth exploration of fewer topics.

The validity of any specific content objective depends on its ecological validity in the real world of the student. Habits are judged by how well they match the challenges presented by the organism's ecological niche. The value of any particular subject matter relates to its instrumental potentialities. Dewey called on teachers to ask themselves how much sense the habits of the mind and heart they were teaching will make in the world of the learner. The secret to developing curricula that will help students acquire important ideas is to develop enterprises that have both internal validity (students develop knowledge and skills and use them to solve the problems within the enterprise) and ecological validity for the world the students will encounter in their own lives outside the classroom.

DEWEY'S NATURALIZED WORLDVIEW

Dewey's conclusions about the nature of knowledge and learning evolved from his basic worldview and his analysis of the nature of experience. Although his analysis of the nature of experience is the cornerstone of Dewey's philosophy, its foundation is his naturalized worldview. In one sense, the word *naturalized* means not supernatural, but it also means operating as a part of and within the dynamic forces of the ecological environment. Dewey viewed all human activity in a natural context: as an organism in its ecological niche acting to adapt to the problems presented by its environment. This naturalistic orientation put him into the world and its problems, especially the problems of education. Dewey's naturalism transformed the way he and his followers viewed every aspect of education. Dewey's naturalism is the source of his belief that *growth* (defined as increased adaptative capacity) is the fundamental goal of education. The first basic principle of the combined constructivist model—that the fundamental goal of education is increased adaptive capacity—is the most basic principle because it represents a total shift of perspective that changes the goals of education and the methods of instruction.

Focusing on people being affected by their physical and social environment and taking action to change the world contextualizes perception, thinking, and action within problem-solving activity. Within this framework, thinking is an activity in the world that is no less natural and no less embedded in the environment than any other human activity. Meaning and action are intertwined (Rosenthal, 2002). Cognitive activities and knowledge objects are in the world and not separate from it (McCarthy & Sears, 2000). For Dewey (1903–1906), "knowing is one mode of experiencing, and the primary philosophical demand . . . is to find out *what* sort of experience knowing is—or, concretely how things are experienced when they are experienced as known things" (MW3:159–160). For Dewey, knowledge is the result of inquiry motivated by a problem that causes discomfort. Dewey's logic is a logic of practice that emerges within the conduct of inquiry (Burke, Hester, & Talisse, 2002). This orientation toward problem solving views knowledge and behavior in terms of its consequences. Dewey's instrumentalism focused him on real-world problems. When inquiry and problem solving are placed within Dewey's ecological perspective, intelligence is behavior (including both thinking and doing) that leads to more successful adaptation. Dewey's particular project was to make practice more intelligent (Eldridge, 1998).

Dewey viewed learning and development from an ecological perspective long before theory and research in human ethology became a major force that shaped our understanding of human development. Influenced by Darwin, he believed that human instincts provide a basic framework for human behaviors that are expressed differently in different cultural environments (Cahan, 1992). From the ecological perspective, growth involves enhancing the learner's capacity to adapt to his or her natural and social environments and to actively create better environments that promote further growth in the future.

THE NATURE OF EXPERIENCE
AND EDUCATIVE EXPERIENCE

Much of the intellectual history of philosophy has explored the definitions of and relationship between objective reality (if there is such a thing) and mind (if the mind ever achieves a measure of independence from its context). The classic positions on this question are empiricism, which gives precedence to the real world, grounding accurate representations of reality once they have been stored (sense experiences are organized into logical structures through a process of induction) and rationalism, which gives precedence to the mind and implicates the mind in the construction of thought processes from perception to the development of "pure" ideas. Kant's synthesis of empiricism and rationalism represented a form of constructivism that asserted that sensory input and mental constructs are both necessary ingredients for knowledge construction. In his philosophy of experience, Dewey addressed this problem by focusing not on the mind or the real world, but at the point of transaction between reality and mind. Yet even this sentence is misleading because it gives the impression that the activity of the mind is not in the world. Dewey (1938b) rejected what he called "the spectator theory of knowledge," where an inner mind knows an outer world. To avoid the inside/outside relationship implied by the word *interac-*

tion, Dewey used the word *transaction* to describe the dynamic nature of the person–environment, mind–reality interface, indicating that the person and environment are a unity within experience (Dewey & Bentley, 1949). Prawat (2002) described this as an "organism/environment co-acting" model. The relationship between mind or the knowledge produced through the inquiry process and the real world is encapsulated within experience. Depending on your perspective, this conceptualization either successfully overcomes the person–environment dualism or cleverly avoids confronting a serious problem by viewing the person, knowledge, and environment as an unanalyzed unity.

Dewey's concept of experience is the cornerstone of his philosophy of education. For Dewey, experience *is* the transaction between the individual and his or her environment—encapsulating an active, two-way interrelationship between the objective and subjective aspects of human life. The transaction places the knowing and the known in a single process (Dewey & Bentley, 1949; see LW 16:272). This places the learner in an active relationship with his or her environment, both affecting the environment and being affected by it. For Dewey (1917), experience is not *in the head:* "In the orthodox view, experience is regarded primarily as a knowledge-affair. But to eyes not looking through ancient spectacles, it assuredly appears as an affair of the intercourse of a living being with its physical and social environment" (MW 10:6). It is not a context observed by the mind, but "an affair primarily of doing" (Dewey, 1920, MW 12:129).

Dewey's (1934/1980) naturalistic view puts people in the world (both in a system and as an active part of a system) seeking harmony with their environments. Although people seek a stable relationship with their environment, Dewey's philosophy focuses its attention on "situations" where people deal with and create disruptions that cause discomfort and doubt. The situation is a field within experience that is defined by inquiry conducted to resolve the problem. It includes both the elements and their relationships (Burke, Hester, & Talisse, 2002). These moments of disruption stimulate emotions and create the potential for reflection, action, and meaning making. As such, they are the key transactions that form the nucleus of educative experiences. In Dewey's scenario, a disruption of harmony creates a problem to be solved. In an educational context, if students see a problem as authentic and relevant, it creates an authentic learning experience. The problem situation is marked by a disruption as a starting point and by goal attainment as an endpoint. The boundaries of an activity from problem creation to resolution define a situation as a meaningful whole. Every meaningful situation, therefore, has form (a starting point, a development phase, and a fulfillment). A situation is like a sonata: It has structure and direction, but it leaves room for creativity. It is dynamic because it moves toward a goal. This has important implications for educational practice. It implies that whatever content we want students to learn, as well as the learning activities we design to promote learning, have to be embedded in a meaningful context (the second basic principle of the combined constructivist approach). Like most fine artists, fine teachers see the art of teaching not as sending a message, but as creating experiences where learning can take place (Dewey, 1934/1980). "There is not, in fact, any such thing as direct influence of one human being on another, apart from use of the physical environment as an intermediary" (Dewey, 1916, MW:9.33). This view of the teacher's role in the classroom is a direct reflection of Dewey's naturalistic, ecological perspective.

Situations are socially and physically contextualized problem contexts for expanding meaning. New meanings are always derived from existing or future meaningful experience (Shook, 2000a). The challenge for Dewey was to create this unity of person and environment without a determinism that would deprive the person of his or her capacity to take independent action. Inquiry is generally thought of as an activity carried out by a group rather than an individual, but the individual retains a capacity for action. For Dewey, involving the organism in a dynamic relationship with its environment, including other actors, does not eliminate the actor, but it does partially embed the actor in a context or situation. The central role of inquiry and problem solving in Dewey's philosophy implies subjects whose actions are an essential ingredient for the transaction to have meaning. The individual's level of autonomy is open to question, but Dewey's sees the person as an actor who is empowered within some arena of activity (as only partially embedded in his or her context). Dewey (1916) clearly saw education as giving individuals and groups increased capacity to take independent action and achieve some measure of independence from their social environment. Logical forms are products of inquiry and provide learners with tools to solve future problems. Most important for educators, Dewey's educational philosophy does not deprive us of students with thinking minds who can function as centers for developing metacognitive skills, constructing mental models, and flexible schema (big ideas and deep principles) that can be used to generalize learning to broader contexts. Dewey's educated person can critique and change his or her own culture (Glassman, 2001).

At its root, Dewey's concept of experience is biological and naturalistic. Although the human environment is primarily social rather than biological, Dewey's ecological view of adaptation as growth offers the best model of the nature of experience, which encompasses the adaptive transaction holistically. This perspective allowed Dewey to identify successful strategies for solving human problems and promoting human growth. The concept of experience is the context for his focus on the use of inquiry to define and solve problems and for defining the nature of knowledge as relative rather than absolute truth, independent of context.

The description of people as seeking harmony does not imply that people seek lives of uneventful homeostasis. We are motivated to create our own disruptions. In fact Dewey (1934/1980) saw a failure to seek variety, growth, and change to be a sign of a life poorly lived. An adaptive person and an adaptive society "troubles itself" by finding problems to solve that enhance their competence to successfully confront new problems in the future (Schutz, 2001). Dewey saw growth as the goal of education, and this means that our goal as educators is to help students enrich their lives through transformative experience. "Demand for variety is the manifestation of the fact that being alive we seek to live, until we are cowed by fear or dulled by routine. The need for life itself pushes us out into the unknown" (Dewey, 1934/1980, pp. 168–169, LW:10.173). This characterization of the nature of the situation or disruption that stimulates inquiry and learning is drawn from Dewey's later work. It is much broader than the "frustration and need-driven-action resolution" model, which he described in much of his earlier work (Prawat, 2002). What separates the spirit of Dewey's later work from his earlier work is the insight that "being in a rut" (deprived of opportunities to create new problems and acquire new knowledge) is a discordant situation for human beings.

Both the scientist and artist are driven to create and solve problems. Dewey's (1934/1980) discussion of the artist's process of creation and the scientist's process of inquiry captures the student's approach to learning in the ideal educational environment:

> Since the artist cares in a particular way for the phase of experience in which union is achieved, he does not shun moments of resistance and tension. He rather cultivates them, not for their own sake but for their potentialities, bringing to living consciousness an experience that is unified and total. In contrast with the person whose purpose is esthetic the scientific man is interested in problems, in situations where tension between the matter of observation and the world is marked. Of course he cares for their resolution. But he does not rest in it; he passes on to another problem using an attained solution only as a stepping stone from which to set on foot further inquiries. (p. 15, LW:10.21)

This quote also reflects Dewey's (1934/1980) general resistance to the compartmentalization that he saw growing out of the division of labor in modern industrial societies. The division of labor in industrial organizations artificially divides art from everyday life, theory from practice, action from imagination, and thinking from feeling. He goes on to comment specifically on the artificial separation of the intellectual and aesthetic in both art and science: "The odd notion that the artist does not think and a scientific inquirer does nothing else is the result of converting a difference of tempo and emphasis into a difference in kind" (Dewey, 1934/1980, p. 15, LW:10.21).

One of the forces that shaped the direction of Dewey's philosophy of education was the effect that industrialization had on the schools. Prior to industrialization, rural children were connected to the organic whole of the community and work life. The division of labor that accompanied industrialization separated children from the experience base that provided a foundation for the largely abstract knowledge they received in school. Dewey thought that rural children found it easier to make their own connections between their school learning and their life outside of school. After industrialization, schools lost their connection to practice, and school knowledge lost most of its usefulness (Dewey, 1902/2001; Schutz, 2001). Dewey (1902/2001) also pointed out that the structure of schools emulated the assembly line and organized itself according to the abstract structure of the curriculum rather than focusing on the student as a whole person (e.g., separating students by age with a teacher for each grade, having teachers teach subjects and pass children from teacher to teacher). The fragmentation of the educational experience was especially inappropriate for students after industrialization. The new administrative structures that made it difficult for teachers to know the whole student accelerated the shift in focus away from the student to the content of the curriculum. With the loss of the whole student, the content of the curriculum became *the whole* that organized the structure of the schools. This led, in turn, to a focus on testing for factual decontextualized knowledge and further fragmentation of the students' school experience.

Dewey (1916) frequently referred to the importance of the concept of experience and indicated that a clear definition was important. Unfortunately, our dualistic language made it difficult for him to develop a clear definition for a transactional concept like experience. An approximate definition of *experience* appeared in *Experience and Education*:

> The conceptions of situation and of interaction are inseparable from each other. An experience is always what it is because of a transaction taking place between an individual and what, at the time, constitutes his environment, whether the later consists of persons with whom he is talking . . . the toys with which he is playing; the book he is reading . . . ; or the materials of an experiment he is performing. The environment, in other words, is whatever conditions interact with personal needs, desires, purposes, and qualities to create experience which is had. (Dewey, 1938a, p. 43, MW:13.26)

Experience contains both the content and process of the person–environment transaction. It is not constructed entirely of cognitively organized knowledge or disconnected, nonreflective acting. It is meaningful and projects itself into the future. Dewey sees experience as "the complex of all that is human" (LW 1:131). Experience then describes the part of the environment that has been made meaningful by human activity. This definition puts self in context, but clearly retains a thinking self who is capable of volitional action. The following quote from *Art as Experience* sheds more light on the dynamic nature of the concept and the active role of the person within experience:

> Experience is a matter of the interaction of organism with its environment, an environment that is human as well as physical, that includes the materials of tradition and institutions as well as local surroundings. The organism brings with it through its own structure, native and acquired, forces that play a part in the interaction. The self acts as well as undergoes, and its undergoings are not impressions stamped upon an inert wax but depend upon the way the organism reacts and responds . . . The organism is a force not a transparency. Because every experience is constituted by interaction between "subject" and "object," between self and its world, it is not itself either merely physical or merely mental, no matter how much one factor or the other predominates. (Dewey, 1934/1980, p. 246, LW:10.251)

Garrison (1994b) emphasized the importance of understanding Dewey's transactional realism to reach correct conclusions about the implications of Dewey's philosophy for education. Garrison characterized Dewey's philosophy as having a constructivist view of knowledge and a behaviorist view of meaning. People construct knowledge, but develop meaning in the context of cooperative inquiry with other people. Following Mead's (1934) social behaviorism, the individual is distilled out of social interaction and achieves some measure of independent self. This process parallels Vygotsky's model, but allows the individual more independence from the culture (Glassman, 2001). Reality is known (made meaningful) through reflective inquiry carried on in a social context. The role of reflection and social interaction, especially language, then are central to inquiry (Dewey, 1925/1958). Garrison (1994b) believes that this social orientation "explicitly rejects the notion of psychic entities (cognitive structures of the type championed by cognitive scientists)" (p. 6). I infer from the context of these remarks that Garrison is rejecting the concept of cognitive structures that are independent and disconnected from the social context. Yet Dewey's emphasis on reflection clearly indicates that some type of in-the-head thinking is involved. Dewey clearly thought of knowledge as structured, but connected to cultural and emotional experience. The debate about whether knowledge can be disentangled from context is important because it relates to the question of whether knowledge acquired in one setting can be transferred for use in another setting. If knowledge is *totally* contextualized in a physical space and embedded in local social practices, it would be difficult, if not impossible, to decontextualize that knowledge to develop abstractions that could be applied to other settings. This is a central issue in debates between psychological constructivists (chap. 3) and socioculturalists (chap. 5).

In Dewey's working model of knowledge acquisition, logical structures are generated in inquiry processes that are embedded in social and meaningful contexts. Because knowledge structures maintain their connections to the social and physical contexts in which they are acquired *and* to the nonreflective web of experience, the epistemological and ontological aspects of knowing are never disentangled. This view explains why the basic principles of the combined constructivist position place so much emphasis on characterizing knowledge as conditionalized and contextualized.

Useful knowledge is produced in particular types of experiences. Some of Dewey's critics found this model difficult to understand because they found his definitions of experience and educative experience illusive. Writing primarily to criticize Dewey's philosophy as compared with Marx's, G. Novak (1975) expressed frustration with Dewey's failure to provide a clear and consistent definition of experience. Novak attempted to provide his own definition from what Dewey had to say on the topic. In many ways, it is an improvement on what Dewey had to say in any one reference:

> He [Dewey] defined experience on a biological basis, as the transaction between an organism and its environment, of which the interaction between humans and their conditions of life is a special case. Unlike the idealists, he did not construe experience as a form of thought; it was a process of action. But he made the monism of experience an "unanalyzed integrity" transcend the real dualism of the subject and the object. (p. 170)

Dewey of course was not the first philosopher to use the concept of experience. Dewey used the concept of experience as a device to escape from a number of dualisms that he believed distorted the nature of the relationship among knowledge, the knower, and the known. Experience is not thought, perception, or nature or a mechanical description of the exchange between thought and nature. Experience encompasses the person–environment gestalt (both aesthetic and rational, both subjective and objective, both the person and his or her environmental context).

Dewey's view of experience differed from the definitions of experience held by many philosophers who preceded him because he saw experience as a transaction between a living organism and a dynamic physical and social environment, rather than as knowledge of the environment housed inside the person (Bernstein, 1966). His view of experience is not a form of idealism. Dewey actively avoided a position that would question the existence of the material world. Yet the real object does not "exist" as part of the individual's meaningful world (experience) prior to reflective inquiry. The world is real, but not known until it is given meaning through inquiry. Dewey is not saying that the real world does not exist, just that things which exist outside experience are philosophically irrelevant (Shook, 2000a).

Dewey's dynamic view of experience tries to avoid both solipsism and determinism. Most important, it allows people to act in and on the world and to actively shape their present and future lives. Dewey's projection of experience into the future is an important shift of perspective from previous views of experience that were bound to the past—to memories of what happened to us (Bernstein, 1966). It is a basic tenet of all pragmatic philosophies that experience is instrumentally oriented toward the consequences of behavior rather than its antecedents (House, 1992).

Dewey's emphasis on the structural and systematic qualities of experience was an important feature of his view of experience that links it to the current constructivists. Dewey saw the elements of experience as a dynamic organized system. The physical and cognitive structures made by people (e.g., houses, languages, ideas) become a part of the natural system within which the person operates. The dynamic and systematic qualities of experience provide experience with the potential for producing learning because experience can be reconstructed. The experience of an individual is continuous with the natural situation within which he or she is a part. Bernstein (1966) described Dewey's conceptualization of the structure of experience as follows: "connections and relations are as much a part of experience as the particulars that we isolate within experience" (p. 209). Again this supports an assertion that Dewey's position combines the two positions held by today's psychological constructivists and social constructionists.

Previous views of experience separated experience from reason. The distinction for Dewey was not between experience and reason, but between nonreflective and reflective experiences. The idea that the organism and the environment are unified within experience is consistent with Dewey's functionalism and his characterization of the person as an active shaper of his or her environment (Bernstein, 1966).

For Dewey, people live in the world of direct experience and a world of secondary or reflective experience populated by transactional objects. The term *transactional object* captures the spirit of the products of inquiry in Dewey's philosophy more than the terms *knowledge object* or *Third World object*. The inquiry process begins in primary experience, moves to secondary experience, and then back to primary experience to confirm the usefulness of abstract objects of inquiry. In each cycle of this process, our perceptions are shaped by and shape our knowledge of the world. For Dewey, secondary experience is "experienced in consequence of continued and regulated reflected inquiry. For derived and refined products are experienced only because of the intervention of systematic thinking" (LW 1:15). Rosenthal (2002) captured the nature of secondary experience:

> What appears within experience, then, opens in one direction toward the structures of the independently real and in the other direction toward the structures of our mode of grasping the independently real. (p. 78)

As they function in the person–environment system, primary and secondary experiences are also transactional: Neither is seen as having a higher status.

Although we might wish it happened more offen, it is difficult to deny the observation that people often learn things in one situation that they apply in different situations. If this implies that there are cognitive structures that facilitate transfer, the debate rests on the degree of independence of these structures (i.e., How portable are they and what conditions facilitate and inhibit transfer?). It is also important to remember that primary and secondary experiences are not separate entities that interact with each other, but components of a whole. All human experience is rooted in our natural situation that includes ourselves and the objects that constitute our secondary experience. Dewey clearly included logical structures in his theory of knowledge, but they were not self-contained, detached mental objects. Dewey (1922) used the metaphor of the organism's relationship to nature as "a plant . . . in sunlight and soil," rather than "coins in a box" (MW 14:204) to capture the "somewhat portable" nature of useful abstractions. I can carry my plant around, but it would die unless I put it in a pot of soil and made sure it got water and sunlight. It is portable, but only under certain environmental conditions. Although some interpretations of Dewey's writings see him as rejecting any type of cognitive structure (e.g., Garrison, 1994a), I think it is more accurate to say that Dewey would not support the existence of mental structures that are totally independent of the environment.

As we move into the discussion of the different versions of constructivism and their relevance to educational practice in future chapters, the reason for the importance of these philosophical distinctions will become more obvious. Psychological constructivist theories include cognitive structures that can function as abstractions that can be applied to a broad range of situations across many settings. In this view, the ability to develop structures with some level of abstraction is the key to the transferability of knowledge from one context to another, especially from schools to the application of knowledge to problem solving in other settings. Combined positions such as the situated cognitive theories maintain a form of cognitive structure, but see knowledge as embedded in its physical and cultural context. Different perspectives within the range of situated cognitive theories have different ways to explain how knowledge can be transferred from one situation to another. Some sociocultural theorists even question whether transfer is possible and whether schools can ever give students useful knowledge.

Let me pause briefly and connect this discourse to its practical implications for the professor in the classroom. Assuming that the important concepts (whether we refer to them as "big ideas," "flexible schemas," or "enduring understandings") and the methods of inquiry we want students to carry from our classrooms to the world of scientific inquiry or professional practice are only semiportable, we need to develop methods of instruction that increase the possibility of transfer. If we adopt the theory that concepts are embedded in the social practices of the learning environment, we might want to change some of the ways that we interact with students in the classroom to match the social practices in the settings where our students will apply their knowledge. It is useful to ask the questions, "How do I expect students to use this knowledge?" and "How do people communicate and work in the settings where students will use this knowledge?"

Another implication of this analysis is that students need to learn to recognize problems that are embedded in complex, unstructured social contexts. In our courses, we tend to pull problems out of their complex contexts and look at them separately. This means that students do not have to recognize the problem embedded in a complex set of other system elements like they will when they try to use the knowledge. Becoming an expert always involves learning to *see* like an expert. Students need to learn to identify and frame problems like the people who inhabit the knowledge communities they will enter when they leave the classroom. Even if we want our graduates to change the way people in their fields approach problems, they have to understand the existing social practices in environments of application. In the "Understanding Organizations" course, I want to help students find new ways to communicate in organizations. It is important for me to embed this change effort in a context that simulates the organizations they will enter after graduation. In effect, they are practicing ways of changing the way they communicate in a context that has important similarities to the settings in which they will work.

Dewey explored both logical structures and the cultural and situational contexts of these structures. For every critic that insists that Dewey would not support even a contextualized version of a cognitive structure, another complains that Dewey was too focused on individual mental constructs. In this regard, it is instructive that he made the following observation late in his career:

> Were I to write (or rewrite) *Experience and Nature* today, I would entitle the book *Culture and Nature* and the treatment of specific subject-matters would be correspondingly modified. I would abandon the term "experience" be-

cause of my growing realization that the historical obstacles which prevented understanding of my use of experience are, for all practical purposes, insurmountable. I would substitute the word "culture" because with its meanings as now firmly established it can be fully and freely carry my philosophy of experience. (Dewey, 1951, LW 1:361)

Educative Experience

As an educator, Dewey, like the rest of us, could see that all experiences did not produce personal growth and increase adaptive capacity. The development of a practical theory of education had to begin with some guidelines for discriminating between educative and noneducative experience. An educative experience arms the learner with habits to successfully adapt to situations he or she will encounter in the future. An experience is *miseducative* if it has "the effect of arresting or distorting the growth of further development" (Dewey, 1925/1958, p. 25, LW:13.11). The criterion for defining an experience as educative was:

> Does this form of growth create conditions for further growth, or does it set up conditions that shut off the person who has grown in this particular direction from the occasions, stimuli, and opportunities for continuing growth in new direction? (Dewey, 1938a, p. 25, LW:13.19)

The learning process begins by finding the basic material for learning within an experience and then actively constructing knowledge through a guided process that gradually approximates the structure of expert knowledge. Dewey (1925/1958) described this aspect of an educative experience as follows: "No experience is educative that does not tend to both knowledge of more facts and entertaining more ideas and to a better, a more orderly, arrangement of them. It is not true that organization is a principle foreign to experience" (p. 82, LW:13.56). Current constructivist theories that include a role for cognitive structures retain this focus on learning as improving the organization of cognitive structures.

The broader definition of experience and inquiry reflected in Dewey's later works gives a stronger picture of the relationship between experience and the transactional objects that emerge from experience through inquiry. The qualitative nature of experience can be lost by readers who focus on inquiry and cognitive structures without considering the "nonreflective matrix of experience" in which they are embedded (Stanic & Russell, 2002). This experiential ether is the source of the emotional/aesthetic energy and sense of being that is a part of the meaning of a cognitive structure. I emphasized the distinction between Dewey's early and later concepts of experience and inquiry because it leads to an increased awareness of the importance of imagination and emotion in educative experience (Stanic &

Russell). Dewey's later work also shifted its emphasis away from prescriptive reason toward the creative problem solving necessary to solve ill-structured problems.

In *Art as Experience*, Dewey (1934/1980) also made a distinction between ongoing experience and *an* experience. Dewey's description of this type of experience gives us more guidance for developing authentic and vibrant educational experiences in the classroom (Jackson, 1995; Wong et al., 2001). *An* experience is experienced as a meaningful whole and moves toward resolution. In *an* experience, the person actively changes the environment to achieve his or her goal, but is also shaped by the environment (i.e., is changed by the experience). Dewey's ideal is a balance between changing (doing) and being changed (undergoing). *An* experience is a product of doing and undergoing in the context of a meaningful activity. Experiences that create meaning require action and reflection. Just doing or just thinking is inert. Dewey's definition of *an* experience is the foundation for the definition of an authentic and meaningful context (the second of the basic principles of the combined constructivist position). In rereading *Art as Experience*, I was struck with how contemporary the following quote sounded:

> Zeal for doing, lust for action, leaves many a person, especially in this hurried and impatient human environment in which we live, with experience of almost incredible paucity, all on the surface. No experience has a chance to complete itself because something else is entered upon speedily. What is called experience becomes so dispersed and miscellaneous as hardly to deserve the name. . . . Resistance is treated as an obstacle to be beaten down, not as an invitation to reflection. An individual comes to seek, unconsciously even more than by deliberate choice, situations in which he can do the most things in the shortest time. (p. 45, LW:10.51)

The learner can make the opposite error by focusing only on receiving and experiencing to the exclusion of action. Information passes through passive learners without taking root. The methods of instruction that Dewey and his followers have developed were derived from their basic understanding of the nature of an educative experience. Within the context of *an* experience, receptivity is not passive, but is tied to the meaningful whole of the experience, and there is no separation between the intellectual and emotional aspects of experience. Concepts are not simply recognized, but perceived and used to reconstruct knowledge.

For an experience to be educative, some aspect of the environment needs to provide resources to help the student connect the learning experience to his or her past and future experience. The resources could be the teacher or some other person with a higher level of expertise than the learner or some element of organization built into the environment by the teacher through the curriculum's design. The student is stimulated to reflect on the situation and take some action, followed by an evaluation of the results of his or her intervention. Engaging in an experience results in changes in the learner's attitude, behavior, or worldview, which Dewey referred to as the transformation and reconstruction of experience.

Education Is Development:
Growth as Increased Adaptive Capacity

One of the reasons I am committed to maintaining a naturalistic position is that I believe the link between experience and education depends on maintaining the beginning point of experience as biological and natural from an ecological systems perspective. The ecological perspective leads naturally to Dewey's primary goal of education: growth as increased adaptive capacity. It also places knowledge as relative to its context rather than as absolute and independent of its situation. From a constructivist perspective, learning is acquiring knowledge and skills to be more successful in a particular life situation (i.e., an ecological niche). The situation is not made up of individual objects or events, or even a collection of objects or events that can be addressed in isolation, but the objects and events as they function as a contextual whole, including the person him or herself as an event in the ecology.

Dewey's naturalistic world has enduring elements, but it is fundamentally changeable, as is the organism and relationship between them (Dewey, 1925/1958). The human organism is naturally inclined to conduct inquiry and acquire knowledge to improve its adaptive capacity, even to alter the environment intentionally (D. J. Simpson, 2001). A key to human adaptation (which is of people in community rather than as individuals) is to create meaning that will "prevail over the instability of events . . . [that is] . . . the main task of intelligent human effort" (Dewey, 1925/1958, p. 49, LW:1.49). This worldview leads naturally to Dewey's definition of *intelligence* as the organism's ability to adapt its behavior to a changing environment and to change its environment to meet its needs. This definition of intelligence as adaptive behavior directly influences the goals of education, the kinds of graduates schools are expected to produce, and the design of the learning environment within the school. Most obviously, schools have to be attuned to the demands of the environments its students will enter after graduation.

Today's corporate environments are designed to emulate the instability of nature rather than to form islands of stability. In times of increasing turmoil and demands for change, the learning environments in schools are getting less like the learning environment in the world of work. The intelligent human organism within this social/ecological context does not benefit from acquiring knowledge that cannot be connected to practice or thinking skills that cannot be connected to practical problem solving. Thinking and inquiry are not seen as separate things (Cahan, 1992).

The Role of Inquiry and the Problematic Situation

The problematic situation and the inquiry it stimulates play a pivotol role in the meaning-making process. It is important to remember that all logical structures emerge within experience as the product of inquiry (Burke, Hester, & Talisse, 2002). A primary characteristic of an educative experience is that it presents the learner with a problematic situation that requires intelligence to solve. Confrontation with a problem or an unusual situation disturbs the flow of habitual behavior and stimulates reflection, which is the foundation of abstraction. As I discussed earlier, Dewey's later works present a broader picture of the nature of the problematic situation/inquiry cycle. Dewey saw inquiry as the activity of intelligence. Dewey did not see intelligence as a noun (i.e., a trait that could stand on its own) but as an adjective that describes adaptive behavior. People can behave intelligently, but they cannot *be* intelligent. This makes intelligence as much a part of the context as of the person. This is a view that is held by most of today's combined constructivists and socioculturalists.

Inquiry is the process that leads to growth, which is the goal of education. Inquiry begins with an indeterminate situation that attracts the learner's attention. The rules of inquiry are not given—they emerge from successful (adaptive) inquiries. Education focuses on developing a logic of inquiry that enhances adaptive capacity (Rosenthal, 2002). The premise that growth occurs through the process of intelligent problem solving in an ecologically valid context begins to provide guidelines for educational practice. The core of this method of instruction is to create situations that demand problem solving through systematic inquiry. Problematic situations must be embedded in a larger enterprise, and learning emerges from work conducted in an ecologically valid context (a context that has structural similarities to the student's world of everyday problems). Defining which structural similarities are important is a goal of research in learning science that is explored in future chapters. The inquiry process should increase the learner's ability to take meaningful action in the future. The *unit* is the best-known feature of the curriculum of Dewey's progressive school movement that survives in American classrooms. On the postsecondary level, problem-based learning provides a good example of a current method consistent with this philosophy.

Meaning, Cognitive Structures, and Experience

A philosophical issue that has a direct impact on how we think about teaching and learning relates to how much of the process of learning involves internal cognitive processing and how much of the process involves activity. Dewey's answers to this question can be confusing because cognitive structures and activity are transactionally related. Dewey's logic is a logic of activity. New meanings emerge in activities where meanings and doings transact within inquiry. Rosenthal (2002) compared the process by which an activity generates a logic of practice to mathematical rules for generating a series of numbers. There is an ongoing dynamic relationship between reflective and nonreflective experience. Knowing and being are not separate realms. Epistemology and ontology are unified within the concrete experience of doing and undergoing (Rosenthal).

I see Dewey's version of mental structures (transactional objects) as part of his conceptualization of the nature of the structure of knowledge rather than as a rejection of the role of mental structures per se. Dewey's concept of understanding involved understanding the connections between a concept and its connection to processes, activities, and social practices. Yet it is clear that Dewey rejected any conception of experience *itself* as being mental. The following quote cited by Shook (2000a) is a good summary of Dewey's thoughts on this issue:

> There was a period in modern philosophy when the appeal to "experience" was a thoroughly wholesome appeal to liberate philosophy from desiccated abstractions. But I failed to appreciate the fact that subsequent developments inside and outside of philosophy had corrupted and destroyed the wholesomeness of the appeal—that "experience" had become effectively identified with experiencing in the sense of the psychological, and the psychological had become established as that which is intrinsically psychical, mental, private. My insistence that "experience" also designates what is experienced was a mere ideological thundering in the Index for it ignored the ironical twist which made this use of "experience" strange and incomprehensible. (Dewey, 1951, LW 1:362)

It is clear that Dewey did not place experience *within* thinking, but it is just as clear that he did include thinking, ideas, and so on within experience. Dewey was not an idealist, but he often discussed cognitive processes in ways that implicated cognitive structures in both the construction of knowledge and in the making of new meanings. Dewey believed that thought increases the meaning of things and that this increase of meaning involves the establishment of relations among them. Although Dewey's perspective clearly included cognitive structures that allow thought to increase the meaning of things, they were not decontextualized structures. Shook (2000a) characterized Dewey's version of thought as highly contextualized:

> He [Dewey] agreed with James's rejection of consciousness as a substantive entity with mental contents, but as radical empiricists, Dewey and James retained the notion of experience in their philosophies. Mind can be discussed, but only insofar as it is a term denoting intelligent activities taking place within experience. Not only was Dewey unwilling to discuss physical entities independent of experience, he was unable to conceive of mental activities occurring independent of experience. Experience is therefore logically and actually prior to knowledge activity for Dewey. (p. 244)

In this sense, ideas are a real thing, although they cannot be fruitfully conceptualized as containable within the head. It makes sense to interpret Dewey's comments on thinking as inferring, at least, that thinking skills (like inferring) and ideas find it difficult or impossible to exist without some form of scaffolding beyond the head, most notably language and culture (which in his later writings he saw as almost synonymous with experience).

For Dewey, the problem of knowledge acquisition is not framed in terms of matching up ideas about the world with the real objects in the world (i.e., he rejected the "spectator theory of knowledge"). The ideas and objects are all part of the same natural system. The test of a theory is its usefulness, and the truth it yields only lasts as long as it has instrumental value. Fortunately, the real world seems to have a lot of enduring structures because many theories are useful for a long time and in a fairly wide range of situations. Otherwise education would not increase our adaptive capacity. The truth endures, but it is not eternal. Truth or, to use Dewey's term, *warranted assertion* does not come from outside of experience, but from the predicable regularities of our transactions with the world.

Both realists and idealists tend to read Dewey's work as opposing their position. When idealists see elements in Dewey's position that sound like realism, they think of him as a traditional realist. Dewey accepts the existence of the real world on a commonsense level, but does not think objects exist for us (i.e., have meaning for us) until we experience them. More accurately, it is meaningless to talk about objects outside the realm of experience. However, Dewey's transactional realism does not eliminate mental states—it naturalizes them. Dewey sees both perception and thinking as natural behaviors (as processes of activities) that take place within experience. Cognitive constructs are tools for enhancing adaptive capacity; they are tools for problem solving.

When realists see points of agreement between the idealists and Dewey, they categorize him as an idealist because they decontextualize his individual points from his broader, naturalized experience framework. The content of knowledge is shaped by constructive processes that use logical forms that are products of previous successful inquiry. The idealists see reality as being shaped by natural preexisting categories (Rosenthal, 2002). For Dewey, thinking and ideas are tools like models, theories, and artifacts. For Dewey then, the objective of knowing is not the real object out there. The transactional object produced by inquiry then becomes a tool available for future inquiry (Shook, 2000a). Thinking as a component of reflective practice or meaningful action plays a central role in bringing about change.

Dewey frequently referred to thinking, but he was clear that thinking is a natural activity (a practice). Although he is clearly a realist, Dewey (1917) acknowledged certain idealistic qualities to his theory. "In so far as it is idealistic to hold that objects of knowledge *in their capacity of distinctive objects of knowledge* are determined by intelligence, it is idealistic. . . . Thinking is what some of the actual existences [people] do. They are in no sense constituted by thought"(MW 10:338,339). Shook (2000b) agreed that knowledge is not constructed by mental states, but said that when knowledge has been constructed it is present as a real object to the knower. This indicates that Dewey would allow for the manipulation of some form of mental structures. Dewey always avoids giving the mind ontological independence (it never operates as a real thing totally disconnected from experience). Yet this does not imply that scaffolded ideas could not function independently enough to facilitate transfer.

McCarthy and Sears (2000) pointed out that the object of knowledge for Dewey is not experience, but a meaningful, and therefore useful, "signforce" of the elements of experience. These are signs of other things not present that represent some at least temporarily dependable regularities in the environment. These signforces are discovered through inquiry. The meaning of these signforces cannot be separated from the process of extracting them (i.e., the logic of inquiry). McCarthy and Sears (2000) provided an excellent metaphor for the relationship between the inquiry process and knowledge objects:

> Data are extracted from the complexity that is the original situation in the same way that pure ore is extracted from the mountain rock. The fact that "pure ore" can be extracted from the mountain does not entitle us to infer that "pure ore" as such was already there, in the mountain. There is a process of analysis in inquiry (an extraction process) that results in the actual occurrence of the "dependable evidential signs"—"elements" (the "pure ore"). (p. 219)

Ronald and Roskelly (2001) pointed out that, like the activity theorists, pragmatists gave mediation a central role in meaning making. Pierce connected language, thought, and action in his "triacity" of sign, meaning, and the inquirer. Coupling this dynamic image of meaning in action with

Dewey's frequent references to the structure of knowledge brings us closer to understanding how a cognitive structure can be both independent and contextualized in praxis. The discussion of Schank's (1999) theory of dynamic memory in chapter 3 presents one version of how this actually operates. As a tool, an idea can be used in a variety of situations, but they all involve using ideas in action rather than detached contemplation (see Dewey, 1934/1980).

ABANDONING ULTIMATE TRUTH AND AVOIDING CULTURAL RELATIVISM

A correlate of Dewey's naturalized worldview and concept of experience is his rejection of the existence of an ultimate or transcendent truth. Understanding is a selective and constructive process. Because meaning is contained within experience, truth is limited to warranted assertions that are bounded by the context of the problem situation. Common sense tells us that some things are true and some things are not true. As scholars and scientists, however, we tend to think of truth as having some limits—some practical and some theoretical. It is only when we stop and reflect on the existence or nonexistence of some absolute or transcendent truth that it becomes obvious that both positions are problematic.

Hay (1996) characterized the assumptions of theories that assume the existence of ultimate truth as follows: "These theories state that there are words in things and in nature that can be abstracted out of them by scientists or prophets. The words then form a structure or framework for knowledge that is ahistorical, cross-cultural, apolitical" (p. 202). Although he was obviously characterizing logical positivism, his statement begins to reveal some of the problems associated with accepting the concept of ultimate truth.

Dewey and the constructivists reject the existence of foundational knowledge and struggle with the implications of this rejection. Criticism of Dewey's philosophy is usually focused on the consequences of accepting his position rather than his rationale for rejecting absolute truth. Conservative critics are concerned about the moral implications of cultural relativism, and radical critics are concerned that Dewey's philosophy provides no justification for the transcendent value of social justice and the common good as criteria for evaluating the quality of a society.

In the educational debates of the early part of the 20th century, Dewey's philosophical position represented a middle ground between the prescriptive essentialists and the nonprescriptive Rousseauians. Throughout the last 100 years, Dewey's positions have been misunderstood and misrepresented by critics from both ends of this spectrum. Conservatives of the early 20th century attacked the progressive schools movement with the same basic concern they have about current programs based on constructivist theories.

They believed that Dewey's philosophy contained a kind of cultural relativism that threatened the core values of the society and left educators with no basis to judge any behavior as unacceptable or immoral. Critics on the left have expressed a parallel concern that Dewey's philosophy accepts the existing social order as "natural" and does not provide access to the universal values that should guide fundamental societal change toward social justice.

Although some of the concerns of the essentialists of Dewey's time reflected a potential weakness in Dewey's philosophy, much of their criticism resulted from the fact that many schools that described themselves with labels like "progressive," "active learning," and "experiential education" were actually following a Rousseauian "freedom to grow" philosophy. This scenario was repeated in the 1960s when many schools adopted the vocabulary of the open classroom movement, but operated schools with a "kids need freedom to grow" (Rousseauian Romanticism) philosophy. This is the source of my concern that the current constructivist reform movement will meet the same fate at the hands of some forms of education growing out of critical theory and postmodernism.

In his day, some of Dewey's critics thought he had a blind faith in the learner's ability to benefit from experience. This inference ignores one of Dewey's basic principles of education: that some experiences are educative and some are not. They incorrectly inferred that his assertion that all learning comes from experience implied that people learn best by following their "gut-level instincts" and "discovering" knowledge as they explore the world without guided reflection. Other critics accused Dewey of putting freedom before discipline and well-organized thinking. This was an especially frustrating accusation for Dewey. As a general principle, this book asserts that Dewey's philosophy, the preponderance of research on learning, and most theories of teaching and learning associated with constructivism indicate that guided (scaffolded) reflection is an essential ingredient for the acquisition of useful knowledge.

A consistent and effective method of attacking constructivist educational programs has been to label them as permissive and laissez-faire. These characterizations of Dewey's philosophy are the farthest thing from what Dewey meant by experiential education. Structure and construction are central to Dewey's view of learning. Knowledge is built by an active systematic inquiry process. In a sense, the learner does *discover* knowledge in the process of constructing it, but he or she does not *find* it unless experiences are structured to facilitate particular learning objectives. Progressivism and constructivism do not reject the idea that there are important things to know (even facts to memorize and skills to practice); they simply place the objectives of education in an adaptive context. They change the criteria for deciding what knowledge is important from an eternal standard to an instrumental standard: what knowledge is useful. They focus education on helping students develop the cognitive and emotional resources they need to successfully adapt to their present and future environment. Neither knowledge nor cognitive structures exist outside the natural environment. Thinking skills are not external structures that are applied by the mind to understand reality, but are part of and derived from an organic whole that includes the activity and logic of inquiry and problem solving. In this sense, Dewey's philosophy has a kind of limited determinism. For Dewey, meanings are created instrumentally through our response to the environment. Our mental structures result from our transactions with the world, but the world does not simply stamp itself on us. Dewey's determinism is limited because the person is acting on the environment as well as being shaped by it. People are partially embedded in their social and historical contexts because the new meanings are constructed out of existing meanings.

The application of Dewey's philosophy to learning in schools must be seen as a special case of his broader analysis of the knower, knowing, and the known. The picture of the process of learning that emerges from this analysis increases our awareness of the complexity of the learning process and makes it especially clear that learning is a complex constructive process. Knowledge construction can more accurately be characterized as taking place at the boundary between the individual and "the nonreflective matrix of experience." As such, learners need environmental support from both teachers and the range of cultural artifacts at their disposal. Given this analysis, it is clear why Dewey did not accept Rousseau's proposition that children have innate capacities that just need to be released. The learning process requires a great deal of external scaffolding.

Dewey experienced as much frustration communicating the practical implications of his theory of education as he did getting other philosophers to understand that his philosophy did not fall into their models of idealism or realism. Even though Dewey spoke out strongly against permissive, unstructured educational programs, he is associated in the public mind with these types of programs. Constructivist and experiential education programs are still having a difficult time avoiding being painted with this brush.

Dealing With the Issue of Moral Relativism

Dewey's philosophy raises important concerns in many readers' minds. What replaces ideal forms and eternal values when philosophy is naturalized and stripped of its certainty? Dewey abandoned the certainty of ultimate truth grounded in the supernatural for the messy world of people in their natural environment. Reason, which had privileged access to Plato's ideal forms *outside* the arena of experience, becomes a practical tool for mean–ends analysis in problematic situations *within* experience (Garrison, 1996). This limits individuals within their perspective in their physical and sociocultural worlds and by their positions within the culture (e.g., dominant or marginalized). Dewey's instrumentalism evaluated attempts to solve problems by their outcomes, but provided no external standard for judging those outcomes.

Despite Dewey's rejection of foundational values, he did express clear values that operate within the context of democratic, face-to-face communities. Democracy becomes a social reality that is defined by certain processes. Within this context, we *should* include all the stakeholders who might be affected by our actions in the process of identifying problems and conducting inquiry. He considered the commitment to the common good a defining characteristic of the form of associated living of democratic communities (Dewey, 1927/1954). Individual and communal growth are *both* promoted by truly adaptive solutions (Henry, 2001). This analysis is the underlying rationale for the goal of establishing new social practices that promote effective inquiry in the classroom. In the "Understanding Organizations" course, this idea is operationalized by adopting Argyris' Model II of communication (high on advocacy and high on inquiry). This sets a standard of communicative action that increases the adaptive capacity of the organizations that are characterized by these forms of communication (Argyris, 1993). In effect, Dewey was saying that the process and criteria for evaluating the quality of communication processes can be defined according to a pragmatic a priori, but the end cannot be established a priori.

Dewey's escape from moral relativism is debatable and tenuous. His solution gives value to a process for reaching consensus on values rather than a set of standards for conduct. For Dewey, the process of reaching agreement on ethical questions is part of a "mode of associated living" within democratic communities (Dewey, 1927/1954; Schutz, 2001). The foundation of inquiry is the community's consensus about which outcomes are desirable based on their understanding of who will be affected by their actions (Dewey, 1927/1954). In chapter 7, I discuss the work of Habermas and others who have focused on how communities can reach consensus on values without access to absolute truth. A successful solution to a problem does not prevent us from reframing the problem context based on a new set of assumptions about the values and facts that define the problem and provide criteria to assess the quality of the outcome. Open dialogue (Habermas used the term *communicative action*) is the process for building consensus within communities on their pragmatic a priori assumptions. When applied to education, this analysis explains the high value given to building diverse classroom communities, promoting open dialogue among community members, and continually examining the assumptions individuals are using to identify problems and evaluate solutions.

The most powerful tools available to human beings for successful adaptation to a wide range of ecological niches are our cognitive reasoning abilities, including our logics of inquiry and our capacity for imagination. These abilities are "natural" because they have developed through inquiry that has led to adaptive solutions to problems. Some emerge in the course of development and everyday experience (e.g., concrete operational thinking) and some require education (e.g., formal operational thinking, dialectical thinking). Imagination is a human capacity that provides a tool for creating values and escaping cultural determinism. In Dewey's (1934/1980) philosophy, imagination is a primary tool for developing new perspectives, understanding the perspectives of other people, and creating new solutions to human problems (Garrison, 1996). Any time that problems or novel situations disrupt habitual behavior, reflecting on possible solutions requires imagining what might happen if we were to try each solution. Schutz (2001) also pointed out that transference requires imagination in the sense that we must disregard the differences between two situations and focus on the specific similarities that would make knowledge acquired in one situation applicable to another. I see the power of imagination as a central principle of Dewey's mature philosophy.

Up to this point, the focus of this discussion has been on Dewey's nonfoundationalism (abandoning ultimate truth). Even if we find an arena for developing some enduring values within a community, we have contextualized the definition of the *right thing* within the boundaries of that community and failed to escape cultural relativism on a broader context. My own summary of Dewey's solution to this dilemma is that he asserts that it is always more adaptive to broaden the boundaries of community to be more inclusive. This means we continue to care about how what we do as a community affects the nation and how what we do as a nation affects the world.

Dealing With Issues of Power and Oppression

Criticism from essentialists who faulted Dewey for failing to defend the canon was matched by critical theorists who faulted him for not attacking it. Many critical theorists believe the canon is not defined by a transcendental ideal, but by a process that designates the knowledge held by the privileged classes as "higher knowledge." Possessing this knowledge is a requirement for access to power, and lack of this knowledge provides "objective" criteria for exclusion from the circles of power (Bourdieu, 1990; Habermas, 1971). Many critical theorists in education do not think that Dewey appreciated the role of knowledge in maintaining the hegemony of dominant groups in society.

Novak (1975) thought that Dewey's instrumental focus prevented him from addressing issues of social justice because it privileged means over

ends. By this, Novak meant that Dewey focused on process in both education and politics rather than dictating the outcome of that process. His critics were uncomfortable with Dewey's faith that the right process would lead
to the most intelligent answer. Much of the criticism of Dewey from the left
was born of their disagreement with Dewey's model for bringing about social change through schools and gradual improvement through cooperative action at the community level. Many of Dewey's critics thought he had a
naive belief in the power of democratic action. They felt he did not recognize the inherent conflicts built into the social structure of capitalism or the
difficulty in translating face-to-face democracy on the community level to
the larger society (Schutz, 2001). Like Habermas, Dewey had a faith that if
we communicate openly, we will achieve just solutions.

Parenger (1990) and Schutz (2001) also thought that Dewey's belief in
the possibility of liberal reform from within established institutions, especially the school, represented a fundamental misunderstanding of the extent to which society's relationships of domination were built into the structure and processes of social institutions. Parenger believed that liberalism
and the pedagogues it spawned inevitably retain the oppressive power relationships built into the social system. He did not believe that Dewey understood the central role of ideology in shaping all of the elements of the educational experience: society, the self, science, and technology.

Parenger (1990) made a specific distinction between Dewey's concept
of a transaction within experience, which is embedded in the natural,
and praxis, which he saw as a stronger concept because it is more clearly imbedded in culture and history. He believed that Dewey's inclusion of the
man-made social environment as the primary component of the human being's environment of adaptation included a tacit acceptance of that environment as a given. He tied the concept of praxis specifically to the idea of
social justice. I do not agree with Parenger's sharp distinction between the
concepts of transaction and praxis, but I agree that most of Dewey's examples of problem-solving situations were narrowly instrumental, rather than
grounded in a broader critique of society and the goal of social justice.
Parenger's analyses of power address the human experience from a different perspective than Dewey's. Because of his brand of naive anarchism,
Dewey did not really address the issues of power that concerned Parenger
because he focused only on modes of association in face-to-face communities. In this sense the criticism was justified.

Yet even if we accept some of Parenger's criticisms as valid, the key question should be whether Dewey's philosophy can be extended to legitimately
position social justice as a central goal of education. Parenger does not give
us much guidance about how to change the way we teach to achieve this
goal except to reiterate the importance of introducing the content of
power and the contradictions of history into the curriculum. He stated, in

fact, that he would not quarrel with the teaching methods Dewey advocated. I would counter with the observation that, within any critical or activity theory, the methods are as important as the content. The problem for the professor in the classroom is: What should I actually *do* to address some of these concerns? Can programs based on Dewey's philosophy restructure themselves to address Parenger's critique or must a totally new model be developed? Throughout this book, I argue against introducing topics like racism, sexism, social justice, and multicultural issues as *content* without restructuring the learning situation to foster social practices that reflect and promote these values.

Habermas (1971) approached the problem of providing a philosophical foundation for moral claims with a special theory of argumentation he called *discourse ethics*. This approach is similar to Dewey's in that it moves the site of ethical decision making from the individual to the group level. Instead of trying to identify specific universal moral principles, he identified a process (a kind of argumentation) that he believed would lead to valid answers to moral questions. The style of argumentation he identified (communicative action) engages everyone involved in and affected by a decision in an open dialogue to reach consensus. The "lifeworlds" (how people experience the world) of the people involved are the contexts for reaching consensus on moral questions. This approach differs from that of other philosophers (e.g., Rawls) because it does not ask individuals to "be objective" and set aside their self-interests. Self-interests that reside in the lifeworlds of participants are legitimate elements of the debate that must be satisfied to reach a true consensus. In the context of the Argyris' Model II used in the "Understanding Organizations" course, students are encouraged to advocate for their own interests as well as inquire about and understand the interests of other students. Habermas (1990) adopted a standard similar to the one Dewey did in *The Public and Its Problems*:

> . . . norm has to fulfill the following condition: every valid (U) All affected can accept the consequences and the side effects its general observance can be anticipated to have for the satisfaction of everyone's interests (and these consequences are preferred to those of known alternative possibilities of regulation. (p. 65)

The recent rise of postmodernism has reintroduced the issues of ultimate truth and nonfoundationalism into the national dialogue about education. Hay (1996) believed that the rise of postmodernism created three crises in education. The first—a crisis of representation—is a crisis resulting from contemporary challenges to traditional theories of truth. Like Dewey, Hay's educational theory assumes there is no universal truth, but only a consensus in a knowledge community. The crisis of representation calls into question what we can teach and how we can represent it to students.

The second crisis is a crisis of authority. If knowledge has no foundation, where do we get the authority to teach it to others? In the past, we based our claim to be teachers on becoming experts in both the knowledge base and the principles of teaching and learning. The third crisis is the crisis of subjectivity. This crisis calls into question assumptions we have made about the self based on a Kantian framework (the autonomous, rational self). The post-modern identity is anchored in the socially constructed world. These crises represent a set of political issues and practical pedagogical problems that the constructivist approaches to education must confront.

Within learning science, theorists and researchers have responded to the growing awareness of the importance of the social context by developing theories that focus on social construction. One way to explore the question of whether Dewey's philosophy can be reconstructed to meet the challenges raised by critical theorists is to examine the two types of constructivism that have emerged from this debate—psychological constructivism and social constructivism—in this context. Psychological constructivists like von Glasersfeld (1995) focused on the processes individuals use to construct reality. Social constructionists like Gergen (1994a) focused on the sociocultural forces that shape the social construction of reality. Psychological constructivists tend to gather data on how individuals develop cognitive skills to increase their problem-solving ability, and social constructivists tend to analyze sociocultural practices and how they influence variables like classroom interaction patterns. Dewey's position represents a compromise or middle-of-the-road position between these extremes. The combined constructivist approaches described in chapter 6 parallel Dewey's approach for addressing issues of values and social justice. When these two branches of constructivism operate together in a complementary fashion, they can tap the strengths of both approaches. Taking Dewey's transactional position gives us a broader range of tools to escape the trap of cultural relativism. It also gives us a picture of students who are capable of escaping their narrow worldviews and committing themselves to social justice and the common good. Exactly what does it mean to choose Dewey's philosophical position and the combined approach to constructivism to develop methods of approaching the issue of cultural relativism? To me it means acknowledging that our sociocultural context is a powerful force that shapes what we think and, possibly more important, what it does not occur to us to think.

Dewey's Concept of Identity

Dewey and the constructivists share the view that we construct our identities by doing rather than finding our "true self." He did not see the self as permanent and independent (Dewey, 1934/1980; D. J. Simpson, 2001), but he gave the individual more agency than the sociocultural theorists that are presented in chapter 5. Both Dewey and socioculturalists held a relationship view of the self and were strongly influenced by Mead's symbolic interactionism. Dewey (1916) stated:

> The identification with the mind with the self, and the setting up of the self as something independent and self-sufficient, created such a gulf between the knowing mind and the world that it became a question how knowledge was possible at all. . . . [And] when knowledge is regarded as originating and developing within the individual, the ties which bind the mental life of one to that of his fellows are ignored and denied. (MW:9.302 and 9.307; Quoted in Packer & Goicochea, 2000, p. 229)

Both Dewey and the theory builders in the various forms of constructivism explored the nature of identity and its relationship to the environment. Transactional perspectives on identity conceptualize the person and the relationship of identity to the world in a way that challenges the Western cultural view. Western cultures tend to hold a highly mentalistic, totally self-contained, individualized version of the self. The boundaries between the self and the environment are sharply drawn. Dewey's concept of the self is closer to current views of identity held by sociocultural, activity, and postmodern theorists. Understanding the way these theories see the identity's dynamic relationship to the environment is critical for understanding all of the concepts associated with these perspectives. As in many areas of Dewey's philosophy, it is difficult to understand Dewey's concept of identity with traditional dualistic thinking. Consequently, as in other areas of his philosophy, Dewey was attacked by critics across the political spectrum.

Marxist educational theorists criticized Dewey's concept of the self because they thought it was too decontextualized and individualistic (Novak, 1975). Today's Marxist critics (Giroux, 1992; McLaren & Farahmandpur, 2000) make the same criticism of psychological and combined constructivist positions on identity. Issues around competing concepts of identity and the self are central to the debate about education reform. Dewey's concept of experience saw people as imbedded in their social circumstances and their mental life as a product of their organized social life. Dewey (1934/1980) did not see "mind" as either developing or operating independently from its environment. Yet Dewey's mental life does develop its own structural integrity that can serve as a foundation for a coherent differentiated identity. For Dewey, the self is partially embedded in its cultural context, but structurally coherent because it functions as a system. By keeping the mind in transaction with the culture rather than synonymous with culture, Dewey recognized that the social milieu is the primary environment that the person must adapt to to survive and flourish. The culture is the soil for growth. In this sense, the identity never really operates outside its cultural context, but it does exist as an active agent defined by action. Most important, Dewey's identity is self-authored by action. This position allows Dewey to maintain an identity with borders (an individual of free will within the force of circumstance who can differentiate thinking from emotion) taking action and constructing ideas that reconstruct experience. This seemingly subtle distinction is important because teachers want students who can create and shape their futures through intelligent practice.

Because Dewey wanted to avoid solipsism and focus on the person as a product of social interaction, his exploration of the identity focused on the construction of identity in a sociocultural context. In fact Bernstein (1966) believed that Dewey and the pragmatists failed to develop an adequate concept of the self because they emphasized the social side of the self to the exclusion of the internal qualities. Yet Dewey's concept of identity was clearly not totally determined by context. The individual exists as an independent identity because he or she can consciously act and adapt. The identity is always transacting with its environment and open to reconstruction. However, it is clear that Dewey saw the integration and independence of the self as a growth objective. The source of the self's viscosity is its ability to make meaning in experience and retain generalizable concepts that enhance its ability to adapt in future situations.

Dewey's view of the relationship between the identity and learning had similarities to current positions held by most socioculturalists and combined constructivists that see learning as the reconstruction of identity. (This position is reflected in the 11th basic principle of the combined position.) For Dewey, the self and the environment were co-constructed. Dewey saw the person as both lost and found in his or her interests and meaningful activities (Hansen, 2002). Our identities are constructed in the meaningful activities that engage us. For Dewey (1938a), "the self and interest are two names for the same fact; the kind and the amount of interest actively taken in a thing reveals and measures the quality of selfhood which exists. Bear in mind that interest means the active or moving *identity* of the self with a certain object" (p. 352, MW:9.361).

DEWEY'S CONNECTION TO THE CONSTRUCTIVISTS

Dewey's philosophy led psychologists and educators toward the view that human development research conducted within living social contexts would yield more relevant results than research conducted in traditional laboratories with more controls, but less connection to the everyday environment. Like most modern learning scientists, especially those with what is called a *situated cognitive view,* Dewey contested the traditional empiricists' claim that knowledge could be created and disseminated free of its context. Dewey's ecological perspective is one of the sources of many of the basic perspectives in modern learning science, most notably, the insight that cognition is "situated" in a social context. This means that the cognitive capacities that have evolved through the organism's genetic and cultural history develop and operate differently in different environments because they operate in active transaction with the environmental context. It is an important principle of many of these theories that the individual and environment shape each other. As people we continually make and are made by our physical and social environments.

The constructivist view of learning science begins with Dewey's insight that the mind exists "in context" and experience does not reside solely inside the mind of an individual thinker. Petraglia (1998) defined *constructivism* as "the interdisciplinary view that we construct knowledge based on our cultural assumptions and prior experiences rather than through the efficient and rational calculation of the information at hand" (p. 4). Other definitions might lean more toward "a cognitive view," but they all involve the learner in an active two-way relationship with his or her environment. The roots of constructivism can be traced from Kant through Dewey, Vygotsky and Piaget, who investigated the ways that people construct meaning from the information they receive and how they integrate this information with their existing cognitive structures. Like Dewey, the constructivists have reframed the goal of education from dispensing knowledge to creating social environments that help students construct their own knowledge (Brown, Collins, & Duguid, 1989).

Today's constructivists have also adopted Dewey's distinction between "useful knowledge" and "inert knowledge" (content that is committed to memory, but cannot be accessed to solve problems in the real world). They also believe that learners must be involved in active construction of their own knowledge in the process of solving personally relevant problems.

Dewey's reconstruction of philosophy, enriched by later research in learning science, reframes the broad goals and specific objectives of education in fundamental ways. Dewey challenged the prevailing model of education that assumed that knowledge can be prepackaged and transmitted to students "passed physically from one to another like bricks" (Dewey, 1916, p. 4, MW:9.7). Fishman and McCarthy (1998) extended Dewey's metaphor to point out that students cannot make use of the bricks they receive unless they understand that they are a part of a building . . . "to even care about bricks, we must have a need to use them" (p. 20). Both the content and structure of knowledge must be meaningfully connected to its use in problem solving. This is a useful metaphor because it also helps us to think about the relationship between the concepts we teach in our courses (the bricks) and the larger models and cognitive structures (big ideas and deep principles) we hope students will acquire.

There are currently a large number of educational philosophers and learning scientists with a range of psychological constructivist and sociocultural theories debating their relevance for education. An equal number of social critics are warning us that these approaches to education endanger the quality of our schools and universities. Most of the constructivists trace their roots back to John Dewey. Many of the critics of constructivism make specific reference to Dewey and the progressive schools movement (Ravich, 2000). The quality of this debate, which has raged over the past 100 years, is always muddied by misunderstandings about Dewey's theory.

Like almost every concept in Dewey's philosophy, the implications of his naturalistic worldview and his attempts to escape all forms of dualism have been difficult for many of his readers to interpret. Because Dewey never placed himself in the categories his readers used to organize and understand philosophy or educational theories, it is easy for supporters and critics from any dualistic position to read him as supporting or opposing their position. Reading key words and phrases from Dewey's extensive writings, they make inferences that move right past the point where Dewey wanted to position himself. This makes reading scholarly work on both Dewey and the constructivists quite frustrating. Much of the literature is of the "he said this" versus "no, he said that" variety, with each position supported by direct quotes that seem to say the opposite thing. There is no uncomplicated way to state the connection between Dewey and the various forms of constructivism and socioculturalism or to say exactly what their implications are for university teaching. As a rule of thumb, it is safe to say that understanding Dewey and his connection to the constructivists always requires that we avoid either/or dualisms.

Chapter 3

Psychological Constructivist Perspectives on Learning

Contemporary theories and research in learning science are connected to the various forms of constructivism that have emerged over the last 30 years. The two basic forms of constructivism that anchor the ends of the continuum of constructivist theories are psychological constructivism, which focuses on internal cognitive structures, and socioculturalism, which focuses on the level of cultural practices. Several other versions of constructivism fall along a continuum between these two positions. Both of the basic forms of constructivism share similarities and differences with Dewey's philosophy. Generally, Dewey's transactional constructivist position falls at the midpoint on this continuum.

Educators who want to explore the question of how these theories can inform university teaching are confronted with a complex and confusing array of vocabulary. Much of the literature is comprised of intense debates between proponents of the cognitive and sociocultural positions. Even my use of the label *constructivism* to cover the broad range of theories from psychological constructivism to sociocultural perspectives may be confusing because the term *constructivism* is often used to refer specifically to psychological constructivism.

I personally favor the combined or transactional constructivist model because it allows me to focus on both internal cognitive processes (the focus of psychological constructivism) and the way thinking is contextualized within culture and social processes (the focus of the sociocultural view explored in chap. 5). Situated cognitive theories are the best-known theories that fall in the middle range on this continuum. Dewey and modern learning scientists like Cobb (1994b) and Greeno (1997) with a combined perspective believe that placing both psychological processes and social practices in a functioning system eliminates the dualism between the individual and his or her context without eliminating the possibility of being. The transactional perspective changes our understanding of the nature of the boundaries between individuals and between cultures from one of walls and fences to one of dynamic transactions. It directs our research agendas toward understanding transactions at the boundaries between individuals and cultures, between cultures, and between communities of practice. It also helps us understand that effective models of teaching and learning depend on understanding the nature of the transaction between cognition and its social context.

This chapter explores psychological constructivist theories and the aspects of combined positions that have strong cognitive components. Other terms used to describe psychological constructivism include *radical constructivism,* the *individual perspective,* or the *cognitive approach.* Psychological constructivism is often associated with the work of Jean Piaget and Ernst von Glasersfeld. Von Glasersfeld's (1995) theory is referred to as radical constructivism because it is sharply focused on internal cognitive structures and processes and the development of an epistemological awareness of the nature of knowledge construction.

Like many other psychological constructivists, von Glasersfeld is a disciple of Jean Piaget and is connected to Kant through Piaget. Piaget (1967, 1970) developed the basic theoretical concepts and methods for studying cognitive processes. Piaget's (1967) theory and research on cognitive development suggested that children move through several distinct stages of cognitive development from infancy through adolescence. Piaget's first stage of cognitive development builds the foundation for conceptual development on action, beginning with the reflexive, sensorimotor actions of infants. Later stages build higher levels of cognition on previously constructed schemes. For Piaget (1967): ". . . to know an object implies incorporation in action schemes, and this is true on the most elementary sensorimotor level and all the way up to the highest logical-mathematical operation" (p. 17). Piaget offered an especially succinct statement of his theory of meaning making: "The mind organizes the world by organizing itself" (Piaget, 1937/1971, p. 311).

Radical constructivism shares many basic orientations with Dewey. Piaget and von Glasersfeld developed their theories from an adaptive and instrumental perspective. Piaget was a biologist and saw cognition as an adaptive, biological mechanism. For Piaget and von Glasersfeld, both organisms and ideas survive if they "work."

That is the difference. Radical constructivism is uninhibitedly instrumentalist. It replaces the notion of "truth" (as true representation of reality) with the notion of "viability" within the subject's experiential world. (von Glasersfeld, 1995, p. 22)

It is von Glasersfeld's instrumentalism that allows him to avoid solipsism (the idea that we live in an entirely imaginary world). All conceptual structures are tied to action (they are action schemes). A concept survives (is viable) if the action it produces is successful in solving the individual's problem (reducing his or her "perturbation").

For readers familiar with activity theory, this may sound like a similar concept. The difference is that von Glasersfeld's environment provides only constraints; the environment of the activity theorist also provides affordances. In the sociocultural model, language and other mediating devices that are produced by social history are appropriated or internalized through social interaction and participation in social practices (Holland, Lachicotte, Skinner, & Cain, 1998). Von Glasersfeld is willing to accept this as a hypothesis, but challenges the socioculturalists to explain how this is accomplished. He wonders how people can have direct access to language and cultural artifacts when they do not have direct access to the real world.

Piaget's theory stimulated a massive body of research on cognitive development in children and adults that transformed the way educators thought about the development of cognitive skills. Von Glasersfeld used Piaget's concepts of accommodation and assimilation as his primary cognitive mechanisms. Von Glasersfeld (1995) referred to his theory as *radical constructivism* to highlight the fact that he believed *all* meaning-making processes take place in the mind of the individual. The two principles of radical constructivism are: "knowledge is not passively received but built up by the cognizing subject; the function of cognition is adaptive and serves the organization of the experiential world, not the discovery of an ontological reality" (p. 18). All constructivist theories reject the idea that cognitive structures are "pictures" or accurate representations of the real world. Perception and conception are constructive. Mental operations do not deal with "raw data" from the "real world." To highlight his position that all mental operations are internal, von Glasersfeld hyphenated representation to read re-presentation. Accommodation (changes in our cognitive structures that represent learning) does not involve a direct confrontation between information introduced from the environment through the senses and existing schema. The "old" and "new" schemas are *both* re-presented, and restructuring occurs internally. Language is important to von Glasersfeld, but it does not function as external scaffolding; it operates internally. Even though von Glasersfeld's model is radically internal, social interactions play a central role in developing viable schemas. He used the term *intersubjective* to substitute for the concept of objectivity in the logical-positivist model. Yet in von Glasersfeld's theory, the intersubjective processes do not operate in the here and now of knowledge construction. They are re-presented within cognitive processes.

There is a substantial body of theory and research on a range of topics related to human learning and cognition. Topics with particular relevance for higher education include intellectual development; analytic, critical, and reflective thinking; concept acquisition and conceptual change; metacognition (thinking about thinking); and epistemological development (thinking about the nature of knowledge). The explosion in research on cognition and cognitive development over the past 20 years makes it impossible to cover this material in one chapter. For the interested reader, *How People Learn* by Bransford, Brown, and Cocking (1999) is a readable summary of theory and research in learning science as it applies to teaching and learning. Rather than attempt a systematic review of this literature, I briefly review the developmental theories that have focused on the cognitive and epistemological development of college students and explore a few specific topics that I believe are the most helpful for thinking about teaching in university courses. I begin with brief overviews of a few important concepts (i.e., reflection, conceptual change, expert vs. novice thinking, and metacognitive thinking) and then I summarize two of the theories that seem most relevant to higher education (i.e., Schank's theory of dynamic memory, Bransford's anchored instruction and situated cognition model). As I move through discussions of these theoretical frameworks, I refer to the basic principles of the combined constructivist approach and to relevant features of the "Understanding Organizations" course. Many of the specific perspectives presented in this chapter are actually combined positions that emphasize both the cognitive and sociocultural aspects of the learning process. In this chapter, I highlight the cognitive aspects of these approaches. Other aspects of these approaches are discussed in later chapters.

DEVELOPMENTAL THEORIES FOCUSING ON COLLEGE STUDENTS

Many theories of cognitive and intellectual development are associated with Piaget's (1952) stage theory of cognitive development and with the large body of work in cognitive psychology and information processing. Piaget's theory of cognitive development proposed that children move through several stages of cognitive development that allow them to think in increasingly sophisticated ways. The stage from Piaget's scheme most relevant for higher education is his final stage of formal operations, which gives adolescents the capacity for formal scientific thinking. Formal operational thinking does not emerge unless people are exposed to formal schooling. When adolescents reach the stage of formal operations, they can manipulate abstract variables and address hypothetical questions. Students who have not achieved this level of cognitive development cannot be expected to conduct systematic inquiry or deal with the types of abstract concepts required of students in university courses. Piaget's research indicated that children who have school experience develop formal operational thinking at about age 12, but many college students do not have well-developed formal operational thinking skills.

Several stage theories have had an impact on our understanding of teaching and learning in universities. Chickering (1969) examined the development of identity and the capacity for mature interpersonal relationships in college-age males. Perry's (1970) pioneering work examined how students' concepts about the nature of knowledge evolve throughout their undergraduate careers. Perry's theory was in the Piagetian tradition and is a precursor to the three most prominent theories of the intellectual development of college students and adults used today: King and Kitchener's (1994) reflective judgment model, Baxter-Magolda's (1999) epistemological reflection model, and Mezirow's (2000) theory of transformational learning.

Perry's (1970) model of intellectual development characterizes undergraduates as progressing through nine positions (he used the term *positions* rather than stages), moving from a dualistic view where they believe all questions have right or wrong answers and authorities like professors are the absolute arbiters of truth to a relativistic perspective where knowledge is contingent and contextual. An intermediate position on the path to relativism is a stage where students conclude that there are no right answers. For many students, this means that they believe that everyone's opinion is equally valid. Their stance toward professors at this point is often to set aside issues of right and wrong and just try to figure out what the professor wants them to say. Because there is no absolute truth to find or defend, they shift their attention from the search for truth to getting a better grade. When students reach the relativistic position, they are capable of true analytic thinking and acquiring metacognitive thinking skills.

King and Kitchener's (1994) model is an invariant stage theory of cognitive development rooted in previous work by Piaget and Perry and linked to Dewey's emphasis on the importance of reflective thinking. They focused specifically on the level of sophistication students bring to evaluating knowledge claims and participating in debates on controversial topics. The theory's usefulness has been enhanced because they have developed a measure of reflective judgment (The Reflective Judgment Scale). Their scale has face validity for most professors because the upper levels of the scale match our definition of analytic thinking.

The seven stages of reflective judgment in King and Kitchener's scale are divided into three general categories: prereflective, quasireflective, and reflective. Students in the prereflective stages have attitudes about knowledge that parallel Perry's dualistic thinkers. These students impose a right or wrong paradigm on unstructured problems. They turn to authorities for correct answers and find it difficult to believe that the nature of these problems does not allow for a specific correct response. It is difficult for students at this stage of development to negotiate a class like "Understanding Organizations" or even to clearly understand what I am asking them to do. The second general level of development in King and Kitchener's model is quasireflective thinking. Students on this level still have difficulty addressing unstructured problems, but they understand that the solution to the problem is uncertain. Students at this stage learn to marshal evidence for their opinions, but they only seek evidence that supports the position they already hold. They can hold two beliefs that are logically inconsistent because evidence is gathered to support a particular position, but two positions are not compared to see whether they conflict with each other. Students in the stages of reflective thinking (Stages 6 and 7) understand how to support their opinions with clear evidence and systematic thinking. These students are able to take strong positions and defend them effectively. They understand that solutions to complex, unstructured problems must be constructed and negotiated among people who have a stake in the solution.

Research using King and Kitchener's Reflective Judgment Scale indicates that few students achieve the level of reflective judgment while they are still undergraduates. This presents a problem to professors because most of our courses assume that students will be able to function on this level. Kegan (2000) also pointed out that there might be a gap between our students' developmental capabilities and the demands we are placing on them. This does not mean that we should give up the goal of developing reflecting thinking skills in our undergraduates. The world they are entering is filled with complex, unstructured problems that require advanced analytic thinking skills. King and Kitchener's work does indicate, however, that we should be more aware that we are asking students to stretch their capabilities to meet our demands.

Baxter-Magolda's (1999) theory of epistemological development represents an extension of earlier work by Perry and King and Kitchener. Her work was also informed by the body of work on women's ways of knowing (Belensky, Clinchy, Goldberg, & Tarule, 1986; Gilligan, 1982). Baxter-Magolda's research indicated that undergraduates progress through four stages of epistemological development from an initial stage of believing that knowledge is certain to understanding that knowledge is uncertain. In the first stage, authority figures like textbook authors and professors (and, in my experience, anyone with a page on the Internet) are seen as infallible. Baxter-Magolda believes that using constructivist pedagogies that encourage students to author their own knowledge is the optimal strategy for moving students to more advanced levels of epistemological development.

Mezirow (2000) developed a constructivist approach to adult learning that has been influential in higher education and adult education. Mezirow's approach combined the basic orientation of Dewey and current constructivists with critical theory, especially the work of Jergen Habermas. He focused on ways of facilitating self-development by changing the ways learners approach and understand the world through reflection. He based much of his theory on Habermas' concepts of communicative action and instrumental learning. His focus on culture and communication also links him to the activity theorists and sociocultural perspectives.

Although I have provided only a brief overview of these developmental theories, I think they provide important insights that can help us understand why our students are struggling with the demands we place on them. I chose to provide limited coverage of these theories because each of these theorists has authored an excellent book that summarizes his or her theories and provides examples of how they can be applied to university teaching and adult education.

REFLECTION

Reflection was one of the central ideas in Dewey's (1910) philosophy. Dewey defined *reflection* as, "Active, persistent, and careful consideration of any belief or supposed form of knowledge in the light of the grounds that support it, and the further considerations that it tends" (p. 6). Many educators inspired by Dewey have also emphasized the importance of reflection. Interest in reflection increased dramatically with the publication of Schon's (1983) influential and widely read book, *The Reflective Practitioner*. Schon's concept of the reflective practitioner is the most frequently cited source of support for the importance of reflection for effective practice. Reflection has also been a central concept in several popular programs focused on higher education (King & Kitchener, 1994).

For Dewey, reflection was a much broader concept than "stopping to think about what we are doing" or "asking yourself how you feel about what just happened." Reflection involves the range of cognitive skills associated with effective inquiry. Rodgers (2002) summarized Dewey's criteria for effective reflection:

1. Reflection is a meaning-making process that moves a learner from one experience into the next with deeper understanding of its relationships with and connects to other experiences and ideas. It is the thread that makes continuity of learning possible, and ensures the progress of the individual and, ultimately, society. It is the means to essential moral ends.

2. Reflection is a systematic rigorous, disciplined way of thinking, with its roots in scientific inquiry.
3. Reflection needs to happen in community, in interaction with others.
4. Reflection requires attitudes that value the personal and intellectual growth of oneself and of others. (p. 845)

These criteria differ from many of the popular uses of the term *reflection* in two important ways. First is the idea that reflection takes place in dialogue with others and, second, that it is characterized as rigorous and disciplined. Dewey's discussions of reflection established many of the basic principles of the psychological constructivist and the combined constructivist approaches. He made it clear that the quality of knowledge depends on how well structured it is (Principle 3). By placing reflection in the context of a community of inquiry and stressing that reflection is a systematic, rigorous way of thinking, he provided the foundation for Principle 5 (that knowledge is socially constructed in learning communities) and Principle 8 (effective learning environments should involve students in productive disciplinary discourse that actively engages them in dialogue about important questions).

Dewey's (1910) concept of reflection includes most of the topics that are addressed by the field of cognitive psychology. For Dewey, reflection included a broad range of thinking skills that describe the dynamic process by which experience is created through the construction of meaning within systematic inquiry. The details of his analysis of topics such as the importance of uncertainty, motivation, inquiry, inference, metacognition, and conceptual development are more profitably explored by examining more recent research. Yet Dewey's definition of *reflection* serves as a general rebuttal to versions of reflection that do not include rigorous thinking. Unfortunately, we still see teachers on all levels misinterpreting the meaning of *experiential education* by offering students experience without thought. They involve students in experiences without systematically connecting them to meaning making. Examples range from young children using math manipulatives without the teacher connecting the experience to number concepts to university students involved in service-learning experiences without systematic reflection that goes beyond asking them how they felt about the experience. Dewey (1910) commented directly on this problem almost 100 years ago:

If physical things used in teaching number or geography or anything else do not leave the mind illuminated with recognition of *meaning* beyond themselves, the instruction that uses them is as abstract as that which doles out ready-made definitions and rules; for it distracts attention from ideas to mere physical objects. . . . A few generations ago the great obstacle in the way of reform of primary education was belief in the almost magical efficacy of the symbols of language (including number) to produce mental training; at present, belief in the efficacy of objects just as objects, blocks the way. As frequently happens, the better is the enemy of the best. (p. 140)

Many educators have emphasized the importance of stimulating students to engage in higher levels of reflection (King & Kitchener, 1994). There are many current models of reflection and logic that update the model Dewey (1910) presented in *How We Think*. Lin, Hmelo, Kinzer, and Secules (1999) described reflection as an "active, intentional, and purposeful process" because it takes place when learners are perplexed about a problem. They would agree with Dewey that, unless people are confronted with a situation that confuses them or interests them, the environment tends to remain outside their consciousness. Effective reflection also involves metacognition (an assessment of how we are thinking). The challenge for university professors who hope to stimulate real reflection is to present students with a problem that successfully competes with the *primary problems* that students associate with the context of schooling—saying what the professor wants them to say to earn a good grade.

Boud and Walker (1998) believed that reflection used in university classes must go beyond the scope recommended by Schon to include critical reflection. They believed it is important to reflect in the context of a particular problem situation and on the broader context of the structure of society. The object of reflection is to examine the phenomena you are studying, not to promote self-examination. In other words, they strongly believe that reflection must include a metacognitive component and apply a conceptual lens to a situation: It should go beyond a statement of "how I feel about this situation." In the example of community service and service learning, they believe students should examine issues around social justice.

In their model of reflective discourse, Zeichner and Liston (1985) developed a hierarchy of four levels of practical reasoning and examined the level of discourse in supervisory situations. The vast majority of time spent in supervisory dialogues was spent in factual discourse (63.2%), which involved contributions that described what had occurred or would be expected to occur in the future and prudential discourse (24.9%), which focused on evaluations of performance and advice about how to achieve objectives. Much less time was spent on justificatory discourse (11.3%) that explored the underlying rationales for actions taken. Almost no attention was paid to critical discourse (0.6%) that probed issues like power and social justice. Their primary observation was that students did not usually engage in higher levels of reflection. One way to describe the change in social practices I was trying to achieve in the "Understanding Organizations" course was to increase the portion of the classroom dialogue spent in justificatory and critical discourse.

Roskos, Vukelich, and Risko (2001) conducted a meta-analysis of research on reflection in education conducted between 1985 and 1999. They found that researchers in the area of literacy generally saw reflection as a problem-solving activity that facilitates bridging of theory and practice. This definition is clearly in the Dewey tradition. Interestingly enough, however, they found that most of this work was more connected to Dewey's early perspective, which focused on psychological construction, rather than his later work, which focused on learning in a community and social context. For example, Roskos, Vukelich, and Risko pointed out that almost all of the data collected in these studies utilized individual writing samples, which pointed the analysis toward internal reflection. In this sense, they would not satisfy Dewey's criteria that reflection takes place in interaction with others within the context of inquiry.

Von Glasersfeld (1995) would see reflection as a primarily internal psychological process in which a "chunk of experience" is re-presented and treated as an object. Abstractions are constructed by organizing these re-presented objects through assimilation and accommodation. Von Glasersfeld's strongly internal model of cognition can be contrasted with the situated cognitive perspective that is discussed in chapter 6. In the situated cognitive model, cognition is not seen as taking place exclusively within the mind of one person. They see reflection as a combination of social construction in dialogue with others and internal reflection (Greeno & the MSMTA Project Group, 1998). In the situated cognitive view, the most basic level of reflection uses language—a cultural artifact—to mediate the transaction between the person and environment. Effective reflection requires social interaction because dialogue exposes students to multiple perspectives and allows them to receive feedback from others on the quality of their thinking. Although von Glasersfeld's specific mechanisms were internal rather than shared, he also emphasized the importance of the learner being able to compare his or her perspective with the perspective of other learners.

CONCEPTUAL CHANGE

In the constructivist perspective, conceptual knowledge includes both what students learn and how it is organized into broader principles (Grotzer, 2002; J. D. Novak, 2002). Yet contributors to the constructivist literature do not always make it clear what level of change they are targeting when they address issues of conceptual change. Building on the work of Ausabell (1963) and Gowin (1981), J. D. Novak (2002) defined a *concept* "as perceived regularities in events or objects, or records of events or objects designated by a label (usually a word)" (p. 550). Concepts are organized into constructs, deep principles, and theories that describe their relationships and how these relationships explain how, when, and why events occur. When teachers help students attach useful labels and signs to regularities and patterns of events, they scaffold students' conceptual development. Because concepts are embedded in larger cognitive systems, their meaning is affected by their placement in these systems and their connections to other concepts and principles and the nonreflective web of experience. The different names given to cognitive structures (e.g., *schema*, *mental models*) try to capture this broader level of meaning connected to conceptual knowledge.

When constructivists describe the process for helping students develop useful concepts, they assume that students are *changing* concepts rather than acquiring new ones. Much of the concern of educators interested in conceptual change has focused on misconceptions that prevent students from adopting concepts and principles that will more accurately explain the events they experience (J. D. Novak, 2002). This orientation acknowledges that learners at all levels usually have conscious or unconscious mental models or "everyday theories" about how the world works. Van Merrienboer, Seel, and Kirschner (2002) defined mental models as "cognitive artifacts or inventions of the human mind that can be considered to be the best-organized representations among declarative learning results" (pp. 62–63). Vosniadou, Ionnides, Dimitrakopoulou, and Papademetriou (2001) defined a mental model as "an analog and generative representation which can be manipulated mentally to provide causal explanations of phenomena" (p. 389). Many constructivists believe that mental models are useful, but caution that they are not accurate representations of the real world that can be "handed to" the student. The student must actively construct them as they inquire about an authentic problem. Lehrer and Schauble (2000) pointed out that giving students a model (rather than helping them construct their own) hides the process that has gone into constructing that model. A simple tool like a ruler contains a long history of theory and practical decisions about measurement. In a situation like measuring a 12-foot room with a 1-foot ruler, young children do not understand that each time they move the ruler they have to place the ruler at the exact spot where they left off. Graduate students make analogous mistakes when they use statistical software.

To design effective learning experiences, it is important to understand that learning involves replacing an existing concept (or more likely a misconception) with a new concept or larger cognitive structure. Seeing learning as replacing an existing concept directs us to start the learning process by trying to understand the students' existing everyday theories and help students become more aware of their own theories. If students share a misconception (if it is common knowledge), it is even more difficult to dislodge the misconception and replace it with a useful concept. Adding this step to the beginning of the teaching process increases our awareness of the common misconceptions and difficult concepts in our disciplines. The constructivist perspective challenges professors to discover what concepts students find most difficult to understand and to identify the most common misconceptions students hold about the phenomena their discipline is organized to understand. It is important for professors to find ways to involve at least a subset of their students in conversations that reveal their conceptual understanding of the subject matter. The basic principle (Number 6) that the acquisition of new knowledge is strongly affected by prior knowledge is supported by this body of work.

Tabor (2001) defined a *cognitive structure* as "the facts, concepts, propositions, theories, and raw perceptual data that the learner has available to her at any point in time, and the manner in which it is arranged" (p. 160). New material is always viewed in terms of the student's existing models. Because these structures are dynamic systems, they resist restructuring and tend to accept compatible new material much more readily than incompatible material (Pendley, Bretz, & Novak, 1994; *The Private Universe Project*, 1989). Tabor (2001) also pointed out that students often plug new material into a model that an expert would see as totally unrelated to the material he or she is teaching.

For me, the most powerful practical implication of research on concept change is the requirement that I spend more time probing students' existing understanding. This is hard for me to do because I am anxious to begin exploring the key concepts and deep principles I want students to learn. There are several exercises built into the "Understanding Organizations" course to help me understand students' everyday theories about how people behave in organizations. In the reflection section of their Personal Organization Papers, students are asked to reflect on the motives of key actors in the three critical incidents they select and develop a personal organizational model that is modified as they move through the semester (see syllabus in chap. 1). The first version of their model helps me understand their everyday theories. For most students, their implicit theory of organizations is a version of the fundamental attribution error. They attribute problems to the stupidity, guile, or emotional instability of flawed individuals. It is their version of the "we need a new dean" solution. During the early part of the semester, I also ask students to respond to a number of simple sentences that describe things they might see in an organization. For each sentence, they are asked why they think the event happened. One item was, "Mary has presented an idea, but Bill is ignoring her input. Why is Bill ignoring her contribution?" The pattern of responses is used as the basis for a discussion of their hypotheses about why things happen in organizations. When I am working with professors in other disciplines, I am always impressed with how shocked they are when they hear the everyday theories that students hold about fairly simple scientific phenomena.

Another important factor in the learning process includes the learners' ability to manage the knowledge acquisition process (e.g., developing metacognitive skills, modeling ability, and intellectual development). The rationales that students give for their conclusions help me understand how they think about information and reach conclusions. King and Kitchener's (1994) reflective judgment scale is a useful way to gather information on how students use (or do not use) information to reach conclusions. Unfortunately, I have found that students resist the idea of using research evidence to influence their opinions. Students, especially males, tend to see the objective of dialogue as "winning the argument" by finding support for their existing opinions rather than expanding their understanding (King & Kitchener, 1994).

There are several models of conceptual change. For example, a model developed by Posner (Posner, Strike, Hewson, & Gertzog, 1982) assumes that learners will adopt a new model if they are dissatisfied with their present model for understanding a situation and they have access to a new model that is intelligible (it does not contradict existing beliefs and the learner can understand the idea), plausible (it is believable), and it is fruitful (they find it useful for solving problems).

Most models of conceptual change make a distinction between situations where the learner makes a small adjustment in his or her way of thinking about a phenomenon and a radical restructuring of the learner's way of thinking (Harrison & Treagust, 2001). These distinctions roughly parallel Piaget's mechanisms of assimilation and accommodation. In assimilation, the students adapt a new idea to their existing cognitive structures. In accommodation, students change their cognitive structure (referred to as a *schema*) in response to the new information. Hewson's (1996) model contrasted situations where new ideas are assimilated without affecting old ideas (conceptual capture) with ones where new ideas replace old ideas (conceptual exchange). Chi, Slotta, and de Leeuw (1994) used the term *branch jumping* for smaller conceptual changes and *tree jumping* for larger conceptual shifts. Many of these theories assume that change is stimulated, at least in part, by cognitive conflict. Caravita (2001) concluded that this is a necessary, but not sufficient, condition for change. She believed that students also need some form of analogy or metaphor to lead them to a viable alternative model. There is also evidence that incompatible ideas can be partitioned into separate categories and held simultaneously (King & Kitchener, 1994). When students are faced with radically incompatible ideas, the easiest solution is to place them in two separate categories: school knowledge and everyday knowledge.

Vosniadou, Ionnides, Dimitrakopoulou, and Papademetriou (2001) and J. D. Novak (2002) indicated that conceptual change is best thought of as an iterative process involving gradual revision of old ideas through a continuing dialogue between teachers and students. This means that knowledge has to be systematically restructured through experience, feedback, and dialogue. The simplest way to describe the kind of dialogue that produces better scientific thinking is that it is characterized by lots of "why" questions and teachers spend more time listening to students' answers.

Our most ambitious course objectives usually aim for at least one important shift in the students' way of looking at the world. It may be unrealistic to hope that this kind of basic change in perspective will come in one course, but a series of courses in a discipline should teach the students the discipline's worldview and its thinking and inquiry skills. In the "Understanding Organizations" course, I want students to acquire a "living systems" perspective of organizations. I favor ecological living systems metaphors over linear input–output models. My own model of organizations and organizational change is built around an environmental adaptation metaphor. One advantage of a living systems metaphor for organizations is that it recasts diversity as an adaptive characteristic rather than a potential disruption to the status quo (Morgan, 1986). I also generally ascribe to a change model that assumes that individuals are only partially embedded in the organizational context and capable of organizing to become agents for change when faced with contradictions (Seo & Creed, 2002). Because research on conceptual change indicates that students are likely to revert to a default model (in this case, a linear cause–effect model; Grotzer, 2002), this is an ambitious goal.

I should briefly mention an issue that may be important in many courses: the possible tension between developing conceptual knowledge and procedural skills. A simple example of this would be understanding the procedures for calculating the standard deviation of a distribution in a statistics class and understanding the concepts behind the formulas. Rich Lehrer (personal communication, March 2003) provided a simple demonstration of this problem in one of our courses. He asked students to perform some simple mathematics problems that involved multiplying and dividing fractions. Because this is part of the fifth-grade curriculum, it is not surprising that they all could do these problems quite easily. He then passed out some strips of paper and asked the students to represent these operations visually. I must admit I was surprised to hear that none of the students could complete this task successfully. I worked out my embarrassment at this lack of mathematical understanding demonstrated by our students by remembering the demonstration tapes produced by *The Private Universe Project*

(1989). In one demonstration, only 2 of 23 Harvard graduates could explain why we have seasons. Most of the MIT graduates they interviewed could not light a small bulb with a battery and a piece of wire.

Most of us would agree that big ideas and deep principles are more important than formulas, but it has not been clear whether it is better to start with the concepts or procedures. Robert Siegler and his colleagues have done a series of studies to explore this question as it relates to teaching mathematics. Rittle-Johnson, Siegler, and Alibali (2001) found that procedural and conceptual knowledge reinforce each other *if* they are mediated by accurate problem representation. They defined *problem representation* as "the internal depiction or re-creation of a problem in working memory during problem solving" (p. 348). This may sound a little abstract, but the examples can be quite simple. For young children learning fractions, it might be the ability to represent a problem on a number line. Students need to learn both concepts and procedures, and the learning of each reinforces the other *if* they have mental models to represent the problem space.

EXPERT AND NOVICE THINKING

One way to think about what we are trying to accomplish in our courses is that we are trying to help novices become experts. Although I realize this cannot be achieved in one course, I want my introductory course in "Understanding Organizations" to start students on the path toward developing real expertise in organizational behavior and organizational development. The course builds on deep principles from previous courses and introduces students to principles that will be embellished and deepened by what they learn in subsequent courses. These principles need to be learned in a meaningful context that organizes the knowledge in a way that resists regression to earlier misconceptions. This means avoiding learning by memorization. One of the negative aspects of learning by memorization (beyond that it is quickly forgotten if it is not used) is that memorization allows knowledge to be stored in a way that it does not confront existing belief systems (J. D. Novak, 2002). To create cognitive dissonance, two ideas have to confront each other in the same cognitive space.

There are several fundamental differences between the way experts and novices approach problems and process information. Experts have many models for viewing a situation, and they know that some are useful in some situations and some are useful in others (Grosslight, Unger, Jay, & Smith, 1991). Novices tend to see concepts as static, and experts tend to conceptualize a phenomenon as a system of dynamic processes. There are also qualitative differences between the way expert and novice information is organized. Novices typically organize information around surface characteristics, whereas experts organize their knowledge systematically (Vosniadou, Ionnides, Dimitrakopoulou, & Papademetriou, 2001). Although even young children can use one object to represent another, children and adult novices without specific training do not construct models that help them distill theoretically important elements, and they do not consciously distance the model from its specific context (Lehrer & Schauble, 2000). Harrison and Treagust (2001) found that using multiple analogies and models for the same phenomena facilitated conceptual change and led to deeper understanding of scientific concepts. They also found large differences in conceptual understanding among students with the same test scores.

Hogan and Maglienti (2001) approached the issue of reconciling everyday theories with scientific theories by comparing the procedures that scientists and nonscientists used when they were presented with a problem and evidence to support a solution. They found that scientists and nonscientists treated their theories about the world differently. Scientists treat their theories as hypotheses to be tested with evidence, whereas nonscientists treat their theories as lenses to interpret what they see. The "Understanding Organizations" course is the third course in a sequence of core courses. One of the recurring themes in these courses is to remind students to "think *about* their mental models rather than just *with* them." Scientists also have an advantage in the area of domain specific knowledge that frees up resources for thinking. Hogan and Maglienti's (2001) research compared the reasoning of scientists with that of students, nonscientist adults, and technicians. They presented their subjects with statements that represented valid and invalid inferences from data and asked them to explain why they thought that the conclusions were justified or unjustified. Students and nonscientist adults tended to evaluate conclusions positively if they agreed with their personal opinions. Scientists judged the quality of the inferences based on whether the conclusion could be supported by the evidence presented. As I discuss further in the chapter on sociocultural approaches, the scientists' responses are not based on superior cognitive development, but on their experience using these ways of thinking while they are conducting scientific research with other scientists (i.e., they are social practices of the scientific community).

Assessment in a constructivist framework is informed by an understanding of the differences between expert and novice knowledge: First of all, expert knowledge is more cohesive than the knowledge of novices. Expert knowledge has more syntactic connectives (interconnections or links between propositions). Gobbo and Chi (1986) measured connectivity by counting the number of connective words students used in their subjects' explanations (e.g., because [causal], if [conditional], then [temporal], or [disjunctive]). They found that 66% of expert propositions were connected compared with 49% for novices. Expert knowledge also included more topics connected to a specific point. The experts were also able to make more analogic comparisons. Gobbo and Chi used semantic comparisons as a measure of how well experts used their knowledge. They compared and contrasted two dinosaurs (either comparing them to each other or to a shared attribute) and asked students to make a judgment about class membership. Students who were experts on dinosaurs were more likely to base sorting on superordinate features, whereas novices focused on explicit physical features and were more likely to create exhaustive categories. This contrast between sorting examples according to deep principles or surface characteristics can be applied to a number of situations across academic disciplines. Once an expert categorical system is established, learners can store much more information and retrieve it in appropriate situations. This reinforces the principle that it is better to learn fewer facts that are well organized than to learn more facts.

Several models are presented in the "Understanding Organizations" course. The four basic organizational perspectives used in the course (i.e., structural, human resource, political, and symbolic) help students understand that organizations and human behavior in organizations can be viewed in a variety of valid ways. They also provide students with a basic framework that will help them begin to understand how concepts in the disciplines are related to each other. The most powerful quality of expert thinking is not the number of facts they know, but an efficient organization of those facts that facilitates future retrieval. It is important to note, however, that, although expertise has more to do with how knowledge is organized than the number of facts known, content knowledge is important to effective problem solving. Thinking is always thinking about something.

One of the conclusions that can be drawn from research on experts and novices is that developing expertise involves "learning how to see" and "learning how to think" as well as acquiring knowledge. This means that learning experiences that are designed to produce useful knowledge must pay specific attention to teaching students how to recognize the meaningful patterns they will confront as they are organized in the real environment (Bransford, Brown, & Cocking, 1999). One of the most important characteristics of expert knowledge is that experts attend to different features of the environment than novices. Assessment practices in constructivist classrooms should focus on what students notice in an unstructured situation (M. Young, 1993). For example, in the "Understanding Organizations" course, I show a video at the beginning of the semester and have students enter all the facts they can retrieve from the video related to organizations and leadership. At the end of the semester, I show the same video and have them do the same task as a posttest.

Bransford, Brown, and Cocking (1999) summarized the following conclusions about experts' performance:

1. Experts notice features and meaningful patterns of information that are not noticed by novices.
2. Experts have acquired a great deal of content knowledge that is organized in ways that reflect a deep understanding of the subject matter.
3. Experts' knowledge cannot be reduced to sets of isolated facts or propositions but, instead, reflects contexts of applicability, that the knowledge is "conditionalized" on a set of circumstances.
4. Experts are able to flexibly retrieve important aspects of their knowledge with little attentional effort.
5. Though experts know their disciplines thoroughly, this does not guarantee that they will be able to teach others.
6. Experts have varying degrees of flexibility in their approaches to new situations. (p. 31)

METACOGNITIVE THINKING

Theories of metacognitive thinking have been important in several instructional programs designed by constructivists (Karpov & Haywood, 1998). On the most general level, metacognition refers to learners' ability to monitor their own learning processes: their increased ability to "think about their own thinking" (Flavell, 1976, 1979). Lin (2001) defined *metacognition* as "the ability to understand and monitor one's own thoughts, and the assumptions and implications of one's activities" (p. 23). This definition is useful because it provides specific areas to guide our dialogue with students to help them improve their metacognitive skills. J. D. Novak (2002) also pointed to the importance of helping students understand the nature of conceptual learning. He and his colleagues developed the technique of concept mapping to help students see how their concepts are organized into deep principles and to serve as a research and teaching tool to understand students' conceptual development. Metacognitive skills are a key component of reflection. Metacognitive skills are especially important for constructivists because they provide a mechanism to overcome the constraints of a conditionalized view of learning. If learning is highly contextualized and conditionalized, learners need metacognitive skills to facilitate transfer and develop the capacity for future learning.

A common method of enhancing metacognitive skills is to make knowledge visible by having students verbalize their thinking while they solve problems. This process also helps us understand and facilitate the structuring of knowledge in content areas. Vygotsky (1978) used the "talk-aloud" method as a way to understand how students were processing ideas. It is important to keep in mind that constructivist approaches to developing metacognitive skills never involve developing thinking skills in isolation from content.

One approach to developing metacognitive skills involves providing students with specific metacognitive strategies. We can model good metacognitive skills by sharing our thinking processes with students. This means going beyond sharing the findings and conclusions of our scholarship and research. We must also share information about the way we approached the problem and the choices we made on the route to reaching our conclusions.

Students need more than modeling to acquire metacognitive skills, however. Bielacszye, Pirolli, and Brown (1995) found that exposure alone was not sufficient. Students need an opportunity to compare their own thinking with the model's. In the "Understanding Organizations" course, students tackle a number of organizational problems. After they have an opportunity to think about how they would approach a problem, other experts involved in the course share their approaches, assumptions, problem-solving skills, and conclusions. In the exercises where students selected examples of important concepts from a set of video clips, I found that students often missed examples that I thought were obvious. It helped when I started going through the clips after the students had selected their clips and explained what examples I saw in the clips. This information was also included in the feedback students received electronically after the presentations were made.

It is also useful to provide students with metacognitive prompts during the problem-solving process. Metacognitive prompts are built into many computer-based training modules (Edelson, 2001; Lin & Lehman, 1999). In classroom dialogues, prompts can help students become more aware of their own assumptions and thinking processes. In the "Understanding Organizations" course, I find that "why" questions can be helpful. I also try to focus on choice points (e.g., What were your options here? Why do you think this was the best approach? Is there a rival hypothesis that could explain what happened?). Asking students to provide rationales for their choices was sometimes effective during the class, but I found that the most useful interchanges took place in the planning meetings, in the computer lab, or during electronic communication with students working on projects.

My most difficult challenge in promoting metacognitive skills was changing the social practices in the classroom to encourage more probing questions from students. This is the arena where individual cognitive processes interact with social practices. It was difficult to establish an atmosphere where prompting and probing questions were viewed as helpful rather than hostile. Ann Brown's Fostering Communities for Learning (FCL) is the best-known model for creating a learning community that fosters meta-cognitive skills (Brown, 1997; Brown & Campione, 1994, 1996). The title of Brown's 1997 article in the *American Psychologist*, "Transforming Schools Into Communities of Thinking and Learning About Serious Matters," provides an excellent summary of the overall goal of the FCL program and my goal for the "Understanding Organizations" course. Brown's approach was designed to create a different type of learning environment in the classroom. Getting students to solve problems together and present their solutions to be evaluated by the larger group is the core of the FCL method. These skills are reinforced in virtual environments like Computer Supported Intentional Learning Environment (CSILE). CSILE gives students an opportunity to compare their thinking and conclusions with experts. Video of experts discussing their approach to the problems students have been addressing can be inserted into virtual environments and can be available through the class Web page. Expert comments are especially useful if they share their thinking and problem-solving processes. The most difficult task for me was getting my students to feel as comfortable confronting each other with "why" questions as the children in FCL classrooms. A more extensive description of the FCL program appears in chapter 6 on combined constructivist approaches.

Georghiades (2000) developed a model for conceptualizing the link between metacognitive instruction, deeper understanding of conceptual material, the successful transfer of the application of concepts to other situations, and the long-term retention of conceptual knowledge. Georghiades used a process that involved establishing short 2- to 3-minute "metacognitive instances" working with students in small groups. Metacognitive instruction involves being reflective, revisiting the learning process, and making systematic comparisons between prior knowledge and current knowledge. Georghiades compared students involved in a series of science lessons using metacognitive instruction with a control group of students who learned the concepts without metacognitive instruction. He found that the students who received metacognitive instruction showed significantly higher levels of knowledge acquisition, increased retention of knowledge over time, and enhanced ability to utilize knowledge in different contexts. Most important, the differences between the control and experimental groups increased over time. Further, he found the most pronounced and enduring differences were in the area of transfer to dissimilar contexts. Bascones and Novak (1985) had similar results in a program that used concept maps to help students gain metacognitive understanding of their concept development processes. In this research, the experimental group's performance was substantially better than the control group's and the magnitude of the differences increased over time.

SCHANK'S THEORY OF DYNAMIC MEMORY

Schank (1992) and his colleagues developed an approach to contextualized learning called *goal-based scenarios*. A goal-based scenario has three parts: (a) a concrete goal that the learners are motivated to achieve, (b) a specific set of target skills that the learners will practice and that will help them reach the goal, and (c) a larger environmental context where the skills the learners have acquired will help them reach the goal. Schank believes the strength of his approach is that it puts the learner in the position of acting on the environment, rather than simply observing it. In this model, students acquire the content of the curriculum while they study a topic that already interests them (Oliver, 2000). Schank's approach is consistent with Dewey's belief that new learning must be connected to students' previous experience, that learning must be experiential, and that knowledge is constructed from previous experience.

Like Dewey, Schank believes that most learning takes place while students are engaged in active goal-directed activity. Schank's goal-based scenarios provide a narrative context for stimulating active knowledge construction through goal-directed inquiry (Basic Principle 4). Schank's theory built on the idea that useful knowledge is embedded in meaningful and authentic contexts (Basic Principle 2) by creating narrative contexts for the development of concepts and deep principles. His theory focuses on how knowledge structures are stored in memory and describes how memory is altered by experience. This theory is referred to as *dynamic memory* because it describes the ways that memories are structured and restructured. The building block of memory in Schank's system is the script. A script is a sequential memory of what we are familiar with and what we expect to happen in a routine situation. When students enter a class, they expect to find a seat and see the professor standing at the front of the room ready to lecture. There are predictable sequences of events we associate with going to class and most of the things we do. Unless something unusual happens, we do not think much about these situations. We use our habits to function successfully.

A central insight that provided a core principle of Schank's theory was the observation that we tend to be surprised by and remember exceptions to these routines (failed expectations) more than we remember events that follow established scripts. Schank believes that failed expectations are retained and more easily retrieved because the script provides a cognitive structure that serves as a coherent context. Failed expectations are stored at appropriate places in the script, and we are reminded of them in future situations at that point in the sequence of activities. The failed expectations are indexed in scripts as exceptions to the normal sequence of events (e.g., the time all the students turned their desks toward the back of the room).

These exceptions generate the stories human beings relate to each other. In addition to scripts, memory contains more abstract structures (e.g., big ideas, deep principles, mental models) that are generalized from experience and built with specific mechanisms. These two types of information in memory are parallel to Dewey's primary and secondary experience.

In our role as professors, we are concerned more about how and when information is retrieved than if it is stored. In courses that are oriented toward providing useful knowledge, we try to understand the types of situations in which the information might be useful. Schank focused much of his attention on the mechanisms of reminding. We can try to understand a failure to access knowledge as defective reasoning or through what Schank called *case-based episodic reminding*. There are several types of reminding, but the most effective and important kinds are attached to processes and narrative contexts. The most obvious is related to expectation failures. Schank believed a system of indexes is developed to point to expectation failures. These indexes unconsciously point us toward remembering expectation failures that occurred at a particular place in the process. If we experience a number of similar expectation failures, they can be grouped to form a generalization. These generalizations guide our behavior when we confront this type of problem in the future. Experts tend to refer to *stories* rather than directly accessing abstract principles when they are solving problems (Klein & Calderwood, 1988). The important thing about this process is that this abstract structure can be used to remind us of the probability of an expectation failure at just the right time; at the point in the process where we need to be reminded of that possibility. For example, my wife and I recently returned from a trip and went out to get a very late dinner on a Sunday night. As we pulled out of the driveway, my wife said, "It's Sunday night, we may have trouble finding a restaurant that's open." She suggested we go over near the campus where restaurants tend to be open late. We "learned that lesson" from just one instance when we returned from a trip and were very hungry and could not find a place to eat late on a Sunday night in our neighborhood. We were reminded of this because we had an expectation failure in our script for going out to eat. We retrieved this knowledge just at the time we needed it because the script provided a rich context of cues. Schank thinks most useful knowledge is acquired and stored in this way.

Another important kind of reminding grows out of situations that involve setting and reaching goals. Schank believes that we also store memories according to the plans we make to reach goals. This aspect of Schank's theory parallels Dewey's analysis of the organizing power of instrumental behavior. Schank agrees with Dewey that we remember situations that are marked as episodes bracketed by the recognition of a problem through the process of directing our resources toward addressing the problem and reaching a solution. The sequence of events (the plan and its outcome) is defined as a unit that becomes salient to the learner. This is a sequential process that provides a set of expectations about what will happen. We especially remember situations where we fail to meet an important goal. Other salient situations occur when we observe another person fail to meet a goal or we find it hard to understand why another person is pursuing the goal they are pursuing. Schank thinks we have a natural curiosity about goal-directed behavior.

Schank's explanation for why much of what we learn in school is inert is that the knowledge is stored in such a way that it must be accessed intentionally. Because the knowledge is not imbedded in a script, there are far fewer indexes available to remind the student to access the knowledge in the context of use. Schank sees useful learning as growing out of a process that involves students in trying to solve a problem or reach a goal. The most powerful learning opportunities grow out of students' reflections on why their solutions failed to solve the problem.

Although Schank's model is powerful, it can be short-circuited in the school environment if students are focused on the consequences of failure rather than the problem. In my experience, students often do not ask themselves why they failed. They are more likely to focus on the negative consequences of their failure or berate themselves for "being stupid." As is the case with developing other metacognitive skills, prompts are required to stimulate metacognitive understanding. I also think it is unlikely that these metacognitive skills will transfer from one domain to another without additional metacognitive training. Experts analyze the reason for their failure and use it as a learning experience, whereas novices are more likely to misdirect their anger to themselves or their teacher.

For learning to be stored properly, the students must figure out why they failed rather than being told by the teacher. The activity of wrestling with the problem and actively reflecting on the failures is what leads to useful knowledge. Schank (1999) used an example of teaching a child to make toast by giving her some bread and telling her to make toast. If the child picks up the toasted piece of bread and burns her fingers, she will be reminded to use the tongs to pick up the bread the next time she makes toast. Most important, that lesson will be marked at the very spot in the process where she needs to remember it. To use knowledge in the future, students have to be able to predict the reasons that they might fail and then develop strategies to successfully achieve their goals.

This analysis of the optimal learning situation indicates that teachers should place students in problem situations with little guidance and let them fail and figure out how to solve their problems on their own. It goes without saying that there are practical limits to this approach. Even if dangerous situations are eliminated, it is not easy to decide how far to take this principle. This was a major dilemma for me in the "Understanding Organizations" course. The first time I taught the course, I decided to let groups fail and give them authentic feedback (e.g., "I'm sorry, you didn't get this consulting contract because you didn't connect the 4Frames.Kamm case study to organizational theories from the course readings"). I balanced this strategy against the realities of the grading system by having the first assignments count much less than later assignments. Unfortunately, my students are not good at formulas that involve weighing some variables more than others (although they could easily solve this problem in a mathematics course). If they got a low grade that was worth 5%, they reacted as if it was worth 20%. The student reaction to this strategy was so strong that it made it counterproductive. Instead of marking their "making a presentation" scripts with "the time we didn't provide the client with a strong justification for our recommendations," they marked their scripts with "the time Bob unfairly didn't tell us what we needed to do to get an A."

Some professors using this approach adopt the "abandon grades" approach. You may think this is a viable option, but I do not think it is realistic. Unless all the courses at a university change their evaluation system, one professor that gives up grading will be eaten alive. In the "Understanding Organizations" course, the students pushed for more guidance on the grading criteria, and I found some of their arguments convincing. Although it might have been the best learning strategy, I could not continue to tell them to do the projects the way they thought they should be done and then tell them their work was unsatisfactory. For me, this did not fall within the limits of a legitimate social contract between the students and the professor at a competitive university. The challenge for me was to find a way to develop standards that would describe the quality of the thinking that I was looking for and not tell them how to do the assignment.

The important issue for most of us who teach on the postsecondary level is finding ways to develop higher level knowledge structures that can be applied to a range of situations. Schank provided some specific models for how this might take place. In Schank's model, a series of prediction failures produces an abstraction ("a goal-oriented, high-level structure"). Schank labeled this structure a *thematic organization packet* (TOP), which contains three types of information: (a) expectations, (b) static information about what is likely to be happening when this TOP is active, and (c) relational information that includes characteristics that help us draw similarities between situations where this TOP will be useful for making accurate predictions. Again my own experience indicates that students have to be prompted to make these types of generalizations. The TOP is used to create a rule about what we should do in these situations. The proverb is one of the most common types of TOPs. Schank's model also includes memory structures that connect other memory structures to each other. He calls these structures *memory organization packets*, which connect a set of scenes organized around a particular goal. They also contain information about where to store new inputs and process information that allows us to make predictions about what future events will occur in other structurally similar situations.

If Schank's basic premise is correct, people should learn from their mistakes. The number of people on the faculty who have married the same type of person over and over again provides anecdotal evidence that refutes this principle. I am often struck by my own ability to get into the same difficulties over and over again. What I think these examples demonstrate is that it takes more than expectation failures to facilitate learning. The learner needs to be directed to some form of problem representation or alternative behavior that might have been more successful. In the "Understanding Organizations" course, student groups met to review feedback from their last presentation before planning their next presentation. I found that taping these meetings and reviewing the tapes helped them to see where their planning process could have been improved.

Another type of reminding that is especially important in the context of university courses is story-based or case-based reminding. Like many other cognitive scientists, Schank emphasized the power of stories in human thinking (Brunner, 1990; Polkinghorne, 1988). Story telling is a universal human behavior. Stories tend to highlight expectation failures because we tell stories about unusual incidents rather than routine incidents. They fit the constructivist model that ties meaning to goal-directed inquiry because so many stories, especially in literature, start with a problem followed by a quest for a solution. Stories are powerful learning tools because they have a structure that relates the parts to the whole and they contain many connections that can be used as indexes for reminding. The most important stories for learning contain elements that we cannot explain. These points of confusion stimulate our need to learn. Generally, stories reflect our beliefs, and one way they are indexed is according to the beliefs they reflect. Schank proposed two types of memory that relate to stories: episodic memory, which stores a story as it is experienced, and semantic memory, which is connected to more than one story and is organized hierarchically.

The teaching method derived from Schank's model of dynamic memory is called *case-based teaching.* He contrasts case-based reasoning with rule-based problem solving (e.g., doing problem sets to test whether content and procedures that have been taught can be correctly applied to solve specific problems). His model tries to explain how it is possible to have highly contextualized learning and still find a way to decontextualize the basic concepts students learn to allow for generalization and transfer. A curriculum built on Schank's model utilizes goal-based scenarios that involve students in authentic problem-solving situations.

The cases and simulations emphasizing role playing that provide the structure for the "Understanding Organizations" course are consistent with

Schank's model. One advantage of this approach is that it allows students to acquire both the knowledge and skills associated with them by reaching a particular type of goal embedded in a context similar to the one where the knowledge and skills will be used. The case format also integrates a range of perceptual and physical cues that help students recognize situations where knowledge can be used. The core idea is to create as realistic a simulation as possible within practical limits. Schank (1999) recognized these limits when he recommended that teachers "replicate as well as possible the breadth of experience an employee needs in an intense, danger free, inexpensive, and timely fashion as possible" (p. 193). Students should not be evaluated on whether they have "the right answer," but on the strength of their thinking and the quality of the evidence they use to support their opinions. The dialogue about the case is the most important way that students index knowledge to the narrative context.

Schank's model fits the "Understanding Organizations" course quite well because the problems presented in the cases do not have one right answer. Edelson (1998) emphasized that good case-based curricula should connect cases from the students' own experience with cases that illustrate important course concepts. Students should leave a course with a library of cases that cover a range of situations. Beyond the presentation of cases, professors must actively link the cases to the specific concepts in the course to help students build useful knowledge structures that are referenced to cases. Linking concepts to cases helps students develop indexes for the cases that will call them to mind in future situations where that knowledge might be useful.

In the "Understanding Organizations" course, the personal organization case and the students' ongoing experience in their simulated consultation organization provide anchors in the students' personal experience. Three critical incidents in the life of the organization are included in the introductory section of the Personal Organization Paper, and these incidents are reedited when each new section of the paper is submitted. The critical incidents represent major problems confronted by the organization. They are also useful because they take the form of stories that can serve as scripts. At each stage in the process of developing the paper (as each frame is applied as a lens to examine the organization and the critical incidents), the students add details to the incidents that fit the frame they are using. A great deal of effort is focused on providing students with prompt and targeted feedback on their assignments throughout the course and through class discussion. I have an opportunity to prompt them with feedback (e.g., You could have mentioned Argyris' Theory X & Y here) and questions (e.g., Why do you think President Bartlett did not share his feelings with the group?). I also insert prompts to alert them to elements that will be good for the next section of the paper (e.g., This will be an excellent example for the Political Frame paper). The other cases in the course (4Frames.Kamm, *West Wing*, and the group organization study) provide comparative and contrasting cases to the personal case (e.g., How did your coach's reaction to your quarterback's arrest compare with the way Dot Kamm handled the crisis with Drew Gooder after his speech to the Chamber of Commerce?).

It is important for students to be involved in problem-based projects and to generate their own solutions to problems. The presentations made by the simulated consulting firms in the "Understanding Organizations" course are the products of these problem-solving processes. The requirement that they include video examples from the *West Wing* case is designed to help them label concepts and tie them simultaneously to at least two cases. According to Schank's theory, the frustrations they experience over failures during the process are the most useful experiences in the course because they are the most powerful forces for constructing indexes.

Edelson (1998) listed four criteria that professors can use to evaluate the effectiveness of the task environments they create in the classroom: (a) opportunities to form and explore hypotheses, (b) opportunities for learning (especially opportunities to learn from expectation failures), (c) authenticity for both the student and the world, and (d) motivation. To motivate students, a task environment must be challenging, must stimulate their curiosity, and must allow them to control the process of inquiry.

Schank (1999) used the theory of dynamic memory to develop his goal-based scenario. The goal-based scenario is a modern version of Dewey's unit. The goal-based scenario is a large simulation that presents students with problems associated with a particular role. For example, Acovelli and Nowakowski (1994) organized a goal-based scenario around a simulation that asked people involved in a corporate training program to play the role of a human resource manager. The participants acquired the knowledge and skills associated with human resource management in the context of a simulation that involved dealing with the kinds of problems that human resource managers confront in their daily lives. The simulation in the "Understanding Organizations" course used a similar approach to teach students organizational theory and develop the inquiry and professional skills they need to identify and propose supportable hypotheses about how to deal with the organization's problems. Students should be able to supply a rationale for why they think the proposed solution will improve the organization that is relevant to the theories and research presented in the course.

The most important question for me to ask about the solutions they generate is, "Why did you suggest that solution?" Students need to develop disciplined thinking skills (both in the sense of rigor and in the sense of learning to think like an expert in the academic discipline) and answers to the "why" questions that index concepts to cases. Edelson (1998) emphasized the importance of what he called *explanation questions*, which highlight the important relationships that define the arena of concern for the discipline. Experts understand what phenomena their disciplines want to understand and what phenomena they can explain. He gives the example that a naturalist's knowledge is organized around the relationship between a plant or animal's physical features and its use. Edelson described a computer-based learning environment that creates a dialogue around features, actions, and behaviors and their functions in nature. The important thing from a teaching standpoint is that the functioning units defined by explanatory relationships, once understood, provide a structure for indexing cases into memory.

The "Understanding Organizations" course could be improved by expanding the number of cases that connect to the core case. Jonassen and Hernandez-Serrano (2002) outlined a procedure for gathering case-based stories from skilled practitioners. Following their suggestions, I plan to interview a number of people with extensive experience solving the kinds of problems embedded in the core case presented in the "Understanding Organizations" course (4Frames.Kamm). It would be helpful to students if they had access to descriptions of a number of solutions to similar problems and their outcomes. The stories of practitioners could then be indexed to determine the larger lessons they contained.

BRANSFORD'S ANCHORED INSTRUCTION AND SITUATED COGNITION

As a program based on the theory of situated cognition, Bransford's approach is also discussed in chapter 6. Bransford and his colleagues have developed instructional strategies that produce generalizable knowledge. Anchored instruction is knowledge centered as well as community centered (Bransford, Brophy, & Williams, 2000). Their focus on perception and action (perceptual learning/tuning perception) rather than decontextualized memory and retrieval (putting facts in students' heads) makes their approach similar to Schank's. One of the teacher's roles is to "tune attention" and perception (teaching students to notice those attributes that are invariant across a range of similar problems). They highlight the importance of learning to identify the salient features from an unstructured problem situation. To use the knowledge and skills they have acquired to solve problems, the first thing learners must do is sort out the relevant from the irrelevant features of the environment.

One of the curricula designed using the anchored instruction model is the Jasper mathematics curriculum. In the Jasper series, mathematics and science "story problems" are embedded in the context of a video story similar to a half-hour TV show. The rationale for embedding the problems in an authentic context relates to the salience of the vehicle of the story and to the authenticity of the story as a situation of application.

Several teaching techniques have been developed to operationalize the concepts of anchored instruction and situated learning. One of the most useful methods is the use of contrasting cases. Contrasting cases is one way to help students notice the theoretically important features of a problem situation. The introduction of contrasting cases highlights the differences that are important to the basic concepts the teacher is trying to convey. For example, in the "Understanding Organizations" course, I asked students to recall examples of effective and ineffective leaders from past organizational experiences. This can be a useful strategy, but it limits students to their own previous experience. More important, they only focus on those dimensions that novices would notice about leadership. They often generated examples that experts on leadership would recognize as misleading or irrelevant to the development of general principles about effective leadership. The contrasting cases technique generates two examples that contrast on a small number of theoretically important dimensions. Bransford, Franks, Vye, and Sherwood (1989) developed cases that allowed students to view situations from several perspectives and highlighted differences that were directly relevant to the objectives of the curriculum. The video clips used in the "Understanding Organizations" course provide many opportunities to position two examples that highlight specific contrasts in areas like management style. Another approach used in the "Understanding Organizations" course is applying a number of concepts to the same set of events. This helps students understand that deep principles can be applied to a number of situations and different principles can be applied to the same situation.

Defining different types of objectives also implies that different types of assessment should be used. Before the lesson even begins, assessment needs to include the assessment of prior knowledge because I assume all knowledge is constructed on the knowledge the student brings to the situation. A general principle of assessment in a constructivist framework is that assessment should measure dynamic rather than static transfer. *Dynamic transfer* refers to skills that efficient learners bring to a learning opportunity that facilitate learning in a new situation. *Static transfer* refers to the transfer of specific facts or specific fixed procedures (Bransford & Schwartz, 2001). This means that assessment should focus on distant transfer rather than specific memorized facts. The question is: How well can the learners apply what they have learned in this class to problems when the specific situation is changed at some time in the future? The ultimate goals of situated learning and anchored instruction programs are long term—particularly to produce life-long learners.

It is also important that assessment include formative assessment (ongoing feedback to and from students during the learning process) as well as outcome assessment. Because effective learning communities make student thinking visible, they provide opportunities for monitoring learning that are not available in traditional classroom environments (Lin et al., 1995). The goal of this kind of classroom is to produce usable knowledge, therefore students need to learn how to monitor their learning and understand the conditions under which it will be useful. Assessment of pure facts is of little value because the important thing the student needs to know is when the knowledge should be used.

In addition to knowledge objectives, most of our courses are also designed to help students acquire the methods of inquiry used in our disciplines. Learning the discipline's approach to data gathering and analysis is often the most important objective of a course. We want our students to learn to think like scientists and scholars in our disciplines. This is what constructivists mean when they talk about acculturating students to the social practices of the knowledge community. Conceptual and procedural knowledge is embedded in our scripts for *doing* chemistry, English, or history.

CONCLUSION

As often as possible, I use art, dance, poetry, music, and literature to provide students with another frame of reference or "way of knowing" to access the "big ideas and deep principles" I would like them to acquire. For me, one of the most productive ways to think about the nature of the relationship among the person, ideas, cultural artifacts (like myths, stories, poems, and art objects), and the real world is through poetry. I would like to use parts of one of my favorite poems by Wallace Stevens (1990), "The Idea of Order in Key West," to explore the relationship between the poet and the poet's being, the real world, the artifact of the poem, and the way that the reader's encounter with the artifact alters the way he or she sees the world. I return to this poem in chapter 6.

Stevens begins "The Idea of Order in Key West" by saying that the real world has an order (a genius) of its own that is totally unaltered by the artifact. The real world, in turn, is not known directly by the poet (referred to as "the singer"). Yet there is some form of relationship. The exact nature of this relationship is the source of the debate between von Glasersfeld and the psychological constructivists and the socioculturalists, which is described in chapter 5. In Stevens' poem, the sea's "mimic motion made constant cry, Caused constantly a cry" (i.e., found some common elements to create some form of connection). "That was not ours, Although we understood, In human, of the veritable ocean." The poet's trope and the author's metaphor connect internal cognitive structures and cultural artifacts that re-present "chunks of experience" from the real world.

She sang beyond the genius of the sea.
The water never formed to mind or voice.
Like a body, wholly body, fluttering
its empty sleeves; And yet its mimic motion
made constant cry, Caused constantly a cry,
That was not ours, although we understood,
In human, of the veritable sea.

Taking a psychological constructivist perspective, Stevens makes it clear that the author and poem are structurally independent from the world they describe. It is interesting to compare the following quote from von Glasersfeld (1995) with the section of the poem that follows it:

The space and time in which we move, measured and, above all, in which we map our movements and operations, are our own construction, and no explanation that relies on them can transcend our experiential world. (p. 74)

The next stanzas of Stevens' poem read:

The sea was not a mask. No more was she.
The song and the water were not medleyed sound.
Even if what she sang was what she heard,
Since what she sang was uttered word by word.
It may be that in all her phrases stirred
The grinding water and the gasping wind;
But it was she and not the sea we heard.
For she was the maker of the song she sang.
The ever-hooded, tragic gestured sea
Was merely a place by which she walked to sing.

Here and throughout the poem, Stevens sounds much like Wittgenstein, Rorty, and the activity theorists who make language and the language game the world we experience.

[We] knew that there never was a world for her
Except the one she sang and, singing, made.

The key question in the poem is a central question for constructivists. I know that real learning occurs, but I cannot really explain this final important step in the learning process: seeing the world in a new way. The methods used in the "Understanding Organizations" course (e.g., the use of media, contrasting cases, embedding content in an authentic context) are designed to transform the future *seeing* of students. Wallace Stevens asks how the poem can change the way we see the world and enhance our life experience:

Romon Fernandez, tell me, if you know,
Why, when the singing ended and we turned
Toward the town, tell why the glassy lights,
The lights in the fishing boats at anchor there,
As the night descended, tilted in the air,
Mastered the night and portioned out the sea,
Fixing emblazoned zones and fiery poles,
Arranging, deepening, enchanting night.

Most of Stevens' poems are considered too deep for university poetry courses, but I wish more students would take the time to understand his work. This penultimate stanza of "The Idea of Order at Key West" reflects my highest hopes for what education and art can accomplish.

Chapter 4

Course Development
Case Study I

This chapter chronicles the decisions I made through the process of designing and redesigning a course entitled "Understanding Organizations," the third course in the program's core curriculum. It follows basic courses in human development and group dynamics.

CASE STUDY OF HOD 1200—UNDERSTANDING ORGANIZATIONS

The following case study describes the problems I confronted and the decisions I made over 3 years of teaching the "Understanding Organizations" course and provides rationales for the changes I made each time I redesigned the course. I use the "Understanding Organizations" course as a case study throughout the remainder of the book and refer back to decisions I made about the course as I move through the topics in the book. The case serves as a concrete example of the abstract philosophical and theoretical principles I present. This version of the case study focuses on aspects of the course that reflect the basic philosophy of John Dewey and the theories discussed in chapter 3 on psychological constructivist perspectives. A final installment of the case study appears in chapter 8, which focuses on aspects of the course that reflect sociocultural and transactional constructivist perspectives.

When I began teaching "Understanding Organizations" again after several years of teaching in the freshman experience courses, I inherited a course that had a history of being one of our most popular, with many creative and innovative features. Terrance (Terry) Deal, a fine teacher and legendary lecturer who was a cowriter of one of the course's textbooks, created the course and established its reputation.

The textbook and course are constructed around looking at organizations from four different perspectives (the four frames): (a) the structural frame that focuses on the structure of organizations, organizational goals, and strategic planning; (b) the human resource frame that focuses on the needs of the members of the organization; (c) the political frame that focuses on issues of power, scarce resources, and negotiation; and (d) the symbolic frame that focuses on issues such as corporate culture and organizational symbols. These perspectives are all related to the overarching theme of organizational leadership. This framework is also used in other courses in the curriculum, most notably during the internship.

All of the sections of "Understanding Organizations" also included several common features: (a) an assignment that asked the students to use the four frames model to analyze an organization they belonged to or once belonged to; (b) an assignment that divided the class into groups and asked each to study an organization in the community and make a presentation about that organization at the end of the class using the four frames model; (c) all of the professors also made heavy use of various types of cases and used video clips to serve as examples of the concepts they were presenting; and (d) most of the sections of the course started off each of the five units of the course (leadership and the four frames) with an introductory lecture and assigned readings. The individual topics addressed within the frames (e.g., strategic planning, systems theory, learning organization, total quality management, situational management) varied according to the professors' assessment of what topics should be covered. None of the sections of the course was as traditional as the sample course included in the first chapter.

MY INITIAL ANALYSIS OF THE COURSE'S OBJECTIVES

The course objectives from one of the sections of "Understanding Organizations" are listed next with my initial reaction to each objective edited from my notes on the course development process:

1. To assess and apply selected classic and contemporary theories of organizations and organizational behavior, including planned change and leadership, to enhance our understanding of actual organizations and how they operate.
2. To assess and understand the interrelationships and interdependencies among core processes and between organizational systems and their environments.
3. To investigate and reflect on, in a systematic fashion, the remarkable impact that organizations have on our lives.

4. To internalize a set of critical thinking methodologies for assessing organizations as dynamic systems and the behavior of individuals and groups within them.

5. To enhance written and oral communication skills, with an emphasis on precision, clarity, creativity, and synthesis.

6. To enhance our abilities to work cooperatively in project-oriented/ investigative self-directed work groups/teams.

Summary of My Notes

The first two objectives provided a general idea of the course's focus and content, but they were too broad to give me much information about the specific content of the course. I also had a general feeling that it would be difficult to cover this much material in a beginning course on organizations, especially with the specific reference to planned change and core processes, which could fill several courses. This is always a problem with an introductory course. I did think that planned change, in a general sense, should be part of the framework of the course, but I did not think it would make sense to try to systematically cover theories of planned change. I was more interested in focusing on change to put the course in a context of identifying problems and conducting inquiries to find possible solutions. I thought students needed to think about how they would change organizations and predict how these changes would affect the organization's success at meeting its goals. The goal of helping students understand the importance of identifying the core processes and key transactions in an organization seems more reasonable than hoping they learned what they are. My notes when I first reviewed the course contained a number of other questions:

Do you try to introduce the range of topics in the field and let future courses fill in the details?

Do students remember anything they learn in courses like this?

What is the proper function of a foundational course?

Do you lay down the main concepts in the field?

Do you establish the preliminary approach to inquiry?

Do you try to identify the overarching ideas in the field?

I need to find a way to define what I want to accomplish that does not start with a list of facts and concepts I want them to learn.

On the positive side, the objectives do focus on applying theory to enhance their understanding of real organizations, and it positions the task as a problem-based inquiry process.

I decided to pick out a few specific topics to cover in some depth. I wanted to see the students improve their systems thinking and develop a systems perspective. We think of the development of a systems perspective as an across-the-curriculum skill in the Human and Organizational Development (HOD) Program. The students in the "Understanding Organizations" course had some background in systems thinking from previous courses. I needed to connect with that content. I was not sure whether I should lecture on systems theory, systems perspectives, and core processes at the beginning of the course. I decided that the students would not really understand these theories disconnected from a meaningful context. I needed to find a way to make it a theme for the entire course. The last four objectives connect broadly to the across-the-curriculum goals of the HOD Program. They reflect a program-wide commitment to building on the students' prior experience, stimulating systematic inquiry, and asking students to reflect on their learning on a number of levels.

By the time the students take this course, they have completed two courses that use the Kolb model to help them ground their learning in concrete experience, reflect on their values and previous experience, apply theory to understand what they have experienced, and develop strategies to take action to solve the problems they have identified. I decided to reintroduce the Kolb model in the introduction to the course. Many courses at Vanderbilt use the challenge cycle from the "How People Learn" framework (Bransford, Brown, & Cocking, 1999). I decided to use the model in a global sense, but to frame it within the Kolb cycle, rather than stating it explicitly.

Other excerpts from my original notes reflect my thoughts on these objectives:

> Writing and oral communication skills are emphasized across the curriculum. We have developed some rubrics to define the various levels of competence. I'm not sure that the rubrics are working very well for the students who don't already have good writing skills. The other students don't look at the rubrics and the guidelines for writing papers until they sit down with a professor to dispute their grade. In these meetings, the students are defensive and find it hard to use the rubric to assess their paper. The students are often confused by the rubric charts and don't feel comfortable admitting they don't understand the criteria. Students often want to use effort as a key factor in determining a grade. Another problem is that the criteria are too general. We have some model papers, but we need to do more work on this. I'd like the course to include more negotiation to clarify what we mean by good work and excellent work.

The First Reorganization of the Course

The following is a summary of some of my notes that capture my thoughts about the course before I taught it for the first time:

1. First of all, I'd like to find a way to focus the course on changing the way students see organizations. I'd like to help them develop templates for understanding what is happening in organizations and identifying problems. I have always used video clips in my lectures to try to ground students in a context. But I have the feeling that the process of finding an example of a problem situation or a concept benefits me more than it does the student who sees the example.

The Vanderbilt (LTC) Group experimented with the development of large video cases (anchors) that serve as an authentic context for problem identification, systematic inquiry, and problem solving. The "Jasper Woodberry" episodes involve the hero in problems embedded in a larger story context that require mathematics and science skills to solve. The Jasper Woodberry episodes are different from traditional story problems in that the problem is embedded in a larger unstructured problem situation. The students have to identify the important variables in this larger context. Generally, I would like to find a large case to serve as an anchor for exploring all the concepts in the course.

2. I like the four frames model. It provides a framework for looking at the organization from different perspectives. The four frames model is not an organizational theory. Rather, it provides a set of categories for ordering other organizational theories. In this sense, it provides a scaffold for students who are looking at organizations systematically for the first time. It is analogous to a table we might give to an elementary school science student who is learning how to look at variables in a complex experiment. The table makes it possible for students to handle more cognitive complexity than they would be able to handle without the scaffolding. Students who would become confused without this external support system are able to control variables systematically to support their thinking. I am also impressed that alumni who graduated from the program 15 years ago can routinely name the four frames and use them to think about organizations.

As I planned the course for the first time, I focused on questions about which theories within each frame were especially important to cover. I was unsure about whether I should lecture on the primary theories or make sure I brought them into the conversation as they facilitate the problem-solving process.

3. I think it is important to get away from the model of doing an introductory lecture on each frame and leadership, plus selected lectures on key topics. I would like to use a model where groups of students are presented with a problem situation and then develop a presentation of their analysis of the problem and suggestions for solutions. My input, as the expert, would come during the class discussion that follows the presentation.

I decided to go ahead and prepare a set of lectures on the four frames, leadership, strategic planning, and Argyris' Models I and II of communication in organizations. I developed Power Point presentations on these topics and stored them on the computer in the classroom so they would be available whenever I wanted to use them.

4. Ideally, I would like the students to have access to expert analyses of the problems presented in the course. This could be accomplished by videotape reactions by experts to the cases, bringing guest experts into the classroom, or setting up on-line access to experts. All these options would be exciting for the future, but, for the short term, I would like to bring in expert opinion through readings. I would also like to encourage students to develop individual areas of expertise that they can apply to the problems we identify.

In the second revision of the course, I decided to establish an official panel of student experts for each frame. Students would be asked to find a current scholarly article that provided theory and research findings that would shed light on the problems we were addressing in the frame.

5. I think it is important for students to take the lead in developing solutions to problems. I would like them to have a way of engaging in active dialogue to identify and analyze problems in groups and developing solutions using the theories presented in the course. The more chances they get to talk about what they think and to reflect on and write about their organizational experience, the more they will develop "big ideas and deep principles" they can use to understand and solve problems in organizations in the future.

6. I would like the students to develop the initial solutions and then I will "label their solutions" with the concepts that have been developed in the community of scholars. I would like to develop some way that students could develop areas of expertise that would allow them to make contributions.

Guided by these initial thoughts, my first task in redesigning the course was to develop a clearer idea of what I wanted the students to learn in the course. My description of the initial course planning process is organized around a model developed by Wiggins and McTighe (1997). The first step in designing a course using this model is to identify the enduring understandings students should acquire in the course. They identify six facets of understanding that can be used to define enduring understandings. These six facets serve as a framework for helping teachers bring their tacit understanding of the course content to consciousness. The "understanding by design" process helps overcome a basic characteristic of expertise that makes it difficult for us to share our knowledge with students who are new to our disciplines (i.e., much of our foundational understanding is implicit). These foundational concepts provide the scaffolding that organizes our knowledge. Without it, our students will find it much more difficult to organize and retrieve the specific theories and facts we present to them.

Six Facets of Understanding

Definition. The commitment of the combined constructivist perspectives to maintain a focus on ideas (Basic Principle 9) is reflected in Wiggins and McTighe's (1997) goal of helping students acquire "sophisticated and apt explanations and theories, which provide knowledgeable and justified accounts of events, actions, and ideas" (p. 34). This means that we want students to be able to answer "why" questions like, "Why do you think Jones found that his productivity increased despite cutting his supervisory staff?" Students should be able to connect findings, especially those that go against their "everyday theories" with the enduring understandings from the course. I worked on developing my statement of Big Ideas and Deep Principles for the "Understanding Organizations" course by thinking about and keeping track of the "why" questions I asked students in the course (see Appendix B).

Constructivist approaches to teaching typically begin by exploring the students' current understanding and immersing them in authentic problem situations. The first steps in the course development process focus on identifying relevant activity systems and thinking about what enduring understandings will help students deal effectively with those situations. After thinking about the situations my students will encounter in their future careers, I listed the problems I thought they might confront where knowledge of organizations and organizational behavior would alert them to important organizational characteristics and patterns of behavior.

Interpretation. Because the goal of constructivist approaches to education is understanding that is anchored in contexts that are personally meaningful to the student, it is important to connect learning to the context of application. McTighe and Wiggins (1999) believed students who acquire useful knowledge "can tell meaningful stories; offer apt translations; provide revealing historical or personal dimension to ideas and events; make them personal and accessible through images, anecdotes, analogies, and models" (p. 38). Narratives and stories are important organizational structures for meaning. This was the central idea behind the goal-based scenarios approach developed by Schank (1999). We hope students will be able to put theoretical explanations into their own personally meaningful narratives. The strong focus on written and video cases as well as the personal and group organizational papers in the "Understanding Organizations" course reflects this orientation.

Application. "The ability to use knowledge effectively in new situations and diverse contexts" (McTighe & Wiggins, 1999, p. 36) lies at the heart of the definition of useful knowledge. The organization of the course around a large simulation (4Frames.Kamm) and asking students to use the theories to analyze two real organizations (their personal organization and their group organization) was designed to assess students' ability to apply theory to authentic contexts.

Perspective. Perspective means critically evaluating the course content from a variety of perspectives and in a larger social context. In addition to being able to examine information from different points of view, perspective means students should be able to base judgments on evidence rather than relying on their personal opinions. According to several theories of cognitive and epistemological development (e.g., Perry, 1970; King & Kitchener, 1994; Baxter-Magolda, 1999), many university students are still in a stage of cognitive and epistemological development that screens out evidence that contradicts their personal opinions.

Empathy. McTighe and Wiggins (1999) believed that "the ability to identify with another person's feelings and world view" (p. 36) is an important educational goal. In the "Understanding Organizations" course, I used Argyris' communication model to help students increase both their advocacy and inquiry skills.

Self-Knowledge. Self-knowledge is defined as the "wisdom to know one's ignorance and how one's patterns of thought and action inform as well as prejudice understanding" (McTighe & Wiggins, 1999, p. 36).

The first stage in the course design process was to use these basic facets of understanding to help identify desired results. This means deciding on a limited number of enduring understandings that represent the most important outcomes. The second task was to decide what evidence would demonstrate that students have acquired these understandings. The specific content and learning activities of the course are organized to support the acquisition of these understandings. The graded assignments in the course and the scoring guide used to evaluate these assignments (see Appendix A) were designed to provide evidence that students had acquired the enduring understandings and skills identified in the Big Ideas and Deep Principles handout (see Fig. 4.1 & Appendix B). The language used

The course presents an "ecological systems" perspective of organizations:
(a) Systems are characterized by interdependent, transactional relationships between sub-systems and a nested relationship among subsystems, systems, and supersys-tems. An "ecological systems" perspective includes seeing an organization and its external (e.g., competitors, government regulations, global economy) and internal contexts as a dynamic ecology.
(b) A systems perspective assumes that each component has a tendency to structure itself as a semipermeable system with structural coupling to other systems on the same and other levels. Students should understand how this creates resistance to change and points to the importance of attending to boundary issues and communication across boundaries.

FIG. 4.1.   Example of big ideas and deep principles.

to express the enduring understandings (big ideas and deep principles) is not transparent to the students when they begin the course. They are intro-duced early in the course, and I refer to them throughout the semester to clarify their meaning and implications. The scoring guide indicates that "an excellent response" ties the case material and course concepts to these principles.

The statement of Big Ideas and Deep Principles for the "Understanding Organizations" course evolved as I developed new insights about what the underlying enduring understandings of the course were. This process was not as straightforward as I expected it to be. I was used to thinking about what content and theories I wanted to cover in a course. I could say why each lecture was important, but I had not connected all the material to a broader set of organizing principles. The specific theories in each disci-pline cluster to reflect the discipline's dominant paradigms and the funda-mental perspectives that lie behind them. As experts we take much of this basic framework for granted, especially the structure of the connections be-tween principles.

An example of how these deep principles are used in the class might be useful. Item b in Fig. 4.1 outlines an aspect of the systems perspective used throughout the course. Students should understand why this characteristic of organizations creates resistance to change and points to the importance of attending to boundary issues and communication across boundaries. This principle is an important organizer of several organizational phenom-ena, such as the tendency of departments within organizations to sub-optimize, focus on their own interests, and create structural barriers to change. In the 4Frames.Kamm case, there is a constant tension between the efficiency and effectiveness of self-managed work teams and the tendency of teams to fight for the same resources and compete with each other in-stead of the corporation's external competitors. All of the students can point to examples of suboptimization (Balkanization) in organizations. Good students can link that tendency to this deep principle. The best students could disagree with this principle and offer an alternative theory about the suboptimization phenomenon.

PRELIMINARY OVERVIEW OF THE DESIGN OF THE "UNDERSTANDING ORGANIZATIONS" COURSE

I problematized the content by developing an overarching simulation for the "Understanding Organizations" course from problems being encountered by real organizations in the current highly competitive globalized economy. To create a mechanism for making knowledge visible that matched a typical situation these students would confront in their careers, I divided the class into six consultation firms. Over the course of the semester, these consultation firms dealt with a series of problems confronting a business called 4Frames.Kamm that developed computer-based learning materials for schools and training materials for corporations. There were four rounds of student presentations focusing on the four frames and their application to organizational leadership from structural, human resource, political, and symbolic perspectives. In each round of presentations, three of the consulting firms were asked to analyze the organization's problems in the selected area and develop solutions based on the theories in the reading.

The six consulting firms were asked to prepare presentations for the management of 4Frames.Kamm to compete for a contract to consult with the organization. On most of the class days, the six student groups each took one of the following roles: (a) presenting consulting firm, (b) management of 4Frames.Kamm, (c) presentation evaluators, (d) experts, (e) holding a planning meeting for the presentation, and (f) meeting in the multimedia lab to prepare the presentation. The experts read articles related to the topic being studied in the management literature and brought this knowledge into the discussions that led up to and followed the presentations. At the end of the semester, each of the groups made a presentation about an organization in the community that they had been studying.

By assigning students projects to complete in self-managed work teams, the course explored a topic in the course (the use of self-managed work teams) and completed a process that mirrored assignments they would often receive during their careers. This process was designed to "involve students in active knowledge construction through goal-directed inquiry" (Basic Principle 4) "in learning communities" (Basic Principle 5) "in an authentic context" (Basic Principle 2). By asking them to analyze each of the cases from several perspectives and analyze the same case from different perspectives, students learned the metacognitive attitude of viewing problems from a number of perspectives.

Summary of the Major Problems I Confronted During the First Year I Taught the Course

The first group of students who took the "Understanding Organizations" course under the new design had a fairly strong negative reaction to the course. Feedback during and at the end of the course registered the following complaints:

• The students thought there was way too much work and too many assignments. Small assignments were due almost every class session. My goal was to force them to address issues and reflect and continually refine their ideas about organizations based on confronting problems, inquiring about them, and finding solutions. I did not think they would learn anything by leaving all their reading until they crammed for a mid-term and a final. Many of the students were used to letting their reading slide and cramming for tests. They experienced the course like a form of Chinese water torture.

• The students thought the grading was too difficult, and they could not understand the grading criteria. I thought they could learn best by getting assignments in the same form they would be receiving them in a real organization. This fit with Schank's (1999) idea of creating expectation failures. I told myself that they would not get a 20-page syllabus with guidelines about how to complete their work assignments in a corporate setting. In the "real world," employees have to figure out how to solve the problem and learn from their mistakes and the feedback they get.

• They wanted more traditional lectures. I provided "mini-lectures" at times when issues emerged naturally, but delivered only one traditional lecture. Even though I kept a log of what had been covered in the class presentations and filled in with additional content that I thought was important, they thought I should be standing at the front of the room telling them things.

Second Revision of Course

When I approached the task of redesigning the course, I was responding to feedback from students that they were confused about exactly what they were supposed to be learning and what criteria were being used to grade their papers and presentations. I was conflicted about this because I thought the confusion and effort they went though to deal with the ambiguity of an authentic unstructured problem was beneficial for them. In the end, however, I decided to develop a set of scoring rubrics that would make the criteria for grading clearer. I did have a goal that made the course different from most organizational settings: I was asking students to use scholarly standards to conduct their inquiries and judge the validity of their evidence. I also wanted the discourse to follow disciplinary standards. This was operationalized in the type of feedback they received on both their presentations and written work. They were repeatedly asked to justify their opinions with evidence. Most of the students made significant progress toward meeting these standards in their written work and in their formal presentations. They had much more trouble incorporating justificatory and critical discourse into their classroom dialogue. I was determined to focus the rubrics on the primary objective of the course: developing concepts, deep principles, and theories and being able to use them to analyze problems in authentic, unstructured organizational contexts (see Appendix A & Fig. 4.2).

---

4 — Good — A–
- Connects specific examples of organizational characteristics, events, and behaviors that fit into the domain of the frame with theories that connect to the examples **and** *explains* **why** *these theories enrich your understanding of the organization, and systematically connects the theory to the case.*
- Demonstrates an ability to explain the same organizational characteristics from *more than one perspective* (using different frames, different theories for the same incident).
- Uses the theories to identify possible problems and identify solutions, says what you would suggest changing **and** *why you think the theory points to your solutions.*

5 — Excellent — A/A+
- Uses the theories to identify possible problems and identify solutions, suggests what should be changed, why the theory points to this suggestion **and** *connects the analysis to the big ideas and deep principles in the course.*
- *Critiques the theories' strengths and weaknesses for explaining the success or failure of the organization.* Explains **why** the theories and the deep principles behind them offer a **good explanation** for what happened in the organization **or why** a theory *fails to increase your understanding* of the organization. (For example, Theory X would predict that employees would be unproductive in this situation, when, in fact, the employees were satisfied and highly motivated. Then go on to say why you think the theory didn't fit this situation.)
- *Challenges theories you disagree with and explains why you reject the theory. Systematically links theory, research, and personal experience to your personal developing model of organizations.*

FIG. 4.2. Sample of scoring guide.

The first task I laid out for myself was to refine the list of Big Ideas and Deep Principles that represented the foundation for the organizational theories and concepts they were supposed to acquire in the course. This was a useful exercise for me because I realized that I had assumed a stronger connection between the deep principles behind the theories and the frames than I had articulated. Most of the theories of human behavior were introduced in the first two courses and followed up as we moved through "Understanding Organizations." I referred to these connections as we moved through the material in "Understanding Organizations." For example, when we studied leadership theories, I referred back to a lecture about human ethology and group dominance structure I had given in a previous course on applied human development. Although the ideas were introduced again in one of the readings for the "Understanding Organizations" course, it is unlikely that most of the students experienced my input as significant. These connections were salient to me because I already had the knowledge from the three courses integrated into one structure. Even the best students rarely referred to any of these deep principles in their papers. I decided I needed to work harder to help the students make the same connections. After I revised the summary of the deep principles, I decided to include it in the syllabus and refer to it throughout the course. I also incorporated specific references to tying theory to deep principles in the rubrics I developed for the course. Giving students these principles helped them make deeper connections between theory and practice. Unless students integrate their knowledge on several levels and connect it to their own past and future experiences, they are unlikely to retain and use the knowledge. They have to connect the ideas in the course to a story that is meaningful to them and develop indexes that will help them connect them to new situations. The course gives specific attention to finding ways to scaffold the structuring of knowledge.

ANNOTATED SYLLABUS FOR HOD 1200—
UNDERSTANDING ORGANIZATIONS

I thought the best form for a case study of the problems I confronted and the decisions I made during the course development and revision of the "Understanding Organizations" course would an annotated syllabus. We are all used to developing and reviewing course syllabi. This section of the chapter is organized around the syllabus for the "Understanding Organizations" course during the third year I taught the course. I put excerpts from the actual syllabus in bold type and describe how each class was conducted, what the assignments were, and describe significant changes from the previous year under each session.

Human and Organizational Development 1200:
Understanding Organizations

See syllabus in chapter 1 for descriptions of readings, objectives of the course, detailed descriptions of assignments, and reading for each session.

Session 1: **Introduction: Review syllabus, course objectives, explanation of methods, review assignments, form teams, set schedule, exercise to pick personal organization.**

Design for Class Session. During the first class, the course design was introduced, I passed out the Big Ideas and Deep Principles handout, and I talked about the course objectives. When they came into the class, the tables were labeled with names and they were already assigned to groups. This matches work situations where employees are assigned to teams. It allowed me to organize teams with cultural diversity and gave me an opportunity to distribute various kinds of talent fairly evenly. Students completed an exercise to pick their personal organization. This has been the primary mechanism for linking the course content to their personal experience in organizations. They each made a list of the organizations they currently belonged to or had belonged to over the previous 3 years. They narrowed the list to three organizations that had been the most personally meaningful to them. Each student then shared his or her three organizations with the group to stimulate more ideas throughout the group. I then talked about the Personal Organizational Paper assignment and discussed the rubrics for grading the assignments to help the students select the best organization. A description of this assignment can be found in chapter 1 under Personal Organizational Assessment.

During this session, I also introduced the primary case for the course—the 4Frames.Kamm case. The case focuses on a high-tech firm that designs and delivers training programs for educational and corporate clients. The company gets it name by combining the Four Frames model used in the course with the name of the company's president, Dorothy (Dot) Kamm. (Dot's name is an example of the many lame attempts at humor in this case that only the professor appreciates.) The case presents the students with a range of problems in a variety of categories. All of the facts in the case, except for Dot's name of course, are drawn from actual events in real companies and corporations (see Fig. 4.3).

I completed this session by presenting several examples of presentations from previous semesters. I showed both presentations to 4Frames.Kamm and final presentations on organizations in the community. Seeing a high-quality final presentation at this point in the semester was designed to help the groups understand what would be expected of them and alert them to

Even though the company has grown rapidly, they haven't really changed the way they do business. They generate a project idea by talking to clients or salespeople, assembling a project team, and finding them some space somewhere. This worked for a while, but now they are beginning to experience some serious problems that threaten their business. A few representative problems are listed below:

First of all, no one in the company at any level is really sure what they are supposed to do. Some projects have been successful, but a project's success depends on the project manager's skill at coordinating work across departments, getting special favors from friends, and successfully outmaneuvering other projects for resources. Some important projects have been completed late and have been of mediocre quality because the project manager could not "work the system" to get his or her project completed. Dot recently intervened and pulled a training package she said was embarrassing to 4Frames and gave the client a public apology and a refund. This made her look good, but was a serious public embarrassment to Ted Nogeek, one of the original partners. Project managers frequently come into conflict about which departments are responsible for different parts of the project and which project has priority for scarce resources. Many of the employees are overworked, while others don't seem to have enough work to fill their time. There is serious competition for resources between the projects, especially for the use of multi-media production equipment. When two projects have the same deadline and need the same equipment, it can lead to serious tension and even the threat of violence.

FIG. 4.3.   Excerpt from 4Frames.Kamm case study.

the fact that the final presentation is a substantial assignment. It is important that they select an organization in the community and begin working with the organization early in the semester. I used these examples to go through the guidelines for evaluating the presentations. I also showed how the Scoring Guide for Application of Theory to Personal Organizations and Other Cases presented in the first session would be applied to evaluating the presentations.

Notes on Design and Changes.   I knew enough about the students to make up groups that were diverse in terms of race, gender, HOD and economics majors, and so on. I tried to give each group at least one excellent student. It is important for each group to have students who can develop more sophisticated conceptual frameworks to help scaffold the knowledge development of other students in the group. This model has worked very well. The mixture of majors and levels of academic ability resulted in groups with distributed expertise to contribute to the group projects. Many of the students from other majors lack some of the group process and communication skills of the HOD students, but they bring important technology skills and knowledge from other disciplines.

I added the exercise on selecting the personal organization in the second year because they needed more help to select the best organization to meet their objectives for getting a good grade and meeting the course's learning objectives. The organization should be important to them, they should have played an important role in the organization, and they should have knowledge of the organization's leader and the problems he or she faced. The Personal Organizational Assessment Paper Assignment is included in the assignments section of the "Understanding Organizations" course syllabus in chapter 1.

Session 2: Introduction to "West Wing"—Introduction to 4Frames and rubrics for written work and presentations.

This class session began by passing out a short handout on the four frames and giving the students a brief introduction to it. Then I introduced the students to the situation and characters from the TV show "West Wing." The show focuses on the problems confronted by the president and the White House staff. "West Wing" provides one of the four "anchors" for the course. These anchors provide the authentic contexts for indexing principles and theories of organizations. At the beginning of each frame, the class saw a 30-minute segment of one of the episodes of the program that contained problems that fell in the domain of the frame we would be using to examine organizations during that part of the course. Using the same program with the same characters over the course of the semester enriched the narrative context and provided continuity in the frames of reference students used to discuss the theories. This first episode contained a number of problems the president would have to deal with in the future. I asked the students to identify the problems, see if they could categorize them by frame, and say what they thought he should do. We explored the solutions generated in this first session for clues about what implicit theories students were using to guide their organizational behavior.

Session 3: Workshop: Editing tapes and making presentations. Leader evaluation pretest. Introduction to the 4Frames.Kamm case and Structural Frame Tape. Pass out 4Frames.Kamm Critical Incident #1. Group 2 planning meeting and Group 4 planning meeting outside class time.

When the student groups were playing the role of consultation firms making presentations to 4Frames.Kamm, they were required to include at least two short clips from "West Wing" in each presentation. These clips were embedded in their Power Point presentation for the frame. Video clips from the "West Wing" segment they viewed in class were digitized and mounted in a project frame in the Apple i-Movie editing system. The clips were available in the computer multimedia lab adjacent to the classroom. Groups had class time to work on editing and developing their presentations, but the clips were also available at any other time in the multimedia lab. This session was a workshop where the students learned how to edit video clips, make them into digital movies, and insert them into Power Point slide shows.

The final 20 minutes of the class session was used to present the "West Wing" episode for the structural frame. Students watched the tape, made notes about the styles of leadership they saw, and identified problems that they thought might fall into the general category of *organizational structural problems* (e.g., mission, goals, organizational design, strategic planning). I also passed out the first critical incident related to the 4Frames.Kamm case. This incident defined the specific problem situation the consulting firms (Groups 2, 4, and 6) would be addressing in their presentations. The planning meetings for Groups 2 and 4 were taped in a meeting room set up for videotaping. Each of the groups reviewed edited scenes from these tapes during their planning meeting for the second round of presentations. I attended these meetings, which were held outside the regular class meeting time.

Notes on Design and Changes. The perceptual and physical act of editing the tapes was designed to tune the students' perceptions to improve their skills at identifying problems in an unstructured problem space.

The dialogue that took place while the groups were discussing what clips they should use and why those clips were the best examples of the course concepts played an important part in the learning process. One problem that often developed after the initial session where the class TA was available to help the groups was the tendency to split up the task of developing the presentation and forgo the conversations that I wanted them to have about the course material. It makes sense for the students to use division of labor to save time in completing the project, but if they complete the projects this way, some of the group members do not really connect the examples with the theory. I try to help them understand that dialogue is a critical part of the learning process.

Each time I taught the course, I reduced the number of student presentations. The first semester, I had three groups presenting each session. The second semester, I cut back to two groups per session. The current version of the course limits the formal part of the presentation to 15 minutes and leaves the rest of the time for questions and discussion. The number of presentations was reduced to respond to complaints that the course had too many assignments and too much work. I think this was a valid complaint. Yet the primary reason for cutting down the presentations was that students were filling up the whole class period with their presentations. The presentations were designed to serve as a stimulus for dialogue, but we never had very much time to talk about the ideas presented and link the discussion to the concepts in the course. The biggest loss in these discussions was that there was so little time for input from the students that were acting as experts. They had so much to offer, and they rarely got adequate time to share what they had learned with their fellow students.

Another problem with the large number of presentations was that the students thought the course was about making presentations rather than organizational theory. It was always a struggle to keep students focused on ideas. This was partly because making presentations was something they knew how to do, and some of the other demands I was making on them were difficult for them to understand. Improving their presentation skills was supposed to be a minor part of the course, but they tended to focus a lot of energy on the appearance of the presentation and too little attention on the substance of the ideas presented. They were confused when a flashy presentation got a lower grade than a less spectacular, but more substantive, presentation.

One advantage of having each group make three presentations over the course of the semester was that I could give them feedback on each of the presentations and create a developmental process that would help them improve the professional and intellectual quality of their presentations. They also stimulated each other to do better. The first set of presentations counted for a smaller portion of their grade than later presentations. Although the presentations do not count for a very large percentage of their grades, they still invest too much time in their surface appearance. As with the expert letter assignment, they invest a lot of effort in an assignment that their fellow students will see. I have been struck by the fact that, despite theory that indicates that professors are seen as authorities, students are much more concerned about work that other students will evaluate.

This session also included an exercise to gather information about the students' initial everyday theories about organizational leadership.

Session 4: **Workshop on Communications—Argyris' Model I & II Introduce Expert Assignments. Pretest for final.**
Assignments Due: **Draft of Section 1 of Personal Paper & Difficult Situations Case.**

This session is the first of two workshops on communication skills and productive disciplinary discourse. I also introduced the Expert Article and Answer Letter assignments. The format of the Expert article is included in the assignments section in chapter 1.

Notes on Design and Changes.   Issues related to communication skills and dialogue are discussed in chapter 8.

The first time I assigned the expert article/response letter assignments, I assumed that the students would know that they were supposed to follow the same guidelines we had used in the two previous courses. In the two previous core courses, we made it clear that we wanted them to use research and scholarly articles with references. We presented clear guidelines that limited the use of Internet, popular magazines, and newspaper articles. When the first assignments came in, most of the students submitted three- or four-page newspaper or magazine articles. Many were opinion pieces pulled from the Internet. The students in the first expert group were angry when I asked most of them to do the assignment again (many of them had received Ds on the assignment). As in many examples of miscommunication between students and professors, my instructions were not more specific because I thought it was "obvious" that they were supposed to read scholarly articles. They were angry (actually furious) with me because I had given them low grades without clear instructions. I was irritated (actually angry) with them because I thought they should have understood that the standards of scholarship they had followed in the last two courses should be followed in all of the HOD courses.

In subsequent semesters, I developed a fairly elaborate set of guidelines for finding articles from a list of journals in our management library. I restricted them to the current organizational and management literature because I wanted them to be exposed to the leading edge concepts in the field. This procedure ensured that the students would find articles that were scholarly and difficult for them to understand. A primary objective of the assignment was to challenge them to wrestle with difficult concepts and help each other understand them. It also connected them to the community of scholars in this field and benchmarked the level of discourse in the field. I have been very impressed with the level of sophistication that the students have been able to handle. After I gave them clear guidelines, the students got very good articles, and the quality of the Expert Letters was generally very good.

Although the process of having students find their own articles was successful in many ways, it presented some problems. First, the students were just learning the theoretical frameworks presented in the course, and some of them had trouble finding an article that linked the right set of theories to the specific problems in the case. I saw this as an important objective of the course, but I was asking the students to demonstrate this skill fairly early in the learning process. Although almost all of them found an article that generally fit the theoretical frame, some had trouble finding an article that also targeted the specific problems in the 4Frames.Kamm organization. If "the experts" had not found an article that targeted the organization's problems, they could not make a strong contribution to the discussion that was relevant to the presenting problem.

The second problem with this assignment had to do with my own workload. The system I set up required that I read 36 articles and grade 64 papers written about those articles in addition to the rather heavy load of grading other papers and presentations in the course. I had to read the articles carefully enough to help the students link specific ideas in the articles to the problems being discussed from the case. I did not mind this if reading the article contributed to my own knowledge and helped me keep up with the organizational literature, but it was difficult if the article was poorly written. Finally, I decided to pick the articles myself. This allowed me to read them ahead of time and reduced the articles I had to be familiar with to 12. The expert group now reads all of the articles related to that frame, and it allows them to focus their conversation more sharply on the organization's problems. During the presentation, the experts question the consultation group about their recommendations for 4Frames.Kamm and present ideas from their reading.

The "West Wing" episode and the 4Frames.Kamm cases provide a context for reading the assignments that cover an introduction to leadership and the structural frame.

Session 5: QUIZ #1—STRUCTURAL FRAME
After Quiz—Group 2—Work Meeting, Group 4—Media Lab—Groups 1, 3, 5, 6 meet to pick outside organization. Group 6—Taped planning meeting outside class time.

This session has a quiz on the readings thus far. It is not designed to test in-depth knowledge, but to check to see whether the students are reading the assignments. After the quiz, we clarify the roles that the different groups will be playing in the next session. Group 2 has the rest of the class period to work on their presentation, and Group 4 goes to the media lab to select their video clips and start assembling their Power Point presentation. The other groups met to discuss possibilities for an outside organization and make initial plans to contact organizations in the community.

Notes on Design and Changes. Introducing the cases and posing organizational problems before the students do the reading primes them with questions that will make their reading more profitable. The quiz is designed to make them read the assignment. The quiz is multiple choice and cannot be defended with any learning theory. My own "action research" indicates that students do not read the assignment without a quiz, and if they have not read the assignment they cannot profitably edit the video clips, find appropriate expert articles, or make meaningful contributions to the class discussions. I have discussed this issue with many classes, and they all admit that they would not read the material without the quiz and their meetings would not be productive if most of the group had not read the material.

Session 6: **Group 2 Presenters, Group 5—Clients, Group 3—Evaluators, Groups 1 & 3A Experts, Group 4 Work Meeting, Group 6—Media Lab.**

Assignment due: **Group 1 & 3A—Expert reports & question letters on the structural frame.**

This was the first of several class sessions that followed the same pattern. The different groups of students in the course played different roles in the simulation in each class session. In this session, Group 2 acted as the consulting firm. The class session started with their presentation to Group 5, who played the roles of the executive team from 4Frames.Kamm. Group 5 was responsible for studying the case and asking questions that would push the presenters to clarify the ideas presented. I encouraged the rest of the class to jump in and ask anyone who spoke to clarify or defend their ideas. Group 4 had a work meeting, and Group 6 was in the multimedia computer lab. The students in Group 3 were evaluators for this session. They filled out observation forms and gave written feedback to Group 2. After the presentation, Group 5 (who played the role of the clients) and Group 3 (who were the evaluators) left for 10 minutes and discussed their respective evaluations of the presentation. They returned and gave feedback to Group 2. While the two groups were out of the room, I asked Group 2 to evaluate themselves and continue the discussion. Groups 1 and 3A were the experts for this and the next two class sessions. After the class, I reviewed the presentation and sent my evaluation and grade to Group 2 through the class Web page. I tried to do this as soon as possible (usually later that day) to give the students immediate feedback. I reviewed the feedback with the group in the planning meeting for their next presentation.

During the class discussion, I presented three sets of guidelines for achieving open discussion. These guidelines are presented and discussed in the next version of the case study in chapter 8, which focuses on issues related to communication and social practices. The central process objective of all of these sessions was to create a series of dialogues that linked concrete examples to deep principles. Embedding discussions of theory in meaningful contexts indexes deep principles, procedural knowledge, and skills to specific organizational cues.

Notes on Design and Changes.   The system used in the class is complicated, but once students have gone through a presentation cycle the first time, they do not have trouble with the simulation. Some students did not like having to think about where they were supposed to be for every class session. Some students did not like having to come to class every session. This is no longer an issue because the student grapevine has made students aware that they have to come to class. Although this section of the class had a heavier workload than the other sections, the impact of the workload was reduced because I was able to organize the work so that it is concentrated in parts of the semester when students do not have other assignments due.

The general design of the presentation days works fairly well, but the student groups (like most professors) tend to try to fit too much content into their presentations. The presentations are professional and impressive. Although it is not part of the instructions or the rubric for assessing the presentations, almost all of the groups dress in business attire for the presentations.

The main problem I had with these sessions during the first year was getting the students to participate in an open dialogue. They were reluctant to push their fellow students to defend their ideas. The issue of finding a way to improve the quality of dialogue in every aspect of the course is the primary problem in making this model work effectively. This issue is addressed in detail in chapter 8.

In the first year I taught the course, I found it difficult to time my input into the stream of student conversation. Scaffolding the emergence of knowledge is an art, and it took me a while to master it. I had a set of mini-lectures prepared that I planned to introduce when the content seemed relevant to the problems being discussed. The first time I taught the course, I also found it difficult to remember what I had talked about before. Unfortunately, the students did not always remember if they had heard it before either. I solved this problem by keeping notes on what I had covered. This worked fairly well, but I still found it hard to stay organized without the support of a structured lecture. It was also more difficult to use the technology effectively because it involved opening a file and finding a spot in the lecture. I am currently organizing an index with hyperlinks to topics to make this process more efficient. When I was able to time my input so that it provided theory that connected well to the discussion, it was effective and reinforced my efforts to keep trying to develop these skills. I originally accepted this awkwardness as a problem associated with this model of teaching, but in the current version of the course this has not been much of a problem. At some point, I began to remember what I had covered and what I needed to cover. I am not sure how this happened, but I assume I reorganized the content of the course and indexed it more efficiently. I benefited from the contextualization of the theory in the narrative context of the course just as the students did. I should add that I am a classic absent-minded professor and found it rather strange to be remembering things.

Session 7: Group 4 Presenters, Group 5—Clients, Group 2, 3B—Evaluators, Group 1 & 3A Experts, Group 6 in Computer Lab
Assignments due: **Answer letters on the structural frame.**

Beyond the procedure already described, I had specific content that I was prepared to introduce each session after the student presentation. The focus of this session was on getting the experts to contribute what they had learned to the discussion. I introduced material on strategic planning during this session. In the first version of the course, I also introduced Argyris' model of open communication at this point in the course. In the current version of the course, I include two full sessions on the Argyris' model and focus much more attention on it to improve the quality of discussion. Details on this aspect of the course appear in chapter 8.

Session 8: **Group 6 Presenters, Group 5—Clients, Group 3—Evaluators, Group 1 & 3A Experts, Groups 2 & 4 in meetings with outside organization. Return for last 20 minutes of the class for "West Wing" introduction to the HR Frame. Pass out critical incident #2.**

Assignments due: **Section 2 of Personal Organization Paper—Structural Frame**

Session 9: **Quiz #2—Human Resource Frame**
After Quiz: Group 3—work meeting, Group 5—Tape planning meeting, Groups 2, 4, & 6—Communications Workshop II. Group 1—Outside organization. Group 1—Planning meeting outside class time.

The first version of the course included an essay quiz at the end of each frame. The essay quiz served as a way to summarize the material on each frame and test the students' ability to apply the concepts to problem solving. The essay question presented the students with a practical problem situation and asked them to apply the theories from the structural frame to understanding the problem and suggesting possible solutions. I eliminated the essay test because I thought I was getting the information I needed about their ability to apply the theories in the Personal Organization papers.

Eliminating the essay test allowed me to add more communications training in the class time. During the third year I taught the course, I also started taping the first and last planning meetings and attending the meetings. During the planning meeting for the second presentation, we reviewed the tape from the first meeting. Details of this process are discussed in chapter 8.

The next 13 sessions repeated this general cycle, with each group rotating through each of the roles twice. The leadership lecture in Session 18 was the only exception to this pattern. (See syllabus in chap. 1 for details of these sessions.)

Session 18: **Leadership Lecture—***Assignments due:* **Section 4 of Personal Organization Paper—Political & Symbolic Frames.**

This was the only time during the semester when I gave a traditional lecture. This lecture, entitled "What I Learned from Basketball," integrated many of the concepts in the course around a "personally relevant and meaningful context" (mostly to the professor). This is an excellent example of "a time for telling." The real reason for giving the lecture was probably because I enjoy doing it so much. Deprived of my center stage for the whole semester, I am the one who most acutely feels that it must *finally* be "the time for telling."

Session 21: **Group 1—Group organization presentation. Groups 2 & 3— Group organizational work day. Group 4—Taped planning meeting outside class time.**

The last six sessions of the course are built around presentations made by the groups on the outside organizations they have been analyzing throughout the semester. Each of these sessions followed the basic organization of this session. Originally, we did the final presentations in the last three class sessions. It was frustrating to hear these rich case studies and have no time to use them to integrate the course material. The discussions around the community organizations the groups had been studying offered rich opportunities to scaffold the development of conceptual knowledge and help students make connections between concrete examples of organizational behavior and the concepts, principles, and theories presented in the course. These discussions were comfortable and productive.

Session 28: **Final Examination**

During the first year, the final exam consisted of having students view the introduction to the "West Wing" video they viewed during the first session of the course. After the first year, I began using another film to serve as a pre- and posttest. During the pretest, they were able to say what they thought about the case in about 20 minutes. On the final exam, students spent 3 to 4 hours on this task. Before the final exam, students were given an outline of the basic concepts in the course. They could either make notes on the hard copy they received or use an electronic copy on the Web site and type in their own notes on the concepts. They were allowed to bring up to six pages of typed notes to the exam. They were encouraged to use an outline form and other devices to organize the material into models. Following Basic Principle 3—that the quality of knowledge depends more on how it is structured than the number of facts accumulated—this exercise was designed to help students organize the course content into an efficient format for retrieval. The students generally do an excellent job of organizing their notes. I am especially impressed with some of the systems of color coding. Many of these outlines are excellent conceptual maps of the course material. The test was administered in the computer lab. This allowed students to type their responses into a template that provided an outline of the scenes from the film. The final exam was scheduled for 2 hours, and most of the students stayed for at least 3 hours to share their ideas about the case. Because the final exam counts for only 10% of their grade, most of the motivation for this extraordinary effort seemed to be intrinsic. I want to emphasize that this task would be difficult without extensive experience at identifying problems in unstructured problem spaces. Their performance on the final exam is very impressive. Many of the students do exceptional work on this exercise, producing 20 typed pages of analysis on five 2- to 3-minute scenes.

Chapter 5

Sociocultural Perspectives on Learning

Sociocultural theories focus on the role of social, cultural, and physical contexts on meaning making with an emphasis on the role of social context and social practices. Other labels applied to these theories include "social constructionism," "social constructivism," "the sociocentric view," and "the interactionist approach." Sociocultural theories focus on the learner's participation in the social practices of the setting, community, and culture. These views see knowledge as developed in discourses carried on by groups of people. Meaning making begins in the cultural context and involves other people in their community of practice, as well as cultural artifacts and symbolic tools. Learning is seen as a process of becoming more centrally involved in a community of practice (Lave & Wenger, 1991)—as "becoming attuned to constraints and affordances of activity" (Greeno & the MSMTA Project Group, 1998). Socioculturalists believe that our sense that our selves and ideas are independent (that we process stimuli and build ideas about things in the world from the inside out) is illusory. They view the mind and cognitive structures (schemas, mental models, concepts) as distilled from participation in social practices rather than as internal mental processes.

As in psychological constructivist theories, there is a range of positions between what might be referred to as a radical sociocultural view represented by Gergen's social constructionism to views like Vygotsky's that are anchored in the social context, but include cognitive structures. Sociocultural theories are historically associated with activity theorists such as Vygotsky and Leont'ev and share many characteristics with modern situated cognitive perspectives. A common thread that runs through these theories is the idea that the mind is not contained totally "in the head." In Vygotsky's theory, the human mind does not make direct contact with the world, but relates to the real world through a range of mediating structures such as language and other cultural artifacts and institutions (Lantolf, 2000). In contrast to psychological constructivist views that focus on how knowledge is structured in the mind, sociocultural and situated cognitive perspectives examine the ways that factors like classroom organization and the patterns of communication in a group help or hinder learning. Many researchers in the sociocultural and situated cognition tradition have examined the process by which novices (especially apprentices) increasingly adopt the system of communication and behavior of experts (Lave & Wenger, 1991). In these models of learning, expertise is not acquired through direct instruction, but through increasing participation in a community of practice. These approaches share Dewey's conclusion that meaning is socially constructed—a product of socially shared behavior (Garrison, 1994a).

Situated cognitive theories and activity theories such as those of Vygotsky (1978) and Lave and Wenger (1991) see internal structures as developing in the activity of social practice rather than as preexisting structures that are shaped by participation in social practices. In other words, these internal mental processes do not exist separately from the social practices in which they are embedded. The idea of context is multidimensional: (a) It includes a range of cultural artifacts including language and macrostructures mirrored in the internal social structure of the classroom, (b) the actual social practices in the classroom, and (c) the environmental context of the concepts being presented. This relates to the specific examples being used, their level of abstraction, and the problem of transfer. A special problem is created if students generally see school as a life world irrelevant to their personal and professional realities. These issues complicate the basic questions we all ask ourselves about the possibility that what we teach will be useful to our students beyond the walls of our classrooms.

VYGOTSKY AND ACTIVITY THEORY

The work of Lev Vygotsky (1978) and activity theorists such as Leont'ev (1981) provides the foundation for current sociocultural theories. Vygotsky's theory is built around the idea that language "mediates" the development of meaning and is therefore central to understanding the learning process (Wertsch, 2000). Activity systems are goal directed, carried out by a group and mediated by tools (e.g., language, signs, mathematical symbols, art), rules (e.g., classroom social practices), and division of labor (i.e., the division of tasks across participants; Jonassen, 2002; Lantolf, 2000; Pang & Hung, 2001; Smagorinsky, 2001). Activity theorists focus on the ways meanings are incorporated into cultural artifacts, and sociocultural processes mediate the development of individual meaning (Cobb, Perlwitz, & Underwood, 1996; Wells, 2000; Wertsch, 2000). Wells (2000) identified three categories of artifacts:

> material tools and the social practices in which they are employed; representations of the tools and practices by means of which activities are organized and their motives, goals and knowledgeable skills passed on to new participants; and the imaginative representational structures in terms of which humans attempt to understand the world and their existence in it. (p. 70)

Vygotsky saw development as shaped by two forces: semiotic mediation and the use of cultural tools that are the vehicles for the transmission of cultural meaning and interpersonal dialogue. Vygotsky's (1981) use of the term *cultural tools* can be traced back to Marx's (1890/1981) description of "man as a tool making animal." Engels (1925) also conceptualized history in terms of tools—human artifacts that make it possible for man to overcome the limits imposed by nature. One form of cultural tool is represented by the person-made environments that we construct to allow us to increase our ability to adapt to the natural environment by creating our own environment. Vygotsky focused his attention on tools such as oral and written language and counting systems, but did not analyze larger human systems such as law, religion, and education. It is important to add the shaping forces of these types of social institutions to our analysis of how education can be made more relevant to life outside the classroom.

Lee and Smagorinsky (2000) identified four core assumptions that provided the foundation for Vygotsky's theory: (a) The learning process involves internalization from the level of social practices to the individual cognitive level. Learning begins on the interpsychological level of the social interaction between people (with cultural artifacts and social processes acting as mediators) and is then appropriated by individuals on the intrapsychological level; (b) The learning process often involves a co-constructive process (as opposed to a transmission process) between a more knowledgeable person and a less knowledgeable person in an apprenticeship relationship. The person with more cultural knowledge is able to provide support (scaffolding) for knowledge development; (c) Knowledge construction involves acquiring and learning to use cultural artifacts and mediational tools (Vygotsky emphasized language as the primary artifact) that have been socially constructed throughout the history of the culture. A corollary to this principle is the insight that cognition is distributed across individuals. The concept of *distributed cognition* is important to many theories of situated cognition; and (d) An individual's learning capacity is seen as a function of his or her previous knowledge and the environmental support provided by social interaction, mediational tools, and cultural artifacts. An individual's capacity for growth is heavily dependent on the environmental supports available to him or her during the learning process.

Vygotsky's (1978) concept of the *zone of proximal development* and Wood, Brunner, and Ross' (1976) concept of *scaffolding* are important for thinking about how the learning environment affects a student's capacity to learn. Vygotsky believed that students should be challenged to reach beyond their current level of development. A more knowledgeable mentor who provides scaffolding for their growth forward provides the support for this leap. Yet a student cannot leap over their zone of proximal development to a more sophisticated level of thinking that is totally beyond their reach. Vygotsky (1978) defined the *zone of proximal development* as:

> The distance between the actual developmental level as determined by independent problem solving and the level of potential problem solving as determined through problem solving under adult guidance or in collaboration with more able peers. (p. 86)

Fernandez, Wegerif, Mercer, and Rojas-Drummond (2001) paraphrased the major functions of scaffolding developed by Wood, Brunner, and Ross (1976):

1. To orientate the child's attention to the version of the task defined by the tutor.
2. To reduce the number of steps that are required to solve a problem, thus simplifying the situation in a way that the learner can handle the components of the process.
3. To maintain the activity of the child as she/he strives to achieve a specific goal, motivating her/him and directing her/his actions.
4. To highlight critical features of the task for the learner.
5. To control the frustration of the child and the risk of failure.
6. To provide the child with idealized models of required actions.
   (p. 41)

Recent interpreters of activity theory have broadened the set of mediational tools available to the learner to include what Lee and Smagorinsky (2000) referred to as "goal-directed mediated action" and expanded their view of learning as a process of inquiry. Leont'ev's version of activity theory shifts its focus to a position that is more closely connected to Marxist thought and emphasizes physical activity and labor. Wells (2000) characterized Vygotky's view of development as involving apprenticeship of new members into a society as they participate in overlapping activity systems. In this sense, Vygotsky tends to see education as incorporating new people into the existing culture rather than changing it as external agents. People are shaped by their active participation in activity systems, and their participation, in turn, reshapes the system. Wells (2000) tied Vygotsky to Dewey when he concluded that the central concept of Vygotsky's theory is "artifact mediated joint activity" (p. 60) and that "inquiry [should be] the organizing principle of curricular activity" (p. 62). Teaching practices derived from a Vygotskian perspective share Dewey's emphasis on beginning the learning process by anchoring the content in the learner's experience and helping students generate "real questions" that motivate them to learn.

Vygotsky's theories embedded the learner in the activity structures in which they participate. Leont'ev and the activity theorists highlighted the goal-directed nature of activity. This reframing of the learning process leads to the conclusion that useful knowledge is acquired through active knowledge construction through goal-directed inquiry, rather than through transmission (Basic Principle 4). Like Vygotsky, Dewey (1934/1980) did not see the mind as totally contained within the person as defined by the border of the head and the skin:

> The epidermis is only in the most superficial way an indication of where an organism ends and its environment begins. There are things inside the body that are foreign to it and things outside the body that belong to it. . . . On the lower side, air and food materials are such things; on the higher, tools, whether the pen of the writer or the anvil of the blacksmith, utensils and furnishings, friends and institutions. (p. 59, LW10:64)

The elements of current constructivist theory and practice that focus on semiotics can be directly connected to Vygotsky. The various versions of the idea that scientific concepts can be decontextualized and operate as abstractions relate to this aspect of Vygotsky's theory. In Dewey's philosophy, the focus on the activity of speaking and its relationship to personal construction can form one side of the transaction that recognizes that people make the world and the world makes people. Vygotsky's emphasis on the role of "talking aloud" reflects his belief that expressing ideas allows the learner to consolidate and clarify his or her thinking.

Participating in dialogue and "making knowledge visible" provides a mechanism to help the learner assimilate the cultural meanings of the community of scholars and a way to allow the learner to play an active role in internalizing and accommodating the shared meaning to his or her existing meaning structures. "Talking aloud" plays an important role as a way for the learners to assume responsibility for self-scaffolding the meaning-making process. This thrust is reflected in many aspects of constructivist teaching models. The most salient feature of these models is the dramatic increase in the students' opportunities to express their ideas to each other and to present them formally. The heavy emphasis on groups of students developing projects and making group presentations is a key feature of many constructivist classrooms and is a key feature of the "Understanding Organizations" course.

The task for the professor guided by these perspectives on learning involves creating a situation where a group of students adopt a "real question" and work together to find a solution. The process starts with everyday experiences and concepts and ties those experiences to scientific concepts. The focus on semiotics emphasizes the process of relabeling everyday experience to link them to the body of knowledge that has been developed in the community of scholars. The professor's focus shifts from transmitting facts to managing the mediating structures that will help the students internalize useful models for understanding the situations they are studying. The professor is the architect and manager of the learning environment and actively participates in the inquiry process with the students.

Another core concept in Vygotsky's work was his assumption that the development of meaning involves increasing abstraction (Wertsch, 2000). Vygotsky assumed that learning involves decontextualization and the acquisition of scientific concepts that could be used to understand a variety of situations. This is parallel to Dewey's concept of secondary experience. This focus on language and its role in abstraction led activity theorists to utilize semiotic analysis of classroom dialogue as a primary research method to understand the nature of learning.

Glassman (2001) asserted that a basic difference between Dewey and Vygotsky is that Dewey used a bottom–up approach to learning, whereas Vygotsky advocated a top–down approach. Dewey placed great importance on the role that interest plays in driving inquiry. Although I think that Glassman characterized Dewey as more student-centered than he really was, Dewey did place more emphasis on anchoring learning in the student's experience and genuine interest.

In a Vygotskian framework (which Cobb also characterized as top–down), the teacher's role is to introduce culturally linked symbols and connect them to the students' experience. The teacher is connecting the cultural meanings (ways of naming things) ensconced in language to the personal meanings of the students. The teacher is an agent for bringing established cultural meanings into the classroom. Cobb proposed an alternative conception of the teacher's role he called a bottom–up approach (Cobb, Gravemeijer, Yackel, McClain, & Whitnack, 1997). In Cobb's model, the teacher facilitates the emergence of meaning as constructed by the students in the classroom. Here Cobb is using Dewey's perspective to inform and enrich Vygotsky's model. Initially, the teacher functions as the architect of the learning environment, designing a curriculum with affordances that help students explore and discover important qualities of the structure of the content. During the learning process, the teacher links the concepts produced by students to the language of the scientific community (the signs and symbols that the community of scholars uses to label concepts). In practice, the teacher is correcting misconceptions, restating the student's contributions, and linking them to the established body of knowledge (Dewey's warranted assertions). Cobb focused on the teacher's role in supporting the emergence of meaning in the classroom (rather than bringing the students into contact with established cultural meaning) and connecting that emerging meaning to the body of knowledge so that students will be able to participate in the practices.

Other versions of activity theory enriched and expanded Vygotsky's theories. Leont'ev's version of activity theory focused more strongly on practical activity, specifically joint collective activity employing cultural tools. In Leont'ev's model, social action mediates the relationship between subject and object (Cobb, 1994b). Leont'ev (1981) expanded on Vygotsky's theory by conceptualizing the transmission process as embedded in the structure of cultural activity. Vygotsky's concepts of artifact-mediated and object-oriented action give substance to transactions involving individuals and social and physical objects. For us, this describes the structuring forces of social practices in classroom communication and the interactions between students and objects like test tubes in the laboratory. These structures are standing between and facilitating the students' acquisition of big ideas and deep principles. Mediation occurs in the person–environment transaction. Mediators include social practices, language, and signs.

Leont'ev also introduced the idea that division of labor as a characteristic of social institutions generates processes that shape the development of cognitive structures (understanding that cognitive structures are not seen as contained within individual minds). Within this frame of reference, cognitive structures are enmeshed with collective activity. Because activities are always seen as involving the cooperative problem-solving efforts of groups of people (rather than one person reasoning in his or her head), we think of activity as involving a community of actors embedded in an activity system of social practices (the division of labor and the rules governing the interactions between people and between people and things). Activity theory tries to understand the transactional relationship between consciousness and activity. In the classroom, activity theory provides a framework for conceptualizing the context of teaching and learning.

Davydov (1972/1990) developed another version of activity theory. The distinctive feature of this approach is Davydov's method of ascent. Davydov's theory has the primary characteristics of Leont'ev's activity theory (e.g., practical activity as the generator of human thought; knowledge building in joint, goal-directed human activity mediated by social practices and cultural artifacts) and Gal'parin's systematic theoretical instruction. Gal'parin's work specifically focused on how particular approaches to instruction increase the quality of the mental models students acquire. Gal'parin's methods introduced abstractions early in the learning process that represented enduring understandings of important phenomena. Gal'parin expanded Vygotsky's work by experimenting with how methods of instruction affect the process of internalizing useful cognitive structures (Arievitch & Stetsenko, 2000). Vygotsky saw the process of abstraction as progressive decontextualization from concrete activity to abstractions. Davydov saw abstraction as proceeding from poorly formed abstractions to well-formed abstractions (scientific concepts). This insight recommends a recursive teaching model that develops increasingly structured abstractions in a series of iterative steps. Davydov saw increasingly complex levels of cognitive functioning as a function of the patterns of environmental practices children were engaged in at different periods of their childhood in the Russian cultural context. Gal'parin and Davydov's view of cognitive development contrasts with Piaget's theory of genetic epistemology, which attributed advances through stages of cognitive development to unfolding genetic capacity and saw the site of cognitive construction "in the head" rather than in social action (Arievitch & Stetenko, 2000). For Davydov, useful abstractions develop through a dialectical interaction between the person's empirical cognition (which interacts with the world to form everyday concepts) and theoretical cognition (which builds increasingly well-structured abstractions that inform the learners' interpretations of concrete experience in increasingly sophisticated ways). Davydov (1972/1990) outlined this concept as follows:

> An idealization of the basic activity involving objects [artifacts] and the reproduction in that activity of the universal forms of things, their measures, and their laws. (p. 298)

The practical effect of Davydov's view is that abstract concepts are introduced into the curriculum at a much earlier stage in the teaching process. Yet it would be easy to misinterpret what actually occurs in a classroom from this description. Students in classrooms using Davydov's curriculum usually begin learning a new topic by participating in an activity that research has indicated will lead to the development of the abstractions the teacher wants them to acquire. Cobb, Perlwitz, and Underwood (1996) compared Davydov to Jerome Brunner and the structuralists of the 1960s by labeling Davydov's position as "structuralism in social action." Davydov's approach shifts the teacher's focus away from defining what the students should know to deciding what the students should do to develop an understanding of the structure of the discipline (e.g., young children may be asked to manipulate Unifix blocks that reflect the qualities of numbers). Because I view learning as an iterative process, I find Davydov's model useful for understanding how to structure learning experiences that help students build helpful mental models.

Rasmussen (2001) presented another alternative to activity theory's linear internalization model. He adopted a systems theory perspective to characterize the relationship between internal psychological structures and social communication structures. Systems theory sees all systems as self-regulating and operating independently. Psychological constructs and social communication systems transact through a mechanism Rasmussen called *structural coupling*. Language is seen as a medium that can connect to both communication and thought. Although his explanations of the actual transactions between internal psychological structures and mediating structures were illusive, Rasmussen's point was that language does not transmit ideas: The teacher and student each construct their own psychological structures using the shared tool of language. The systems theory approach avoids ideas like *intersubjectivity* and *shared life world* that strike me as mystical. If *shared life world* is a metaphor for the transaction between people, I would rather find a term that moves me closer to understanding the nature of that transaction. From a systems perspective, the shared space for distributed cognition is in the social communication system. The psychological and social systems are autonomous and interdependent (co-evolutionary). Rasmussen saw communication as *mutual scaffolding*. This allows for situations where experts and novices interact in a zone of proximal development, but also for co-construction by peers in cooperative learning environments. For Leont'ev, students appropriate cultural processes into their internal mental operations. Both Vygotsky and Leont'ev saw language and symbols as carrying cultural meaning into the students' thinking. Rasmussen (2001) replaced this metaphor of transmission to emphasize that both the psychological and communication structures are informed by transactions with mediating structures like language. For me, the most productive model for thinking about this transaction combines Davydov's iterative process and Rasmussen's co-evolutionary systems model. The structural coupling is at the point of transaction between semi-autonomous systems. Understanding the dynamics of this transaction is the key to improving the effectiveness of classroom social practices.

Although Rasmussen's model is closer to psychological constructivism than socioculturalism, a systems perspective provides a mechanism for combining the sociocultural and psychological constructivist perspectives. It allows the social context to be the arena for meaning making, but provides a mechanism to connect social structures to both physical and cognitive structures. Meaning-making processes are always both natural (connected to the material world) and cultural (what they mean for us in the context of our social groups). Our ecological niche is always an eco-social system. This means that understanding the meaning-making process forces us to account for the structural qualities of both the physical environment and cultural system. As structures that interact, the physical and cultural environments assume the characteristics of all systems. First of all, they are self-organizing. In this sense, all systems have some form of intelligence beyond the intelligence of the actors within the system. They are not shaped by some larger intelligent guidance. Bourdieu's concept of the *habitus*, presented later in this chapter, is a useful model for understanding this broader perspective of intelligence.

GERGEN'S SOCIAL CONSTRUCTIONISM

The sociocultural position (social constructionism) is often represented by the work of Kenneth Gergen (McCarty & Schwandt, 2000). Gergen (1994a) developed a form of socioculturalism that incorporated many of features that characterize sociocultural positions: a focus on language and social practice, along with elements of critical theory, poststructuralism, and post-modernism. In contrast to von Glasersfeld, Gergen situated meaning making in the discourses within human relationships. He focused strongly on language and culture and largely eliminated the role of individual mental processes (McCarty & Schwandt, 2000). By situating experience totally within culture, language, and social processes, Gergen, in effect, eliminated any direct experience of our participation in the natural world (or at least made direct knowledge of the nature of reality unknowable). Gergen (1994a):

> places the locus of knowledge not in the minds of single individuals but in the collectivity. It is not the internal processes of the individual that generate knowledge, but a social process of communication. It is within the process of social interchange that rationality is generated. Truth is the product of the collectivity of truth makers. (p. 207)

Gergen (2001) did not deny the existence of internal cognitive structures and a stable, enduring self-concept, but he did not use these concepts or think they are useful for understanding human behavior. He anchored his entire discussion in the processes of human relationships. For Gergen (2001), "all claims of knowledge, truth, objectivity, or insight are founded within communities of meaning making" (p. 2). Language about psychological entities is part of the discourse of psychologists, and their usefulness is limited to the language game of psychologists. Words like mental model, idea, and self do not represent real things that exist in people's heads. Attitudes, beliefs, values, and emotions are never seen as expressions of an internal structure or as the cause of actions, but as ways that people negotiate meaning. He tried to understand human meaning making by looking for regularities in patterns of interaction in social situations. This view also led Gergen to a strong form of nonfoundational relativism on moral values (Gergen, 1994a). Questions of right and wrong can only be negotiated by communities.

Gergen's (1994a) first assumption of social constructivism shows a point of agreement with von Glasersfeld and the radical constructivists: "(1) The terms by which we account for the world and ourselves are not dictated by the stipulated objects of such accounts" (p. 49). For Gergen, words are never about the thing in itself, whether it is a physical object or cognitive structure. Gergen accused von Glasersfeld of giving the mind ontological status. Gergen's second assumption moves him away from radical constructivism by moving the focus of meaning making out of the head and into the social world: "(2) The terms and forms by which we achieve understanding of the world and ourselves are social artifacts, products of historically and culturally situated interchanges among people" (p. 49). All meanings are derived from social context. They are not shaped by any predetermined genetic or structural characteristics within the individual. Meaning is based on the structure of human relationships and is not predetermined. Gergen specifically sought to "denaturalize" meaning making. In this respect, his position is fundamentally different from Dewey's position. Gergen's third assumption was: "(3) The degree to which a given account of world or self is sustained across time is not dependent on the objective validity of the account but on the vicissitudes of social process" (p. 51). Gergen's fourth and fifth assumptions were: "(4) Language derives its significance in human affairs from the way in which it functions within patterns of relationship" (p. 52) and "(5) To appraise existing forms of discourse is to evaluate patterns of cultural life; such evaluations give voice to other cultural enclaves" (p. 53).

Gergen's position has similarities with Dewey, Mead, and Vygotsky, but he specifically rejected the aspects of their positions that involve the use of cognitive entities like self-concept, abstractions, and cognitive processes. He focused his analysis entirely on microsocial processes. Although he rejected most forms of instrumentalism because he saw them as individualistic, his view is instrumental in the sense that he focused on the social consequences of discourse about cognitive entities, rather than the entities (which may or may not exist). He measured the value of a discourse by asking "what forms of cultural life are suppressed or sustained by such discourse?" The value of different forms of cultural life is negotiated within communities of practice.

Despite some differences, there are strong similarities between the ways Gergen and Dewey conceptualized the process of acquiring knowledge.

Like Dewey, Gergen rejected the empirical model of taking in representations of reality in favor of a focus on process (acquiring the capacity to take certain actions to address problems) and instrument (judged by how effective the action is at solving the problem). Gergen (2001) dissociated himself from instrumentalism because he saw it as aligned with individualism, but Dewey's brand of instrumentalism was strongly linked to community. Dewey would agree with Gergen's (2001) statement that "constructivism [emphasizes] meaningful action embedded within extended patterns of interchange" (p. 35). On this point, both Dewey and Gergen replaced the goal of storing inert knowledge in individual learners with the goal of reaching understanding in learning communities. Specifically, this means that learners increase their capacity to recognize the problematic features of a situation and take action to address problems.

Both Gergen and Dewey saw problem solving as a community activity, but Gergen placed more emphasis on positive outcomes related to increased capacity to communicate and work with others toward shared goals. Students have new tools to see the old world in new ways and develop new questions: "What is going on here that I find problematic (or should find problematic from a critical perspective)? How can I fix this situation so that we (as a group) can enhance our adaptability?" Gergen identified two instrumental criteria that serve as indicators of positive growth that reflect the shift from inert knowledge production (e.g., reciting memorized facts) to understanding: (a) *generative capacity*, the ability to generate more opportunities for dialogue to expand our social constructs; and (b) *transformative force*, creating positive changes in society to increase social justice and reduce oppression. This shift in the nature of educational goals requires a parallel shift in the methods of assessment used in the classroom and a reconceptualization of how we define *transfer*.

Gergen's goals for understanding also seem reasonable and consistent with Dewey's, but it is hard to understand the rationale for selecting these goals within a theory like Gergen's, where people's values seem to be totally determined by their cultural context. However, I am not sure that Dewey did a much better job of justifying why he anchored his philosophy in democratic social values. For reasons that I discuss in chapter 7, I support Gergen's emphasis on expanding the scope of dialogue to other cultural groups and marginalized individuals within the culture. Based primarily on Habermas' analysis, I assert that open dialogue is the primary mechanism for escaping the oppressive aspects of a culture that would otherwise be blind to those who participate at the cultural core. Dewey's analysis of this issue is similar to Gergen's in some ways, especially in its implications for classroom practice. An important difference is that Dewey maintained a naturalistic position that includes culture and the "language game," but is not partitioned within the language game. Although I believe our genetic history is value neutral, I repeat my assertion from human ethology that our genetic history and our status as members of the natural systems in the world can provide as many affordances that we might see as positive human tendencies (e.g., the predisposition to want a sense of community) as negative human tendencies (male dominance). Any nonfoundational philosophy will have difficulty explaining the origin of positive social values. Dewey's perspective does not allow us to receive positive social values from someplace outside our experience as people in community in the natural world.

SITUATED COGNITION

As a category of constructivist views of cognition, situated cognition includes a group of theories that see learning and cognition as embedded in larger social processes. Most situated cognitive models lie between the psychological constructivist and the sociocultural models. In this sense, situated cognition belongs in the next chapter on combined approaches. Because most of these theories see cognitive structures as evolving *from* social interactions, however, they are closely linked to sociocultural theories. Most situated cognitive theories include specific elements of mediation by language and artifacts that also link them to activity theory. When situated cognitive perspectives are used to understand educational practice, these theories can be differentiated according to their frame of reference. Some theories focus on the level of the classroom, and some focus on a broader context of power relationships in society. These differences in frame of reference can mask the similarities between the positions.

Situated cognitive theories are distinguished by their focus on intact activity systems that include, but go beyond, the individual. This involves a shift in perspective from examining the behavior and cognition of individuals to analyzing behavior patterns in systems in which individuals are embedded (Greeno & the MSMTA Project Group, 1998). This shift refocuses the definitions of many basic educational terms like *learning, transfer,* and *abstraction* out of the head and into the social context.

The research and writing of socioculturalists and situated cognitive theorists has expanded and enriched Dewey's ideas about the nature of knowledge as contextualized, conditionalized, and situated. The term *conditionalized* indicates that, in addition to being imbedded in the experiential context and being organized around central concepts that "hold it together," knowledge is bound to the specific conditions of its use. Some critics think that this means that knowledge acquired in one situation cannot really be transferred to a different set of conditions (Anderson, Reder, & Simon, 1996). Several proponents of the situated cognitive view dispute this assertion (Greeno, 1997; Kirshner & Whitson, 1997). At a minimum, the situated cognitive analysis implies that learners need to acquire both content knowledge and knowledge of the conditions of its application (Bransford, Brown, & Cocking, 1999).

Tripp (1996) attributed the early thinking on situated cognition to Michael Oakeshott (1962), who asserted that knowledge does not exist apart from its application and is created within a community of practice. Brown and Duguid (1996) also pointed to Oakeshott's work by reviewing his ideas on the difference between technical and practical knowledge. Oakeshott (1962) saw practical knowledge as existing only in practice. Writing from the perspective of political philosophy, Oakeshott saw society as guided by an unfolding tradition. Brown and Duguid supported Oakeshott's assertion that the only way that practical knowledge can be acquired is through some form of apprenticeship relationship, not because the expert can actually teach it, but because it can only be acquired by continuous contact with someone who is practicing it.

Brown and Duguid (1996), like Dewey, argued that abstractions are not universal truths, but "the products of complex practices. They make sense only in the context of these practices" (p. 170). This perspective fits Oakeshott's assertion that technical training "remains insoluble until it is immersed in the acid of practice." Situated cognitive theorists define representations and abstractions differently than psychological constructivists. Rather than seeing learning as the development of cognitive structures that can be applied to a number of situations, situated cognitive theorists focus on teaching students ways of interacting and participating that foster successful participation across communities of practice (Greeno, 1997). Rather than teaching students abstractions and rules for when to use them directly, teachers with situated cognitive perspectives "engage students in representational practices that make up competent activity in some subject matter domain" (Hall, 1996, p. 230).

Brown and Duguid (1996) asserted that it is problematic to apply an abstraction to a new field of practice. At times these theorists seem to be saying there is no way students can acquire abstract concepts that will serve them across settings, especially from school to work. Yet most situated cognitive theorists actually do think it is possible to acquire "transferable" abstractions (Greeno, 1997). Although the situated perspective does not preclude the possibility of acquiring these abstractions with some level of portability, it highlights the difficulty in designing learning experiences that give students useful abstractions (big ideas and deep principles) that can be broadly applied.

An interesting and provocative assertion that grows out of this perspective is that only people who already know how to do something can understand abstractions about practice. I suspect this might be true, but I do not think this means that students cannot develop useful models and abstractions. I think abstractions can be identified and enhanced in a recursive process that alternates concrete experience with model building, including activities that promote discovery and communication that label and enhance the complexity of transactional objects. This transaction between abstraction and practice can lead to enriched understanding of both theory and practice and make abstractions increasingly portable.

Like other constructivist theories, situated cognitive views oppose any mind–body dualism that disconnects cognition from bodily experience and the sociocultural context. To understand the process of learning in the real world outside the classroom, many of these theorists have examined the situation of apprenticeships. These theories move the unit of analysis from the individual to the sociocultural level in which the individual is embedded.

To summarize the discussion thus far, all constructivist theories, including Dewey and Piaget, recognize the social environment as a key part of the learning environment and focus on the interaction between the individual and the social and physical environments. Some theories place more emphasis on internal thinking processes, and some (like Gergen's) are almost totally oriented toward social practices. Situated cognition theories give varying degrees of emphasis to the arena of social practices. It is important to understand that the world of social affairs includes all situations governed by social practice, including the use of language, symbolic representations, cultural artifacts, and mental models evolving out of intersubjective action and is not restricted to situations where people are in physical proximity to each other. Rather than seeing learning as the acquisition of facts, a permanent change in behavior, or improved organization of cognitive structures, sociocultural views tend to see learning as increasingly successful participation in social practices and the development of an identity as a member of a community of practice (Cobb & Bowers, 1999; Greeno, 1997; Lave & Wenger, 1991).

Research on situated cognition may address questions at several different levels of analysis. Cobb (Cobb & Bowers, 1999) and Brown (Brown & Campione, 1994) focused their analyses of social practices on the level of the individual classroom or place. Other theorists such as Lave and Wenger (1991) focused on the broader sociocultural context. Parenthetically, readers might wonder why these fine distinctions should make a practical difference to teachers. The short answer is that, if learning is seen as situated at several levels of analysis, we can no longer view knowledge as a separate thing (like Dewey's bricks) that can be passed to students. To design effective courses, we have to think about a number of other environmental variables and decide how they might apply to our particular teaching situation.

BOURDIEU'S CONCEPTS OF HABITUS
AND SOCIAL CAPITAL

The notion that ideas and thinking are not activities totally contained "within the head" represents a paradigm shift in our thinking about thinking and the nature of knowledge. It requires what Chi, Slotta, and de Leeuw (1994) called *tree jumping* rather than *branch jumping*. Pierre Bourdieu's (1990) concept of the *habitus* provides a perspective that can help us make this leap. The habitus is the internalization of the social order, including the relationships of power and domination that occur through socialization. His description of how habitus is structured offers a model of how collective practices are internalized. The influence of Bourdieu's work on sociocultural theory has increased substantially over the past two decades.

Bourdieu (1990) defined *habitus* as:

> systems of durable, transportable dispositions, structured structures, that is, as principles which generate and organize practices and representations that can be objectively adapted to their outcomes without presupposing a conscious aiming at ends or an express mastery of the operations necessary in order to attain them. Objectively "regulated" and "regular" without being in any way the product of obedience to rules, they can be collectively orchestrated without being the product of the organizing action of a conductor. (p. 55)

I would highlight in this definition that the core of the habitus is not specific principles and practices, but the principles that "generate and organize practices and representations." The habitus contains the "programs" that generate strategies for solving problems without bringing themselves to consciousness. This is an efficient (i.e., adaptive) system when the strategies match the problem situation. *Doxa* is Bourdieu's (1990) label for that portion of the habitus that goes completely unquestioned because the behavior is in harmony with its current environment: "It is because agents never know completely what they are doing that what they do has more sense than they know" (p. 69). The "sense" comes from the organizing principles of the habitus rather than conscious formal logic. Bourdieu's "logic of practice" is efficient in the sense that it allows members of a culture to assimilate knowledge, skills, and subjective awareness through participating in the practice of the culture without bringing very much of the material to consciousness. Both our perceptual sets (our predispositions to see the world in ways characteristic of our cultures) and our subjective reactions (how we react emotionally and aesthetically to the world) are built into our habitus. Once acquired, habitus structures the generation of new ideas and consequently defines the structural limits of what seems natural to us (what "makes sense" to us) and what we are capable of thinking of at all. An arbitrary social norm embedded in habitus is seen as necessary, as the natural order of things, and therefore not open to examination on moral grounds. Habitus provides the mechanism by which history generates more history. It ensures that new practices produced by individual agents will be limited by the basic structure of society. This has the advantage, for the dominant class, of freeing them from having to use their energies to maintain the social order. The existing order "makes sense" to everyone.

One way to look at Bourdieu's work is to see the habitus as a model for the way that habits operate in a cultural context that combines Dewey's general ideas about habits with a Marxist perspective. Bourdieu can be seen as a neo-Marxist because he sees power and domination as the seminal source of all of society's structures. He adds an important dimension to Marx by expanding the types of capital that classes can use to maintain their dominant position. In addition to economic capital, Bourdieu (1977) analyzed the ways that cultural capital, social capital, and symbolic capital are used to maintain the hegemony of the dominant class. *Cultural capital* refers to the tastes and conventions of high culture, *social capital* is the network of friendships and "connections" that facilitate success, and *symbolic capital* is the individual's presentation that identifies him or her as a member of the dominant class (e.g., ways of speaking, posture, appearance).

Bourdieu's (1990) perspective on the "logic of practice" parallels Dewey's work in the sense that he strongly emphasized that habitus is seated in the body as well as the mind.

> Thus the dualistic vision that recognizes only the self-transparent act of consciousness or the externally determined thing has to give way to the real logic of action, which brings together two objectifications of history, objectification in bodies and objectification in institutions. (pp. 56–57)

The transaction between habitus and the field (i.e., the environmental context of behavior) is the arena where implicit knowledge (Bourdieu's "feel for the game") constitutes expertise. This explains why experts cannot fully explain their behavior. It is also the source of the position held by many socioculturalists that describes the acquisition of expertise as a movement from legitimate peripheral participation to central participation in a community of experts (see Lave's work described later in this chapter).

Bourdieu (1990) paraphrased a quote from Proust that captures the transactional relationship between mind and body: "the arms and legs are filled with numb imperatives" (p. 69). When an imperative like "sit up straight" is uttered within a cultural context (a habitus), it can evoke a whole set of unconscious scripts related to cultural behavior. For Bourdieu (1990), "the body is . . . constantly mingled with the knowledge it reproduces, and this knowledge never has the objectivity it derives from objectification in writing and the consequent freedom with respect to the body" (p. 73). Bourdieu's description is reminiscent of Dewey's discussion of the logic of experience.

An important question about Bourdieu's theory is the extent to which it expands or contracts the possibility of agency. This is a debate that surrounds all sociocultural theories. The two general positions of constructivism—psychological constructivism and socioculturalism—also represent modern versions of theories that "lean toward" individual agency and theories that "lean toward" determinism. The issues of determinism and relativism become more problematic for constructivist theories as they move along the continuum toward highly situated and sociocultural views.

Bourdieu's habitus clearly limits agency, and some critics think that it eliminates the possibility of meaningful choice and the possibility of changing the existing social order. For Bourdieu (1990), the individual is embedded in the habitus (which produces him or her and is in turn produced by his or her action), but the nature of the relationship between the individual and the habitus also contains the potential for agency:

> Because the habitus is an intimate capacity for generating products— thoughts, perceptions, expressions and actions—whose limits are set by the historically and socially situated conditions of its production, the *conditioned and conditional freedom it provides* is as remote from creation and unpredictable novelty as it is from simple mechanical reproductions of the original conditioning . . . habitus . . . cannot be described either as the autonomous development of a unique and always self-identical essence, or as a continuous creation of novelty, because it arises from the necessary yet unpredictable confrontation between the habitus and an event that can exercise a pertinent incitement on the habitus only if the latter snatches it from the contingency of the accidental and constitutes it as a problem by applying to it the very principles of its solution. (p. 55)

The "unpredictable" nature of the interaction between the habitus and the environment is Bourdieu's "window of opportunity" for escape from determinism. For Bourdieu, as for Dewey, the source of individual agency comes from the transactional (two-way) relationship between the person and his or her environment. The structuring forces of habitus are open to shaping by the person who is only partially embedded in the structuring process because he or she is *doing* the processes. Bourdieu's "logic of practice" is "fuzzy" enough to give the actor some freedom to act within the field of the activity. Individuals do not "exist" in the same sense as they do for the existentialists, but they do have some measure of freedom. I am not sure how different Bourdieu's freedom really differs from Sartre's freedom within the "force of circumstance," but Bourdieu's agent is much more contextualized. The potential for change resides at the boundaries of discourse. For Bourdieu, "social sense truth" is contextual. It can be challenged by participation in alternative discourses in other contexts. Given Bourdieu's assertion that the internal standards governing social practices are opaque to observers taking an "objective" position from outside a habitus, he does not provide much hope that cross-boundary discourses will happen very often. Bourdieu's reliance in the potential of cross-boundary discourse is essentially the same mechanism adopted by Dewey and Habermas. For me, this assertion has the status of a "hopeful hypothesis." At best, I have found that it is difficult to promote dialogue across boundaries. I have seen few instances where cross-boundary dialogue created a change of consciousness, and most of these instances did not take place in the classroom.

Bourdieu (1990) believed that the self-producing structure of the habitus and its transactional relationship with the environment contains the seeds of an arena where freedom can be exercised:

> . . . a habitus that so perfectly possess the objectively available means of expression that is possessed by them, so much so that it asserts its freedom from them by realizing the rarest of possibilities that they necessarily imply. The dialectic of the meaning of language and the "sayings of the tribe" is a particular and a particularly significant case of the dialectic between habitus and institutions, that is, between two modes of objectification of past history, in which there is constantly created a history that inevitable appears, like witticisms, as both original and inevitable. (p. 57)

I still do not think this "window of opportunity" sounds like a very big window. Within this system, for the individual to take action against the existing order, he or she has to overcome the tendency to reject information that challenges the existing order and avoid being exposed or perceiving this information (Bourdieu, 1990). Adding to the barriers to consciousness raising, the individual is not aware of this process of screening contradictory information. Behavior produced by the generating mechanism of the habitus is most apparent when individuals are in a context that is quite different from their habitus because they will produce inappropriate, nonadaptive behaviors (e.g., Don Quixote). The typical response to this problem is to return to the original environmental niche. The person tends to behave in the way he or she always has and seek environments where that behavior will lead to successful adaptation.

The most important transactions take place at the interface between cognitive structures and activity (between formal logic and the logic of practice) and between internalized structures of the habitus and the actions they create and that in turn create them (Bourdieu, 1977). The nature of the balance between habitus and action determines our ability or lack of ability to possess rather than be possessed by the dominant mental models in our culture. The exact nature of the relationship defines the subtle difference between a sociocultural theory and a combined position like Dewey's.

The effects of habitus are felt most strongly in the area where students (especially college students) are most resistant to change. In Bourdieu's terms, the logic of practice that produces the behavior of students in the classroom is unconscious and interlaced with the structural aspects of cultural capital. Changes in classroom behavior are even more difficult to affect because schooling is a key mechanism for achieving and maintaining cultural and symbolic capital and the power differentials related to class, race, and gender. A major implication of Bourdieu's analysis for education is that it highlights the particular difficulty we face when we try to change classroom social practices that students consider necessary and sensible. Bourdieu's analysis highlights both the barriers to and the positive potential of creating dialogue across cultural boundaries.

COMPARING PSYCHOLOGICAL CONSTRUCTIVISM WITH SOCIOCULTURALISM

Constructivist perspectives developed as what Cobb and Bowers (1999) referred to as the second wave of the cognitive revolution. They compared this second wave of situated approaches to the information-processing models of "the first wave" by comparing their underlying metaphors. Cobb and Bowers described the underlying metaphors for knowledge in the cognitive perspective and the situated learning perspectives as:

> [in the cognitive perspective, knowledge is] an entity that is acquired in one task setting and conveyed to other task settings. In contrast, a primary metaphor of the situated learning perspective is that of knowing as an activity that is situated with regard to an individual's position in the world of social affairs. (p. 5)

Again knowledge is an activity rather than a representation of a real thing. Kirshner and Whitson (1997) also compared situated cognitive theories to earlier cognitive theories:

> Traditional cognitive psychology conceives of cognition intrapsychically. The extent that social context is considered in such an analysis, it must be decomposed into discrete facts or rules that can be entered into the individual's cognitive system. (pp. 5–6)

The information-processing model focuses on how internal cognitive processes mediate the organism's response to environmental circumstances. In contrast, situated views of cognition emphasize the link between knowledge and the context in which it was acquired. Representations and abstractions are "simultaneously physical, social, and cognitive . . . [and] . . . constructed in people's activities" (Hall, 1996, p. 230) rather than directly taught.

Situated cognitive theories differ from psychological constructivist and information-processing theories on the importance they give to internal cognitive structures and their explanations of the origins of internal cognitive structures. In contrast to a sociocultural analysis, an information-processing analysis of a particular situation would focus on how each individual person processes information from the environment and how this information affects his or her schema and behavior.

Internal cognitive and information-processing perspectives can be contrasted with a sociocultural analysis of two groups of students learning mathematics in Nepal conducted by Beach (1995). One group was made up of traditional students learning mathematics "for its own sake" in a traditional schooling situation. The other group was made up of shopkeepers learning mathematics to use in their businesses to improve their profits. Rather than focus on how individual students processed information while they were solving mathematics problems, Beach looked at the reasoning of the two groups in the context of the social practices of shopkeepers and students. Beach's work includes an analysis of individual meaning acts, but places these acts in the context of social practices (Cobb & Bowers, 1999).

Cobb (1994b) compared and contrasted the sociocultural view with the view of psychological constructivism:

> Socio-cultural and [psychological] constructivist theorists both highlight the crucial role that activity plays. . . . However, socio-cultural theorists typically link activity to participation in culturally organized practices, whereas [psychological] constructivists give priority to individual students' sensory-motor and conceptual activity. Furthermore, socio-cultural theorists tend to assume from the outset that social and cultural processes subsume cognitive processes. In doing so, they adhere to Vygotky's (1978) contention [that] . . . the "individual dimension of consciousness is derivative and secondary." (p. 14)

One way to understand the differences between the range of constructivist theories is to categorize the theories according to their conceptualization of the site of knowledge construction (i.e., in the individual, in the culture, or in some combination of the two). McLellen (1996) provided a basic definition of situated cognition derived from the pioneering work of Brown, Collins, and Duguid (1989):

> The model of situated cognition is based on the notion that knowledge is contextually situated and is fundamentally influenced by the activity, context, and culture in which it is used. (p. 6)

For those theories on the sociocultural end of the continuum that see cognition as enmeshed in the physical and social contexts where learning takes place, we can also ask, "Just how situated is cognition and knowledge?" "Does the theory say that cognition is so situated in its context that I can't hope to give my students knowledge they can use in another context?" There are a number of ways to think about *where* cognition is situated and the nature of its relationship to its context. Even the idea that cognition is a separate or separable structure from its context can violate many models of situated cognition. Some proponents of the situated cognitive view see cognition as situated completely within the cultural, sociopolitical context of social practice. Another view holds that cognition can be situated within some combination of the person's physical, genetic, and cultural environments.

The role of genetics in cognition is a controversial issue in the debate among proponents of the situated cognitive view. Gergen (1994a) took an extreme position on this question when he "denaturalized" his theory to eliminate any consideration of genetic influences on behavior. Many situated views are closely associated with poststructural and critical theory and are hostile to any form of naturalism because they see genetic context as a source of justification for oppression. Vygotsky's theory included a genetic component to the person's predisposition to appropriate their cultural practices. Bereiter (1997) provided a good example of a situated cognitive theory that incorporates the impact of both physical and genetic contexts. I also found his example to be useful for thinking about the concept of situated cognition in general. Bereiter referred to early research on cognition in rats from the "rat maze era" of psychological research. He pointed out that rats are naturally good at learning mazes even when they are left to run around the maze without any reinforcement. Other examples of ways that genetic predisposition provides scaffolding for learning include the fact that children under 3 are naturally good at learning and incorporating the sounds of the languages they hear, and people are naturally good at remembering faces and not very good at remembering meaningless words (St. Julian, 1997). The rat's natural environment consists of mazelike structures like those found in the walls of buildings. This accounts for the rat's genetic predisposition to be good at learning to find their way around mazelike structures (to escape from enemies, to find food, etc.). The rat's learning is situated both in the mazes it is learning in in an experiment and in its genetic history of maze-learning skills. Bereiter believed that human learning also has a genetic component that is shaped by our genetic history.

Connectionism is a form of constructivism that focuses on the capacities of the brain. Connectionism makes an active connection between the physical characteristics of the brain and the cognitive processes of the mind. Connectionism reconceptualizes the relationship between mind and brain in a way that is parallel to the way that situated cognition blurs the distinction between the individual and the environment (St. Julian, 1997). These skills are much more pragmatic than Kant's transcendental structures and are anchored in the natural world rather than the supernatural world, but they can serve something like the same function as a foundation for constructive activity and as a route to escape cultural relativism.

Greeno (1997) and many of the current constructivists place the concepts of activity and mediation in a central position in their description of the process of knowledge acquisition. Greeno viewed the individual as acting within a system of social practices. Both the individual and system of social practices are changing and affecting each other in a transactional relationship. Lemke (1997) emphasized the importance of seeing cognition as embedded in "a larger meaning-making system of which our bodies and brains are only a part" (p. 37). It is not only what we do that impacts the knowledge students acquire, but also the meaning they give to what is happening in the classroom. As professors, if we shift our view of the classroom to see it as a community of practice where people behave in a certain way and in a different way than they behave in other settings, this frees us to view the issues and problems we are facing both more objectively *and* more personally. If students and professors are meaningfully engaged in a community of practice, our active participation changes the students and us. As Lemke (1997) put it: "Our identity-in-practice develops, for we are no longer autonomous Persons in this model, but Persons-in-Activity" (p. 38). Lemke did not provide a precise description of whether cognitive structures in this situation are independent and structurally coupled, semiindependent, or totally enmeshed.

LAVE'S APPRENTICESHIP MODEL

Lave and Wenger (1991) developed one of the most influential sociocultural theories of learning. Lave's model moves away from traditional classroom teaching to describe learning as entering and participating in a community of practice. Lave's work focuses on the idea that new participants in an activity structure learn the proper way to participate in that structure through an apprenticeship relationship with established actors in the system. Lave's work in legitimate peripheral participation has been influential in the development of situated cognitive theory. Much of her work has focused on how novices learn from experts in craft apprenticeships and the implications of this type of learning for understanding meaningful learning, especially outside of school settings. Although Lave tended to deny the legitimacy of schooling where students try to learn by listening and watching rather than doing, she did see her work on apprenticeships as affecting the way schools operate. Lave used the term *legitimate peripheral participation* to refer to the position of novices in a social structure of practices carried out by a community of experts. Novices move from the periphery to the center of the community of practice as they acquire expertise. As the participant moves from peripheral to full participation, he or she constructs an identity as a member of that community of practice. The identity development process is central to Lave's concept of learning (Manyak, 2001).

Lave's analysis of the nature of knowledge in the context of practice was heavily influenced by the work of Marx, Vygotsky, and Bourdieu. Lave's theory assumes that learning and ways of thinking are generated in social practices where the specific characteristics of the situation are part of the practice. Like other activity theorists, Lave and Wenger (1991) did not mean that social practices *shape* internal cognitive structures and processes that function as separate entities from those practices. They meant that learning *is* developing new ways of participating in social practices (Cobb & Bowers, 1999).

Many educators are skeptical about Lave's apprentice model because it implies that knowledge can never be separated from the context where it is acquired. Professors see themselves as being in the business of teaching decontextualized knowledge that is generalizable. Although many educators are skeptical about how much light Lave's work can throw on the learning process within school settings, there is growing interest in connecting her research to educational practice across several disciplines and levels of education (e.g., learning math by doing what mathematicians do by "engaging in structure-finding activities and mathematical argumentation typical of good mathematical practice") (Lave & Wenger, 1991, p. 17). In the classroom, this points professors with this perspective away from lecturing and toward creating, modeling, and fostering productive disciplinary engagement (Engle & Conant, 2002). The classroom becomes an arena for dialogue about important questions in our disciplines that mirrors the best discourse in our fields. On the other hand, Davis and Sumara (2002) questioned whether this theory, which is primarily descriptive rather than prescriptive, can be profitably applied to teaching.

Lave's work on legitimate peripheral participation examined a range of situations from the curriculum of tailor's apprentices to the use of mathematics among Weight Watchers. In her work on Weight Watchers, one of Lave's (1990) major conclusions was that there was a remarkable lack of transference between the mathematics subjects learned in school and the use of math in the real-life situations of using math in dieting (e.g., measuring the amount of food). (This may also explain why no one ever seems to lose any weight.) Several variables that we might logically think would be associated with the level of transfer from formal mathematics training to the use of mathematics in practice did *not* correlate with the successful use of math in the real world of dieting: (a) age, (b) number of children at home, (c) dieter's years of education, (d) amount of weight they had lost, (e) amount of weight they planned to lose, and (f) scores on the arithmetic test. Lave's two major conclusions were that (a) people were able to develop effective ways to deal with math problems in everyday life, and (b) math activity was stimulated by dilemmas, and the nature of the dilemma shaped the practice that was developed. Scribner's (1997) observations of dairy workers also revealed that dairy workers developed strategies for dealing with mathematical problems that did not correspond to the mathematical practices of schooling.

Although I do not think that most people "figure out" how to use mathematics effectively in their everyday lives, I agree that the decontextualized way that students learn mathematics in school accounts for the fact that most people do not understand how to use mathematics to solve everyday problems. Yet the most important thing about the "memorize and recite" teaching methods that are often used in mathematics teaching is that they do not help students acquire deep mathematical understandings. This is obvious to any of us who try to teach statistics and research design to otherwise bright undergraduates. My interpretation of many purely sociocultural approaches is that they do not have a systematic way to ensure that students acquire the basic enduring understandings that serve as a foundation for the development of expertise. I would assert that unless people are going to stay in the same job for their entire lives, it is not adaptive for them to know how to solve a problem unless you know *why* that solution is effective.

Lave (1988) characterized the relationship between the individual and the context as dialectical: as mutually co-constructive. She contrasted a situation where the person and environment have a mutual effect on each other with a dialectical relationship where the components are created and brought into being only in relationship to each other. This is parallel to Dewey's contrast between an interactive and a transactional relationship. Because Lave (1988) held a strongly sociocultural view, she is often accused of denying the existence of individual cognition. Her work focused almost exclusively on social practices and sounds deterministic. Yet Kirshner and Whitson (1997) pointed out that Lave's ultimate objective is to "propound a theory that fully realizes individual agency in its social make up" (p. 23). The problem of individual agency is a critical point because it is hard to see how sociocultural, critical, and postmodern theorists find a mechanism in their own theories to foster the kind of individual agency required to ferret out and confront the social injustice and oppression they would like to eliminate from society.

Kirshner and Whitson attributed confusion about Lave's theory to the fact that the intellectual roots of situated theories can be traced to highly deterministic theories from critical anthropology and neo-Vygotskyian sociocultural theory. Lave used a range of theories to develop a theory of activity that links local settings to a broader social context.

> The supermarket [for example] as an arena is the product of patterns of capital formation and political economy. It is not negotiable directly by the individual. It is outside of, yet encompasses the individual, providing a higher order institutional framework within which setting is constituted. At the same time, for individual shoppers, the supermarket is a repeatedly experienced, personally ordered and edited version of the arena. In this aspect it may be termed a "setting" of activity. (Lave, 1988, p. 151)

For Lave, the social environment contains structuring resources that shape individual cognition and behavior. It is not always clear how strongly these resources structure the cognition and behavior of those who participate in the setting. Therefore, it is easy to see how some critics would infer that the individual within Lave's theory has no capacity for independent action.

Although Hay (1996) saw great value in Lave's work, he questioned whether it can be seen as a model for educational practice. A primary problem that Hay recognized with the legitimate peripheral participation model is the lack of power that the student possesses in relationship to the experts in the community. The apprentice only has the power to participate or not to participate. Hay did not believe this really constitutes a choice. I had the same concern reading Lave's work. Lave clearly has an appreciation for the systems of power and oppression built into the social structure, but it is not always clear how she thinks this can be dealt with in a learning situation. This is an example of the general difficulty facing many sociocultural theories like Lave's and Bourdieu's, which emphasize the importance of overcoming marginalization, but include features (e.g., the idea that cognition is highly contextualized) that seem to prevent people from raising their consciousness about these problems in society. In Lave's theory, the apprentice seems to be at the mercy of whatever attitudes are incorporated into the expert system. Because sociocultural theories are by nature nonfoundational, they have to find some alternative, if temporary, version of "the right answer." Most educators are predisposed to want to make a difference. Many sociocultural theories do a good job of describing "the way it is" and why, but seem fatalistic about the chances of changing the system. Many of their descriptions of learning rely heavily on the use of experts. This presents a problem because experts are, by definition, representatives of some form of establishment that marginalizes nonexperts. Because the power arrangements in society lead to marginalization of certain classes of people, class tends to correlate with level of expertise. These forces can produce *permanent peripheral participation* for marginalized classes.

Lemke (1997) voiced a similar concern about Lave's work when he pointed out that not all peripheral participants in a community of practice can really achieve full participation. Some participants, like women and minorities, may not really be welcome. Others, like most university students who do not want to become scientists or professors, may not buy into the basic rules for participation. In the case of students, they may have different reasons for participating than professors. In traditional approaches to higher education, students typically learn about these practices rather than participate in them.

Commenting on Lave's research with apprentices, Lemke (1997) provided further insight into the relationship between the person and the physical and social environments in situated cognition theory:

> They are functioning in microecologies, material environments endowed with cultural meanings; acting and being acted on directly or with the mediation of physical-cultural tools and cultural material-systems of words, signs, and other symbolic values. In these activities, "things" contribute to solutions every bit as much as "minds" do; information and meaning is coded into configurations of objects, material constraints, and possible environmental options, as well as in verbal routines and formulas or "mental operations." (p. 37)

Lemke's analysis of the learning process includes a clearer explanation of the role played by internal mental processes. Although Lave did not focus on cognitive structures, her structuring resources include the range of environmental forces described by Lemke—they exist in the activity's structure, in the physical setting, and as appropriated into the cognitive structures of the person.

Moore, Lin, Schwartz, Petrosino, Hickey, Campbell, and the Cognition and Technology Group (1996) addressed another issue in Lave's model when they questioned whether learning can rely exclusively on modeling. Their research showed that teachers who taught only by modeling achieved less transfer. In Vanderbilt University's Cognition and Technology Group model, the teacher provides a model as a problem solver, but not as the sole method of instruction. The value of a model depends on the knowledge base of the people doing the observing. First of all, novices do not have the ability to see what an expert would see. The researchers of the Cognition and Technology Group pointed out that there are many situations where "non-real-world" learning can be useful if it is actively linked to "real-world" activity:

> In any event we do not claim that non-school activities guarantee better learning. For example, in airline crew training, simulation allows rehearsal of procedures for high-risk situations. Simulations can also expand and contract

space and time, and permit control over "real world" complexity that can hinder learning. (p. 129)

They prefer a model that tries to help students learn to see a problem in new ways by having them try to solve the problems before they see a model address the problem. Students have a different view of a problem after they have attempted to solve it themselves. Approaching the problem in this way gives students a personal interest in solving the problem, and the discomfort they experience motivates them to acquire knowledge that will help them solve the problem.

In addition to the shaping forces of the physical and cultural environments, Lemke's (1997) version of the person-in-activity theory includes both the person as defined by his or her behavior in this setting and his or her continuity of identity across settings. Lemke's analysis highlights that, as professors, we are dealing with individual people who have individual reactions to the learning environments we create. Like Vygotsky and Dewey, Lemke acknowledged that some of the lenses that shape our perceptions are genetic, but believed that most are shaped by participation in cultural activities. Also, the external environment is "real" in the sense that it provides affordances and constraints that shape cognition, but the shaping forces of the culture are more powerful. Each of our students comes to us with a unique identity shaped by the social environment we create in our classrooms, the social practices they associate with previous educational experiences, and their previous life experience that shapes their individual identities. One of the most important differences between traditional teaching methods and constructivist approaches is that we find ourselves in the classroom with "real people"—a situation that is at once frightening and rewarding.

Walkerdine (1997) examined the semantics of meaning making in social institutions. Rather than drawing on the "dialectical tradition of social thought" as Lave did, Walkerdine (1997) drew on French poststructuralists like Foucault. Walkerdine drew on Foucault's (1973) analysis of the process by which medical students (novices) become full-fledged members of a medical community. Foucault's analysis uses the metaphor of seeing. Dewey would support the idea that the transactional nature of our relationships to physical and social objects is a two-way process. Experience shapes our way of seeing the world, and that framing process shapes our future behavior. The transformation from medical student to doctor involves developing the "gaze" of a doctor—seeing the world as a doctor sees it. The doctor's seeing is mediated by language or other meaning structures that shape the things seen. In this frame of reference, knowledge is developed at the lens where language and seeing intersect.

Our way of seeing the world is transformed by learning, and our new way of seeing transforms our relationship to the thing or person seen. Through

Foucault's (1973) lens, the patient is created by the doctor's gaze. In similar ways, many of the labels we use to categorize people are dependent on the context of a social institution (e.g., the label *mental retardation* exists within the social object of the school and does not exist when school ends). This transformation process has both positive and negative aspects. The doctor recognizes symptoms of diseases, but also assimilates the biases of medicine and has trouble seeing things that do not fit the mold of medicine. Expertise focuses perception and automaticizes many basic skills out of conscious awareness. Walkerdine used Foucault's ideas to focus on the processes by which the "student" is produced by the gaze of the teacher in settings like the classroom. The people in charge (teachers) behave in a way to produce the student they expect.

Lemke (1997) explored the ways that history, culture, and biography operate in "the here and now of situated activities" as forces that structure thought and behavior. His approach—social semiotics—examines language usage in particular situations and particular cultures. When we function as members of a social system, we participate in activity networks that span the communities of practice within the larger community. By networks, he meant heterogeneous (across different types of systems) event structures. Participation in different activities in different communities of practice may be interdependent (e.g., we have to take chemistry to become a doctor). We learn in activity and a community of practice. Engaging in these practices shapes our identities: "We always perceive, act, and learn by participating in the self organization of systems that are larger than our own organism" (p. 52). Lemke was also influenced by Foucault's concept of subjectivation: the social forces that impact us during a culturally embedded activity fix our subjectivity in a particular historical context, making us historically constructed beings. This subjectivity supplements the elements of identity that are more within our cognitive control. Lemke (1997) asserted that:

> In an ecological systems model, the primary units of analysis are not things or people, but processes and practices. It is the processes and practices that are interdependent, linked, creating the emergent properties of the self-organizing system. (p. 47)

Moore, Lin, Schwartz, Petrosino, Hickey, Campbell, and the Cognition and Technology Group (1996) provided further insights about the structural dynamics (environmental affordances and constraints) that shape thinking and behavior by pointing out that all settings provide some level of scaffolding for cognition. Some settings provide little support for novices, and some provide a systematic support system that provides a lot of support for newcomers and slowly withdraws that support as new members become competent in the community's social practices. This is important because it helps clarify that there are many types of scaffolding for promoting competent participation in a community and many levels on which it can be provided (e.g., physical space, logic of inquiry used, communication patterns, rules of participation). This is an important insight for educators because it challenges the generalization held by Lave and many socioculturalists that schools are so unlike the real world that they are inherently poor places to learn. It also gives us a perspective to analyze the support provided by any environment where we expect learning to take place, irrespective of whether the environment is in a school setting or a setting outside the school. Apprenticeships in the "real world" have a range of levels of support (scaffolding) just as classrooms do. Moore et al. (1996) asserted that observing people who are competent in other settings does not necessarily lead to more competence for the learner than traditional school learning does. In some instances, apprenticeship models with few supports for learning are really in-the-world versions of the spectator model of learning that Dewey questioned in the schools. Moving the spectator model of learning from the classroom to the real world does not enhance its effectiveness.

LEARNING AS THE CONSTRUCTION OF IDENTITY

The sociocultural perspective introduces a broad set of issues about identity and the teaching–learning process. Because the transmission model sees the student as an empty vessel to be filled with knowledge, it does not raise concerns about who the students are. Within this framework, curriculum development focuses almost exclusively on deciding "what the students should know." Knowledge is stored in a person with an enduring self.

In the sociocultural perspective, identity, like other kinds of knowledge, is constructed in activity (Packer & Goicochea, 2000). Learning is characterized as increasingly "effective participation in practices of inquiry and discourse" in a community of practice (Greeno & the MSMTA Project Group, 1998) and "a process of coming to be, of forging identities in activity in the world," and learning environments are referred to as "central identity-generating activities" (Lave, 1992). Identities are embedded in social contexts like classrooms, and developing new identities depends on changing the social practices in the classroom. Issues of identity and self can play a major role in an individual's ability to negotiate life successfully. New views of identity formulated by socioculturalists and postmodernists have challenged traditional views of the stable and enduring self and replaced it with multiple identities embedded in social contexts. Transcendental and universalist models see the self as stable and built on a spiritual foundation or a complex of structures and processes with genetic underpinnings.

Socioculturalists are also concerned about how the social practices in the classroom reflect the power relationships in the larger society and contribute to the disempowerment of certain marginalized groups. Gergen (1994a) shared the view of many postmodern theorists such as Bourdieu that the shared theories of the self held on the societal level define the cultural limits of the definition of preferred and acceptable human behavior.

Our age has been characterized as the age of the "empty self," where inner resources and a focus on seeking meaning have been commodified and replaced with a self defined by material goods and "lifestyle" (Cushman, 1990). The effects of the dominance of the empty self thwart our efforts to motivate students by authentic learning experiences. Students who exemplify the "empty self" are more likely to focus on grades than learning.

Sociocultural perspectives have focused a great deal of attention on the construction of identity. Constructivists in general and socioculturalists in particular reject the idea that the self is a stable, enduring construct that operates independent of context. This view stands in sharp contrast to the ideals of personality integration and the "solid self" forwarded by traditional psychological theorists (e.g., Erikson, 1968; Rogers, 1961). For constructivists, the self has no ontological status. Discussions about the self and identity raise important issues in constructivist approaches to teaching in the university. A primary concern has been understanding how participation in social practices embedded in educational processes affects the construction of identity. The shaping forces of social participation in the classroom impact the construction of positive or negative identities as learners, the construction of students' identities as members of a professional community of practice, and raise issues related to the negative consequences of the sustained marginalization of certain classes of students.

An area of disagreement within constructivism is the extent to which the identity formation process is embedded within the social context. Some constructivists characterize the self as "self-authored" (Baxter-Magolda, 1999). For psychological constructivists like von Glasersfeld (1995), identity is an internal psychological construct like other cognitive structures. The individual has an awareness of his or her own experience to use as a foundation for constructing the self. Gergen (2001) specifically asserted that the self is *not* self-authored.

Like most socioculturalists, Gergen (1994b) denied the existence or desirability of maintaining a stable, coherent identity. He took an agnostic position about the existence of all mental structures including the psyche. Socioculturalists understand human life solely through human relationships. Gergen (2001) called his view "the relational constitution of the self." This perspective excludes examination of the range of emotions, personality traits, and inner thoughts associated with most characterizations of the self. Rather than theorizing about the nature of an individual's inner experience, Gergen focused on the discourse about experience that takes place in human interaction. Gergen (1994b) proposed:

> a relational view of self-conception, one that views self-conception not as an individual's personal and private cognitive structure but his *discourse* about the self—the performances of languages available in the public sphere. I replace the traditional concern with conceptual (self-concepts, schemas, self-esteem), with the self as a narration rendered intelligible within ongoing relationships. This then is a story about stories—and most particularly, stories of the self. (p. 185)

Gergen viewed the self as totally embedded in public discourse, but he denied that his view is totally deterministic. The self is not self-authored, but is co-authored in interaction with other people. He drew a parallel between the function of self-narratives for a person and oral histories for a society. He did not see a group of people as individual identities interacting, but as "a network of reciprocating identities." For Gergen, the concept of an individual identity is meaningless. Gergen (1994b) believed:

> persons in this case do not consult an internal script, cognitive structure, or apperceptive mass for information or guidance . . . they do not author their own lives. Rather, the self-narrative is a linguistic implement embedded within conventional sequences of action and employed in relationships in such a way as to sustain, enhance, or impede various forms of action. (p. 188)

Gergen's (2000) basic premise—that we make ourselves and our worlds through discourse—focused his attention on speaking and writing. He believed that changing patterns of communication lead to action and cultural transformation. In essence, Gergen saw his ideal of relational selves as a way to overcome the challenges to the traditional view of the ideal self as stable and coherent. He advocated for the desirability of a flexible identity to deal with the disintegration of coherent identities in postmodern life. Although the traditional view of the self champions the desirability of the "solid self" and sees shifting identities to adjust to different contexts as a problem or symptom of pathology, Gergen saw a flexible identity as adaptive in postmodern times.

A large body of research by social constructionists focuses on the study of identity construction in classrooms. Much of this work is focused on ideological critiques of the current system showing how the dominant hegemony of the culture is played out in the classroom discourse. Most of this work is descriptive and does not make recommendations for change. Many socioculturalists, in fact, seem to be antagonistic to the idea that they should be thinking about changing the curriculum to avoid these problems.

Lave, Walkerdine, and other social constructivist theorists examine the identities of students on the level of the classroom. Walkerdine's (1997) perspective on identity as it relates to education is nested in her strong sociocultural position and the way she sees the subject defined in the context of classroom practices. She challenged the model that places thinking "in the head" and asserted that cognition is produced by the activity of classroom practices. Most important, she rejected the idea that cognition is produced by the internal processes of abstraction associated with schooling. She believed that the schools' focus on abstraction serves the interests of power holders in society rather than producing learning. People in power are invested in upgrading school-based reasoning skills and downgrading the everyday practices ("street smarts") associated with oppressed people. She is interested specifically in how cognition is produced in everyday practice compared with the conception of cognition expressed in classroom practice that separates cognition from context, especially the social world of the student.

Walkerdine's position on identity can be clarified by comparing it to Lave's. Walkerdine stated that Lave's idea of analyzing learning in everyday practice is important, but does not go far enough because it understates the role of activity and does not include an analysis of how subjects are produced in practices. Walkerdine criticized Lave's position, which posited a dialectical relationship between the person and his or her environment. She objected to the use of the term *dialectical* to describe the person–environment relationship because Lave did not explicate the processes occurring. She thought Lave's concept of activity fell short of providing an adequate explanation of the subject–environment relationship. In effect, she was afraid that Lave's analysis provided a word to explain the person–environment relationship, but not a real analysis of the processes involved. To Walkerdine, Lave's inadequate analysis provided no way to avoid traditional dualism because "neither the person nor the setting is theorized." For Walkerdine, the subject is produced within discursive practice. Although all practices are created through the exchange of signs, practices are both material and discursive. In other words, the interactions take place in a physical setting as well as within a language and activity structure that subjectificates. If we alter the physical, communication patterns, processes, and so on in a classroom, it creates a new expectation that different behaviors will occur. The teacher's view of the cause–effect relationships in the classroom can be greatly distorted. The practices that are designed to discover certain behaviors may actually produce them.

Walkerdine's (1997) theory is strongly situational—denying the existence of practices or cognitive structures that are independent of setting. For her:

Situated cognition . . . is not people thinking in different contexts, but subjects produced differently in different practices, in which certain transformations are necessary to turn, for example, nonschool mathematical into school mathematical practices. These transformations are in the relations of signification that produce different subject positions and different truth conditions. (p. 65)

Walkerdine's conceptualization of the subject is quite different from prevailing models such as Piaget's, which saw the capacity for scientific reasoning as genetically determined and the most advanced stage of thinking. In this sense, Walkerdine saw Piaget as legitimizing the enlightenment ideal of the rational man of science. Piaget's psychological constructivist position saw the subject as internally constructed and then understanding the world. Following Foucault, Walkerdine contrasted this approach with one where different identities emerge in different historical-cultural contexts. The most immediate implication of this analysis is to recognize that the "self" we encounter in the classroom is at least to some extent "produced" by our classroom practices. To the extent that we find that self problematic, we must assume some of the responsibility for producing the problems we encounter.

Walkerdine has also questioned the "rational man" as the guiding principle of education. She based her criticism of the rational man ideal on Foucault's idea that the accepted rationality within a culture is defined in a way that promotes the interests of the existing power structure in a society (i.e., schooling perpetuates the existing social order by exalting the knowledge and cognitive skills possessed by the people in power and by downgrading the skills held by the people who are not in power). Foucault also introduced the idea that governments wanted to avoid basing their system of conformity on policing people. They wanted people to police themselves. In the Victorian era, the concept of the self riddled with dangerous unconscious urges justified both state and self-control (Cushman, 1990). The unknown, a natural fear for humans, migrated from its position as an external threat to an internal threat (e.g., Freud, 1930). Modern populations are controlled more by cultural definitions of normalcy. The shaping forces in the culture can then be coordinated by this definition of normalcy, and efforts to shape behavior to fit the mold can be seen as attempts to help people with problems.

The "regulation of practices" in settings like classrooms also categorizes people and creates negative definitions of some categories of people, disadvantaging certain kinds of people in line with the oppressive structure of the larger society. Walkerdine saw the subject as "historically and socially produced—produced, furthermore, not through natural processes and behaviors, but in and through discourses and practices." She cited a specific example of what she meant by this. She looked at the historical degrading of skills like calculating when capitalism moved from a merchant class to one of large-scale manufacturing. Beginning in the 19th century, reason was seen as the key to access to the society.

The societal elements that shape the modern empty self discussed by Cushman (1990) interact with the social practices in the classroom to produce the "student selves" we encounter in the classroom. The role of the professor in reinforcing behaviors and attitudes associated with the empty self is also an important part of the dynamic of the empty student. For us, this is the most important part of the process because it is the part we can affect most directly. We can look for clues about the role we play in producing the problem of the empty student by revisiting Walkerdine's assertions about classroom practice and applying it to our own situation as university professors.

Walkerdine (1997) linked the work of Bhabba (1984) and Fanon (1967) to the process of producing students in classrooms. Bhabba and Fanon described how the oppression of colonial people is orchestrated by stories containing negative stereotypes about what "the natives" are like. The colonialists' tales of native indolence and cheating do not sound that different from professors' stereotypes and storytelling about what students are like. For example, Sacks' (1996) book, *Generation X Goes to College*, is an account of the frustrations professors express when they encounter students whose values and objectives are so radically different from their own. Without denying the validity of the Sacks' descriptions of empty student behavior, the parallels between our stories and the colonialists are striking. The analyses of the forces that produce the empty self and the empty student are important starting places for an understanding of the dynamics of today's university classroom. Yet it is just as important to recognize the fact that if all we do is stereotype this behavior, we are using our stories to avoid confronting the process of change or even justifying some of the most serious shortcomings of the research university for undergraduate students.

CONCLUSION

Phillips (1995) identified several continua on which constructivist theories could be compared with each other and with other types of theories of knowledge acquisition. Phillips' analysis provides some additional dimensions (other than the continuum from psychological constructivism to socioculturalism) to examine constructivist theories. Exploring these dimensions further clarifies both Dewey's position and the exact locus of various constructivist philosophies and theories.

Phillips' first continuum contrasted theories that focus on how individual learners construct knowledge with theories that focus on how bodies of knowledge are constructed (e.g., Popper, Kuhn). On this continuum, Vygotsky and Piaget, usually presented as contrasting theories on the individual–social continuum, are both interested in how individual knowledge is constructed, even though their theories are quite different in other ways. Here we can ask whether theories that focus on individual knowledge necessarily assert that knowledge is constructed by individuals. Dewey, Vygotsky, and the socioculturalists see knowledge as constructed in some form of group activity, but some of these theorists (like Dewey and Vygotsky) see it as ultimately expressed in individual cognition. Although this complicates the description further, individual cognition functions at least partially within the individual mind, but always maintains some connection to the larger social context. To some extent, an individual's "good thinking," "problem-solving skills," or "adaptive intelligence," and even the coherence of their sense of self (Dewey, 1934/1980), become less functional, dysfunctional, or even disappear when he or she is placed in a different setting. Piaget's theory deals primarily with the construction of internal mental structures (schemas), whereas Vygotsky focuses on sociocultural influences on learning. For Vygotsky, the internal structures are a product of the larger cultural context (they are internalized from social practice). Vygotsky placed most of the constructional processes on the group and cultural levels. Vygotsky, like Dewey, saw the child's internal psychological structures as growing out of communication patterns between people (Vygotsky, 1981). The child is genetically predisposed to appropriate cultural practices and acquires truth through language (Wertsch, 2000). Vygotsky's rich description of the mediation process enriches Dewey's theory.

Glassman (2001) saw a difference between the way Dewey and Vygotsky viewed cultural tools. For Dewey, culture provides a toolbox available for solving problems. Dewey's learner can make more independent judgments about whether the tools are useful for problem solving and is much more likely to use education to change society. Combined positions like Dewey's and those described in the next chapter offer some escape from this determinism. Vygotsky's learners are more embedded in their cultures and have less capacity for independent action.

In his review of constructivist theories, Phillips (1995) concluded that most constructivist theories were "rational" in the sense that knowledge is seen as organized and manipulable by some form of systematic operations. Yet theorists who take a strongly sociocultural view assert that, because cognitive structures and processes are constructed and sustained within the context of social relations, they are heavily influenced by the power relationships in the society. Whether the knowledge is seen as being constructed within the individual or on the social level, there is some social consensus about what is reasonable and "obvious."

Dewey would not have great difficulty with the socioculturalists' strong orientation toward placing experience within culture. He would agree that meaning making is primarily an intersubjective rather than a subjective process (generated by inquiry in a community of scholars). Jackson (2002) completed a detailed analysis of Dewey's long struggle to provide readers with a clear definition of what he meant by experience. Jackson examined four revisions of the introduction to *Experience and Nature*. Twenty-five years after the book was first published, Dewey began his final attempt to rewrite the introduction with the following sentence:

> Were I to write (or rewrite) *Experience and Nature* today I would entitle the book *Culture and Nature* and the treatment of specific subject matters would be correspondingly modified. (LW1,361; Quoted in Jackson, 2002, p. 51)

This change was stimulated both by frustration stemming from his inability to communicate what he meant by experience and by shifts in the generally accepted meanings of the words culture and experience. By 1950, culture had taken on a meaning that covered the breadth of human experience, and the meaning of the word *experience* had narrowed to imply psychological experience. Dewey's unpublished introduction also liberally quoted Malinowski's contribution to the 1931 edition of the *Encyclopedia of Social Science*, including Malinowski's statement that "culture is at the same time psychological and collective" (LW1, 364; Quoted in Jackson, 2002, p. 52). This statement clearly supports an assertion that Dewey saw most of experience as being subsumed within culture. It is also important to note that he never considered taking the word *nature* out of the title. He would not have called the book *Experience Is Culture* or *Culture Is Everything*. Dewey never gave up the basic naturalism that Gergen and the postmodernists seem to reject. Dewey's learner functions within experience that includes the real world and the learner's genetic and cultural histories.

Effective learning in supportive environments provides the optimal level of scaffolding for learners. Models for understanding the processes of learning from a structural scaffolding perspective can help us think about what is going on in our classrooms. The most important general principle that can be extracted from this research is that some of these environments—both in school and community settings—provide scaffolding to support reasoning in a particular context that increases the learner's capacity for behaving in more intelligent ways and some do not.

Packer and Goicochea (2000) provided an excellent summary/collage of the range of theories, ideas, and jargon associated with socioculturalism:

From this perspective, cognition "is a complex social phenomenon . . . distributed—stretched over, not divided among—mind, body, activity and culturally organized settings (which include other actors)" (Lave, 1988, p. 1). And, learning is "an integral part of generative social practice in the lived-in world" (Lave & Wenger, 1991, p. 35), the result of "guided participation" (Rogoff, 1990) or "legitimate peripheral participation." Brown, Collins, and Duguid (1989) argue that "understanding is developed through continued, situated use" involving "complex social negotiations" (p. 33), so that "learning and cognition . . . are fundamentally situated" (p. 32) in activity, context, and culture. Learning involves "enculturation": picking up jargon, behavior, and norms of a new social group; adopting its belief systems to become a member of the culture. (p. 229)

Given this summary of the epistemological perspective of the socioculturalist position, Packer and Goicochea (2000) pointed out that sociocultural theories also have fundamental ontological implications. This is why most socioculturalists see learning as a process of developing an identity as a full participant in a community of practice. Packer and Goicochea saw psychological constructivist views as retaining a dualism between the person and the world, which they find unacceptable. Sociocultural perspectives recognize the role that participation in social practices, purposive activity, and human relationships play in shaping the identities of people. For me, the important overall implication of theory and research drawn from the sociocultural literature is the critical role of dialogue in learning. Almost everything we do in organizing the learning environment in constructivist classrooms is designed to create conversations about important topics. Chapter 7 focuses on issues related to dialogue, and chapter 6 explores models that combine the psychological constructivist and sociocultural perspectives.

Transactional Constructivist Perspectives

This chapter explores transactional constructivist perspectives on learning that combine the psychological constructivist and sociocultural positions. The sociocultural perspective provides a rich source of new insights about the dynamics of learning environments in university classrooms. It highlights many issues that are especially relevant to higher education and its relationship to the larger society. Yet it is also clear that adopting a strong sociocultural view that rejects a focus on the development of portable abstractions would be unacceptable to most professors. I believe a useful model that draws on the strengths of both perspectives must maintain a focus on ideas and make a clear statement about the status of cognitive structures and their relationship to social structures.

Combining the psychological constructivist and sociocultural positions is not a straightforward task. The extreme forms of the two positions define learning in different ways. Psychological constructivists tend to view learning in terms of the organization of cognitive structures, and socioculturalists see learning as increasingly successful participation in a community of practice (Greeno, 1997; Greeno & the MSMTA Project Group, 1998; Lave & Wenger, 1991; Wenger, 1998). Pragmatists think of learning as acquiring new meanings that reconstruct experience. Learning is documented only when new meanings are applied to problem solving in new situations (Gregory, 2002). Both views are different from the implicit models that guide most teaching practice in universities: the direct transmission view and the information-processing view. I would characterize the direct transmission view as telling, memorizing, and telling back. When the students have told us what we told them without the benefit of notes, we assume they have acquired knowledge. The information-processing view pays more attention to the process of helping students acquire the mental representations (concepts, theories, mental models, etc.) and procedural knowledge that they can use to understand and solve problems in the future. In the information-processing model, the professor teaches his or her students the mental representation, and the students complete assignments that require them to solve problems using these mental representations (Hall, 1996).

It was difficult to place the range of constructivist approaches into the chapters labeled as the psychological constructivist, sociocultural, and transactional constructivist perspectives. Most did not fit neatly into one category. Most constructivist theories can be characterized as combined models. My categorization related as much to the elements of the theories I chose to highlight as the theories themselves. The theories included in this chapter specifically emphasize the value of understanding learning as grounded in both social practices and individual cognitive structures.

There is a history of debate between advocates of the psychological constructivist and the sociocultural positions about which model best describes the dynamics of learning. More recently, an increasing number of authors (Anderson, Greeno, Reder, & Simon, 2000; Cobb, 1994b; Greeno & the MSMTA Project, 1998; Hall, 1996; Kirshner & Whitson, 1997; Packer & Goicochea, 2000; Prawat, 1995) have argued for the value of combining the psychological constructivist and sociocultural positions. Cobb (1994b) concluded that both perspectives offer important insights to practicing teachers. Cobb believes that some form of combined position is emerging as the dominant constructivist position in education (Cobb & Yackel, 1996). Kirshner and Whitson (1997) are in basic agreement with Cobb.

Four prominent learning scientists who have debated the merits of the competing positions (Anderson, Greeno, Reder, & Simon, 2000) recently asserted that both the individual and sociocultural positions provide important insights about learning. They acknowledged that readers could find the actual implications of these theories confusing because advocates of both perspectives (psychological constructivism and sociocultural) focus on different aspects of the learning process. They pointed out, however, that most theorists who focus on either the psychological or social dimension do not deny the role of the other. They concluded that learning situations should be analyzed by considering both the individual cognitive perspective and the social practices that influence learning. I believe there is a transactional relationship between knowledge structures and social practices and social discourse. Knowledge is structured within individuals through social practices that reach beyond the individual. People live in experience (past, present, and future), and experience includes both our cultural and genetic histories.

Reynolds, Sinatra, and Jetton (1996) developed a categorical continuum for positioning the range of constructivist theories about how knowledge is acquired and represented. Their continuum provides a framework for mapping a useful position that combines psychological constructivism and socioculturalism. In their own exploration of Cobb's (1994b) question, "Where is the mind?", they placed the range of constructivist theories on a continuum from experience centered to mind centered. They placed situated cognition in the center of the continuum (equally mind centered and experience centered). Critics of the situated perspective often attack these theories specifically because they see the situated position as too close to the experience end of the continuum (Anderson, Reder, & Simon, 1997). Although I would also reject a position that eliminates the individual mind because it would leave no role for reflection, I do not see the situated cognitive theories as overly experiential; they fall in the middle of the mind–experience continuum with Dewey and other theories that take a transactional stance. Piaget's schema theory and von Glasersfeld's psychological constructivism are examples of constructivist theories that fall closer to the mind-centered end of the continuum because, for Piaget and von Glasersfeld, knowledge acquisition involves internal constructive processes that capture and *re-present* the interaction between the person and the environment. Sociocultural theories such as Gergen's and Lave's fall at the experience end of the continuum. Leont'ev's theory is similar to Vygotsky's, but strengthens the aspects of the theory that assert that learning occurs within the context of activity. Many of the situated cognitive theories are closely linked to the activity theorists who extended Vygotsky's work. The model I propose uses aspects of all of these perspectives because it utilizes cognitive structures in the context of activity structures anchored in social contexts.

Supporters of the psychological constructivist and sociocultural positions have also addressed the issue of which position is most strongly supported by Dewey's philosophy. As I stated in chapter 3, my own interpretation of Dewey's work led me to the conclusion that he would support what Cobb (1994b) referred to as the emergent or combined position. Other theorists have also reached this conclusion (Hall, 1996; Prawat, 1995). The strength of Dewey's position, and the reason he is still relevant today, was his attempt to understand how the elements of an educative experience (concepts, ideas, thinking, mind, physical and cultural context) could simultaneously establish a dynamic unity and maintain their separate identity within experience (Hall, 1996).

Prawat's (1995) analysis of Dewey's philosophy connected Dewey to Vygotsky and the activity theorists. Dewey consistently gave a larger role to perception and activity than he did to representation (Kirshner & Whitson, 1997), and he placed the development of useful representations in the context of the social processes of inquiry. This links Dewey's concept of learning to today's situated cognitive theories (Hall, 1996).

Prawat (1995) defined *rationalism* as the position that the mind (by establishing "coherence and logical fit") is the yardstick of truth and *realism* as the position that "truth ... reflects correspondence between structures present in the mind and those present in the world" (p. 14). Dewey's transactional realism eliminates this dualism. Although Dewey is connected to psychological constructivists like Glasersfeld by his focus on the structure of knowledge, he would not have supported a totally rationalist "in-the-head" position. Prawat (1995) characterized Dewey as solving the mind–world problem by proposing "a triangular relationship between individual, community, and the world mediated by socially constructed ideas" (p. 14). I agree with this characterization. This position ties Dewey's position to activity theorists like Leont'ev and to current situated cognitive theories. These theories can be used to expand and enrich Dewey's work without doing an injustice to his basic positions.

Transactional approaches like Cobb's and Dewey's highlight the importance of defining the relationship between psychological and social structures. When both types of structures are acknowledged as important, the precise nature of the transaction between psychological and social structures becomes the central theoretical problem. Kirshner and Whitson (1997) acknowledged the importance of defining this relationship when they made a distinction between what they characterized as Cobb's position of *coordination* of psychological and social positions and their model that involves an *integration* of these positions. Because Cobb considered the relationship between individual construction and social construction to be reflexive, his model sounds much more dynamic than the word *coordination* (or combined) would indicate. Neither Cobb nor Kirshner and Whitson provided a detailed model for the transaction between cognitive structures and social practices. The fact that they thought it was important to make this fine-grained distinction highlights the importance of the issue. I see this as the principal challenge facing researchers in learning science who want to develop a viable and useful combined model.

BASIC PRINCIPLES OF A COMBINED CONSTRUCTIVIST APPROACH

At the risk of being redundant, I think it would be helpful to restate the basic principles of a combined constructivist approach introduced in chapter. The discussion of the combined model that follows is designed to integrate concepts from the various versions of constructivism to support these principles.

1. The fundamental goal of education is increasing the learner's adaptive capacity.

2. Useful knowledge is embedded in an authentic and meaningful context. Contexts should be authentic in three ways:

    a. be relevant to the students' interests and concerns,

    b. be relevant to disciplinary discourse and methods of inquiry, and

    c. have important similarities to contexts of application.

3. The quality of knowledge depends on how well structured it is.

4. Useful knowledge is acquired through active knowledge construction through goal-directed inquiry, rather than through transmission.

5. Useful knowledge is socially constructed in learning communities. The process of knowledge construction is embedded in social processes and mediated by socially produced cultural artifacts. The role of dialogue and productive disciplinary discourse is a central factor in understanding the development of productive learning communities.

6. The acquisition of new knowledge is strongly affected by prior knowledge.

7. All knowledge is conditionalized and contextualized. The fact that knowledge is embedded in the conditions and context of its acquisition makes it difficult to transfer knowledge to applications outside the school setting.

8. Effective learning environments should involve students in productive disciplinary discourse that actively engages students in dialogue about important questions.

9. Combined constructivist approaches maintain a focus on ideas.

10. Knowledge is constructed through a recursive, iterative process that fluctuates between empirical and theoretic knowledge.

11. It is important to use multiple perspectives for addressing ill-structured problems.

12. Establishing a productive dialogue across boundaries (cultural, communities of practice, from experts to novices) is the most difficult challenge for constructivist approaches. There are significant forces that make it difficult to foster open dialogue across cultural boundaries and communities of practice. Social practices, especially patterns and styles of communication, are maintained to preserve the interests of dominant groups. The success of combined constructivist approaches depends on being able to foster conversations that traverse these barriers.

13. Learning involves the construction of identity.

14. There is an inherent contradiction between the two goals for the ideal classroom discourse of promoting communication across cultural boundaries and creating productive disciplinary discourse. This is particu-

larly challenging because disciplinary discourse is shaped by the values of the dominant culture.

THE TRANSACTION BETWEEN COGNITIVE AND SOCIAL STRUCTURES

As I discussed in chapter 2, Dewey overcame the dualisms of previous philosophical positions by encompassing the old dualistic elements within experience. Dewey described this relationship as "transactional" to indicate that the relationship between mental and social structures is two way and more intertwined or mutually embedded than would be indicated by words like *interacting, coordinating,* or even *integrating.* I interpret Dewey's transactional constructivism as a living systems perspective because the dualisms (e.g., mind and the real world, rationalism and realism, psychological and social) are unified to operate as one system, but each element also structures itself as a coherent system. It is the requirement that all structures adapt to the contexts in which they are embedded that creates forces for change.

Setting aside the question of which learning theory best describes learning in university classrooms, the combined perspective is the most complex approach to understand and implement. Each move from a transmission model to a behaviorist model to a cognitive model to a transactional model demands an increasingly complex explanation of the learning process. The transmission model assumes that intact, preorganized knowledge can be "told to" students either through lectures or reading. If the students listen, pay attention, memorize, and do well on the test, they will have the knowledge in their heads, and they will be able to retrieve it at the appropriate time "because they know it." Professors using the information-processing model also "tell" students about concepts and procedures for solving problems and guide the process of using these concepts and procedures to solve problems (e.g., doing problem sets; Hall, 1996). Behavioral approaches factor the knowledge and skills to be learned into small subunits, set behavioral objectives, and design learning experiences to reinforce students for learning each skill. The subskills are then systematically assembled to produce expert behavior (Gagne, 1968). Psychological constructivist models like Piaget's and von Glasersfeld's need to explain how processes like assimilation and accommodation operate to alter or replace students' existing ideas. The socioculturalists broaden the context of learning to focus on improving the students' sensitivity to the constraints and affordances of a particular context by moving toward legitimate participation in a community of practice (Greeno & the MSMTA Project Group, 1998; Lave & Wenger, 1991). All of these models can produce useful knowledge. They all work under certain conditions to reach certain learning goals. Yet none of these models seems applicable to all of the learning situations we confront. If we decide we want to increase the probability that a student will elicit a particular response in a defined stimulus situation, the behavioral perspective is clearly indicated. If I wanted to help someone overcome a phobic fear of snakes (or constructivism), I would use a behavioral approach. Yet behavioral approaches do not seem to be appropriate for teaching responses to complex unstructured problems. The sociocultural positions bring important new insights to our teaching, but some of their explanations of learning seem as simplistic as the transmission model. All of these perspectives have strengths and weaknesses for designing effective educational environments in university courses.

Most situated cognitive theories characterize internal cognitive structures as developing through some form of internalization of social practices and cultural artifacts within an activity structure (Greeno, 1997; Greeno & the MSMTA Project Group, 1998). Internalization is not a transfer of knowledge to an existing plane of consciousness, but the process by which consciousness is formed (Confrey, 1995). There is a range of explanations for how these structures get "in the head" and how much independence they achieve. A key question is whether cognitive structures can critique the social structures that spawned them (e.g., Bourdieu's habitus is a box that seems difficult to escape). The credibility of combined constructivist models depends on their ability to describe the nature of the transaction between the learner's existing cognitive structures (wherever they are and wherever they came from) and social practices and cultural artifacts. A comprehensive model describing this transaction is potentially mind-boggling.

Because I do not want my mind boggled, I have not tackled the task of developing a comprehensive theory or model for the relationship between ideas and social practices. Yet I do think it is important to have a way of thinking about this relationship that guides my thinking about teaching and learning. A fairly detailed set of hypotheses about the dynamics of this transaction is important to understanding several key processes in the transactional constructivist model (e.g., the "zone of proximal development," communication across the boundaries between cultures, the space between the teacher and the students, or the expert and the novice during any type of scaffolding). If I imagine that I am going to design an experience that radically changes the way students see and understand something in the world (I want to stimulate "tree jumping," not just "branch jumping"), I need to have a fairly clear picture of how this type of change occurs.

Most constructivist approaches include an explicit or implicit systems theory. There are structures at some level (either cognitive or social) that become more organized and resist change (e.g., von Glasersfeld's schema and Bourdieu's habitus). Readers are given the impression that these authors know how these structures function and interact with other systems, but key details are missing. It would be helpful if more authors would try to articulate the dynamics of these processes in clear language or simply admit that they are not sure exactly how these systems operate. My own working hypothesis, based on research and everyday experience, is that both cognitive structures and social structures tend to organize themselves fairly autonomously and are difficult but not impossible to change. Using the term *structural coupling* may link me too closely to classical systems theory and, by inference, to psychological constructivism, but I am comfortable using this term. The important point I would like to make is that the key to understanding learning is understanding the nature of transactions across boundaries.

Several transactional and sociocultural theories refer to some form of life world, blended space, or hybrid space where various types of transactions take place. I think it is important to avoid an explanation that characterizes this space as created "out there" in some magical way beyond individuals. This is tricky because the space *is* "out there" in the sense that a single person cannot maintain the space by him or herself, but it is not a magical space or central mind. I find many of Habermas' ideas to be helpful, but some of his references to a "shared lifeworld" sound too much like a magic space floating in the air between the individuals. Fauconnier and Turner (1998) defined a conceptual blend as a "projection between different cognitive/linguistic structures. Projection is a general process of relating one viewpoint or frame to another" (p. 664). I am not clear what they mean by projection. Because I take a systems view, I think the blended space has to exist for each actor. The specific nature of the structural coupling between the individual's cognitive structures and the blended space is transitory because the blended space can only be maintained while support is present. Fauconnier and Turner (1998) described the way this blended space is created:

A particular process of meaning construction has particular input representations; during the process, inferences, emotions, and event-integrations emerge which cannot reside in any of the inputs; they have been constructed dynamically in a new mental space—the blended space—linked to the inputs in systematic ways. (p. 135)

Fauconnier and Turner identified three types of mental spaces that interact in blended space: *Input spaces* are "particular configurations of events, emotions, meaning, and inference." Linking to this space links to the being of the person. This is important because it retains Dewey's (1934/1980) transactional relationship between conceptual knowledge and the matrix of experience that includes the direct experience of the emotional/body complex and the unity of epistemological and ontological aspects of learning (Packer & Goicochea, 2000); *generic space* "maps onto each of the input spaces, and consists of what these input spaces have in common. Generic spaces "can become powerful conventions, used as resources in cross-space articulations in new networks." As I understand it, the generic spaces are analogous to Bourdieu's habitus; *Blends* are "a new formation produced in relation to the inputs" (p. 137).

Leander (2001) used Fauconnier and Turner's blends and Bakhtin's similar concept of the hybrid space to analyze a particular situation involving a trip by a group of African-American high school students to visit the site where Martin Luther King, Jr. was assassinated. The particular discourse described in Leander's article involved a lesson that took place on the bus. The teachers were drawing parallels between the bus trip and the freedom rides that took place over 30 years earlier and trying the help the students personally connect to the civil rights struggle and the pain of King's assassination. The teachers helped the students draw on their own experiences of loss to understand the feelings of loss felt by an associate of King's (Reverend Kyles) whom they would be meeting on the trip. The dialogue that took place is parallel to many situations that all of us encounter in our classes. Leander analyzed several "stories" that were told to the students and told by the students and how they were connected and elaborated by the teacher in the blended space. In one dialogue, the teacher asked the students to imagine that they are with their best friend when the friend is shot. In Leander's analysis, the *generic space* had four elements (two people, traveling, waiting for ride, one assassinated in front of the other). I connect this to Schank's scripts because it represents a normal script—two people waiting for a ride to go to dinner, with an unusual twist "the time when someone shot my friend." The *1968 assassination space* included six elements (Reverend Kyles with MLK, traveling for activism, waiting for a ride, plans for dinner, MLK shot in front of Kyle's face, 30 years of painful "what if" reflections). The *1998 imagined vacation space* had five elements (self with best friend, shared home space-times, traveling on vacation, waiting for ride, friend shot in front of your face). The *blended 1968/1998 space* included six elements (self/Kyles with best friend/MLK, travel as vacation/activism, best friend/MLK shot in front of face, painful "what if" reflections, plus the teacher's elaboration: "do not take life for granted"). To successfully blend these spaces and connect to the teacher's elaboration (Schank's moral of the story), the students have to connect the key parallel elements of the historic example to their personal experience.

The blending process involves selecting and seeing similarities between particular elements. From my perspective, these spaces have a structural predisposition to remain closed and contextualized. To create useful knowledge, a blended space with a key elaboration needs to have a structural coupling to a class of "real-world" situations. Leander's scenario serves as an example that highlights Packer and Goicochea's (2000) observation that combining the sociocultural position with the psychological constructivist position involves a shift in both ontological and epistemological perspectives. The knowledge these students acquired was intertwined with changes in their identities and their sense of being.

However, this portion of the lesson did not demonstrate connections to scientific concepts. What are the enduring understandings about facilitating social change that students should learn from the civil rights movement that can guide their own attempts to address current social problems like the mass incarceration of African-American males? I do not mean to criticize this specific lesson because I have taken it out of context to make a point that is unrelated to the focus of Leander's analysis. The position of Leander's rich description in this text just happens to provide me with an opportunity to make a point about a potential weakness of classroom practices that are exclusively derived from sociocultural perspectives. If this description were typical of the "lessons" connected with this trip, I would ask where the big ideas and deep principles were. If dialogue is only about opinions that do not change and emotions that do not inform and alter future behavior in an adaptive way, I would not judge an experience to be educative. The art of combining sociocultural and psychological constructivist positions is to develop ways to embed important concepts in rich social contexts. Although it is important, it is not enough for students to understand how someone feels in a situation and how that connects to how they feel. If this story were not connected to any meaningful generalizations, I do not think it would help these students to more effectively identify and confront a problem in the future.

COLLABORATIVE LEARNING

Collaborative learning is an approach to teaching that is built on philosophical positions like Dewey's, Vygotsky's, and Habermas', which assert that knowledge is socially constructed within a community of learners. One of the most fundamental principles that can be derived from this constructivist literature is that dialogue has a privileged position in learning. If knowledge is socially constructed in learning communities, an important feature of any method of teaching within this framework is to promote meaningful dialogue among students. If effective learning environments involve students in productive disciplinary discourse, that discourse should be directly related to the professors' learning objectives. Bruffee (1993) listed three strengths of collaborative learning: (a) Students make their learning visible to each other, (b) students model learning activities for each other, and (c) students are required to voice their positions publicly. Assuming that professors and fellow students push students to examine their thinking, this type of public reflection promotes metacognitive awareness and encourages students to correct their own misconceptions.

In addition to the work of Vygotsky (1978), Bruffee (1999) discussed the work of two other educators who strongly influenced the development of collaborative learning in higher education. He traced the understanding that dialogue is critical in higher education to research conducted by Abercrombie (1960) with medical students at the University of London. She changed the way rounds were conducted when she found that students learned diagnostic skills better when they worked collaboratively in small groups. Instead of asking one student to make a diagnosis, she asked the group to discuss it and come to consensus. Bruffee also pointed to work by Treisman at UC Berkeley, who hypothesized that Asian students did better in math because they were in constant conversation among themselves about the subject matter. An intervention to promote dialogue among North American students raised their performance significantly. Models of collaborative learning must provide specific training and guidance to offset the individualism that characterizes North American culture and schooling (Hogan & Corey, 2001).

There are several models of collaborative learning: peer tutoring, collaborative project work, writing peer reviews, consensual response to lectures, and consensus groups. Bruffee (1999) described the process he uses to organize consensus groups: (a) Begin by creating small groups of about five students. He advises against making groups larger than six students to ensure that all of the students have an opportunity to participate in the dialogue. In general, group performance and learning are enhanced if the groups are more diverse. It is also important to allow consensus groups to function without the professor sitting in on the discussion; (b) The professor assigns the groups a discussion question that captures an important element of the lesson. In most cases, the topics presented should be ill-defined problems with no specific correct answer. The conversations should engage students in a truly constructive process of exploring a solution that uses their own experience and the content of the course. Before they come back to a large-group discussion, the group should ask the recorder to rehearse the report they will give to the entire class. This gives the small group an opportunity to check on the report's accuracy and test whether it really represents the group's consensus view; (c) The small groups' discussions are then shared in a large-group discussion. During the large-group discussion, the professor's role is to record the observations made by the class and connect the language invented by the students to the language and concepts used by experts in the field. The professor should also explore disagreements in the group discussions. In this phase of the process, the professor represents the view of the scientific community in his or her discipline by comparing what the students say with the current set of warranted assertions from the research literature and introducing the vocabulary used in the discipline to label the concepts the students have generated. If the student groups have arrived at a consensus that differs from the predominant scientific view, the groups should be sent back into a discussion to explore the reasons their opinions differed from that of the experts; and (d) This phase is followed by a research phase, where group members divide up the task of researching expert opinion on the topic.

The professor can also serve the role of pointing out the quality of the internal logic of the responses and making process observations about the dynamics within the small groups. It is particularly important for professors to provide scaffolding for learning during the discussion that follows group work. This relates to what Vygotsky called the *zone of proximal development*. Semiotic and linguistic theories provide a framework for guiding professors' attempts to support conceptual development in open discussion.

Another type of discussion question suggested by Bruffee is to provide student groups with a position that is generally supported by scientific research and ask them to generate an explanation for how and why the experts reached the conclusion. What reasoning would someone use to make this assertion? A variation of this technique is to create a two-step process where students discuss an open question and are then provided with a set of scientific conclusions related to that question. Then students are asked to explore the reasoning that the experts might have used to reach their conclusions. Collaborative learning can be a powerful strategy for getting students involved in the process of constructing their own knowledge.

An important practical issue in any teaching practice derived from a constructivist perspective that begins with the students' ideas and experience is the relationship between everyday knowledge (empirical knowledge gained from experience) and abstract scientific concepts. Vygotsky thought students should get precise definitions of scientific concepts early in the learning process (Karpov & Haywood, 1998). Cobb (1994a) and many current constructivists recommended beginning with student inquiry and then connecting the students' ideas to scientific concepts. I have settled on a middle ground influenced by the work of Davydov: introducing simple abstractions early in the learning process and helping students construct increasingly sophisticated abstract concepts throughout the course (through a recursive, iterative process that fluctuates between empirical and theoretical knowledge). Cobb made it clear that when he advocated turning Vygotsky's model on its head (replacing Vygotsky's top–down model with a bottom–up model where students initiate a learning process grounded in their own experience) he did not reject Vygotsky's central premise that semiotic mediation is a critical step in the process of conceptual development. In

Cobb's bottom–up model, the teacher manages a chain of signification by connecting the students' emerging understanding to increasingly abstract symbol systems (Cobb, Gravemeijer, Yackel, McClain, & Whitnack, 1997).

Cobb and Bruffee built many of their collaborative learning strategies on the linguistic theories of Saussure and the structuralists and poststructuralists who followed him. Saussure began his analysis with the idea that words take their meaning from their context and knowledge is dependent on the conventions that are negotiated among and inherited by knowledgeable people. Cobb was also influenced by van Oer's (1996) theories of distributed cognition that link the process of concept formation with symbol formation. This negotiation process is reproduced in classroom dialogue.

As professors we have the problem of managing both the semiotic (helping students attach symbols to concepts) and perceptual (tuning the perceptual systems) processes to help students see structures that have meaning. By adopting a combined position, we can use methods from psychological constructivism (perceptual tuning) and socioculturalism (semiotics) as long as we also conceptualize and understand the transactional relationship between individual thinking (that is not really totally contained "in the head") and social practices (that are, in turn, affected by the action of the students and professors).

Instituting a collaborative learning model requires that a new set of social norms and classroom practices be introduced to the students (Cobb, McClain, & Gravemeijer, 2003). Cobb, Gravemeijer, Yackel, McClain, and Whitnack (1997) reported on their attempts to move students into a new way of learning mathematics. They began by assuming that the students would be attracted to the new more social environment of the classroom and would readily adapt to the new way of operating the class. They reported, however, that:

> it soon became apparent that the teacher's expectations that the students would verbalize how they had interpreted and attempted to solve tasks ran counter to their previous experiences of class discussions in school . . . students took it for granted that they were to infer what the teacher had in mind rather than articulate their own understandings. (p. 155)

At the point at which Cobb et al. recognized that the students were not willing to change their classroom practices, the teacher stopped to systematically present and negotiate a new set of classroom norms. Yet it is difficult to renegotiate classroom norms with college students. As our students enter their careers in the university setting, they have 12 years of successful acculturation and skill building at inferring "what the teacher has in mind," rather than "articulating their own understandings." It is difficult to break students away from this mindset. We think we are "shaping the students' understanding of our subject matter" and "connecting their experience to scientific knowledge" while our students are "figuring out what the professor wants them to say." In this case, the professor and student only appear to be engaged in a joint communication process; they are actually playing completely different games and have completely different interpretations of what is happening.

Like many constructivists, Cobb and his associates began the learning cycle by involving students in collaborative problem solving in small groups followed by large-group discussion of the solutions processed by the teacher. Maintaining high-quality participation by all of the students is an indispensable ingredient for successful collaborative learning. If students are to become actively involved in constructing their own knowledge within the context of a knowledge-building community, they have to change their typical classroom behavior in fundamental ways. They have to listen actively to what other students have to say and be willing to ask questions until they understand the positions of their fellow students. Most important, they must be willing to challenge the positions and thinking of other students. Students are expected to ask for clarification from other students if they did not fully understand what they were saying.

The class in which Cobb, Gravemeijer, Yackel, McClain, and Whitnack (1997) conducted their research came up with the following set of communication norms:

> (1) explaining and justifying solutions, (2) attempting to make sense of the explanations of others, (3) indicating agreement and disagreement, and (4) questioning alternatives in situations where a conflict in interpretations had become apparent. (p. 155; numbers added)

Students cannot conform to these norms unless they have the ability to judge and articulate the quality of the other students' thinking. Fernandez, Wegerif, Mercer, and Rojas-Drummond (2001) developed a similar set of criteria and provided students with training in what they called *exploratory talk*. They contrasted exploratory talk with disputational talk, which involves patterns of asserting opinions and not really listening to what other students are saying, and cumulative talk, which involves students taking turns making contributions that are loosely linked to the previous speaker. They defined *exploratory talk* as:

> participants engage critically but constructively with each other's ideas, offering justification and alternative hypotheses. Knowledge is made publicly accountable and reasoning is more visible in the talk, and the progress results from the eventual agreement reached. (p. 42)

An important focus of the Fernandez et al. research was to explore a re-definition of Vygotsky's zone of proximal development to account for mutual scaffolding and co-construction of knowledge in cooperative learning groups. Vygotsky's original idea focused on situations where an expert was supporting the growth of a novice. In this situation, the zone of proximal development is seen as the difference between the individual's level of knowledge and the distributed expertise of the group in a blended space they called the *intermental development zone*. The intermental development zone is described as "a dynamic contextual framework of shared knowledge, created through language and shared action" (p. 42). Given the right type of group communication style (i.e., exploratory talk) embedded in goal-directed activity, they believe that the growth of individual students can be scaffolded by the shared cognition of the group. From the combined perspective, dialogue is seen as embedded within activity structures (Confrey, 1995).

Hogan and Corey (2001) believed that norms of communication need to be supplemented by clear norms of scientific practice (e.g., a commitment to rigor in collecting and analyzing data). Engle and Conant (2002) labeled this type of dialogue *constructive disciplinary engagement*. This concept emphasizes the importance of fostering classroom practices that follow disciplinary norms related to issues like how evidence is used to support assertions. In most university courses, this would be an essential criterion for evaluating students' work.

In the "Understanding Organizations" class, I incorporated workshops in the areas of reflective thinking, metacognition, and group process feedback. In addition, students need some disciplinary guidelines about what standards are used to judge the quality of a response. In the mathematics class where Cobb and his associates were conducting their curriculum development and research (Cobb, Gravemeijer, Yackel, McClain, & Whitnack, 1997), the students had to learn enough about mathematical thinking to be able to judge what counted "as a different solution, an efficient solution, and an acceptable explanation" (p. 157). Each discipline has a parallel set of criteria that have been developed within their scientific community. Students are expected to assimilate these standards through participation in the dialogue of the community.

In the "Understanding Organizations" course, new classroom norms were reinforced by communication skill building, coaching during group work, and follow-up discussions about the learning process and the quality of the products produced. These norms were reinforced by written assignments where students read articles designed to give them expertise around a particular problem. They then wrote an "expert letter" to another student explaining what they understood about the concepts in the article and what concepts they found confusing or challenging. A fellow student read the same article and composed an "answer letter" to explain his or her understanding of the concepts. These dyadic discussions were then brought into large-group discussions scaffolded by the professor.

Although the collaborative learning model has great promise as a method for reforming higher education curriculum, the approach also presents challenges that can be difficult to overcome. First of all, collaborative methods can be difficult to implement because it is easy for students to approach the time they spend in collaborative work groups as social time. They often divide the labor of completing a task rather than solving it collaboratively. Professors cannot expect students to make the transition from traditional courses to collaborative courses without a systematic acculturation process. Dewey (1938a) recognized this problem when he wrote, "the removal of external control" [cannot ensure] "the production of self-control" (pp. 64–65). Bruffee (1999) echoed this concern when he criticized the innovations attempted in the 1960s because the implementers failed to replace the old classroom practices with new conventions to govern student behavior in group situations. Collaborative models change the authority structure in the classroom. Students need considerable training and ongoing support to learn to control learning activities within their own domain. In the "Understanding Organizations" course, I participated in selected group meetings to provide process support.

For Bruffee (1999), the paramount responsibility of the teacher in the collaborative classroom is to ensure that all students participate in the classroom dialogue. This is a critical issue in a model that requires dialogue for knowledge construction. This issue cannot be overemphasized because it represents the Achilles' heel of the model. Bruffee (1999) identified two primary barriers to student participation in collaborative learning: (a) They are used to giving authority only to the teacher, and (b) they have not learned to trust the power of dialogue to bring out the best of what the group has to offer. At every stage of the learning process, it is important to create structures that support processes that promote learning. It is not enough to put students in a group and ask them to discuss a topic.

ANCHORED INSTRUCTION AND GUIDED DISCOVERY IN COMMUNITIES OF LEARNERS

Several models have emerged that apply the range of psychological constructivist and sociocultural theories to curriculum design. Two models that have both cognitive and sociocultural influences were introduced in chapter 3 on psychological constructivist perspectives: Schank's theory of dynamic memory and Bransford's anchored instruction and situated cognition. These models were discussed in chapter 3 to introduce their cognitive aspects. Bransford emphasized that his model includes elements of both the psychological constructivist and sociocultural views when he described his model as "knowledge centered," "learner centered," and "community centered" (Bransford, Vye, & Bateman, 2002). Students in both these programs engage in forms of collaborative learning. Both anchor student inquiry processes in an authentic problem context.

Brown, Collins, and Duguid (1989) developed a framework for a model of instruction based on theories of situated cognition. Within this framework, the concept of a learning community and the cognitive apprenticeship is an overarching approach to linking experience to abstractions by making knowledge visible. A key feature of the cognitive apprenticeship is placing tasks that link to abstractions within authentic contexts and presenting learners with a range of problems that facilitate generalization (Collins, Brown, & Holum, 1991).

To be effective, a learning community must create a supportive social network. An active network of communication and participation scaffolds knowledge construction across the entire learning community, rather than by one-to-one links from the professor to each student (Bransford, Vye, & Bateman, 2002). A basic assumption of this approach is that a learning environment built on the learning community model will produce more students who can flourish in the learning organizations they will confront after they leave school (Lin et al., 1995; Popkewitz, 1998).

The following principles of the learning community can be derived from the literature: (a) Students are provided with the opportunity to plan and organize their own independent and group research and problem solving (Brown & Campione, 1996; Lin et al., 1995). However, professors are still responsible for presenting students with the problems they must solve and evaluating their success in solving these problems. (b) Students work collaboratively to achieve important goals. (c) The learning community utilizes the distributed expertise of its members. Collaborative learning does not assume that all students will learn the same material at the same depth (Lin et al., 1995). When they have developed expertise in an area, students share their expertise with their classmates. Access to expertise should be extended beyond the classroom through mechanisms like online consultation and cross-age teaching (Brown & Campione, 1996). This allows the professor to create situations in the classroom that are much closer to the patterns of communication and social practices students will encounter after they leave the university and, therefore, increase the probability that learning will transfer to the new setting. (d) An overall goal is for students to learn to interact with each other as well as teachers and other experts (a reciprocal exchange of ideas, data, and opinions; Lin et al., 1995). (e) Sharing is motivated by some consequential task (e.g., presentation, test, producing a joint project) that demands that all students have learned about all aspects of the joint topic (Brown & Campione, 1996). (f) The teacher must model critical thinking and self-reflection (Brown & Campione, 1996).

Ann Brown and her colleagues developed their Fostering Communities of Learners Program (Brown & Campione, 1994) around the idea of the cognitive apprenticeship. They engage students in teams to address important problems that require application of basic principles for their solution. The specific learning objectives are embedded in the larger problem that is fixed in a realistic context. In this case, "realistic" or "authentic" has more to do with organizing a setting that demands the cognitive skills, communication skills, and social practices of the target setting than directly simulating all of the specific characteristics of the target setting. Students form research groups to address questions they have generated about the basic problem presented. Here the resources available in the learning environment (e.g., lectures, reading, links to experts in the community) and the skills required to explore and organize knowledge become part of the students' process of seeking a solution to the problem. They use several specific methods to create community and facilitate the problem-solving process: (a) *Reciprocal teaching/crosstalk* involves asking student-led groups to master and use strategies to comprehend difficult material and teach it to others or make reports on their progress to other groups. The reporting process gives other students an opportunity to challenge their thinking. They clarify their thinking by explaining the concepts and answering questions from other students (Brown & Campione, 1996). (b) In *jigsaw teaching*, different student groups focus on different areas of a single topic area. True jigsaw teaching lessons are difficult to design because the model demands that each subunit be independently coherent so that a group can conduct research on it. At the same time, each subgroup combines with others to cohere to a higher level of meaning (Brown & Campione, 1996). (c) The *collaborative database* (e.g., CSILE) uses technology to build a database that represents the student learning community's store of knowledge.

Instructional strategies that are similar to Ann Brown's guided discovery in learning communities have been the most common form of combined constructivist approaches. For some socioculturalists, these approaches are too cognitive. Karpov and Haywood (1998) expressed the opposite concern—that these approaches do not give sufficient focus to the development of theoretical knowledge. They pointed out that most applications of Vygotsky's theories outside of the former Soviet Union represent only one of the two approaches represented by his followers. They categorized Brown's approach and most of the constructivist approaches as forms of metacognitive mediation. They feel that these approaches tend to ignore the other strand of neo-Vygotskian thought, cognitive mediation, represented by the work of Russian psychologists like Galperin and Davydov.

Galperin and Davydov emphasized the importance of developing theoretic knowledge and introducing abstractions early in the learning process. I would agree that more systematic attention needs to be paid to the development of scientific concepts in some constructivist approaches. Domain-specific problem solving requires extensive conceptual and procedural knowledge mediated by appropriate problem representations. My working model introduces basic abstractions early in the learning process that are embellished through a recursive process that modulates between concrete (primary) and abstract (secondary) experience. Much of this model was derived by extending a model developed by Edelson (2001). This model is discussed in detail in chapter 9.

DOROTHY HOLLAND'S COMBINED POSITION ON IDENTITY

The idea that learning is the construction of identity is drawn from sociocultural theories that see learning as acculturation to a community of practice. It is also included in most situated cognitive and combined positions (Greeno, 1997). Dorothy Holland and her associates crafted an interdisciplinary model for the construction of identity that incorporates and integrates ideas from Mead, Bakhtin, Vygotsky, and Bourdieu. Her model captures and enriches Dewey's view of the self by giving a prominent place to imagination and emphasizes both the shaping power of culture and the potential agency of the individual. Her view specifically combines psychological constructivist and social constructionist perspectives.

Holland's definition of *identity* focuses on the transactions that embody identity rather than treating identity as a quasireal thing: "Identity is one way of naming the dense interconnections between the intimate and the public venues of social practice" (Holland, Lachicotte, Skinner, & Cain, 1998, p. 270). From her disciplinary perspective as an anthropologist, she rejected the pure essentialist position that culture dictates behaviors but leaves the dynamics of social positioning unexamined, as well as the pure social constructionist view, which ignores the durable aspects of the self altogether. Holland adopted a transactional view of the relationship between the person and the culture, choosing to describe the process of identity development as co-development rather than using Foucault's term *suturing,* which is much more deterministic. For Holland et al. (1998),

Identity is a concept that figuratively combines the intimate or personal world with the collective space of cultural forms and social relationships . . . identities are lived in and through activity and so must be conceptualized as they develop in social practice. (p. 5)

This focus on social practices and developing identities in social relations ties her view to Mead and her focus on activity and conceptualization growing out of social practice connects her view to Vygotsky and Bakhtin.

Holland et al. (1998) compared and integrated two sometimes opposing perspectives on the focus and shaping of personal identity: (a) theories of cultural logic that describe how cultural constraints "suture" individuals to predetermined social roles and societal positions, and (b) constructionist and postmodern positions that focus on how issues of power and influence shape discourses to place certain categories of individuals in designated subject positions. Her academic training as an anthropologist predisposed her to focus on cultural regularities. Her experiences in the field forced her to look for additional theories to account for instances of innovative behavior, resistance, and change. Holland used perspectives such as Vygotsky's analysis of the role of play in development and Bakhtin's explorations of creativity and imagination to explain how individuals and groups escape determined perspectives and bring about social change. Holland did not believe, however, that individuals are totally free to reinvent new subjectivities:

> The possibilities of heuristic development do not mean that humans are free to develop whatever subjectivity they wish and do whatever strikes them at the moment. Far from it. One's history-in-person is the sediment from past experiences upon which one improvises, using the cultural resources available, in response to subject positions afforded one in the present. The constraints are over powering, yet not hermetically sealed. Improvisation can become the basis of reformed subjectivity. (p. 18)

Different versions of critical and postmodern theory have focused a great deal of attention on the power negotiations that take place in face-to-face discourses, such as those that occur in the classroom. Foucault's observations in a number of settings have increased our awareness of the role of power in social relationships and spawned the development of identity politics built around issues of race, gender, culture, and sexual preference. In the version of identity development described by many constructionist and postmodern thinkers, the categories of power relationships in the dominant culture are "inscribed" on interpersonal discourses and shape the structure of institutions. Power discourses and cultural artifacts construct identities. This process is played out in classroom discourse just as it is in other social settings. When students talk to each other, their speech makes claims about their social standing as well as sharing information.

Holland and her associates focused their attention specifically on the development of identity in what they called *figured worlds*, which are "socially produced, culturally constructed activities" where behaviors and social positions are structured. A figured world is not a bounded physical space, but is structured by a web of meaning that incorporates structural constraints and affordances (e.g., the world of academia, the world of romance, the game of Dungeons and Dragons, the classroom). For Holland et al. (1998), "Figured worlds rest upon people's abilities to form and to be formed in collectively realized 'as if' realms" (p. 49). They define a figured world as:

> A socially and culturally constructed realm of interpretation in which particular characters and actors are recognized, significance is assigned to certain acts, and particular outcomes are valued over others. Each is a simplified world populated by a set of agents (in the world of romance: attractive women, boy friends, lovers, fiancées) who engage in a limited range of meaningful acts or changes of state (flirting with, falling in love with, dumping, having sex with) as moved by a specific set of forces (attractiveness, love, lust). (p. 52)

Identity is constructed through dialogical relationships with others. Individuals position themselves through speaking and answering in ways that reflect their social rank. A major problem that is explored in more depth in chapter 7 on dialogue is that individuals who are marginalized in figured worlds tend to be ignored and silenced. Subtle dynamics in dialogic situations work to perpetuate existing social structures. The silences produced in classroom discourses short-circuit opportunities for learning and perpetuate dysfunctional identities. Education can organize itself to give voice to marginalized groups. Incorporating creativity and play and highlighting cultural contradictions can create authoring spaces for students if they are provided safe spaces for expression (e.g., Bakhtin's carnival). To bring about change in identities, students need to be able to imagine themselves in new ways. Vygotsky's zone of proximal development tends to be a vehicle for expressing existing social structures because expert competencies capture elements of the social system in which they are embedded. Yet if the more knowledgeable person presents an alternate view, he or she can create a leading edge for movement toward liberation.

To summarize Holland's model of the co-construction of identity, Holland et al. (1998) identified four contexts of identity: (a) *Figured worlds* provide the "frames of meaning" for identity construction. It is not impossible for an individual to buy a self-help book and change his or her identity, but it is difficult. In the examples of Alcoholics Anonymous and Weight Watchers, webs of meaning maintained by social practices are much more successful at establishing new identities than individuals working on their own. Traditional models of higher education are highly competitive and individualistic. Constructivist approaches include a variety of group activities that can be the sight of transformative discourses. (b) *Positionality* expresses the systems of power, status, and oppression of the larger society in figured worlds. Without some active intervention and change in the social practices in classrooms, it is unlikely that they will provide spaces for authoring new positive identities in students who challenge the existing order. (c) *Spaces for authoring* must give flexibility to students in how they respond to problem situations. They must provide opportunities for students to explore and challenge existing knowledge and develop creative solutions to problems. (d) *Making worlds* expresses their confidence that, although creative behavior is heavily constrained by existing structures, it is possible to create new worlds through "serious play."

TRANSFER IN COMBINED CONSTRUCTIVIST MODELS

Transfer is an important issue for a combined constructivist perspective on learning because the theory both emphasizes the importance of transfer and makes it theoretically problematic. Because we claim that we are producing useful rather than inert knowledge, enhanced transfer from school-based learning environments to "real-world" settings is a primary selling point used by proponents of constructivism. The advantage of constructivist approaches is that the knowledge acquired will be accessible to learners in future problem situations because it is acquired in authentic contexts and indexed to those contexts. Students will be reminded of the knowledge they have acquired and use it in real-life situations because constructivist learning environments have important similarities to the settings where the knowledge will be applied.

At the same time, however, constructivist theories of learning, especially situated and sociocultural approaches, emphasize the difficulties of decontextualizing knowledge. Some critics even charge that this view precludes transfer from one setting to another (Anderson, Reder, & Simon, 1996). If knowledge is not "in the head," but scaffolded by its physical and social contexts, it is not that easy to keep it alive if it is "ripped from its soil and deprived of its sunlight." Whereas transmitted knowledge gets stored in Dewey's "water-tight compartments," constructed knowledge "dies on the vine." At the least, these theories highlight the real problems associated with the application of knowledge in contexts that are removed from or dissimilar to the original learning environment.

Most proponents of combined and situated cognitive perspectives place their analysis of abstraction and transfer within the concept of activity. This connects these issues to the work of Vygotsky and activity theorists. A cornerstone of Vygotsky's theory was his distinction between everyday concepts (Davydov's empirical knowledge) and scientific concepts (Davydov's theoretical knowledge). Vygotsky's theory rested on the assumption that the development of meanings involved increasingly abstract relationships between signs and the linguistic and nonlinguistic objects to which they referred. Everyday concepts are acquired through contact with things in the world, and scientific concepts are acquired by moving from the concept to the thing. Scientific concepts begin to form when signs refer to systems of things rather than just one thing that is experienced directly (Wertsch, 2000). It is important to connect this discussion to current research in learning science that has found that useful knowledge requires *both* primary experience and secondary experience. Experience, in itself, is not always a good teacher. Without theoretical knowledge, we do not have the "knowing gaze" that calls our attention to salient features in the environment that organize an expert's way of seeing a situation.

Debates about the issue of transfer are complicated by the fact that different perspectives on learning define transfer differently. Rather than focusing on whether a cognitive structure can be transported, connected to, and used to understand a different situation, situated and sociocultural perspectives focus their analysis on environmental variables that support or do not support transfer. Greeno and the MSMTA Project Group (1998) stated that transfer "depend[s] on attunement to constraints and affordances that are invariant or modifiable across transformations of a situation where learning occurred to another situation in which the learning can have an effect" (p. 11). This statement reflects a different perspective than traditional discussions of transfer. Greeno (1997) reframed "the transfer question" from, "Does knowledge transfer between tasks?" to a form that reflects the situated cognitive perspective: "When someone has become more successful at participating in an activity in one kind of situation, are there other kinds of situations in which that person will also be more adept?" (p. 11). Instead of focusing on the construction of internal knowledge structures independent of context, the situated view embeds cognition in "patterns of participatory processes" (p. 12). If these patterns are consistent across settings, transfer will occur; if they are inconsistent, transfer will not occur. In the situated cognitive view, representations and abstractions are embedded in participatory patterns in activities. A completely decontextualized abstraction is not useful because it is separated from its meaning context. An important part of the research agenda for proponents of combined and situated perspectives is understanding how representations and abstractions function in activity structures, especially in dialogue.

Bransford, Brown, and Cocking (1999) summarized several of their key conclusions about the characteristics of learning and transfer that have the most important implications for teaching: (a) For transfer to occur, students must acquire and understand a threshold level of knowledge; (b) knowledge that is learned "with understanding" is much more likely to transfer to other situations than material that is simply memorized; (c) knowledge that is connected to a number of different contexts helps students develop abstractions that are not bound to one situation; (d) transfer is facilitated when teachers help students recognize underlying themes and deep principles and tie knowledge to the conditions where it can be applied; (e) it is important to assess dynamic transfer (how learning affects further learning in a new situation) as well as static transfer (how well knowledge learned in one situation can be used in another); and (f) all learning involves transfer from previous learning situations. Teachers should assess students' prior knowledge, promote positive transfer of accurate existing knowledge, and help students change misconceptions.

To promote transfer, students need to go beyond memorizing facts to understand their relationships to real-world problem contexts. This is why it is so important that knowledge be presented in as many contexts as possible. Otherwise students will link the specific knowledge to the specific context and will not be able to untie the concept from the single context in which it has been presented (i.e., Dewey's water-tight packages). As an example, in the "Understanding Organizations" course, I ask students to apply the course concepts to several different organizations, and then we follow up these exercises 2 years later when they are working full time in their internship settings.

Putnam and Borko (2000) addressed the issue of transfer within the framework of the debate about what constitutes an "authentic" classroom environment. One way to judge whether a classroom learning situation is "authentic" is whether the classroom learning is useful to the students in future problem-solving situations outside the school setting. There are a variety of ways to think about what qualities need to be present in the learning experience to facilitate transfer. One approach represented by the work of J. S. Brown (Brown, Collins, & Duguid, 1989) started with the idea that the social practices in the classroom need to match the social practices in the setting where the knowledge is used. From this perspective, the professor needs to analyze the qualities of the social environments students will enter after graduation, such as the leadership styles, group structure, patterns of communication, and decision-making styles used in corporate environments. Jonassen and Rohrer-Murphy (1999) identified four characteristics that learning environments should attempt to produce: (a) activity structures, (b) tools and sign systems, (c) sociocultural rules, and (d) community expectations. Looking at learning from this perspective radically affects the look and feel of our classrooms.

Several cognitive scientists have pointed to the obvious differences between the way that inquiry, problem solving, and learning take place in schools and the way learning takes place in a typical work setting (Pea, 1993; Putnam & Borko, 2000; Resnick, 1987). School learning is highly individualistic; work-site learning has a high degree of social scaffolding and is usually carried out in cooperative work teams.

Bransford and Schwartz (2001) broadened the scope of the discussion of transfer by posing new questions about the link between how knowledge is acquired and how transfer is measured. The power of many instructional methods associated with constructivism comes from the way concepts are acquired (e.g., becoming involved in a group project that involves systematic inquiry and solving an authentic problem embedded in a meaningful context). Bransford and Schwartz questioned whether the ways that most research measures transfer are appropriate to measure learning in classrooms using constructivist perspectives. In this context, real transfer involves more than the application of knowledge to new situations; it includes increased ability to identify problems and ask appropriate questions, better ways of approaching and framing problems, and skill at gathering new information.

Bransford and Schwartz (2001) specifically addressed the conditions under which transfer should be measured. They pointed out that, in most research, transfer is assessed in "sequestered problem-solving" situations. In a sequestered situation, a student is asked to retrieve knowledge and solve new problems without access to reference materials or dialogue with fellow students. This makes the transfer task different from either the learning situation or the typical situation in which knowledge would be applied. If the initial learning task takes place in an authentic context, the retrieval task should also be authentic. Given the differences between the nature of the learning situation and the nature of sequestered problem-solving situations that rely on retrieving memorized facts, we might expect that students in a constructivist curriculum would perform more poorly on the transfer task than students in traditional programs. For example, their research on the use of the method of contrasting cases to help students learn to identify the salient features of a problem situation found that the students in the program did not exhibit superior performance until their next attempt to learn new material. They recommend broader use of dynamic assessment techniques. This type of assessment asks students to learn something new and measures their ability to acquire new knowledge rather than asking them to demonstrate what they have already learned. Transfer is evidenced by increased capacity to learn in the new situation.

Another perspective on transfer is represented by the work of Ann Brown (Brown, Ash, Rutherford, Nakagawa, Gordon, & Campione, 1993). In this view, the focus is on reproducing the kinds of problem solving that will be required in the postgraduation environment. Using this approach, it is not necessary that the activities engaged in by the students are accurate simulations of the activities of people in the application settings. Many professors, especially those teaching in liberal arts programs, are preparing students to enter a wide variety of settings. It is obvious that they cannot re-create a range of settings that students will enter after graduation, but they can create situations that demand the kinds of communication, thinking, and problem-solving skills that will serve students well in other environments.

CONCLUSION

The next chapter focuses on an area of particular concern for constructivist theories of teaching and learning. Chapter 7 addresses issues related to dialogue and diversity. This is important because so much of the success of learning in a combined constructivist classroom depends on the quality of the dialogue, particularly the quality of dialogue across cultures, classes, and communities of practice.

Open Dialogue, Disciplinary Discourse, and Diversity in the Learning Community

No curriculum is really defined by the specific teaching techniques it uses. Effective teaching methods are aligned with theory, but embedded in the context of their use. The effectiveness of any specific method of instruction, like lecturing or working in small groups, depends on when and how it is used. Traditional lecturers think they can transmit what they know directly to the learner. Most lecturers have not done a lot of thinking about exactly how this might work, but I suspect a lot of professors using group work could not articulate the processes of meaning construction taking place in student problem-solving groups. The Achilles' heel of the lecture method lies in the difficulty and talent required to connect with and motivate students who do not happen to have a pressing problem that the content of the lecture will help them solve. The problem of promoting the proper types of dialogue between students, especially between students from diverse cultural backgrounds, is the most important and difficult challenge facing professors who want to implement a teaching model derived from a constructivist perspective.

The proponents of each theory of learning and model of teaching tend to focus on its strengths and success stories. This book highlights the advantages of seeing learning through a transactional constructivist lens. Like every approach, a teaching model developed from a combined constructivist perspective has weaknesses as well as strengths. Every model, in fact, faces some daunting threat to its success. The real challenge of implementing any model is identifying and addressing the problems presented by the elements of the model that are most likely to fail. This chapter focuses on the theoretical and practical significance of open dialogue and productive disciplinary discourse.

The conversations that take place in classrooms play a central role in achieving learning objectives and overcoming the forces that can short-circuit learning. It is difficult to promote open dialogue across cultural barriers in any setting. This task is even more daunting in classrooms because it is also important to foster productive disciplinary discourse. Because disciplinary discourse is shaped by the values of the dominant culture, the two objectives can come into conflict. The bulk of this chapter addresses issues of dialogue and diversity, but it is important to keep in mind that conversations in university classrooms are about important disciplinary questions. They have to move toward forms of discourse that reflect the way that the discipline approaches and addresses problems. One of the most important roles professors play in classroom dialogues is to manage this paradox by mediating between the classroom learning community and disciplinary standards (Gregory, 2002).

This chapter provides philosophical, theoretical, and research support for the assertion that the quality of dialogue and disciplinary discourse in small groups and class discussions is the most problematic aspect of the constructivist models. If it is clear that the lecture may not reach a large portion of the students, it is also clear that cooperative learning does not work well unless it is done correctly. Despite their enthusiasm, research does not always support the methods touted by constructivists. In a meta-analysis of research on methods of teaching science problem solving, Taconis, Ferguson-Hessler, and Broekkamp (2001) found that having students work in small groups had a negative effect on the development of scientific problem-solving skills unless other features were present in the teaching methods used. They identified attention to schema construction, external guidelines, and immediate feedback as the key factors. All of these features were included in the model for the "Understanding Organizations" course.

The bulk of this book has focused on why I think methods derived from a combined constructivist perspective will produce more useful learning. A key element in the learning process in classrooms informed by this perspective is the quality of dialogue in the learning community. The students who read newspapers in our lectures may end up talking about fraternity parties in our small-group activities. It is important to acknowledge that it is difficult to promote open communication in learning communities.

OPEN DIALOGUE IN A COMMUNITY OF LEARNERS

Dialogue is important in constructivist models in two separate but interactive ways. First, productive disciplinary dialogue plays a central role in the process of building new knowledge structures. For example, when professors help students develop a useful sign system by scaffolding the significa-tion process from concrete experience to an abstract sign system, it re-quires a certain type of dialogic interaction. The professor's skill at managing the dialogue can be the difference between the students storing inert knowledge or finding more adaptive ways to solve problems that tran-scend but stay connected to students' previous knowledge.

Just as Dewey (1927/1954) defined democracy as a mode of associated living, our students' experience with open dialogue can build essential democratic citizenship skills. Unless educational institutions can develop the skills needed to communicate across cultural boundaries, education's potential for advancing the cause of social justice will be neutralized. If edu-cation is to play a role in developing a more effective democratic society that utilizes the talents of an increasingly diverse population, it has to play a role in increasing communication and understanding across cultural boundaries. This can only be accomplished by creating open communica-tion that at least partially transcends the structural boundaries of the domi-nant culture.

The two functions of dialogue (increasing conceptual understanding through disciplinary discourse and enhancing mutual understanding) are enmeshed because students' inability to communicate with each other im-pacts the inquiry process and consequently affects their ability to acquire useful knowledge. There is a transactional relationship between the con-ceptual development and the cultural boundary-crossing functions of dia-logue that can enhance its effect in either a positive or negative direction. The students' ability to coordinate the inquiry process and the effectiveness of students' ability to help their fellow students across the zone of proximal development depend on their ability to communicate with each other across cultural barriers. Communication feeds back into the goal of pro-moting a more democratic and competent society because the communica-tion skills required for effective learning are practical skills for working to-gether in society.

Dewey, Vygotsky, and the constructivists view learning as an intersub-jective activity: as knowledge construction in a community of inquiry. Com-munication around meanings, the methods of inquiry, and the process for reaching agreement on how conclusions will be assessed are central to the learning process. Dialogue is seen as the primary mechanism for reaching a shared understanding about what questions should be addressed (Wells, 2000).

Transmission models of teaching are embedded in a system of social practices that discourage authentic knowledge construction. By this I mean that the social relationships and styles of communication that are part of the structure of the social practices of the traditional classroom are in-authentic in two important ways. First, they disconnect students from communicating with each other in ways that facilitate knowledge building in a community of cooperative inquiry. If Dewey and the constructivists are correct about the conditions under which useful knowledge is developed, competitive classroom environments that pit students against each other rather than engaging them in cooperative inquiry are not effective learning environments. In traditional classrooms, fairness means that each individual student has equal exposure to the course content under the rules of the game, not that each student gets the resources he or she needs to learn the material.

Traditional classrooms are also inauthentic in the sense that they embed knowledge in a social communication context that is quite different from the problem-identification and problem-solving environments students will encounter outside the school. In most professional work situations, we frequently consult with each other to check our approaches to solving a problem. The "rules of the game" for school are quite different than the rules for academic activities like writing a journal article, where input from colleagues makes a legitimate contribution to the quality of the final product. In school, students are supposed to communicate their knowledge in what Bransford and Schwartz (2001) called a "sequestered problem-solving environment." Cooperation is seen as a form of cheating. Learning to solve problems cooperatively is an important skill for working successfully in a learning organization.

THE ROLE OF DIALOGUE IN DEWEY'S PHILOSOPHY

Young (1992) labeled the traditional classroom that focuses on eliciting "correct" answers from students the *method classroom* because it focuses on methods of teaching rather than the learning process. Dialogue in the method classroom is characterized by what Dewey referred to as *mechanical communication*. Mechanical communication is designed to manipulate the listener. Dewey (1916) compared normal communication between people with mutual concern for each other with mechanical communication:

> By normal communication is meant that in which there is a joint interest, a common interest, so that one is eager to give and the other to take. It contrasts with telling or stating things simply for the sake of impressing them on another, merely in order to test him to see how much he has retained and can literally reproduce. (p. 217, MW: 9.225)

Dewey believed that inquiry and learning are inherently social and always involve meaningful communication. Much of the communication in the traditional classroom, especially the communication directed from teachers to students, is not meaningful to students because no specific mechanisms are provided to connect new learning to the student's personal experience and existing knowledge. Both Dewey and the constructivists put dialogue, especially dialogue between students, in a central position in the learning process. Dewey, the activity theorists, and supporters of the situated cognitive positions also share a view of thinking as socially distributed rather than completely contained within the minds of individuals. Thinking and reasoning, especially in the early stages of the learning process, do not occur totally or even primarily "inside the head."

Educational models based on transactional constructivist theories cannot overcome the existing social practices of schooling that work against cooperative learning unless they can promote certain types of dialogue. Nonfoundationalist learning models like Dewey's believe that we justify our beliefs through a social consensus-building process, rather than by comparing the knowledge to some universal standard. There is an inherent tension between the development of meaning within cultural boundaries and the necessity of promoting inclusiveness across boundaries to develop adaptive solutions to important problems. Classroom communication must awaken and contribute to students' self-motivated efforts to construct their own knowledge. If teacher communication is designed to transmit knowledge out of context, it will be disconnected from the students' experience and will remain inert in the sense that it will not be available to facilitate problem solving in the future. This is the basis for Dewey's privileging of dialogue in the educational process.

Dewey's focus on the importance of democracy and his careful attempts to define what he meant when he used the term *democracy* acknowledge his awareness that our natural tendency to form communities may be too fragile to survive without support from strong institutions (D. J. Simpson, 2001). A viable democracy is the necessary context for a society that enhances the development of its members. In the classroom, strong structural supports and specific communications skill development are required to maintain the types of social practices that enhance learning.

There is a strong link between the way Dewey conceptualized democracy and the types of classrooms he designed. Classrooms in progressive schools, like today's constructivist classrooms, were characterized by groups in dialogue to solve meaningful problems. Eldridge (1998) summarized this view:

Democracy is the best form of shared experience because, through its open processes of consultation and change, individuals and groups can expand their common interests and common space. Democracy is thus the social manifestation of intelligence—that is, the deliberate reconstruction of experience by a group. It is the way in which collectives adjust themselves over time to the new situations in which they find themselves. (p. 27)

For Dewey, democracy was a superior social arrangement because it was the most adaptive social arrangement (i.e., it would promote growth in its citizens).

Dewey's focus on communication was connected to his commitment to and faith in democracy as a way to live in a community. Dewey saw democracy as the optimal way to build cooperative communities on the local, face-to-face level. Democracy requires people to engage in dialogue to define problems, negotiate change, and reach consensus on their common interests. The processes of democracy expand intelligent behavior from the individual to the group level and allow the positive effects of distributed cognition to increase the adaptive capacity of the group as a whole. The group as an adaptive unit is more powerful than the individual. In the natural environment, the individual increases his or her chances of survival by connecting to the group.

> The principle that development of experience comes about through interaction means that education is essentially a social process. The quality is realized in the degree in which individuals form a community group. (Dewey, 1938a, p. 58; LW: 13.36)

Dewey believed that learning takes place in the context of social communication. Dewey's (1927/1954) concept of cognitive processes matches the distributed cognitive model of many of today's situative cognitive models:

> Their final actuality is accomplished in face-to-face relationships by means of direct give and take. Logic in its fulfillment recurs to the primitive sense of the word: dialogue. Ideas that are not communicated, shared, and reborn in expression are but soliloquy, and soliloquy is but broken and imperfect thought. (p. 371, LW: 2.271)

Dewey's vision of experience shaped his faith in democracy. Bernstein (1971) summarized Dewey's belief about the overall goals of democracy by saying that it should create a "freer and more human experience in which all share and to which all contribute" (p. 224). Dewey's philosophy focuses on the picture of people as actors that can shape their lives for the better. Yet because we are social animals, change must come about by reshaping our institutions so they are places where people can achieve positive growth. We need to develop a genuine community of inquirers. Dewey's model indicates that the professor should create a learning community in the classroom and challenge students to solve problems in ways that promote adaptive growth.

Within Dewey's philosophy, creating situations where different kinds of people are engaged in face-to-face, undistorted communication is an indispensable feature of an educative experience. We need communication between diverse people because we need to hear ideas that disrupt our ways of seeing things. For Garrison (1997), the key factors that allow people to escape cultural determinism are the power of the imagination and exposure to other perspectives through open dialogue. This applies not only to communication across cultural barriers like race and gender, but to communication across the communities of practice of students and disciplinary scholars.

The idea that the classroom should function as a learning community is linked to several of the basic philosophical positions held by constructivists—most notably the idea that knowledge is contextualized, the social context of knowledge building, and the importance of dialogue and reflection for building both useful knowledge and metacognitive skills. The nature of a learning community is to build a culture characterized by critical thinking and reflection that fully utilizes the expertise distributed throughout the group.

VYGOTSKY'S VIEW OF CLASSROOM DIALOGUE

Many of the basic ideas presented about Vygotsky's theory in previous chapters have direct implications for constructivist views of dialogue and its central position in the learning process. Vygotsky reversed the traditional model of language and thinking by saying that we can think because we can converse: Thinking is internalized conversation. As we internalize speech, we construct knowledge and internalize the social structure of the culture by learning and using the language according to the social practices of the culture. In essence, we make our minds by talking. We are participating in the context of the culture even when we think to ourselves because we are using language—a cultural artifact.

Placing learning in a social context leads to increasing recognition of the central role that language and other cultural artifacts play in mediating learning. Many of the specific methods employed in constructivist classrooms (e.g., having students work in small groups, having groups of students make presentations of their projects) are based on the assertion of Vygotsky and other theorists that articulating ideas externalizes thinking and facilitates knowledge construction. In Vygotsky's educational model, "making knowledge visible" is an important mechanism for organizing knowledge.

Recognition of the central role of dialogue in knowledge construction is historically associated with Vygotsky's view that cognitive development is imbedded in the social environment, particularly the linguistic/cultural environment. The individual's mental structures are internalized from social practices that are imbedded in the context of cultural practice. It is not just the words that are internalized, but the structure of the dialogue and the whole matrix of meaning associated with it. The mechanics of internalization involve mediational tools, especially language, that link lower functions to higher functions. Several of Vygotsky's key concepts depend on a permeable boundary between the person and environment. Vygotsky's best-known teaching principle—the zone of proximal development—depends on the idea that the mental structures of an individual can be actively shared and supported by/with other minds and other supportive mediational tools (e.g., tables, templates) during the concept construction process. Another person (e.g., teacher, coach, fellow student) with a more organized knowledge of the subject under study can provide scaffolding for the learning process to support the development of structures while they are "under construction." Newman, Griffin, and Coleman (1989) provided a good definition of *zone of proximal development* that captures this perspective:

> [the zone of proximal development] refers to an interactive system within which people work on a problem which at least one of them could not, alone, work on effectively. . . . [T]he zone is considered both in terms of an individual's developmental history and in terms of the support structure created by other people and cultural tools in the setting. (p. 61)

The thinking person in Vygotsky's framework is always seen as a person actively transacting with the environment, rather than as an isolated individual manipulating pieces of ideas into a structure inside his or her own mind.

HABERMAS' VIEW OF DIALOGUE

Habermas' view of the role of dialogue was compatible with Vygotsky's and Dewey's in the sense that they all diverged from traditional epistemology to view knowledge as socially situated (R. E. Young, 1990). Habermas (1984) identified two types of social action: (a) strategic action that is oriented toward meeting a goal and achieving success, and (b) communicative action that is oriented toward reaching an understanding. Dialogue in classrooms should be about reaching mutual understanding; it tends to be about achieving individual success. In communicative action, participants "are not primarily oriented to their own individual successes; they pursue their individual goals under the condition that they can harmonize their plans of action on the basis of the common situation definitions" (Habermas, 1984, p. 286). Here Habermas referred to consensus decisions, not compromises and coerced agreements. In this situation, the worldviews of individuals meld and become one worldview. Reaching agreement on this level involves agreement on all three levels of validity claims: (a) objective reality (truth), (b) social reality (rightness), and (c) inner reality (truthfulness).

Habermas' belief in the possibility of open communication is similar to Dewey's commitment to participatory democracy. Habermas' communicative action offers a mechanism for creating the type of community Dewey strove to achieve. Habermas and Dewey both followed Mead's assertion that individual identity emerges from social interaction. This implies that we are made by our actions, rather than acting on the basis of who we are. "Habermas understands human subjectivity out of human intersubjectivity, and understands intersubjectivity in terms of action, albeit mainly in terms of speech acts" (Biesta, 1994, p. 311). To develop adaptive people and an adaptive democratic society, education should be built on purposeful social cooperation rather than pure cultural transmission. In traditional education built on the transmission model, students will develop "objective habitual identity," but no "reflexive self-conscious identity" (Biesta, 1994). Within an ideal democratic society characterized by communicative action, personal growth and the needs of all individuals can harmonize with values that promote the common good and the needs of the community.

Habermas' ideal of open communication is similar to several other models of communication. Some of these models are derived from Habermas' work and some come from other sources. Several models of open communication come from theories of psychological development. These models are grounded in developmental theory modeled after the reciprocal communication that characterizes secure attachment relationships that foster the optimal development of children (Bowlby, 1969). Mead's symbolic interactionism—one of the forerunners of Habermas' philosophy—also used our genetic predisposition to seek attachment and friendship as a foundation for our predisposition to communicate with each other. More recent open communication models are based on research in human ethology that supports the genetic need for attachment and community (Bowen, 1978; Gordon, 1970).

Habermas (1971) identified three interests that lie behind human action including our educational efforts: (a) the societal interest in controlling and shaping the learner's behavior to conform to society and prepare him or her for the workplace, (b) an interest in increasing understanding, and (c) an interest in reducing injustice and promoting liberation. R. Young (1992) pointed out that these three objectives can be separated for analytic purposes, but they are all actually present in all human activities. The classroom characterized by communicative action moves away from an exclusive focus on the first objective to focus more attention on the second and third.

Habermas (1990) developed a set of rules for argumentation that can serve as guidelines for classroom dialogue designed to facilitate a dialogue that fits the definition of *communicative action*:

1. Every subject with the competence to speak and act must be allowed to take part in the discourse.
2. (a) Everyone can question any assertion whatever.
   (b) everyone is allowed to introduce any assertion whatever.
   (c) everyone is allowed to assert his attitudes, desires and needs.
3. No speaker shall be coerced in any way (internally or externally) from their rights set out in 1 and 2. (p. 89)

Because Habermas' communicative action is initiated with the goal of reaching mutual understanding between actors about their common situation, it contains the potential for escaping a perspective bound by individual and cultural interests. As such, communicative action provides a process for reconfiguring social relationships between people with different cultural backgrounds. Communicative action, as a change strategy, is qualitatively different than strategies that add information about other cultures to the content of the curriculum. There is a difference between viewing another group of people's situation objectively (as content in the curriculum) and understanding the multiple perspectives of different actors in the same situation. Treating the problem of learning about other cultural groups as content removes the student from a position of subjective understanding of the other person's human experience (R. E. Young, 1990). The goal of praxis is precisely the opposite—to objectify the materialized world (rather than the other person) and allow people to reclaim their being within it.

If communicative action, as a process, can be incorporated as a core activity, it creates a vehicle for building a pedagogy of social justice. The concept of communities of inquiry is central to Dewey's educational philosophy. The critical importance of this issue is captured by Dewey's assertion that diversity is important because it is pedagogical. This statement supports the contention that Habermas' philosophy can be viewed as a natural extension of Dewey's. Without a method for reconstructing Dewey that resonates with the other elements of the model, the social justice theme is "tacked on" as content. This isolates social justice as something that will be transmitted to the students rather than lived in community. Adding social justice as content rather than process is using an essentialist method (transmission) in a constructivist model—making social justice an inert part of the curriculum. If the problem-solving process within a constructivist curriculum model is coordinated by communicative action, mutual understanding can be organically integrated into the lived experience of the classroom. Ideally, open dialogue includes an exploration of the ways that disciplinary conventions reflect and further existing power relationships. This conversation can then be extended to explore ways of involving marginalized groups as equal partners in inquiry (L. D. Brown, 1985).

It is important to understand that Habermas did not believe that pure communicative action could really be achieved. It is a model of communication for which we should strive (R. Young, 1992). In practice, the structural forces of the culture keep asserting themselves into efforts to maintain open communication. In research on a method that was specifically designed to give voice to marginalized students, Hawkins (2000) found that societal status hierarchies were re-created within the dialogues in student collaborative work groups. Although the tasks were designed to give equal validity to the input of all participants, the group members with the best traditional academic credentials tended to dominate the communication in the groups. This was not only because these leaders took control. The groups tended to turn to the students they viewed as "the smartest" to help the group succeed. This strategy makes sense if they assume they are "playing the school game" of "what does the teacher want?" (i.e., achieving individual success rather than reaching mutual understanding). The smartest student (and the other students) will usually be blind to the value of input from marginalized students. One reason for this, beyond the society's status structure, is that the marginalized group members do not know how to put their input in the "proper form." Turning to the smartest student makes sense if the goal is to get the best grade. They have proved themselves to be the best "grade getters." As a professor, I hope that the most competent students will scaffold learning in the areas where they really have the greatest skills. It is just as likely that he or she will take over the group and do the work to ensure that the group does not bring his or her grade down. An important goal of constructivist approaches is to access the "funds of knowledge" of students who have been marginalized in traditional classroom settings (Moll, 1992).

DEMOCRACY, DIVERSITY, AND SOCIAL JUSTICE

Dewey's (1927/1954) concepts of democracy and community focused on the way that people associate with each other in face-to-face communities rather than on democratic practices like voting. For Dewey, "a democracy is more than a form of government; it is primarily a mode of associated living, of conjoint community experience" (MW 9:93). Dewey (1927/1954) saw democracy as:

> a wider and fuller idea than can be exemplified in the state even at its best. To be realized it must affect all modes of human association, the family, the

school, industry, religion (p. 143) . . . regarded as an idea, democracy is not an alternative to other principles of associated life. It is the idea of community life itself. (p. 148, LW: 2.325 & 328)

The important implication of this stance for education is to understand that Dewey did not want schools to adopt democratic procedures. He did not want students to "vote on" the design of the curriculum. He wanted schools to create communities characterized by the forms of association that define the heart of democratic community life.

Long before human ethologists made this observation, Dewey (1927/ 1954) saw that individuals do not form groups—they develop in groups and live in groups from the beginning to the end of their lives. He was suspicious of the ability of big government to represent people unless it was an extension of dialogue in local communities, rather than an attempt to represent groups of individuals organized around special interests:

The Great Society created by steam and electricity may be a society, but it is no community . . . new and relatively impersonal and mechanical modes of combined human behaviors are the outstanding fact of modern life. (p. 98, LW: 2.297)

Later in *The Public and Its Problems,* he stated:

Till the Great Society is converted into the Great Community, the public will remain in eclipse. Communication can alone create the Great Community. Our babel is not one of tongues but of the signs and symbols without which shared experience is impossible. (p. 142, LW: 2.324)

There are important similarities between Dewey's ideas about democratic community life and the picture of the learning community drawn by modern learning scientists. Dewey's view of education makes it impossible to separate content knowledge from the process of learning and dialogue or the cultural artifacts that mediate its production. Experience is a system within which all other elements are embedded in a dynamic relationship. Because meaningful experience is defined by purposeful activity, values and content knowledge cannot be disentangled or decontextualized. When Dewey said that diversity is pedagogical, he was defining the conditions under which learning can occur. He believed that real learning could not occur without open dialogue between people who are different in some important way. Recent calls for a shift from the machine metaphor of organizations to a living systems metaphor that values diversity as adaptive are natural extensions of Dewey's insights (Senge, 1999).

The barriers to open communication are complex. Changing any kind of preexisting theory requires experience and participation in a learning community characterized by certain forms of association and communication. This is also true of our personal theories about proper ways to communicate and our stereotypes about other groups of people. Much of this knowledge operates on the unconscious level. The whole learning experience needs to support the goals of achieving civic responsibility, democratic participation, and commitment to social justice.

It is important not to interpret these statements as supporting educational experiences that merely "expose" students to diversity outside the context of real relationships and genuine communication. In the context of true dialogue, diversity can function as a catalyst for stimulating new ways of thinking and seeing the world; it cannot have this effect in either the transmission or spectator models of education. Gadamer (cited in Biesta, 1994) believed that it is important to communicate with other people within the context of understanding their entire life world. Understanding people within the context of their broader life world is important because meaning exists in context. Gadamer identified three ways we might experience other people that represent levels of understanding. Only the third level has real educational value: (a) knowing typical behaviors (we can predict how they will act); (b) acknowledging the other as a person, but only in a form of self-relatedness (he placed many forms of sympathy in this category); and (c) acknowledging our mutual positions as part of a different legitimate tradition. This is the highest form of hermeneutic experience. Achieving mutual understanding on this level requires communicative action: a two-way, sensitive-responsive dialogue.

Dewey's focus on transactional processes oriented him toward wanting to understand the processes of learning across structural boundaries. The role of dialogue across boundaries is similar to, but broader than, Vygotsky's analysis of what occurs at the leading edge of the zone of proximal development. As Cobb, Gravemeijer, Yackel, McClain, and Whitnack (1997) pointed out, Vygotsky's concept of teaching was a top–down model. Dewey saw learning as a two-way transactional process. Using a combined constructivist model, the way the experience is organized to scaffold learning and the way the dialogue in the learning community generates ideas allow the teacher to stimulate and guide the emergence of meaning. Creating an arena for dialogue around problems gives the professor student-generated ideas to link to scientific theories and research relevant to the problem under consideration. If the presenting problem engages students in meaningful problem solving, the professor's role can change from the authority figure who tells students the truth to a coach who helps them solve problems that genuinely interest them.

Habermas' transcendental approach reframed the problem of finding a foundation for a commitment to social justice by shifting the focus from the content to the process used for reaching agreement on ethical issues. He identified a set of rules for a communicative process that would yield a consensus decision that is fair to all the participants. Apel (1980) introduced the idea of "the ideal community of communication" characterized by unimpeded and uncoerced communication between people. Habermas and Apel developed a set of standards by which people should view each other and a set of rules of open communication that provide a transcendental critique to replace the critique based on absolute truth (Biesta & Stams, 2001). In this system, ethical disputes are settled when all who would be affected by a dispute have a free and open discussion and reach consensus on a solution. This is similar to Dewey's (1927/1954) solution. In Dewey's instrumentalism, all those who are affected by an action should be involved in the process of problem identification and inquiry to find a solution. This is not really a moral imperative. Dewey thought this is the process that will yield the most adaptive response. A solution that does not serve all of the constituencies will create tensions that will eventually be maladaptive. For Dewey, in the long run, working for the common good yields the most adaptive solutions.

Although Dewey carefully holds onto the individual's ability to take meaningful action, the person is highly contextualized in the community (both by nature and by culture). Dewey's naturalistic perspective is based on the fact that individuals are embedded in cultural groups and connected to groups by the mechanisms of adaptation and genetics. Working for the common good is adaptive, but not in the "survival of the fittest individual animal" sense. Within a cultural context, successful adaptation takes place on the community level and promotes the common good because the definition of a problem is anchored in culture and groups of people solve problems through inquiry. Individuals are not seen as growing if their learning isolates them from open communication and participation in community life or reduces the adaptive capacity of the community as a whole.

The problems of learning to function in a learning community whose members are drawn from different cultures are clear if we return to Petraglia's (1998) definition of *constructivism* as "the interdisciplinary view that we construct knowledge based on our cultural assumptions and prior experiences rather than through the efficient and rational calculation of the information at hand" (p. 4). Cross-cultural communication is problematic because mental models are highly scaffolded by cultural artifacts and language. If different cultures and communities of practice have different artifacts and language, they have to struggle to find common ground. Our stereotypes about ourselves and categories of other people shape our mental models of the communication we expect and "approve of." In addition to people of other races, religions, and genders, there are significant cultural gaps between professors and students as groups of people from different communities of practice with different ideas about how we should communicate.

Dewey and the constructivists shifted the focus of education from transmitting knowledge to creating environments that help students construct their own knowledge (Branford, Brown, & Cocking, 1999). Students in an ideal learning community are communicating openly in an inquiry process. Learners have to share a common problem definition and adopt a group goal. Within this framework, difference and diversity enhance the learning potential of the group if individuals contribute freely and listen openly across cultural barriers. If knowledge is constructed through social practices, the nature and quality of those practices are critical to learning. Dewey saw the relationship between knowledge structures and social practices and discourse as transactional. In Lave's terms (Lave & Wenger, 1991), the environment contains structuring resources that shape the cognition and behavior of participants. If learning is indeed dependent on developing new ways of participating in social practices (Cobb & Bowers, 1999), then reshaping social practices becomes a primary instructional goal.

Traditional learning theories tend to separate issues of learning from issues like freedom, social justice, and civic responsibility. Because Dewey and the constructivists see learning as an intersubjective process (rather than an intrasubjective process), classroom practices, diversity, social justice, and communication are all intimately involved in the learning process. The learning process occurs within the context of the learning community, therefore all these issues are part of the dynamics of the learning process. Experience within the cultural and naturalistic context is the ether for learning as growth and adaptive capacity.

Issues of social justice and diversity are central to both a functioning democracy and the classroom because they describe the way people should relate to each other and live together if they want to promote the positive growth of everyone in the community. The meaning of the word *diversity* in this context is not synonymous with race, gender, religion, and sexual preference. It is a much broader concept that seeks to include people with different ideas and different ways of thinking. Yet Dewey (1916) clearly thought that the democratic principles of association and open communication are "equivalent to the breaking down of those barriers of class, race, and national territory which keep men from perceiving the full import of their activity" (MW 9:93). Race, gender, and religion are important dimensions of diversity in our culture because they define the boundaries between people that have been problematized in this society. They form the patterns of inclusion and exclusion that function as barriers to open communication in our classrooms.

NEGOTIATING COMMUNICATION ACROSS
CULTURAL BOUNDARIES

A primary concern related to the functioning of effective learning communities is the systematic marginalization of certain categories of people. In Lave's apprenticeship model (Lave & Wenger, 1991), apprentices are seen as "legitimate peripheral participants." As apprentices move toward acquiring expertise, their participation becomes more central and more meaningful. You would expect to see the same process when new members join a learning community. However, this process of increasingly meaningful participation is often stunted because systems of power and oppression that exist in the larger society are imported into the group. This is not surprising because these unequal social relationships are interwoven in the culture and incorporated into the cultural artifacts that facilitate communication. Typically, groups that are marginalized in the larger society continue to be marginalized in the learning community and develop a pattern of *sustained peripheral participation.* This is a paradox because the same diversity that is essential for meaningful learning and finding effective solutions to difficult problems promotes exclusion.

Boud and Walker (1998) highlighted the complex difficulties involved in operationalizing Dewey's model when they pointed out the special problems involved with pushing students from oppressed cultures to reflect. If the students we label as diverse are also members of groups oppressed by the dominant majority in our society, open reflection may increase their vulnerability. This often places professors in a paradoxical position. Do we encourage vulnerable students to expose themselves "for the good of the community"? Habermas (1987) referred to this as the "colonization of the life world." In some cases, demands for reflection represent an intrusion of institutions like the school into the proper personal domain of the student. This makes it especially important for professors to clarify the boundaries of reflection.

The difficulties of promoting productive disciplinary dialogue across boundaries of culture and communities of practice is exacerbated by the fact that the standards we use to judge the quality of disciplinary dialogue are highly enmeshed with the conventions of the dominant culture. Because universities are major producers of cultural capital, they tend to foster standards that support the communication styles of the dominant culture. Most professors come from the dominant culture, so it is hard for us to separate "sound thinking" from "right thinking." This is an issue that cannot be resolved, but we can raise our consciousnesses about the inherent paradox we are dealing with when we try to foster disciplinary discourse across cultural barriers.

Derrida (1978) and the deconstructionists acknowledged that we can never totally escape the boundaries of our own system of thought. Any system that uses language as a way of thinking would find it hard to escape the conclusion that language is a cultural artifact and incorporates many of the structural elements of the culture. Derrida's approach deconstructs the structure of the language and the culture to turn them "on their heads." Deconstruction reveals the unspoken elements of the culture by bringing out what was silent and centralizing those who had been marginalized to reveal the injustices that are part of the structure of the system. Derrida and the postmodern thinkers place more emphasis on the particularity of the individual than on the fairness of the system, which is Habermas' focus. Unlike Habermas, postmodern theorists have abandoned the Enlightenment project and have less faith in the power of reason. They have developed a series of other strategies to account for and overcome the systems' power to obscure the existence of competing interests. Derrida added a dimension to the ethical debate when he added a focus on the uniqueness of the individual. Derrida replaced a focus on equal treatment as an ethical standard of fairness with a focus on caring. For Derrida, a focus on equal treatment threatens the autonomy of the individual person. In this frame of reference, we are obligated to care for other people on the basis of their need rather than simply making sure that every person has an equal right to speak (Honneth, 1995).

Lothstein (1978) asserted that Dewey saw "the concept of structure as processional, and the concept of diversity as pedagogical" (p. 57). Diversity is pedagogical because it plays a critical role in the development of communicative action in a community of learners. The dimensions of diversity represented in a group may or may not conform to definitions of diversity that promote particular political goals. Although it is reasonable to assert that groups of people disenfranchised by the dominant culture would bring a different and valuable worldview to the classroom dialogue, there may also be other groups with less political visibility whose worldviews would make powerful contributions.

The patterns of communication embedded in the social practices of classrooms reflect the patterns of privilege in society. Brickhouse (2001) pointed out that, although identities belong to individuals, they are crafted in social activity. This means changing patterns of dialogue so they do not reflect oppressive patterns in society is important because they reinforce negative patterns in individual identities. Because of their central importance in understanding identity and the dynamics of group process, focusing on understanding the dynamics of boundaries and ways to bridge them is the most fruitful way to understand the learning process.

Bruffee (1999) made a distinction between normal discourse (within a knowledge community and within that context accepted by the community as foundational) and boundary discourse at the edge of a knowledge community or between knowledge communities (e.g., scientists in a theory crisis). He used the example of the problems in crossing knowledge community boundaries experienced by writers like Richard Fynaman, a physicist, who attempted to write about biology. The problems and rewards of working across interdisciplinary boundaries have their parallels with students working across cultural boundaries. It is difficult and frustrating, but it can reap great rewards.

PRODUCTIVE DISCIPLINARY DISCOURSE

To achieve the specific goals of most university courses, students must acquire concepts, generalizable abstractions, and enduring understandings that can be used to frame and solve future problems. This statement would be accepted by most professors and most constructivists, with the exception of those holding strong sociocultural positions. Idea-focused constructivist approaches such as the combined and situated cognitive perspectives place ideas in social contexts. This focuses attention on the quality of disciplinary discourse.

Boxtel and Roelofs (2001) presented one set of guidelines that are representative of criteria used to assess the quality of disciplinary discourse:

1. The amount and type of discourse about the concepts that have been appropriated . . . 2. The amount and type of elaboration . . . 3. The amount and type of co-construction . . . 4. The use of available tools. (p. 56)

In its most general form, the first guideline indicates that we want students in our classes to discuss the problem situations they are addressing using concepts related to the course. For the most part, we expect those concepts to be drawn from the body of knowledge in our disciplines. We hope that the discussion moves beyond the concrete example to address the meaning of the concepts and their relationships to each other and the class of problems being discussed. Useful abstractions must be well structured and systematically connected to the types of problems they can be used to address. The professor and knowledgeable students play a critical role in linking concrete examples to abstractions and helping students understand how specific problems fit into a class of problems. In a situation where a professor has effectively scaffolded the development of understanding and corrected misconceptions, the new concepts will be more resistant to reverting back to the students' original everyday theories. It is especially important for professors to be aware of common misconceptions. One way we get information about common misconceptions is by paying attention to incorrect answers on examinations. Models of instruction that increase the amount of dialogue in the classroom provide an even richer arena for understanding student misconceptions.

Boxtel and Roelof's second criterion for increasing the quality of disciplinary discourse (the amount and type of elaboration observed) provides a marker for identifying more sophisticated discourse. If a student connects his or her remarks to a previous student's comments in a way that links both comments to course concepts, it is evidence that the class has moved from serial storytelling to Boxtel and Roelof's third criterion (co-constructing knowledge). We want to move our classes from the usual pattern of expressing unsupported opinions and telling self-referenced stories that are loosely related to the concepts in the course to reasoning together about important problems. This will only happen if students inquire about and actively listen to their fellow students. Boxtel and Roelof's final criterion (the use of available tools) provides further evidence of productive disciplinary discourse. If students refer to the readings, lectures, cases, and so on used in the course, they show evidence that they can use disciplinary resources to solve problems.

Following Vygotsky's (1978) model for the internalization of concepts and principles from dialogue, the quality of classroom discourse about important disciplinary ideas is central to the development of disciplinary understanding. Wertsch and Toma (1995) identified two basic forms of classroom communication: (a) univocal (one-way) communication that characterizes transmission styles of teaching, and (b) dialogic discourse (transactional, two-way communication) that represents the goal of teaching models derived from constructivist perspectives. Wertsch and Toma made a key theoretical point when they pointed out that dialogic communication both scaffolds the development of useful abstractions and internalizes the form of dialogic discourse as an internal cognitive capacity. Good thinking skills are internalizations of good dialogic skills.

It may be difficult to facilitate the development of and promote the use of dialogic discourse. Blanton (2002) found that dialogic discourse facilitated the development of mathematical understanding in an undergraduate geometry course, but she also found that increasing dialogic disciplinary discourse required specific methods to focus students' attention on the quality of their own dialogue. She had students code transcripts of their class discussion as univocal or dialogic. Coding data on their own dialogue increased the students' awareness of this distinction and increased the amount of dialogic disciplinary discourse. This style of communication also transferred to discussions around pedagogy.

Engle and Conant (2002) tied productive disciplinary engagement to the instructional strategies used by constructivists. They identified four ways to foster productive disciplinary engagement in classrooms: "(a) problematizing subject matter, (b) giving students authority to address such problems, (c) holding students accountable to others and to shared disciplinary norms, and (d) providing students with relevant resources" (p. 399). In essence, they were saying that if we create authentic problem spaces for students and provide them with resources to address these problems, they will be motivated to become actively engaged in solving these problems. If we hold students "accountable to others and to shared disciplinary norms," their discussion will help them develop the communication and metacognitive skills to become legitimate participants in productive disciplinary learning communities. If this acculturation process were successful, we would expect students to exhibit increasingly competent argumentation skills. We would also expect them to show increasing ability to use other students' ideas and the ideas of the discipline to inform their own thinking.

Although we encourage students to challenge ideas from the established body of knowledge, these challenges should be addressed on the level of theory and evidence rather than on unsubstantiated opinion. In the specific example Engle and Conant (2002) discussed, they stimulated discussion about the classification of animals in a biology class. One of the types of evidence they want students to bring into the discussion is anatomical evidence. A contribution that qualifies as legitimate disciplinary discourse has to connect the anatomical feature of the animal under investigation to the classification system. Knowing the criteria and understanding its relevance to a broader discussion of adaptation is evidence that the student is acquiring useful knowledge related to the focus of the course. Connecting opinions to evidence is a primary goal of most university courses. In the "Understanding Organizations" course, these principles were articulated within the Argyris II model of communication and the criteria for dialogic discourse. In Argyris' system, *high advocacy* includes explaining the reasons why you hold your position and presenting evidence to support it. *High inquiry* means listening until you understand the speaker's position well enough to paraphrase it to his or her satisfaction.

DIALOGUE IN CURRENT TEACHING MODELS
DRAWN FROM CONSTRUCTIVIST PERSPECTIVES

Hawkins' (2000) example of the reassertion of status hierarchies in student discussion groups has parallels with many academic conversations both inside the classroom and among professors. Many academic interchanges are part of "the academic game" rather than being a learning experience. This is what Keefer, Zeitz, and Resnick (2000) labeled *eristic discussion*. Eristic discussions are situations where the objective is to "win the argument," rather than gain deeper understanding. The problem of achieving open communication in a group is complicated by the fact that discourse includes communication that expresses the identities of the group members (Lee & Smagorinsky, 2000). Communication is mediated with language and other cultural tools. These are the tools we use to understand ourselves and other people. It is important to keep in mind that threats to identity will be met with heavy resistance. To the extent that a person's identity is tied to their social status (and it almost always is), he or she will resist any situation that threatens that status.

Lemke (2001) also pointed out that the two areas of knowledge construction and communication across boundaries strongly interact with each other. The process that teachers use to negotiate their social relationships with students creates the arena for teaching and learning. The social distance between students and professors in traditional classrooms is large. If the distance is extended by basic cultural differences, the task of bridging that gap is even more formidable. In each instance of dialogue, it is difficult to move past games and barriers erected by cultural differences and group members defending their identities. Creating communicative action within dialogue is even more difficult because so many structures operate outside our consciousness.

Lemke's (2001) research on discourse analysis demonstrated a close relationship between learning and the way that students and teachers negotiated their social relationships. Lemke concluded that students, especially marginalized students such as those who were less fluent in English, needed more time to acquire concepts than the other students in the course. There is a "Catch 22" between Lemke's findings and Hawkins' (2000) observation that hierarchies reassert themselves within student groups. There is no easy solution to this problem, but it is important to be aware that social hierarchies are always present and threaten the quality of the learning experience.

In combined constructivist models of education, the primary dialogic roles of the professor in the classroom are to renegotiate the norms of social practice, provide support for new modes of interaction between themselves and the students and between the students, and "label" knowledge constructed by students to link it to the body of knowledge in the field under study. In instances where students have developed misconceptions about the best solution to a problem, we enter the dialogue as experts. Students can then compare their ideas with our ideas. This is an example of Cobb's bottom–up version of Vygotsky's procedure for linking student experience to the body of knowledge. Although this could be perceived as stopping to say, "Oh, here is the *right* answer," it is different psychologically. The students have their own ideas that are connected to their own experience, "out on the table." These ideas are available to compare with the knowledge that has been developed in the community of scholars in the discipline. In this situation, the new knowledge may be rejected, but there is much less chance that the expert knowledge will be categorized as "school knowledge," which does not have to be considered because it has nothing to do with life outside the school.

Learning how to time and articulate professor input is tricky. Students have been playing the "What answer does the teacher want?" game all of their lives. It is difficult to change well-honed social practices and create dialogic discourse (Blanton, 2002). I found that creating this type of classroom dialogue was a new skill that took a while to develop. It was difficult for me to learn new ways of communicating in the classroom (at first, quite unsuccessfully) with students complaining and asking me to go back to my old way of teaching.

MODELS OF COMMUNICATIVE ACTION
IN THE CLASSROOM

Dewey and Habermas shared a faith in the possibility of open, undistorted communication as a foundation for a well-functioning democratic society. Biesta (1994) used the term *practical intersubjectivity* to describe a concept she developed by integrating ideas from Dewey, Habermas, and George Herbert Mead. Her project was to develop a synthesis of critical theory and pragmatism called *critical pragmatism*. This concept has two elements: (a) Intersubjectivity—We should not begin with a self-conscious individual subject to understand human relationships, but the other way around. We should understand human subjectivity by beginning with human interaction. (b) Practical intersubjectivity—We should understand the process of "human intersubjectivity in terms of action" (p. 301; communicative practice). We should understand the development of practical intersubjectivity in the context of joint activity in a purposeful social context. Biesta's synthesis was an attempt to overcome some of the biases that exist in present theories of action. Her view of the self is similar to Dewey's. She wanted to avoid seeing the person as a totally independent actor "deciding" to act, but also rejected determinist structural theories that do not recognize human agency. She argued for a position like Habermas' that focuses on communicative action designated to increase "mutual understanding." Her view of education as a "co-constructive process in a symmetrical relationship" is supported by research in cognitive science (A. Brown, 1997; Bransford, Brown, & Cocking, 1999).

Bereiter (1994) outlined a model of progressive discourse that shows the connection between open communication and knowledge building. He presented guidelines for progressive discourse as a social contract that confirm the responsibility of participants to act in a way that promotes effective inquiry. These guidelines represent the type of dialogue required for productive inquiry:

1. To work toward common understanding satisfactory to all;
2. To frame questions and propositions in ways that allow evidence to be brought to bear on them;
3. To expand the body of collectively valid propositions;
4. To allow any belief to be subjected to criticism if it will advance the discourse. (p. 6)

Wells (2000) used these guidelines to conduct a progressive discourse as part of his model of the "spiral of knowing." Wells saw curriculum planning as creating arenas for dialogue around mutually important problems. The spiral of knowing is similar to the iterative/recursive constructivist learning model presented in the last chapter. Learners cycle through experience (e.g., group inquiry), information (e.g., reading and lectures), knowledge building (e.g, progressive dialogue), and understanding.

Several key teaching strategies employed by combined constructivists share an assumption with Vygotsky, Dewey, and Habermas that knowledge is socially constructed. This assumption places communication and dialogue in a privileged position in the learning process. This is a key issue when it comes to dealing with some of the most difficult problems with the basic philosophy of constructivism. Rejecting the idea that knowledge is foundational and emphasizing the important role of dialogue between students who are constructing their own knowledge change the role of the teacher. This shift away from the teacher as the transmitter of truth to the teacher as architect of the learning environment and participating member of the community of learners leaves most educators on unfamiliar ground unsure of where their lines of authority begin and end. In the real world of the classroom, teachers have authority to develop curriculum, set objectives, and evaluate student performance. Experiences have to be organized to produce knowledge, and teachers need to know what learning is essential and possible in each lesson. However, if students are going to be recognized as competent partners in the learning process, it will require a renegotiation of the relationships among teachers, knowledge, and students.

R. Young (1992) developed a model for classroom discourse based on Habermas' philosophy. He characterized the traditional or method classroom as being dominated by manipulative communication that treats students as objects. Young cited the following description of the tasks of the traditional method classroom from research conducted by Smith and Geoffrey (1968). Teachers in these classrooms saw their roles as "covering" the content in the curriculum and keeping the students under enough control to allow them to reach the curriculum's objectives as measured by their performance on achievement tests. Young cited several classroom studies published over a long period of time that matched his own finding that at least 75% of classroom time is devoted to teacher talk. Most teacher talk consisted of questions that were designed to elicit material students had committed to memory (Hoekter & Ahlbrand, 1969; Stevens, 1912; R. Young, 1992). In my own experience of gathering data using interaction analysis techniques in a variety of classrooms, teacher talk always made up 80% to 85% of the total. Invariably, however, teachers were under the impression that their talk and the students' talk were about equal.

In observations of traditional method classrooms, R. Young (1992) found that a large portion of student communications could be characterized as "looking for the right answer" and "guessing what the teacher thinks." These "classroom games" are at the heart of the analysis of why school learning fails to produce useful knowledge. The way school material is usually memorized is strongly tied to the particular context of the school, the course, and the testing situation. Students leaving an exam often joke that they need to quickly erase all the material from that exam so they have room to store what they need to learn for tomorrow's exam. Unfortunately, this is not far from the truth. Students have honed their study skills to achieve success in a very narrow set of circumstances. The attitude of "guessing what the teacher wants" is even more destructive to the development of useful knowledge structures because it removes the entire process from the arena of ideas and their application to problem solving. The problem presented by the professor is replaced by the problem of guessing what the teacher thinks. The students are playing a perceptual matching game rather than working to integrate the new ideas with their existing concepts and experience. Their attention is directed at the guessing game. Many of the skills students acquire for playing this guessing game have to do with looking for nonverbal cues from the teacher, rather than thinking about the ideas under consideration.

Managing a classroom discourse is problematic because it is difficult to push students to use better inquiry and thinking skills without triggering the "what does the teacher think" sequence. The student does not have any precedent for interactions with teachers that are more egalitarian. When the communication becomes more transactional and the social distance between the professor and student is reduced, students are rightfully suspicious. Students expect professors to fall back on their position of authority if their intellectual expertise is questioned. Challenging the teacher can be a dangerous game. I found that it was easier to produce this type of conversation in the "Understanding Organizations" course if I introduced questions that I was actually still confused about myself. The students seemed to know when I was sincerely unsure of the answer to a question, and the quality of the conversations was much richer. There are many areas in organizational theory where the research evidence is fairly unclear and the opinions of researchers vary. In discourse classrooms, special attention is paid to maintaining the positions and views held by people, with every participant having an equal opportunity to make their case. The professor's authority in these dialogues does not come from their position as the teacher, but by demonstrating that his or her expertise is useful and his or her thinking is sound. The professor's view is expressed but submitted for evaluation just like the students' views. For example, Young (1992) found that when teachers in constructivist classrooms summarized their conclusions, they frequently invited students to say whether they personally agreed or disagreed with the teacher's conclusions. Classrooms characterized by high-quality discourse also had higher incidences of students asking questions of the teacher and other students. In my "Understanding Organizations" course, I hoped that students would ask clarifying questions of other students and ask students why they held the opinions they did, rather than simply replying with their own opinions.

Chapter 8

"Understanding Organizations" Case Study II

Although this book makes a strong case for a combined constructivist approach to teaching and learning, I would be the first to acknowledge that the transition from a transmission to a constructivist model is difficult for both professors and students. For reasons discussed in chapter 7, the most difficult behaviors to change are patterns of communication and other classroom social practices. The social context provides one of the most important supports for learning.

I am convinced that the teaching model I used in the "Understanding Organizations" course was effective for producing useful knowledge. I have seen clear evidence that the students in the course dramatically increased their ability to use theories to understand organizations and propose solutions to organizational problems. After a rocky beginning in the first year I taught the course, students produced increasingly impressive work and developed a much richer understanding of the enduring principles. Their ability to identify problems in unstructured problem situations improved considerably. The quality of their written work and their ability to justify their observations and recommendations with research, theories, and deep principles has been especially impressive. My course ratings dipped during the first year I taught the course, but were strong for the latest version of the course despite that my section of the course required more work and the average grade in the course was lower. Student satisfaction with the course is now equal to or better than the satisfaction of previous students in courses that I taught using more conventional designs.

In contrast to my satisfaction with the course's success in the area of conceptual development, I would characterize my efforts to improve the quality of the disciplinary discourse in large-class discussions as a "work in progress." The quality of dialogue and disciplinary discourse in small-group discussions has been much better, but still falls short of my goal. As this aspect of the course has improved, I see a clear connection between the quality of the dialogue and the quality of the students' learning.

BASIC ASSUMPTIONS OF A COMBINED
CONSTRUCTIVIST APPROACH
TO UNDERGRADUATE TEACHING

This chapter explores some of the challenges I faced when I attempted to change the social practices in the "Understanding Organizations" course. First, I revisit the basic assumptions of a combined constructivist approach that relate directly to issues of social practices, identity, dialogue, and disciplinary discourse. I reflect on how well the "Understanding Organizations" course was able to function in a way that exemplified each of these assumptions.

The fifth basic assumption introduced in chapter 1 was that useful knowledge is socially constructed in learning communities. This principle highlights a central theoretical premise of the combined model. It reflects the assertion that knowledge construction is embedded in the social practices of the classroom. A growing appreciation for the implications of this principle reshaped my own definition of what it means to be "an architect of the educational environment." As a teacher and consultant designing open classrooms early in my career, I viewed instructional design as orchestrating an encounter between curriculum materials and the students' ideas. I would stand in classrooms and imagine how students would approach and encounter the physical materials I had left for them to explore. If I designed a science activity, I tended to think first about how my instructions and the way the materials were organized would stimulate certain kinds of thinking, inquiry, and discovery. I would ask myself whether students would discover and internalize the deep principles that underlay the solutions to the problems I would present to them. I focused my attention on what students would do when they interacted with my design. Although the problems I designed for open classrooms were almost always solved by groups of students, and I imagined they would discuss alternative approaches and solutions, I did not fully appreciate the importance of the dialogue. Now I tend to see almost every element of a course design in terms of the kinds of *dialogue* it will create.

In the "Understanding Organizations" course, the *classroom* extended to a network of learning environments that reached into meetings held outside of the room where the class was scheduled and outside the normal class time, to Internet communication, and into interviews with managers in organizations in the community. Conversations about the course content were always anchored in the various problem contexts presented in the cases. This put dialogue and disciplinary discourse in the context of goal-directed group activity. The personal organization case connected the other cases in the course to each student's previous organizational experiences. Conversations in groups and the standard that asked students to draw parallels between their personal case and the other cases helped students integrate and reconcile their past, present, and future experiences. The focus on dialogic communication and productive disciplinary discourse as a definition of an ideal learning community has increased each time the course has been taught. The most recent change in the course has been to add a simple observation tool to help focus the students' attention on the importance of high-quality dialogue. This tool is described later in this chapter.

The eighth principle listed in chapter 1 was that effective learning environments should involve students in productive disciplinary discourse that actively engages them in dialogue about important questions. As professors, we tend to take it for granted that all of the conversations in our classes should focus on important disciplinary questions and that the discourse should follow standards established by the discipline. In hindsight, I am not sure why I ever thought that the standards of productive disciplinary discourse should be "obvious" because I do not see people, even professors, using these standards in their everyday conversations outside of their disciplines. I now think that every course must devote some time to helping students become acculturated to the discipline's standards of evidence and discourse. This is based on an understanding that the structure of a conversation about a set of ideas is part of the knowledge. It is not enough just to hear about an idea; students have to engage in dialogue about ideas. Dialogue allows students to internalize the structure of the disciplinary discourse and eventually develop the ability to have these conversations "in their own heads" to continue to refine their knowledge and integrate it with their previous understanding. This also explains why it is much more effective to focus on learning metacognitive thinking skills by learning to converse within a particular disciplinary domain.

In the early days of the Human and Organizational Development Program, I taught a separate thinking skills course. This course had no effect on the students' thinking beyond the course. Now I understand that thinking is always thinking about something. Thinking skills cannot be developed in isolation. Students also need help developing a metacognitive awareness of the similarities and differences between the various types of disciplinary discourse and how those styles of communication link to the methods of inquiry in the disciplines. Teaching an interdisciplinary course like "Understanding Organizations" gives me opportunities to point out the differences between the way that researchers from different disciplines gather and interpret data. Class discussions around recommended solutions to organizational problems provide arenas for discussing the standards of evidence used in academic and private and public sector organizations. The rubrics for the class provide one standard for disciplinary discourse that can be contrasted with the "rules of evidence" used in other disciplines and nonacademic settings.

The twelfth principle was that establishing a productive dialogue across boundaries (cultural, communities of practice, from experts to novices) is the most difficult challenge for constructivist approaches. Most of my experience with the "Understanding Organizations" course affirmed this principle and highlighted the barriers to fostering open dialogue within groups and across cultural barriers and communities of practice. I teach in a university with high tuition and a predominantly affluent student body. There is little economic diversity except for students on academic and athletic scholarships. This has created forces that make it difficult to achieve the cultural diversity required to promote productive dialogue about important societal questions. This lack of diversity creates special problems for the implementation of constructivist teaching models.

I also think that students who are in a cultural minority may avoid classes built around small-group work because it puts them in situations where culturally dominant students fail to acknowledge the value of their input. This can be especially frustrating when these students are in situations where they have special areas of expertise to contribute to the group. In my class, for example, students who have worked in organizations have a distinct advantage in understanding the issues in the course. Although many of the students with high levels of cultural capital have not been employed in a "real job," they rarely seek information from students with a more extensive work history. This creates a dynamic where these students assume that their contributions are not valued or wanted. When they withdraw, their behavior is seen as refusing to contribute to the group effort. It is especially ironic when their fellow group members schedule meetings at times when they are working. This was one of the reasons I reorganized the class to include more meetings during class time and at preset times outside the class.

My observations of students working in groups in the "Understanding Organizations" course conform to the patterns that would be predicted in the literature on diversity. It is difficult to prevent students who are in the cultural minority from withdrawing and playing a passive role in the group. By the time students reach the university, they all seem to be cooperating in a dance that privileges the dominant cultural interests. This effect is exaggerated when race, ethnicity, and class are confounded. When low participation fits stereotypes about other groups of people, experiences that are designed to promote cross-cultural dialogue may actually reinforce the negative stereotypes that justify the existing social order (Bhabba, 1984).

I should not leave the impression, however, that this pattern of marginalization and withdrawal is the usual pattern of behavior in this class. The model used in the "Understanding Organizations" class leaves many more opportunities for mining the "funds of knowledge" of all of the students in the class. These opportunities can be leveraged to facilitate boundary-crossing dialogue. Although I am disappointed when this does not happen, I am much more satisfied with the quality of dialogue across cultural boundaries in this class than in any other course I have taught.

The effect of the thirteenth principle, learning involves the construction of identity, strikes at the core of why it is so difficult to change social practices in classroom settings. One of the reasons that it is difficult to create productive dialogue across boundaries of culture and communities of practice is the central role of dialogue in the construction of identity. Students' and professors' identities are deeply embedded in their positions in the social environment. The structure of identity is scaffolded on the structure of conversations in social settings. Our students are also at a place in their development when "style" may be more important than substance. Their identities are highly dependent on "acting like" the person they are (playing their roles in Holland's "figured worlds"). They also cling to whatever cultural capital they have that can bolster their sense of self-worth. Because school is a primary societal institution for developing social capital and preserving the definition of what counts as cultural capital, it is a difficult arena for changing these standards. For many students, especially students at an elite, private university, the purpose of the institution and the reason for paying exorbitant tuition is the university's role in preserving the status quo and enhancing their cache of social capital. Students with minority status have long experience with schooling and have developed successful strategies for dealing with the schooling situation. The problem is that some of these strategies are adaptive within the context of schooling, but will be maladaptive in work settings outside the school.

All students have "funds of knowledge" that give them important resources for problem solving, but schools tend to value only knowledge that fits the dominant cultural template (Moll, 1992). Bringing marginalized funds of knowledge and styles of participation into a central position in the dialogue requires rebuilding the school identities of both majority and minority students. There is no way to accomplish this successfully unless both the dominant and marginalized groups benefit. If identities are developed in figured worlds where people play established roles, as Dorothy Holland proposed, students are unconsciously committed to the roles they are playing (Holland et al., 1998). Even if we are convinced that new patterns of communication are "good for" the students, they will not take our meddling in their identities lightly.

The reason that I decided to have the students participate in gathering data about the quality of classroom discourse was that my efforts to promote this type of dialogue seemed to be "falling on deaf ears." The students did not seem to understand what I wanted them to do. My own involvement in small-group meetings (which contradicts Bruffee's, 1999, recommendation about professors' involvement in collaborative learning groups) was designed to support the exploration of different identities and roles in the dialogue. This can be as simple as acknowledging the value of a student's input or asking a student a question that highlights his or her practical experience. Reading the students' personal organization papers gave me knowledge of each student's organizational experience. As the semester progressed, I was able to bring this into the conversation by asking students questions that would allow them to bring their own experience into the discussion.

I also attempted to create what Bakhtin (1981) called "spaces for authoring" in the classroom, where new behaviors and identities could be constructed. I did not like the idea that students would need to work to avoid being "ventriloquated by one and then another authoritative voice." This phrase struck home because it seemed to capture the way many students deal with the classroom. They parrot "right answers" and "correct behavior" in the school setting. As a teacher, I also reacted emotionally to Habermas' (1987) characterization of our role in promoting the "colonization of the life world." This forces students from other cultures to double index both the dominant culture and their primary culture to protect their identities. My observation and participation in groups in the "Understanding Organizations" course indicate that all these dynamics shape communication in class discussions. I hope that my increased awareness of these dynamics helps me to create spaces where these patterns could be relaxed enough to allow for fuller participation by more students.

Changing the basic expectations of what goes on in a classroom has a strong impact on students. In the early part of the course, they tend to be confused and anxious. After they become accustomed to the routines, they begin to relax and take advantage of opportunities to use other parts of their personalities in the classroom. There are many more opportunities for casual conversations and humor. The new structure creates more opportunities for expressions of different identities. After the first 2 weeks of the "Understanding Organizations" course, I start to see different personalities emerge from students. The contrast between their "formal classroom identities" and these emerging expressions of alternative identities is sometimes dramatic.

The last basic principle of the combined constructivist model is that there is an inherent contradiction between the two goals for the ideal classroom discourse of promoting communication across cultural boundaries and creating productive disciplinary discourse. This is particularly challenging because disciplinary discourse is shaped by the values of the dominant culture. Many of the issues raised by this principle have been addressed in the discussions of the two previous principles. The important thing for me to acknowledge is that I have retained a respect for the adaptive power of reason. Although I can use my powers of argumentation to define the limits of reason, the postmodernists have not convinced me that the Enlightenment project "was a total failure." This insight (that I am an old-fashioned, modern man) makes me especially sensitive to the need to be cautious about using my own rationality to judge the behavior of other people. On one level, I agree with most of the insights of the postmodernists. The standards of evidence within a particular discipline are culturally specific "reasonable" standards. I understand that "what makes sense" is always scaffolded by culture and supports the established order. "The disciplines" are cultural inventions that by definition support some "establishment." We do not think of our own discipline as "*the* establishment," but it probably is. The contradiction here is obvious (and a little irrational at that). If we see the classroom as a cognitive apprenticeship, we are, by definition, imposing our rationality on our students.

However, disciplines and their current set of warranted assertions have survived in the war of ideas because they have been useful in some way. They may have been used to advance the hegemony of the powerful classes or the careers of professors, but they have also helped us solve important problems. They have proved to be adaptive ideas within certain contexts. I do not know of any way to deal with this paradox except to find ways to raise my consciousness about the broader context of my worldviews, especially about the ways that my view of reality serves my self-interests and the interests of the dominant culture.

There are many reasons that it is difficult to change the social practices and patterns of communication in the classroom. Students have ideas about how they should communicate with each other in school, and those ideas will not change without some systematic intervention. In the "Understanding Organizations" course, several changes were required before any change in classroom practices was accomplished: the communications training using Argyris' communication model, the analysis and feedback of taped planning meetings, the briefing sessions with the client and expert groups, and including the standard that presenters find ways to stimulate dialogue in the rubric for class presentations. The sessions where groups reviewed selected taped segments from their first planning meetings were especially helpful for initiating discussions about classroom social practices. Both the quality of disciplinary discourse and the general quality of dialogue in small-group meetings improved slowly as I learned how to give students feedback about social practices.

Attending the planning meetings was a problem for me because it was time-consuming, but it also allowed me to establish a different type of relationship with students. The increased levels of trust allowed them to share their thoughts more freely and gave me more information for understanding what was occurring in the classroom. I made little real progress toward changing the social practices in the large-class situation until the third time I taught the course. Even then, the class did not have the kind of diversity required to really test the limits of the model.

DIALOGUE CATEGORY SYSTEM

My struggles with issues related to classroom dialogue motivated me to develop a category system to increase my awareness of the dimensions and dynamics of classroom social practices. To understand what types of social practices I wanted to increase and communicate my expectations more clearly to the students, I developed a framework for categorizing the types of dialogues that I might encounter. After experimenting with various category systems and developing training modules for improving the quality of disciplinary discourse using Argyris' model, I developed a simple observation tool that the students could use to observe their own discourse. The tool combined Wertsch and Toma's (1995) basic categories of univocal (one-way) and dialogic communication using Argyris' criteria for high-quality communication (high advocacy and high inquiry). The key criteria for defining a statement as high advocacy was that it used evidence to support assertions and positions (theoretical and research support) and identified the rationale for the inferences that were made. The key criteria for high-inquiry statements were "asking for clarification" and "asking why questions." Dialogic communication is high on advocacy and high on inquiry. Students were expected to defend their positions and listen to other students until they really understood why the students held the positions they did.

The simple instrument described earlier gave students a tool for examining the quality of their own discourse. To give myself more information about the social practices in the classroom, I developed a more detailed observation instrument. In the future, I plan to use this to conduct a formal research study in the class. For the present, I have been using it to evaluate the "teacher experiments" I have been conducting to try to understand how to improve the quality of classroom dialogue. Some of the students in the evaluation role in the simulation used this instrument to gather data on the classroom discourse and give feedback to the rest of the class.

I began developing the observation instrument with a system developed by Keefer, Zeitz, and Resnick (2000). They developed a model for examining four types of dialogue: (a) critical discussion, (b) explanatory discussion, (c) eristic discussion, and (d) consensus dialogue. A *critical discussion* involves students in a discussion of the ways that they disagree on their interpretation of the text under consideration. For their purposes, the critical discussion was considered the most appropriate type of dialogue to discuss literary texts. As in Argyris' model, the participants in this type of discussion are expected to support their opinions, but also listen carefully to the arguments presented by other group members and be open to changing their positions in the face of convincing evidence. An *explanatory dialogue* is appropriate when some group members do not have knowledge in a particular area. The goal of the dialogue is to share and acquire appropriate knowledge. I would expect to see this type of dialogue if students were helping each other move into their "zones of proximal development." *Eristic discussions* occur in conflict situations, where the participant's objective is to win the argument rather than gain new knowledge or find the best solution to a problem. These dialogues are characterized by clever intellectual sleight of hand, personal attacks, and dazzling mental agility. I am afraid a large percentage of university dialogues fit into this category. The aim of the *consensus dialogue* is to reach mutual understanding and consensus. This category captures discussions that represent Habermas' communicative action. There are many situations in the "Understanding Organizations" course where critical, explanatory, and consensus dialogues are appropriate. Keefer, Zeitz, and Resnick's system was developed to observe dialogues in student groups. I added additional categories to capture the roles that teachers play in classroom dialogues.

I added two more categories to this list that describe two roles that teachers play in interactions with students in traditional (method) and constructivist (discourse) classrooms: (e) teacher right answer, and (f) teacher scaffolding. The *teacher right answer dialogue* is initiated by the teacher and involves the students in a guessing game about what the teacher wants them to say. *Teacher scaffolding* represents the type of open dialogue where a teacher helps to promote the students' knowledge construction by linking the students' experience to the existing conceptual framework in the field under study or supports the quality of the discourse. I would like to explore the relationship between these two types of "teacher talk" and quality of dialogic communication among students.

Keefer, Zeitz, and Resnick (2000) made the point that students need to learn to understand that there are different types of dialogues and they are appropriate for different types of situations. If the situation changes during the conversation, students need to be able to recognize the change and execute a change in the type of dialogue they are using. Keefer, Zeitz, and Resnick examined both the appropriateness of the type of dialogues employed and the quality of the arguments made by students. When they used their system to conduct observational research on student dialogue in literature courses, they found a strong relationship between the style of argumentation used and the depth of the conceptual analysis exhibited by the students.

R. Young (1992) also developed categories that were helpful additions to the categories developed by Keefer, Zeitz, and Resnick. Young conducted observational research in classrooms and identified several categories of classroom dialogue that are typical of the traditional method classroom:

- The Question–Answer–Reaction (QAR) sequence was the most common. In this sequence, the teacher asks a question, the student answers, and the teacher responds with some type of evaluation of the adequacy of the student's response. These sequences of questioning are often repeated in rapid-fire fashion interspersed with teacher minilectures and transitions to new lines of questioning. This is the type of interaction students expect when they hear a question from a teacher and they naturally fall into this pattern.

- When students are cued that a QAR sequence is beginning, they tend to fall into the Guess What the Teacher Thinks (GWTT) sequence. This sequence may initially appear to be a more open question, but students know that teachers are usually leading students toward a particular conclusion. Young called this "being Socratized." My experience as a professor has led me to the conclusion that Guess What the Teacher Thinks is the dominant cognitive stance of university students.

- Administrative–Procedural (AP) sequences are exchanges where the teacher needs routine information from students (e.g., "John, did you bring your textbook with you today?").

From a cognitive perspective and from the perspective of professors meeting their teaching objectives, the perceptual and cognitive orientations of the "looking for the right answer" and "guessing what the teacher thinks" games will not lead to the development of useful knowledge.

- The final sequence Young identified, Discourse (D), is dialogue that approximates Habermas' ideal speech situation. These interactions are seen in the ideal discourse classroom. In discursive dialogues, the teacher engages students in a conversation designed to help them understand the course content in the context of their own experience. Young identified three kinds of questions within the discourse category: (a) What Do You Think? (WDYT) questions, (b) the Methodological Challenge (MC), and (c) the Procedural Question (P). The WDYT question is a truly open probe to find out what students think about an issue. In discourse dialogues, student contributions are not evaluated as good or bad (as fitting the correct answer or not), but students are continually challenged to explain why they hold the opinions they do. In the MC, the professor or another student challenges the student to explain the basis on which he or she has reached a conclusion, without invalidating his or her personal experience.

Combining categories developed by Keefer, Zeitz, and Resnick and Young with my own yielded a set of behavioral categories I found useful for understanding the dialogues taking place in the "Understanding Organizations" course. This system is summarized on the following chart.

Date _____ Time _____ Context _____

Classroom Discourse Checklist

Initiator	Initiations	Responses						
Teacher	What do you think?	High Advocacy Statement						
		Research						
		Theory						
		Reasoning						
		Experience						
		Unsubstantiated Opinion						
	Providing Information (Lecturing)	No response						
	QAR Sequence	GWTT						
		"Correct answer"						
	Procedural?	Factual Statement						
Either Circle Teacher	Unsupported Opinion	Unresponsive unsupported declarative opinion						
		Scaffolding						
	Factual Statement	Clarification?						
Student Circle Teacher	Procedural?	Factual Statement						
	High Advocacy Statement	High-Inquiry Statement						
	Research	Methodological Challenge						
	Theory	Active Listening						
	Reasoning	Clarification						
	Experience	Connected Point						
	What is the answer?	Factual statement/"correct answer"						
	What do you think?	Scaffolding	Ideas					
			Process					

General Discourse Category — Dialogic ( )   or Univocal ( )
Dialogue Type   Critical Discourse ( )   Explanatory Discussion ( )
       Consensus Discourse ( )   Eristic Discussion ( )
                               Procedural Dialogue ( )

REFLECTIONS ON DIALOGUE IN THE "UNDERSTANDING ORGANIZATIONS" COURSE

I originally introduced the standards for classroom dialogue in the first class session. In the current version of the course, I introduce the discussion of standards for classroom social practices in the third week of the semester. Students tended to listen and agree with the standards as part of the established conventions of classroom behavior. Unfortunately, they quickly forgot the conversation and it did not affect their behavior. For the students, the initial conversation was not about making a commitment to behavioral change; it was about agreeing with the teacher. There is no link between "guessing what the teacher thinks" and behavior change. Guessing correctly marks the end of the game.

I originally presented Habermas' guidelines for communicative action to the class in the beginning of the semester and asked them to discuss the feasibility of making standards like these the standards for dialogue in our class. These guidelines were:

1. Every subject with the competence to speak and act must be allowed to take part in the discourse.
   (a) everyone can question any assertion whatever.
   (b) everyone is allowed to introduce any assertion whatever.
   (c) everyone is allowed to assert his or her attitudes, desires, and needs.
2. No speaker shall be coerced in any way (internally or externally) from their rights set out in 1 and 2. (p. 89)

These standards were too abstract for the students to agree or disagree with in the first class session. For the students, they were rules for conversations they did not expect to have.

There are several models of communication that try to develop a rationale and process for establishing open, uncoerced communication in an organization. We have been using Argyris' Model I and Model II communication model in the HOD program as a practical model of open communication. Argyris' model is easier to understand than most of the other models and communicates well to students and nonacademic audiences. He also has well-constructed training materials and training methods. The department's faculty has been involved in training under this system over the past year, with the objective of using it for our own communication within the faculty and as a shared system and vocabulary across the program's curriculum. It also links up nicely with the communication skills curriculum and the theories presented in the courses in the freshman experience. In the "Understanding Organizations" course, it also has the advantage of being grounded in a corporate context. Most of the examples in the training materials describe communication in business situations. For many of the students, this makes it more legitimate than ideas associated with counseling or psychology.

That being said, I was not satisfied that the workshops were having much effect on their communication in the class. The students took notes on the system and could state the principles, but it did not affect the quality of communication in the group. Part of the problem was that I did not allocate enough class time to complete the exercises and practice the skills. I wanted to create an electronic dialogue as a vehicle for reaching these objectives, but I did not think I could add any more work to the course, and I was not sure I could integrate it into the simulation in an authentic way. The real problem is that adopting Argyris' guidelines for communication represents a radical change in the social practices of the classroom and the student community. It was difficult to find a way to make real progress toward furthering the goal of open communication. Eliminating the essay tests during the class allowed me to add more communications training to the class time. During the second year that I taught the course, I also started taping the first and last planning meetings and attending the meetings. During the planning meeting for the second presentation, we reviewed the tape from the first meeting. I used Argyris' system to guide my feedback about their dialogue. These sessions generated the best discussions of communication styles.

The personal case assignment that was included in the first Argyris workshop provided a vehicle for addressing issues related to productive disciplinary discourse. In the first 2 years, the workshop worked well, but the examples tended to be personal situations involving a failure to communicate with a friend when they should have been more assertive. Because many of the students had been involved in active listening and assertiveness training modules in earlier HOD courses, they tended to connect the content of the module to their personal communication rather than to the social practices of the classroom. This semester, I asked them to develop an example that involved communication in a classroom situation. Rather than giving the students a general instruction to "Think about a situation where you disagreed with someone, but didn't voice your disagreement openly and made assumptions about why they held the opinion they did," I asked them to think about situations when this happened in a class discussion or group project situation. This focused the conversation on classroom social practices and made it easier for them to relate the content of the workshop to classroom social practices.

In the "Understanding Organizations" course, personal experience in organizations is a legitimate source of data, but I want students to understand both the importance of this experience and the limitations of personal experience for making generalizations. I want them to construct a chain of evidence to support their assertions that connects concrete experience with theory, deep principles, and research support. In terms of Argyris' system, I wanted students to articulate the "ladder of inference" they were using to reach their conclusions. I wanted them to avoid voicing unsubstantiated opinions or making the fundamental attribution error by being too quick to conclude that problems resulted from individual personality characteristics.

In the "Understanding Organizations" course, the quality of the dialogue improved as students generated more possible explanations for the same sequence of events, provided other students with a rationale for their opinions, or changed their opinions based on valid evidence presented by other group members. I would also identify "attending to other participants' arguments" as an important characteristic of a high-quality dialogue. This was expressed as the standard of high inquiry. Many of the students in this class were trained in interpersonal communication skills and group dynamics in two previous courses. Consequently, they had a set of criteria for evaluating the quality of a group member's active listening skills, assertiveness, and performance of group roles. This orientation helped establish a foundation for a culture of advocacy and inquiry in the course.

The design of the course (organizing observations around four organizational perspectives) facilitated the generation of alternative explanations for the same behavior. These types of statements increased throughout the semester. However, the students seemed to avoid pressing each other for evidence to support their statements. In the small-group setting, they tended to respond by giving an alternate opinion, rather than probing their fellow students for evidence to support their opinions. The groups almost always mysteriously found a consensus without debating the issues directly. Direct criticism of a student's ideas was even less common in the large-class situation, although the written feedback to students by evaluators often included fairly caustic assessments of the quality of evidence for recommendations. One student in last semester's class was quite confrontive with groups that were presenting in the beginning of the semester. His fellow students complained that he "was rude." Despite my efforts to encourage him to continue his questioning, the class quickly extinguished this behavior. Although I agreed with some of his critics that his style was problematic, his questions were good, and I was disappointed that I could not help him reshape his style and encourage more students to join him in his questioning.

The dialogue that took place in the planning meetings and in the media-lab sessions played an important role both in conceptual change and in shaping social practices. In the sessions where I sat in with the group, I was able to connect the guidelines in the communication training with the conversation. It was more difficult to do this successfully in the large-group session.

From the beginning of the course, students were aware that they would be working in groups and making presentations. The students do not like being assigned to groups, but they generally accepted my rationale that they would not be able to pick their other team members in their future work sites. It is also important for each group to have enough diversity to produce dialogue across cultural boundaries. The fact that the class does not usually draw a highly diverse group of students has been a problem in assessing the elements of the model that relate to communication across cultural boundaries.

Although I believe that a combined constructivist model is a richer and more powerful model for producing meaningful and useful knowledge, the costs of adopting this model must be weighed against the real gains achieved. Adopting a constructivist perspective means trading a simple model for an extremely complex picture of the learning process. It would be naive and counterproductive to assume that a change of this magnitude could be accomplished without some adjustment period for both professors and students. I completed the transformation to a course design consistent with a transactional constructivist perspective on learning in manageable steps. I think it is important to develop a systematic, gradual transition from one model to another. The next chapter provides a summary of the learning principles and the teaching model I arrived at after experimenting with the "Understanding Organizations" course over a 3-year period.

Chapter 9

Developing a Transactional Constructivist Teaching Model

I personally find models to be useful ways to organize my own understanding of the dynamics of a system. This chapter describes the construction of the model I presented in the first chapter. The theories presented in the previous chapters provide the philosophical and theoretical foundation for this model. This chapter gives the reader an opportunity to judge whether I have successfully supported the model. This teaching model was informed by a transactional constructivist perspective on learning. The model was derived from the theories presented in previous chapters and the work of several other constructivist model builders. A good part of the model was constructed from Edelson's (2001) "learning-for-use" model.

Edelson's (2001) model was developed to provide a framework for designing inquiry-based learning. The model guides instruction through a three-step process: (a) motivation, (b) fostering knowledge construction, and (c) knowledge refinement. Edelson's model utilized Schank's theory of dynamic memory and his method of goal-based scenarios. It was specifically geared to help teachers design curricula to meet national science standards intended to "develop deep, interconnected content knowledge and inquiry skills through activities that incorporate authentic scientific inquiry" (p. 356). The principles that Edelson used to develop his learning-for-use model fit well with Dewey and a combined constructivist view that is oriented toward developing both metacognitive skills and conceptual understanding:

1. Learning takes place through the connection and modification of knowledge structures.

2. Knowledge construction is a goal-directed process that is guided by a combination of conscious and unconscious understanding goals.
3. The circumstances in which knowledge is constructed and subsequently used determine its accessibility for future use.
4. Knowledge must be constructed in a form that supports use before it can be applied. (p. 357)

Edelson's list covers many of the basic principles of a transactional constructivist model. The first of these principles is consistent with most psychological and transactional constructivist positions, but would not fit strong sociocultural theories. Revisioning education as crafting knowledge structures in the context of cultural artifacts and social processes points toward a learning process that alternates experience that connects students to their present ideas with communication with other students and professors that helps students reconstruct experience. New structures are developed incrementally. As the second principle indicates, students are not consciously aware of some of the processes they use to make sense of their learning experiences. Positioning learning in the context of goal-based scenarios provides a narrative context for indexes that serve as reminders that point to the knowledge in situations where it will be applied. Because much of this process is unconscious, it is important that in-class simulations contain as many similarities with the context of use as possible.

STAGE 1: THE MOTIVATION STAGE

The motivation stage is designed to stimulate the students' motivation to engage with the specific content of the course by immersing them in a context and a problem situation where that content will be useful. This would usually be a case-based scenario, a problem case, a simulation, or a video anchor. In this first stage, the curriculum designer "creates demand" by creating an authentic context and "elicits curiosity" by defining specific problems or asking students to identify specific problems. The professor "plants problems" in the case that require specific knowledge to solve. To elicit curiosity, students have to be alerted to the fact that they will confront problems that will be important to them that they do not know how to solve. The problem situations should be complex enough to result in some expectancy failures. Schank emphasized the critical role of expectancy failures in indexing contextualized knowledge.

In my "Understanding Organizations" course, nearly all of the students had encountered organizational problems they had been unsuccessful in solving, although many of them were not really aware that their solutions were not very effective. The initial step in the learning process for the course was to try to connect students to an important organizational experience and help them become more aware of their own theories about organizations. The initial stage of the process must contain some strategy for helping students recognize gaps in their knowledge.

A common strategy in constructivist teaching is to establish an unstructured problem situation that serves as an "anchor" for identifying problems. The anchor that Edelson (2001) provided as an example came from a computer simulation called the Create-A-World Project, which focused on the relationship between geography and temperature. Students were challenged to use a computer-based model to explore and learn about global temperature and ultimately to use that knowledge to create a world with certain temperature characteristics. The computer simulation gave students feedback on whether the new world they had created would result in the temperature patterns they predicted.

In the "Understanding Organizations" course, there were four organizational anchors for developing deep principles about organizational behavior: the personal organizational case, the 4Frames.Kamm case, the video case from the "West Wing" TV show, and the group organizational case. In each part of the course, students reanalyzed their personal case from a new perspective. At each stage, the students were asked to revisit the organization that had the most personal meaning to them.

Edelson's motivational stage presents its own set of problems for the professor using the model. The learning experiences must be authentic enough to create real motivation. In Dewey's terms, the presenting problem needs to create an authentic "perturbation" or intriguing problem that will stimulate intrinsic motivation grounded in the problem. The problems in the "Understanding Organizations" course were all drawn from real problems in four organizations I used to construct the case. I was careful to use problems that had really occurred in organizations like 4Frames .Kamm. This made it easier for me to convince the students that the problems in the case were similar to problems they would confront after graduation. "Experts" who visited the class or communicated with class members electronically consistently confirmed that even the most dramatic events in the case were typical of what they had experienced in their organizations.

Wong, Pugh, and the Dewey Ideas Group at Michigan State University (2001) drew on Dewey's (1934/1980) *Art as Experience* to clarify Dewey's definition of an authentic experience (Dewey used *an* experience to distinguish an educative experience from an *ordinary* experience). *An* experience involves the person emotionally and stimulates goal-directed behavior that is carried through to fruition. The instrumental nature of *an* educative experience imbues the experience with a sense of anticipation that keeps the endpoint in view and refers back to the presenting problem to give an overall unity to the experience. Completing the cycle from motivation to goal setting to goal attainment stimulates thinking and meaning-making and so-lidifies the experience into a unity that can serve as a narrative context for organizing knowledge and linking it to opportunities for application. Wong et al. (2001) emphasized that, to create authentic educational experiences, teachers must stimulate emotional involvement and the commitment to solve the problem. For Dewey, "*an* idea" creates a situation that has the power to create anticipation and stimulate problem-solving behavior.

Wong et al. built on Dewey's concept of *an* idea to develop guidelines for motivating students. This approach favors concepts over facts because con-cepts are structurally connected to larger knowledge structures. They pre-fer ideas to concepts because they connect the whole learner to the inquiry process. They pointed out that Dewey rejected the idea that mental models mediate between the person and the world. For Dewey, activity, emotions, mental structures, and the world operate as a system. They contrasted Dewey's model with the traditional picture of the world feeding data through mediating structures into an internal psychological process that serves as the site for knowledge construction. Dewey's transactional rela-tionship between the person and the world is characterized by both action on the world (doing) and being shaped by the world (undergoing). Mean-ing involves action as well as cognition. That is why role playing is such an important part of effective problem-based learning. It was also one of the sources for my hypothesis that students would learn more if they selected and edited their own film clips to use as examples of the concepts in their presentations in the "Understanding Organizations" course. Although they think concepts are important as elements in knowledge structures, ideas fuel educative experience because they excite the students' anticipation, motivate action, and unify experience. For Wong, Pugh, and the Dewey Ideas Group at Michigan State University (2001), "The goal is to teach the students to more fully perceive the world by teaching them how to see it through the lenses of powerful ideas" (p. 330). One way to do this is to con-nect students to the excitement we feel when we create new ideas. Part of this involves sharing the discovery process from our perspectives as scholars and then "putting them in the drivers seat" within an authentic educational experience.

STAGE 2: FOSTERING KNOWLEDGE CONSTRUCTION

Edelson's second stage is fostering knowledge construction. This stage involves students in *observation* and *communication* to build knowledge struc-tures. By *observation*, Edelson meant "making observations" in an active ex-ploration and discovery process, rather than more passive forms of observa-tion like watching a demonstration. To avoid confusion with what Dewey called "the spectator model of education," I substitute the longer phase "exploration and discovery" to describe this type of knowledge construction. Like Dewey, Edelson wanted to involve groups of students in systematic inquiry around authentic problems. To the extent possible, he wanted to create situations where students can physically engage the environment and get feedback when they attempt solutions. It is easier to envision these types of situations in the sciences than in other fields. In cases where actual lab work is not practical, computer simulations can give students feedback. In Edelson's Create-A-World simulation, students were able to change the shapes and locations of land masses and their physical characteristics. The computer program then generated data about the effects these changes would have on temperature.

Hershkowitz, Schwartz, and Dreyfus (2001) presented another model for understanding knowledge construction they called "abstraction in context." I used this model to add detail about mechanisms for knowledge construction within Edelson's stage of fostering knowledge construction. Hershkowitz, Schwartz, and Dreyfus described a teaching model that focuses on building useful abstractions (in the sense of "big ideas and deep principles" or enduring understandings) that "vertically reorganize previously constructed [knowledge] into new structure[s]." New abstractions must be constructed by organizing existing abstract structures. They placed this process in the context of activities and social practices. Following Davydov, they saw abstraction as a recursive process where poorly formed abstractions are refined and expanded through a cycle of moving back and forth between empirical thought (that engages the world) and theoretical thought (that constructs useful abstractions). They called this process a "dynamic nesting of epistemic actions" (p. 218). They identified three epistemic actions: constructing, recognizing, and "building with." I see "recognizing" and "building with" as nested within Edelson's stage of constructing. At each stage of the process, the student can use the abstractions that they have constructed in previous stages. This process is not a decontextualization process in the Vygotskian sense, but a process of "abstraction in context" in the tradition of Leont'ev and Davydov. Hershkowitz, Schwartz, and Dreyfus' (2001) model has a transactional concept of abstraction similar to Dewey's that positions the transactional object in the process of abstraction that merges the concrete and abstract. The context contains all of the actors' personal, genetic, and cultural histories, as well as the artifacts and social practices that make up experience. These constructs are similar to what Greeno (1997) referred to as *schemata*. The stage of recognizing occurs when the student has acquired a preliminary abstraction.

Hershkowitz, Schwartz, and Dreyfus believed that much of the preliminary structure may be at the level of empirical thought. Yet the act of recognizing "a class of things" and using these primitive abstractions can help facilitate the process of clarifying small structures. The "Four Frames" used in the "Understanding Organizations" course are not theories, but a vehicle for helping students recognize "a class of things." Forms of communication (e.g., dialogue to promote reflection and signification) and active inquiry and problem solving are needed to move from "building with" to constructing new objects. In practice, constructing, recognizing, and "building with" are nested and interactive. In the "Understanding Organizations" course, the activity of reviewing and editing video clips and using the clips as examples represents a process of recognizing and "building with" basic concepts to construct deeper principles.

The three epistemic actions that operate in context to build useful abstractions (*constructing, recognizing,* and *building with*) provide some detail to enrich the model developed by Edelson. Hershkowits, Schwartz, and Dreyfus saw these processes as operating in a "dynamic nested model" reflecting that learning is a recursive process. *Recognizing* and *building with* are nested within constructing. In von Glasersfeld's model, an individual sees common characteristics of specific concrete examples and extracts them to develop an abstraction. Abstraction is a one-way process from the concrete to the abstract. The sociocultural view introduces complex mediators into the process.

In the "Understanding Organizations" course, I experimented with a progressive model-building exercise to test the hypothesis that models, if they are self-constructed, can scaffold the development of useful abstractions. My experience with the "Understanding Organizations" course indicated that some combination of all the approaches reviewed seemed to help students understand the material more deeply. I think it was important to link students to their personal experience in organizations at the beginning of the course, but I do not think that staying on the level of empirical thought for an extended period of time is productive.

Staying on the personal experience level quickly degenerates into random storytelling. This is both the strength and weakness of the narrative form. It is easy for the internal coherence of the form of the story to break free of its connection to principles and ideas. We need to help students keep some of their cognitive resources focused on the level of reflection. This allows them to explore and further develop their personal theories that are informed by scholarship and scientific research. I think it is more useful to move to the theoretical level fairly quickly and then return frequently to the concrete, empirical/experiential level to continually link experience to theory as a vehicle for viewing experience from different perspectives.

Reading analyses of classroom discourses such as Leander's (2001) description of the lesson on the bus to visit the site of Martin Luther King's assassination has focused my attention on the strengths and weaknesses of the use of stories in classrooms. This is important to me because I make heavy use of stories in my teaching, both during lectures and through video and written cases. It is always "obvious" to me how my stories connect to the deep principles in the lecture, but it may not always be obvious to my students. I try to be explicit about what I want students to get out of the stories I tell, and I ask students to think about what the stories they tell mean and how they connect to the topic being discussed. The three critical incidents that students write to anchor their analyses in their personal organization papers in the "Understanding Organizations" course are an example of my attempts to highlight these connections.

When I started teaching the "Understanding Organizations" course again, I changed the way the personal organization paper was written—from one paper at the end of the course to a series of shorter papers on each frame. This allowed me to give students feedback on each section and make suggestions about ways to link the events they were describing to abstractions in this and future sections of the paper. I allowed them to rewrite each section based on my feedback. This procedure transformed the assignment into an iterative learning process where students increased their ability to use abstractions to recognize concrete examples and "build with" those abstractions to build more complex organizational models. Feedback about what constituted a "good response" and an "exceptional response" served as a vehicle for establishing the standard that connecting theory to practice was the core objective of the course and coached students about how to reach this standard. A student made a "good response" when he or she recognized something he or she described as an example of one of the concepts or theories from the course. This was an example of Hershkowitz, Schwartz, and Dreyfus' standard of *recognition* in their abstraction in context model. An "excellent response" or an "extraordinary response" involved levels of richness or creativity in connecting concrete descriptions to broader principles of human or organizational behavior and using these insights to develop new ways to take action to solve problems. Higher level responses indicated that students were beginning to *build with* and *construct* increasingly useful knowledge objects. At each stage of the process, students also rewrote the three critical incidents from the "concrete experience" section of their personal organization papers based on their unfolding theoretical understanding. This process reinforced the cycle of recognizing and "building with" by connecting it to the cycle of concrete experience, reflection, abstract conceptualization, and active experimentation. The entire process is designed to index abstractions to a meaningful narrative.

The work of activity theorists like Leont'ev and Davydov alerted me to the importance of activity as a *maker of mental structures*. Schank's theory of dynamic memory provides a model for how mental structures and indexes are developed. This perspective moves us away from seeing learning as transmitting what we know to the students to organizing activities where students can construct their own understanding of the subject matter. We begin to see perception (recognition) as organized through activity to see and give meaning to the salient features of the environment, rather than as a filter that distorts the "real world." In the "Understanding Organizations" course, students learned to view organizations through a variety of different frames of reference. My decision to have the students develop presentations and edit examples of course concepts from film clips was stimulated by the activity theorists' emphasis on engaging students in joint, goal-directed activity. Discussion among group members about which scenes represented examples of particular concepts is an example of the second type of knowledge construction in Edelson's model (communication), which is explored in the next section.

Regardless of what specific teaching model we use, we have to start by trying to articulate the enduring understandings we want students to acquire in our courses. Planning courses involves mapping backward from the outcomes we expect to produce at the end of the course to the motivating ideas we think will enliven the course's activities with excitement and anticipation. The activities students engage in during the course should also be consistent with the behaviors and thinking skills we want them to exhibit when they use the knowledge being conveyed in the course. The individual steps in the recognizing and building with cycles within the knowledge-construction process always have to be connected to the larger context of the motivating ideas and enduring understandings that represent the link between the students' existing interests and the goals of the course.

Because we are experts in our fields, we might think it is a relatively simple task to articulate the enduring understandings in our courses. Yet as experts we often have knowledge that is so well integrated into our worldviews that it does not function on a conscious level. These ideas also have to be translated from jargon into a more understandable form. This translation can be difficult for us because it sacrifices some of the precise meaning that is so important within the community of scholars in our disciplines.

A simple example might be useful. A lesson described by Cobb, Gravemeijer, Yackel, McClain, and Whitnack (1997) began with an "anchor" story about Mrs. Wright, a candy factory owner, who packed up pieces of candy in rolls of 10. The children moved through a sequence that progressed from concrete to abstract representations of the story. They started by physically packaging the candy, moved to Unifix cubes, then to picture collections, then to a sign system (r = roll, p = 1 piece of candy). Cobb and his associates analyzed the concept development process in their classroom using Walkerdine's (1988) adaptation of Lacan's (1977) chain of signification. The following diagram outlines the chain of signification involved in this lesson.

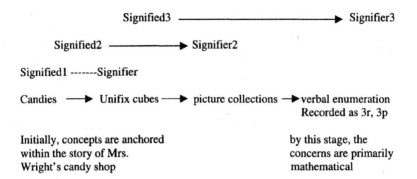

This chain of signification offers an account of the process by which students develop an understanding of a mathematical sign (a sign is a unification of a signified/signifier pair). At each stage in this process, the preceding sign (a union of a signified and signifier) becomes signified to a new (more abstract) signifier and forms a new combination that was originally grounded in a particular example (an anchor that places the concept in a context, both the context of the story and the context of the learning community) that was connected to the students' experience. Cobb, Gravemeijer, Yackel, McClain, and Whitnack (1997) described this process as follows:

> It is important to stress that Walkerdine's (1988) notion of a chain of signification offers an account of the process by which signifiers can gain independence from their signifieds and take on a life of their own, freed from the domination of signifieds that might have initially provided realistic grounding for the mathematical signs established by the classroom community. (p. 218)

Many of the relationships and practices of the classroom community that impact the learning environment can be better understood by using an analysis like Cobb's, which combines insights from both the psychological constructivist and sociocultural positions. Cobb believed we can understand and improve classroom practices by analyzing both the psychological (how individual students construct knowledge) and social aspects. By coordinating these two positions, Cobb's research seeks to clarify the relationship between the signification process and cultural reorganization. For the professor, it is important to know exactly how semiotic mediation operates within the context of social practices in the classroom setting. Cobb's analysis of the process by which students incorporated an understanding of mathematical signs into their own thinking through participation in a particular set of classroom practices shows how the process of signification incorporates both social and psychological views of knowledge construction.

In addition to understanding how the knowledge-construction process nests within the context of enduring understandings, we must also understand how it nests within the social practices of the classroom.

Communication is the second element of the Fostering Knowledge Construction stage of constructing knowledge in Edelson's learning-for-use model. Edelson used the term communication in the sense of *telling*. He made a similar point that Schwartz and Bransford (1998) made in their article "A Time for Telling." Once students are involved in pursuing the solution to a problem, they are receptive to information from a variety of sources that will help them understand the phenomena they are studying.

I would modify this part of Edelson's model to include *dialogic inquiry* and *semiotic mediation* as forms of communication that facilitate knowledge construction. Some theorists would make the case that semiotic mediation is a way of refining knowledge rather than constructing knowledge, but I think it fits best under knowledge construction. Dialogic inquiry and semiotic mediation are primary mechanisms that help students craft the deep structures that represent real understanding of the subject matter.

STAGE 3: FOSTERING KNOWLEDGE REFINEMENT

The third stage of Edelson's learning-for-use model, fostering knowledge refinement, contains the processes of reflection that are part of the knowledge-construction process. In Hershkowitz, Schwartz, and Dreyfus' model, knowledge refinement involves the process of "building with." Edelson placed these processes under fostering knowledge refinement to recognize Davydov's idea that more elaborate abstractions are refinements from existing abstractions. Much of what the professor does in a class discussion is foster reflection and facilitate signification.

In the "Understanding Organizations" course, I found that the process of fostering knowledge refinement involved learning to "think on my feet" in a new way. I had to improve my ability to recognize students' input as examples of concepts in the course, and I had to articulate the connection clearly enough so that I connected with students at various levels of sophistication. I did this more effectively the second time I taught the course, but I found it to be much more challenging than moving through a lecture in a linear fashion.

In the application substage of Edelson's fostering knowledge-construction stage, students should be able to use knowledge to understand the phenomena they are studying and make predictions about how different changes would affect the systems they are studying. The litmus test of an abstraction is that it is structured in a way that supports use. In Edelson's Create-A-World simulation, students could apply a solution based on one of the deep principles they had learned and get feedback to see whether it yielded the results they predicted. In the "Understanding Organizations" course, the presentations by the simulated consultation firms emphasized assessing organizational problems and making recommendations for change. Unfortunately, there was not much opportunity to test these recommendations and see their effects. I could only comment on their recommendations as "an expert" with knowledge of organizational theory and research. We were also able to get some input from outside experts and parents of students working in the corporate world through answers to e-mail questions. In the best of all possible worlds, I would have a computer simulation that would give students feedback on the probable effects of the changes they recommended. In the next redesign of the course, I hope to build more case studies of the effects of organizational change efforts and establish electronic connections with organizational leaders and experts to get their feedback on the probable effects of recommended change efforts. I would also like to assemble a library of digital video clips accessible through the class Web page that would give the reactions of experts and organizational leaders to the dilemmas presented in the case studies.

SUMMARY OF MODEL

1. *Stage 1: Motivation*
   (a) Present students with an intriguing problem to solve that has the potential to become "*an* experience" (e.g., a problem-based scenario, case-based scenario, a video anchor) that creates an authentic context for learning, elicits curiosity, and stimulates goal-directed behavior.
   (b) Help students generate cases and problems from the students' experience that connect to the anchor.
2. *Stage 2: Fostering Knowledge Construction*—Building new abstractions through epistemic actions
   (a) *Exploration and Discovery (Observation)* as part of a systematic inquiry.

   Progressive model building
   {
   - recognizing (acquires a preliminary abstraction and uses it to recognize examples of concepts)
   - "Building With"
   }

   (b) *Communication* ("telling," dialogic inquiry, and semiotic mediation to further develop and refine enduring understandings—deep principles and big ideas).

3. *Stage 3: Fostering Knowledge Refinement/"Building With"*—The role of the professor: telling, semiotic mediation, fostering dialogic inquiry, disciplinary discourse, and communicative action.

   (a) Students *use knowledge to understand new situations.*

   (b) Students *make predictions and test them* (students get feedback on how useful the concept is for solving a problem in the real world).

APPLYING CONSTRUCTIVIST THEORIES TO TEACHING

In all of our disciplines, we have both knowledge and a logic of inquiry that shape the way we see the world and the way we improve our conceptual vision. A primary methodological bias in constructivist approaches is to move away from a model where students passively receive knowledge they can store in "water-tight packages" (Dewey's bricks) to a model where students are invited to participate in the inquiry activity of the discipline. It is not possible to really understand the perspective of any discipline without actively participating in its logic of inquiry. In most cases, there is a fundamental mismatch between the way a student learns to see and the way a scholar approaches the problem of learning in his or her discipline. It takes an intensive apprenticeship process to acculturate graduate students into the thinking styles and inquiry practices of a scholarly discipline. The problem is compounded when we deal with undergraduates who are with us for only a short time.

It is clear that constructivist theories have important implications for teaching practice. In most cases, a lesson does not begin with a lecture. The professor using this approach presents a problem, allows students to wrestle with it, and then participates in a dialogue initiated by students and provides scaffolding for reflection, reasoning, and knowledge building. Much of the professor's "telling" comes after students have begun to address a problem and made an initial attempt to find a solution. The professor's role often involves correcting misconceptions, relabeling student input to link it to their discipline's body of knowledge, and guiding students toward the development of useful abstractions. In practice this means creating a norm where everyone in the classroom learning community (both the professor and students) listen to each other and ask each other *why* they hold the opinions they do.

Cobb's "bottom–up" method does not mean that students create and are left with their own naive explanations of the events under investigation. Yet it does recognize that we need to start with the way students view a problem situation before they are exposed to the course content. A lesson usually begins by finding out what students' "everyday" knowledge tells them about a problem situation. Then groups of students are given a chance to use the discipline's logic of inquiry to explore the problem. In a history class, groups of students might begin by sharing their knowledge and opinions about a historic event and then examine a set of primary documents related to that event. An introductory course might begin by examining some salient event that occurred on the campus and generating a set of interpretations of that event. The student's methods of inquiry and standards of interpretation are then compared with the established theories of history and the established methods of conducting historical research.

One of my first experiences with this method came during my first year as a fifth-grade teacher. I used a "historical event" of great local significance to introduce my students to the idea of "doing history" (as opposed to memorizing history). In Michigan where I was teaching, students waited eagerly for the first big snowstorm that would launch the first "big snowball fight" followed by an endless debate about which team won. I asked some of the kids to generate primary accounts of the "battle" from their own perspectives. We appointed reporters to cover the event and created a class newspaper. The reporters interviewed several of the "soldiers" who bravely fought on both sides. With these and other materials, the historians set about determining what really happened that day and why it happened. This gave us a context for understanding how historians construct their descriptions of historic events.

USING THE MODEL TO DEVELOP PROCEDURES FOR COURSE DEVELOPMENT

The following list of steps for developing a course based on the combined constructivist model was presented in chapter 1. If my presentation of the theories and models used to develop this list has been clear enough, the logic behind these steps should now be obvious. I am reminded of a story a friend from Cambridge University tells about Leibnitz. As the story goes, Leibnitz was presenting a proof to a group of students when one of the students said that he did not understand how he had reached his conclusion. Leibnitz reportedly said, "it's obvious." When the student responded that it was not at all obvious to him, Leibnitz sat down and stared at the proof for 20 minutes. He then rose and said, "Yes, it's obvious." Like Leibnitz, I hope the list is now obvious. It may not even be obvious why that story had "anything to do with this topic."

Steps in the Development of a Course Based on Constructivist Principles

1. *Predict the types of situations in which your students might predictably and profitably use the knowledge and skills they might acquire in the course.* Identify a

set of problem situations where you imagine the knowledge and skills might improve the probability of adaptive solutions.

2. *Define the enduring understandings (big ideas and deep principles) you want students to acquire.* Many experiential educators believe students should dictate or play a key role in selecting learning goals and work with teachers to define performance criteria. Within limits, this is an important process, but I am taking the position that professors should establish the broad learning objectives of their courses.

3. *Problematize the content by "anchoring" it in an authentic context* (e.g., problem situation, research question, strong narrative context connected to a personally relevant problem).

4. *Assess students' current understanding* (everyday theories). The first step in engaging students with the course content is to elicit the students' previous experience related to the content. Students should generate cases and problems from their own experience that connect to the authentic context. We should spend time helping students generate personally relevant questions and systematically articulate their "everyday theories."

The rest of the steps in the process are presented linearly, but it would be more accurate to present them as a circle or spiral. Through all these steps, professors need to provide students with the informational resources, technological resources, conceptual resources, communication training, and methodological guidance they need.

5. *Scaffold the development of abstractions while students are involved in an active inquiry process using methods appropriate to the discipline.* Involving students in active problem solving defines the experience as authentic. The discipline's ways of observing, exploring, and discovering patterns in information as part of a systematic inquiry tie the problem to disciplinary norms. The professor's role is to support links between the inquiry process and the development of useful representations, abstractions, and enduring understandings. The professor needs to *facilitate abstraction in context* (cognitive mediation to enhance the development of theoretical knowledge) by helping students link the course's enduring understandings (big ideas and deep principles) to problems in the context of activities and social practices. The professor's role is to foster *progressive model building* by helping students use preliminary abstractions and "classes of things" to recognize examples and concepts in unstructured problem situations.

6. *Provide resources for knowledge construction.* The primary role of the professor is to function as an architect of the educational environment, rather than as a transmitter of knowledge. In addition to resources like research tools, readings, and simulations, the professor becomes an expert resource to facilitate problem solving.

7. *Provide students with training in effective communication, metacognitive thinking, and disciplinary norms for inquiring and discourse.* Most students are not equipped with the communication skills they need to perform successfully in cooperative learning environments. They need training in both basic communication and the norms of productive disciplinary discourse. They do not understand the standards of evidence used in the discipline. It is helpful if they are provided with rubrics that capture the higher order thinking and standards of evidence we want them to exhibit. The content needs to include introducing students to new social practices (new communication structures) that redefine the roles of teachers and students.

8. *Involve students in collaborative learning* (create learning communities where students can develop expertise). For collaborative learning to successfully achieve course objectives, it is importance to promote meaningful, transactional dialogue across boundaries of culture and communities of practice as well as promoting justificatory (why questions) and critical discourse (addressing issues of power and social justice). If students are going to learn from each other, their groups need to create a "zone of proximal development" where students learn from more competent students and "instrumental development zones" where students bridge the gap between their individual knowledge and the total expertise distributed throughout the group.

9. *Communication* (transactional telling and scaffolding of knowledge construction). An important organizing principle of constructivist approaches to education is to create "times for telling," where students receive information from professors, reading, and experts at a time when they need this information to solve problems that are important to them. The professor plays an important role in the *dynamic nesting of epistemic actions* by scaffolding connections between concrete problem-solving experience, conceptual, and procedural knowledge (e.g., semiotic mediation that links examples to concepts, orchestrating dialogic inquiry, "Just in time" lectures are matched to the students' information needs).

10. *Create arenas for making knowledge visible.* Students in constructivist classrooms are involved in projects that produce significant products and are encouraged to make their knowledge visible through mechanisms like making presentations to the rest of the class. The professor's role in this stage is *fostering knowledge refinement* by helping students use the knowledge they have acquired to construct new knowledge (*building with*) and *fostering productive disciplinary engagement* around the issues raised by the presentation.

11. *Application.* In the application phase, students use knowledge to understand new situations. This is often used as an assessment of transfer. Students make predictions, test them, and receive feedback about how useful the concepts and ideas are for solving real-world problems.

CONCLUSION

The social practices of inquirers in an academic discipline, executives in a corporation, and doctors in hospitals all represent a context and set of factors associated with learning in which the signification process is embedded. These arenas of application usually have different norms and communication patterns than the social practices associated with schooling. It is difficult to create classroom environments that connect to these future environments of application. In the "Understanding Organizations" course, I tried to create an overarching simulation by asking the students to imagine that they were six consultation firms vying for the 4Frames.Kamm account. Solving the problems presented in this simulation required the enduring understandings I hoped they would acquire in the course. Many of the usual structural qualities of a course were changed (e.g., the students rarely meet in the same room at the same time). The overall goal was to embed the facts, concepts, principles, and theories acquired in the course in an authentic context that shared important similarities to the organizations they would encounter in the real world.

One problem I experienced with the "Understanding Organizations" course was created by a conflict between the social practices I wanted to create in the simulation and the established social practices of schooling. The structural changes I made in the course made the students uneasy, and they began to test the environment to understand "what the teacher wanted them to do." I increased the students' anxiety by sending them mixed messages. I was trying to reframe the class as a simulated organization that had real problems to solve, but I evaluated their products with academic criteria that rarely operate in business settings (although I think they should). Most important, I assumed a role as evaluator of their work that pushed them toward applying more academic rigor to their thinking. I said, "Be creative, come up with your own way of approaching the problem as though you were a management consulting firm." I "assumed" that they would also understand that they had to demonstrate that they could link their recommendations to the theories in the readings. In effect, I negatively evaluated their admittedly creative presentations because they were "light on theory." If they did not see the way I wanted them to see, I would give them feedback that their analysis was shallow and they needed to look a little harder. They would respond with frustration and ask that I tell them exactly how to complete the assignment. "How many pages does this assignment have to be?" "How many theories do we have to cite?" To me it was "obvious" that their papers on each frame would be evaluated by how well they linked the theories presented in the course to the events in the organization they were studying. I had stated this as *the* primary objective of the course in the syllabus and on several other occasions, but many of the students did not really understand what that meant.

On reflection, I realized that this was not entirely surprising considering how much of their schooling had involved memorizing theories and defining them on a test. Yet I did not want to stop pushing students to produce highly theoretical explanations for organizational behavior. Contrary to some characterizations of constructivist approaches to education (Terhart, 2003), they do not abandon academic rigor. This teaching model does put me in the position of behaving in ways the students associate with schooling (e.g., giving them low grades for work that failed to support assertions with theory and research support) and then asking them to eliminate other schooling behaviors (e.g., asking them to make presentations and evaluate each other's work). When I started teaching the course, I underestimated the magnitude and complexity of the change I was asking the students to make. They were frustrated with low grades, and I had trouble understanding why many of the students continued to have difficulty understanding what I wanted from them. On the positive side, this frustration created several dialogues in the class that spanned the boundaries usually maintained between students and faculty.

A key insight from Dewey and the constructivists is that students come to classrooms with ideas about how things work and how to address problems. These worldviews are not easy to change especially if students see the ways of thinking, the social practices, and the worldview of the classroom as separate from their real-world problems. As professors, we are constantly confronted with the problem of creating new patterns of participation while inertia keeps returning students to the problem of figuring out what answer we want from them. It is difficult to disconnect students from this perspective and adopt the problem as their own problem. At a minimum, this requires that we find a way to put academic learning in the context of our students' lives.

Many problems are introduced into the learning environment because students are trying to make sense of their broader experience as students, as well as attending to the specific content of the course and the problems embedded within a simulation. Although we may want students to focus on the complex unstructured problem space within the simulation, much of *their* problem space has to do with the social guessing game of "what does the teacher want me to say" and the high-stakes game of "getting good grades." When the class makes no sense to them, they intensify the "social guessing game." They push for clearer standards of performance and quicker feedback.

In the "Understanding Organizations" course, I wanted to give students open-ended assignments and problems to solve that were closer to the kinds of assignments and unstructured problems they would face in their organizational experience. I also wanted to hold them to standards of academic rigor. Their response to the anxiety that my intentionally ambiguous assignments engendered was to push for more clarity about what they were supposed to do. I am trying to find the best model to balance the advantages of creating situations that cause expectancy failures and the realities of the grading system. The following quote from Brousseau (1985) highlighted this dilemma:

> The more explicit I am about the behavior I wish students to display, the more likely it is that they will display that behavior without recourse to understanding which the behavior is meant to indicate; that is, the more likely they will take the form for the substance. (p. 40; quoted in Cobb, Perlwitz, & Underwood, 1996)

Looking to the constructivist literature for help with this issue, I found that most programs turned to developing scoring rubrics. I have been using rubrics for a number of years. They help students understand the evaluation criteria, help me clarify my standards, and cut down on the number of arguments with students over grades. They are essential for increasing reliability with teaching assistants on grading standards. I have had the feeling, however, that they sometimes shape the students' behavior without expanding their understanding. My biggest dissatisfaction with the rubrics that I found in the literature was that they did not direct students toward higher levels of thinking. I finally decided to try to develop a scoring guide that would help students understand what types of thinking I wanted them to produce. I am somewhat satisfied that the scoring guide I developed for the "Understanding Organizations" course does a fairly good job of helping students understand what is expected of them (see Appendix A).

This book has explored the implications of a constructivist perspective on learning for designing and conducting individual undergraduate courses. The final chapter briefly addresses some of the issues involved in expanding the scope of education reform beyond the level of an individual course.

Chapter 10

Curriculum Reform
in Higher Education

The primary focus and objective of this book has been to review recent literature in learning science and explore its potential for developing more effective ways of teaching in colleges and universities. This book was organized to build a systematic case for adopting a particular version of constructivism—transactional constructivism—to inform undergraduate education reform. Although I have addressed the book to an audience of professors who are interested in reforming their own teaching, I am aware that broader education reform will require intervention on the systems level. This chapter explores issues related to curriculum reform in higher education.

Although this chapter broadens its focus beyond the level of the individual course, I do not address the range of issues related to designing curriculum across several courses within a program of studies. This is an important topic that would require an extensive discussion. Effective program development and curriculum design are strongly embedded in the contexts of local settings and disciplinary communities of practice. An adequate presentation of this topic would require a number of examples from a range of disciplines and the discussion of a number of issues that go beyond the scope of this book.

Because change is a form of relearning, it can be viewed through the same lens that we use to understand any kind of learning. The combined constructivist view sees learning as embedded in activities and social practices. This perspective leads most naturally to a social practices perspective of organizational change. As Fullan (2001) asserted, education reform requires "reculturing rather than restructuring." New approaches to teaching must be developed and adapted to local circumstances, and the meanings associated with new behaviors have to be articulated and explored in face-to-face communities. In this chapter, I make a case for a change model that does not rely on top–down leadership.

The formula for reforming undergraduate education presented in this chapter contradicts the conventional wisdom about the importance and role of leadership in bringing about change in organizations. Many professors assume that they are powerless to influence the educational climate in their institutions beyond their own courses. My own view is that the most effective change starts with individual professors, especially with groups of professors organized into learning communities. Although the support of formal leaders is essential, change may be initiated from anywhere in the system. The formal leaders' most important role is to create a culture that fosters and celebrates conversations about teaching and learning. I believe that administrators and individual professors interested in improving the quality of both research and teaching should focus on establishing and nurturing viable learning communities.

THE CURRENT STATUS OF UNDERGRADUATE EDUCATION REFORM

There has been a long-standing and growing concern about the quality of undergraduate teaching and learning in North American colleges and universities (Association of American Colleges, 1985; Boyer, 1987; Gaff, 1991; Gardiner, 1994; McKeatchie, Pintrich, Lin, & Smith, 1986; National Institute of Education, 1984; Shulman, 1993; Wingspread Group on Higher Education, 1993). Department chairs believe the most important way they can improve the quality of their departments is to improve the quality of their faculty's teaching (Lucas, 1989). Despite these concerns, higher education curriculum has received remarkably little attention over the last 30 years (Stark & Lattuca, 1997). This lack of attention to curriculum is most pronounced in the areas of teaching and learning. Consistent with the dominance of the transmission model of learning among higher education faculty, discussions about the college curriculum invariably focus on what courses should be offered and what content is "essential," rather than how courses should be taught (Stark & Lattuca, 1997). Endless debates about the content of the required core dominate the discourse about curriculum, although course distribution requirements have not produced the types of knowledge faculty desire (Astin, 1993; Boyer, 1990; Gardiner, 1994).

Despite strong research evidence that the lecture produces disappointing results, compared with approaches like collaborative and problem-based learning, there has been little change in the teaching practices used in colleges and universities (Berger, 2002; Cohen, 1998; Gardiner, 1994, 2000; Halpern & Hakel, 2003; National Center for Postsecondary Improvement, 2002; Pascarella & Terenzini, 1991; Stark & Lattuca, 1997). A study conducted in 1980 indicated that between 70% and 90% of professors relied on lecturing as their primary teaching method (Blackburn, Pellino, Boberg, & O'Commell, 1980). There is no evidence that much has changed since then.

Recently, however, the growing body of research in learning science has stimulated calls for extending the innovations being implemented in other parts of the educational system to teaching in colleges and universities (Gardiner, 1994, 2000; Halpern & Hakel, 2003; Krockover, Shepardson, Eichinger, Nakhleh, & Adams, 2002; Marchese, 2003; National Center for Postsecondary Improvement, 2002; Pierce & Kalkman, 2003). The most widely read list of recommendations, "Ten Ways to Change Undergraduate Education," outlined in the Boyer Commission on Educating Undergraduates' (1999) *Reinventing Undergraduate Education: A Blueprint for America's Research Universities*, reflected the basic thrust of constructivist views of learning and their implications for postsecondary teaching. The report urged universities to move away from the lecture as the dominant form of instruction and promote more active modes of learning. The report specifically recommended increasing the use of inquiry-based and collaborative learning. Despite evidence of increasing interest in applying theory and research in learning science to teaching in higher education, a recent report issued by the National Center for Postsecondary Improvement (2002) indicated that little progress has been made toward changing what is actually happening on the classroom level:

> However natural it is to suppose that teaching should be informed by knowledge of how knowledge occurs, this principle seldom aligns with actual practice in higher education. During the 1990s, a considerable body of research was produced on the neurological processes within the brain that produce learning, as well as research by psychologists on situated learning as it occurs in different contexts ... Unfortunately, institutions and academic departments have seldom taken responsibility for applying the findings of such research to pedagogical practice. (p. 13)

Arthur Chickering and Zelda Gamson's (1987) *Seven Principles for Good Practice in Undergraduate Education* has been widely circulated as a guideline for reforming higher education:

1. Frequent student–faculty interaction in and outside the class that helps to motivate and involve students.

2. Cooperation between students, rather than competitive and isolated study.

3. Active learning through discussion, writing, and application of what is learned.

4. Prompt feedback on student performance to help students assess their existing knowledge and competence.

5. Emphasis on time on task—that is, helping students learn to use their time effectively.

6. Communication of high expectations to all students, from the poorly prepared to the bright and motivated.

7. Respect for diverse talents and ways of learning that students bring to college. (p. 3)

Braxton, Eimers, and Bayer (1996), however, did not find normative support for a similar list of basic principles that are compatible with a movement toward approaches to teaching that are informed by a constructivist perspective. Participatory, student-centered approaches received the least support from faculty in research universities. One reason for this lack of support was the faculty members' perception that student-centered approaches are more time-consuming and require more effort. Braxton, Eimers, and Bayer (1996) summarized their concerns about the difficulty of accomplishing curriculum reforms in institutions that did not support essential norms to support these reforms:

The lack of normative support for a concern for the "improvement of teaching" may be one of the significant findings of this study. It posits that faculty did not consider it "inappropriate" if they avoid reading about college teaching, bypass professional development opportunities to enhance their own teaching, and/or refuse to incorporate new teaching methods or procedures into their own classroom. (p. 619)

Surveys of professors and administrators in research universities indicate that, although an overwhelming majority believe that more time should be given to teaching, they also believe that attention to teaching would hurt their chances of achieving promotion, tenure, and competitive salary increases (Gray, Frohl, & Diamond, 1992; Stark & Lattuca, 1997). Professors often complain that time spent on teaching interferes with their research and scholarship. Yet Stark and Lattuca (1997) found that, although most respondents complained that the time spent on administrative duties like committee work interfered with their ability to improve their teaching, no respondent complained that research prevented him or her from devoting time to teaching. To me, this indicates that any solution to the problem of improving teaching cannot compromise our ability to conduct high-quality scholarship and research.

Many of the objections to implementing new teaching models are practical rather than theoretical, but the practical environment is produced by the habitus of the university. Before I address the issues involved in bringing about change on the systems level, it is important to acknowledge that individual professors face systems-level barriers to implementing several of the methods described in this book. As the "Understanding Organizations" case illustrated, the struggle between learning and the "game of schooling" is a difficult problem for any new approach to teaching and learning. I have been involved in a tug-of-war between learning and "school games" the entire time I have been experimenting with new ways of teaching.

The constructivist perspective also demands that individual professors become reflective practitioners who are aware of why they are using specific methods for achieving their goals. We must focus the same kind of rigorous scholarship on teaching that we apply to our other scholarly work. Few professors can sustain the effort required to make these changes without an active supportive environment.

It is also important to avoid blanket criticisms of any method of teaching without accounting for the situation in which it is used. It is absurd to assert that "no one ever learns anything from a lecture." All of us can cite examples of times when our lives were changed when a lecture or reading connected a vital concern or answered an important question. We know that lives can be transformed by ideas because it has happened to us and our students tell us it has happened to them. The most effective lectures and art touch more people because they have universal themes that connect with the concerns of many people. Yet it is important to remember that this connection depends on a serendipitous match between what we say and our students' concerns.

As my discussion in the last chapter acknowledged, there are legitimate concerns about the difficulties in managing the quality of dialogue and disciplinary discourse in the various forms of collaborative learning. There are many reasons that it is difficult to change the social practices and patterns of communication in the classroom. As I reported in the case study in chapter 8, changing the social practices of the classroom requires training, negotiation, monitoring, and feedback to students. Because the identities of both students and faculty are scaffolded by the existing patterns of communication in the classroom, restructuring these patterns requires considerable attention and effort. It is not reasonable to expect that professors will embark on this difficult process without a well-developed support network. Furthermore, the new patterns must ultimately provide both students and faculty a more rewarding experience in the classroom. Although I argue against a model of change initiated and championed by administrators, it is clear that college and university administrators must establish a general atmosphere of support for innovations initiated by faculty.

RESISTANCE TO CHANGE AT THE SYSTEMS LEVEL

There are a number of factors on the systems level that prevent curriculum reform. One of the reasons that it is even more difficult to promote education reforms on the postsecondary level is that neither the promotion and tenure of individual professors nor the reputation of the university rests on teaching. Despite rhetoric to the contrary, colleges and universities do not offer powerful incentives for good teaching. Furthermore, professors' loyalties align them more with their disciplines than with the colleges and universities that employ them. Disciplinary incentives focus on research and scholarship, rather than teaching (Cohen, 1998). The tendency for communities of practice to be more salient than formal organizational cultures is even more pronounced in universities than it is in other types of organizations (Brown & Duguid, 2001; Strauss, 1984). The power of what Knorr-Cetina (1999) referred to as "epistemic cultures" made up of scientists in the same field has been strengthened by electronic communication and the increased competition for and mobility of top scholars. Brown and Duguid (2001) found that information often flows more freely through broader "networks of practice" than within individual organizations.

The recent rash of budget crises and the rapid increase in the number of courses being taught by adjunct and part-time faculty members has been an additional impediment to systematic change efforts. There has been a 40% increase in the use of part-time faculty and a sharp increase in the number of non-tenure-track faculty and staff who are shouldering a growing portion of the undergraduate teaching and advisement duties in research universities (National Center for Postsecondary Improvement, 2002). These trends have weakened the power of local organizations in relationship to wider communities of practice and have made it increasingly difficult to maintain viable face-to-face learning communities.

Organizational Change

Although I do not attempt to review the literature on organizational change, it is important to touch on a few of the classic ideas on planned change and resistance to change before addressing the issue of change in higher education. Most discussions of planned change begin with Lewin's characterization of change as a process of unfreezing, changing, and refreezing (Schein, 1969). Lewin's model has provided a basic framework for thinking about change as a process. It is a fairly simple model, but it focused the attention of change agents on some important dimensions of organizational change. It was important at the time it was formulated in the 1930s because it helped early change agents understand that (a) people need to become aware of the need for change before they are open to change, and (b) change will not endure if it is not institutionalized. Research in learning science has highlighted the strong tendency for learners to return to their previous understandings and ways of behaving. The work of Lewin and his followers focused attention on the importance of avoiding resistance by removing barriers to change, rather than meeting resistance with coercive power (Bennis, Benne, & Chin, 1961).

Katz and Kahn (1978) identified six sources of resistance to organizational change. Most analyses of sources of organizational resistance to change that followed were similar to Katz and Kahn's. Most of these points also have special aspects that relate to the specific situation of bringing change to colleges and universities.

Overdetermination. The standardization and control mechanisms that organizations use to maintain their stability can be the source of strong structural forces that resist change. Job descriptions and expectations are both formal and informal. Any professor who has struggled to implement an innovative way to teach knows the amount of frustration these situations can generate. Even change efforts initiated by administrators often fail to incorporate the other changes needed to facilitate the new methods. The criteria for promotion and tenure may penalize professors who implement innovations (e.g., professors who implement cooperative learning techniques may be penalized because their course ratings drop when students complain that they had to teach the content to themselves; National Center for Postsecondary Improvement, 2002).

Narrow Focus of Change. It is important to consider not only the person making the specific change, but all the other people who might be affected or need to change their behavior to facilitate that change (e.g., the size of the technology staff is rarely increased enough to support efforts to increase the use of technology in teaching).

An awareness of the importance of systems-level issues is one of the reasons that many theorists think change must be managed by top managers (Wallace, 2003). My own perspective is that the most effective change efforts, especially in higher education, are not led from the top. Even change agents who are not at the top of the organization need to educate themselves about systems-level concerns (Senge, 1999). I do not think professors should "let the dean worry about the budget." For change agents in educational settings to be successful, their proposals have to be reasonable from a budgetary perspective. This might mean including some lectures in the overall design of a course. Learning science does not recommend using large lectures, but it can help us to maximize their effectiveness when they are a budgetary necessity.

Group Inertia. Colleagues may resist making changes in their own behavior that allow the key person to carry out the change. This is a special problem in the area of innovations in teaching because the culture of the university places less value on teaching than on competitive activities.

Threatened Expertise. This is an especially strong factor in resistance to change in higher education. Professors have an enormous investment in the lecturing and group discussion skills they have developed, and their students and colleagues respect these skills. New methods of teaching often require new skills that are difficult to acquire (e.g., I found it very difficult to learn to deliver "just-in-time" minilectures; during my first year of teaching the "Understanding Organizations" course, I was even concerned that I lacked the natural cognitive ability to master this skill).

Threatened Power. In this category, Katz and Kahn referred to the redistribution of power to make decisions about work. A key feature of their general recommendations for improving organizational effectiveness was a shift in decision making down the organizational hierarchy. Their research indicated that increased participation in decision making led to higher job satisfaction and increased productivity. In essence, they recommended giving workers more decision-making power about how they completed their own work. Although this downward shift in decision making increased workers' productivity, job satisfaction, and "behavior above and beyond the call of duty," it was not always accepted by supervisors who lost power. In most universities, professors have a great deal of freedom to regulate their own work. The issue of power comes up more often at the interface between professors and students. We are the supervisors who might resist giving students more decision-making power.

Resource Allocation. Resources are a serious problem in most higher education institutions. Even in well-funded research universities, resources for teaching are often poor. A colleague of mine once complained that because we had invested in technology, he had to buy his own chalk.

Mintzberg and Westley (1992) developed a broader framework for organizational change that has been useful for developing strategies for change. They made a specific distinction between deductive change that moves from concepts to practical implementation and inductive change that begins on the level of practice. I would assert that if innovations by small groups of professors are informed by theory, an inductive change process can move forward with much more ecological validity and lead to effective systematic reform. This change theory is parallel to the iterative-recursive learning model I have been using to develop instructional strategies. I do not think a list of "teaching tips" or "things that work" that are disseminated throughout the system can lead to meaningful change. Yet a "theoretically informed" change initiated on the local level can have systematic effects if it is shared in a way that includes both the how and why of the methods used.

Mintzberg and Westley (1992) identified three approaches to organizational change: procedural planning, visionary leadership, and inductive learning. Procedural planning is similar to classic "rational" strategic planning. This approach is characterized by planned change efforts initiated from the top of the organization designed to meet particular organizational objectives. Visionary leadership is change inspired by a leader who can create an image of what is possible by "telling a story" that has broad appeal in the organization and creates a shared vision of where the organization should be moving (Gardner, 1995). Planned change resulting from strategic planning efforts and visionary leadership dominates the literature on leadership and change. Although these approaches have been championed and romanticized, they have been largely unsuccessful in colleges and universities, and I do not think they represent the most promising approaches to change in higher education. Beer and Nohria (2000) estimated that 70% of organizational change efforts fail to achieve their objectives. If this rate of failure exists in corporate environments with considerable leverage over employees, the chances for the success of top–down change efforts in universities are small. Even in private sector organizations, most successful change probably results from leaders appearing to lead change that would have happened naturally (Ogbanna & Harris, 1998).

Mintzberg and Westley's third approach, inductive learning, seems like a more appropriate change strategy for colleges and universities. Inductive learning takes place during experimentation in subunits of the organization. In the typical example, a middle manager recognizes an important innovation on his or her own level of the organization where the key transactions are carried out.

Eckel, Hill, Green, and Mallon (1999) summarized the results of a large evaluation of planned change efforts conducted in 26 colleges and universities. They identified nine successful change strategies. Most of these strategies fit into the procedural planning and visionary leadership approaches (e.g., "Leaders make a clear and compelling case to key stakeholders about why things must be done differently" [p. 2], "Change leaders craft an agenda that both makes sense and focuses on improvement without assigning blame" [p. 3]). Other successful strategies represent a more inductive approach (e.g., "Change leaders develop connections among different initiatives and individuals across campus that create synergy and provide momentum for the initiative" [p. 4], "Collaborative leadership identifies and empowers talent across campus and at a variety of levels," "Leaders develop supporting structures, create incentives, and provide resources for change efforts" [p. 6]). These formulas for success highlight the paradoxes that need to be overcome to implement change. Traditional dualisms must be transcended to develop what Peters and Waterman (1982) called *loose-tight organizations*. Because I believe effective organizations are organized to understand and facilitate their key transactions, I think resources should be organized to help employees responsible for these transactions to develop effective and creative ways of improving the quality of their work. In colleges and universities, resources should be organized to focus resources on supporting teaching and research. I believe organizational leaders need to formulate, communicate, and create consensus on the broad vision of the institution. Beyond that, organizational leaders in higher education should manage their organizations in ways that encourage innovation on the departmental and program level (Del Favero, 2002).

The key transaction of teaching takes place with professors and students in classrooms. This is the arena where powerful teaching experiments can be conducted and guided by theory/practice transactions and the ongoing face-to-face dialogue necessary to weld theory and practice in a recursive process. The constructivist view does not hold that theories can be applied hierarchically to practical situations. Instead theories are grounded in experience and altered and instantiated in transactions within the dynamics of local communities of practice. In these instances, local experiments are highly conceptual (idea-focused), rather than "just practical." In the particular instance of change in teaching and learning practices, ideas about how to teach that are disconnected from answers to "why questions" are of little value. Theory does not dictate practice; it is a lens that helps practitioners develop practices that fit local environments.

Mintzberg and Westley specifically saw inductive approaches to change as effective in professional organizations such as universities. In a case study of McGill University, Mintzberg and Rose (1992) found that most innovation bubbled up from the work of faculty in individual courses. Leaders who encouraged and nurtured innovation and provided the resources to evaluate its effectiveness were able to disseminate innovations throughout the system that fit their overall vision. The advantage of grounding innovation in the best local practices is that the innovation has already proved its ability to adapt to the local environment.

The Nonconforming Enclave

Mintzberg and Wesley (1992) made a case for the idea that systems that endure must have an ongoing strategy for managing change that balances the need for continuity and the need to adapt to external environmental pressures. They used examples from major world religions that have survived for thousands of years by successfully maintaining this balance. Each of the three strategies they identified has been employed by one of the world's great religions: cloning by the Protestants, uprooting by the Buddhists, and enclaving by the Catholics.

Cloning refers to instances where a push to change is dealt with by spinning off a new organization. As in the case of the proliferation of the Protestant denominations, the new organization is structurally detached from the original organization, but retains key core principles. Uprooting occurs when organizations are disbanded completely and a new organization is formed that responds to new environmental pressures. The revolutionary nature of uprooting preserves the visionary leadership and passion associated with a new enterprise and prevents bureaucratic ossification. Although there are many examples of cloning and uprooting in education, they cannot serve as models for managing change within an existing educational institution that wants to preserve itself.

Innovations within the Catholic Church were often dealt with by enclaving. New variations of Catholicism were given the status of orders within the church. Nonconforming enclaves are partitioned from the mainstream of the organization. Over time they tend to get less radical as they adapt to the environment of the larger organization. As long as they are not seen as a direct threat to established power bases, enclaves may even be valued by the more conservative parts of the organization. The enclave can be used as an example of its creativity when the organization wants to portray itself as being on the leading edge of innovation (e.g., normally marginalized service-learning projects are the subjects of a large number of public relations stories released from universities). Nonconforming enclaves can also serve as a source of vicarious pleasure for employees who must function under more constraints (e.g., those crazy guys with the ponytails in Information Technology who bring their dogs to work).

Most important, nonconforming enclaves can serve as vehicles for incubating new ideas. Ideally, they can serve as the site for "power experiments" guided by the attention to theory and the ongoing inquiry necessary to weld theory and practice in a recursive process. Powered by energy created by dialogic communication, the ideal enclave functions as a cohesive learning organization that develops new visions for the future.

Enclaving is a natural partner of inductive learning. Because colleges and universities are loosely organized, underbounded systems whose members place a high value on preserving their autonomy, they tend to tolerate the development of nonconforming enclaves. These enclaves are partially isolated from the primary system, but available as models for change in times when the organization recognizes the need for change. Innovations functioning as nonconforming enclaves will not be institutionalized unless they are needed to resolve a crisis. It is the local program director's job to perfect the model and be "ready to move" in times of organizational opportunity or crisis.

ORGANIZATIONAL CHANGE IN COLLEGES AND UNIVERSITIES

The literature in higher education contains several descriptive models of curriculum change that define the steps in the change process (e.g., Stark & Lattuca's [1997] model of the stages of curriculum change: [a] the initiation [awareness] stage, [b] the screening [adaptation] stage, and [c] the adoption [confirmation] stage). Even when details are added to these types of models, however, they do not have any particular power to inform someone who wants to promote a basic change in the way undergraduate education is conducted. Stark and Lattuca's model describes the way innovations like the option to take a course on a pass/fail basis or the requirement that all students take a multicultural awareness course are approved by the faculties of various institutions across the country.

Morrison (1998) developed a list of sources of resistance to change in educational organizations that is parallel to the list originally produced by Katz and Kahn (1978) for organizations in general:

1. *Value Barriers.* Value issues can create powerful forces for opposition to change in higher education. Commitment to traditional models of education can be based on strong values connected to identities. The principle of academic freedom and the fact that professors are protected by tenure gives them more autonomy and they are less willing to capitulate.

2. *Power Barriers.* Participants tend to oppose change efforts that reduce their power. Because professors have little formal power, they tend to focus on maintaining their autonomy. Changes that reduce autonomy usually meet with strong resistance.

3. *Psychological Barriers.* This category relates to issues of comfort and a sense of well-being. Curriculum reforms inspired by constructivism ask professors to acquire new skills and develop different types of relationships with students, faculty, and staff on teaching teams. These changes can increase uncertainty and anxiety.

4. *Practical Barriers.* The general overload in educational systems also accentuates practical barriers to efforts to provide professors with new skills. Educational organizations are often short on technical support, teaching space, and planning time.

Cohen and March (1974) conducted the classic analysis of the forces for continuity and change in colleges and universities. Since that time, little has changed in higher education that would challenge their characterization of colleges and universities as "organized anarchies." Cohen, March, and Olsen's (1972) *garbage can* model of organizational choice has also survived the past 30 years as a useful metaphor for understanding day-to-day life on university committees. Weick's (1976) description of educational organizations as "loosely coupled systems" is a third image of the university that still captures the frustrations of deans and college and university presidents who often describe managing change in higher education as "herding cats." More recent analyses based on systems thinking (Senge, 1999) and chaos theory have fostered hope that sweeping changes will grow out of small local events (Cutright, 2001). I sometimes fear, however, that it would be much easier for a butterfly in Asia to cause a hurricane in Texas than to change the way professors teach in universities.

Colleges and Universities as Organized Anarchies

Cohen and March (1974) developed their analysis of the nature of higher educational organizations on the premise that colleges and universities find it hard to set specific objectives and engage in meaningful strategic planning because their purposes are ambiguous. Rather than having a single coherent purpose, postsecondary education provides a vehicle for satisfying many conflicting societal needs. This ambiguity of purpose fosters a state of organized anarchy. This phrase recognizes that anarchies are not really chaotic, but organized around local communities of practice. They resist control above the level of face-to-face communities. The ambiguity of purpose in higher educational organizations produces an ambiguity of power and responsibility. College and university presidents, deans, and department chairs generally resonate to Cohen and March's description of their role as "the driver of a skidding automobile."

Cohen and March concluded that leading successful change in an organized anarchy is more difficult and demands different strategies than organizations with clearer objectives. Higher education organizations are always overloaded and have a severe shortage of energy to direct toward operating and changing on the systems level. Change efforts must take advantage of the fragmented nature of the system. Because most of the energy in the system is directed at individual teaching and research efforts linked to national disciplinary agendas, few organizational issues are important enough to rise to a visible level in the system.

Cohen and March's most useful recommendation is that change agents need to be persistent and concentrate their efforts on selected change efforts. If change agents have a clear goal and are persistent and willing to do the work to implement change, they will eventually succeed. This can be a frustrating process because we all know that almost anyone can stop a proposal from getting through a committee. Yet persistent change agents know that if one committee does not approve the change, another one will. Colleges and universities also operate with a weak information base. Change agents are often the only people with specific information related to their proposal. Successful change agents in universities not only need to "do their homework," they need to "overdo their homework." A key delaying tactic during a committee meeting is to ask for more information. If the change agent has the information requested, it neutralizes resistance.

Cohen and March also pointed out that the ambiguity of the system tends to elevate the importance of status concerns. They recommended that change agents "exchange status for substance." Letting other people take the credit can be a powerful tool for facilitating change. It has been my experience that the chairperson of an academic committee will be glad to let someone else write a report, as long as his or her name is on the cover, even if it contains ideas he or she does not actually agree with or totally understand. Colleges and universities admittedly have a great deal of inertia. Change takes a great deal of effort, but it also takes a great deal of effort to reverse a change once it has been achieved.

Meetings as "Garbage Cans"

Cohen, March, and Olsen's (1972) *garbage can* metaphor also provides an important insight that helps change agents avoid the pitfalls and frustrations they can confront while negotiating change through committees. In an organized anarchy, problems and concerns tend to float in the system without a clear place to be expressed. Any proposal submitted to a committee tends to attract these concerns. The most visible proposals (and the first item on the agenda) tend to create garbage cans for these concerns. Cohen, March, and Olsen recommended creating other arenas to catch this garbage (and avoid being the first item on the agenda). I think we also need to create legitimate arenas for exploring these concerns. If professors are deeply concerned about sexism, racism, social justice, falling academic standards, and a number of other important issues in the university, these issues need to be addressed in a meaningful way. As it stands, any new course proposed to the college curriculum committee will become the arena for a debate on *all* these issues.

Colleges and Universities as "Loosely Coupled Systems"

Weick's (1976) characterization of the educational organization as a "loosely coupled system" has also been influential in efforts to understand institutions of higher education. Weick applied systems theory to educational institutions and concluded that educational organizations have few mechanisms to span boundaries. Educational systems are not characterized by the exercise of authority that actively binds the parts of the organization together.

The loosely coupled system is usually characterized as a problem for managers, but Cutright (2001) pointed out that the loose coupling and organized anarchy of educational organizations also make higher education systems flexible and highly adaptive. In loosely coupled systems, subsystems can develop innovative solutions to problems that adapt to local pressures without greatly affecting the whole system. Loosely coupled systems are more open to the development of nonconforming enclaves. However, loosely coupled systems resist standardization that might bring important efficiencies to the system.

Chaos Theory

Some attempts are being made to reframe change strategies by reexamining postsecondary institutions using chaos theory. Despite the lack of change in the core educational processes in higher education, administrators see themselves as experiencing enormous pressures to make profound changes or risk the survival of their institutions (Barnett, 2001). Dever (2001) believed that chaos theory provides clues to the mechanisms that colleges and universities might use to facilitate adaptive change. He pointed to the primary mechanisms of chaos theory (feedback loops and strange attractors) as potential sources of leverage for change. Dever introduced the variable of human agency into the formula for change that in many interpretations of chaos theory are both random and determined. Leadership in this model harnesses the creativity and energy of individual actors and groups of actors. Leadership must help group members see the winds of change before it destroys them and harness these energies to find new ways to use their own energy and the energy of the prevailing winds to chart new courses for education. A driver of a skidding car or a sailor tacking into the wind may seem to be at the mercy of the unmanageable forces, but their knowledge and skill can take them where they want to go.

Griffith and Lemisko (2001) provided an optimistic picture of how the set of forces at play in higher education could bring beneficial change:

> Exhilarating and empowering ways of thinking and doing in higher education could arise out of a combination of seemingly random strands: new technologies, post-Fordist economic influence, constructivism, and the notion that chaos theory can be applied to social institutions. The convergence of these strands creates the possibility for a bright future for higher education— a future where students are part of the process of discovery, planning, and reshaping along with faculty, administration, and boards of governors. (p. 175)

Griffith and Lemisko (2001) analyzed the emerging and future ecology of higher education as much more dynamic than it has been over the past

60 years. They saw the external demands of a post-Fordian economy as in constant flux. The move toward increased flexibility and rapid responses to changing markets creates organizations that need "just-in-time" knowledge, employees, and manufacturing. They believe constructivist learning theory and information technology can create an information-rich environment in the university that will prepare students to succeed in this type of economy. Their call for a "planning not a planned" organization is reminiscent of Dewey's "planning not a planned society." These are dynamic, process-oriented systems where information is widely available and used as feedback rather than to reach static conclusions. In this kind of a system, dissent and conflict are seen as potentially creative and adaptive forces. Constructivist learning theory and information-rich environments also create forces that make top–down change strategies counterproductive. The impossibility of "knowing everything" in an age of information overload creates forces that facilitate the development of learning organizations where students, faculty, staff, and administrators learn together.

Post-Fordian economics is "just-in-time" economics. Just-in-time knowledge use makes different learning skills adaptive. The new economy shifts the emphasis from static knowledge to increased ability to gather, evaluate, organize, and utilize new knowledge. Leadership as seen through chaos theory involves sensitivity to emerging patterns and possibilities that can be leveraged to create new synergies. Mossberg (2001) echoed these sentiments: "Today's institutions are becoming larger, more diffuse, more porous in their borders, more distributed, sowing new schools and practices and complex new educational formats" (p. 205). Succeeding in these types of organizations demands a different kind of learning (Barnett, 2001). The view of organizations and change forwarded by chaos theory sees leadership as leveraged from anywhere in the system.

College and university administrators who want to improve the quality of teaching and learning face a number of structural and cultural barriers. Watson and Stage (1999) recognized this fact and called for administrators to target their efforts toward supporting and enhancing the key transactions of teaching and learning. Administrators can create an environment that supports a culture of teaching (Centra, 1993).

Research on knowledge-intensive private sector organizations also indicates that leaders should focus on developing strong cultures and minimize top–down control, creating structural supports that facilitate rather than limit creative behavior (Cunha, 2002). Grant (2003) found that even large oil companies have abandoned top–down "rational" strategic planning models for planning strategies that emerge from local ecologies. Professors in colleges and universities have even more power to resist top–down change efforts than members of private sector organizations. Given the considerable barriers to change in the university, a coherent alternate change strategy is required that fits its organizational realities. Trowler (1998) found that using top–down reform strategies in educational organizations was ineffective because educators had a broad range of effective ways of undermining the reforms they did not support. Top–down change efforts also suffer from the tendency of all significant proposals to become garbage cans for a range of ideological issues floating around in the system (Knight & Trowler, 2001).

A Social Practices Perspective on Change in Learning Organizations

Knight and Trowler (2001) presented a social practices perspective on change that is derived from the sociocultural perspective. This approach conceptualizes teaching as an activity structure that involves the development of professors' identities. Any change in the primary mediating structures, especially the social practices of communication, has a profound impact on the meaning of the activity. The most obvious example of a change that has taken place in recent years has been the effect of the rapid adoption of e-mail on patterns of communication between professors and students (Sproul & Kieslers, 1991). A sociocultural perspective predicts that the most profound systems-level changes result from changes in communication structures rather than systematic, top–down change efforts (by reculturing rather than restructuring). The social practices perspective fits well with change models based on the inductive approach to change and the practice of nurturing nonconforming enclaves.

The social practices perspective contrasts with the technical-rational approaches that dominate the change literature. In professional, loosely coupled systems, it is more effective to provide facilitative leadership that harnesses the competence and creativity of people across the system. In educational organizations in general, and particularly in colleges and universities, top–down change strategies usually fail (Fullan, 2001). Wenger (1998) concluded that organizing change efforts around top–down strategic planning and efforts to overcome resistance to change are based on certain assumptions about people in systems:

> if we believe that people in organizations contribute to organizational goals by participating inventively in practices that can never be fully captured by institutionalized processes, then we will minimize prescription, suspecting that too much of it discourages the very inventiveness that makes practice effective. We will have to make sure that our organizations are contexts in which the communities that develop these practices may prosper. We will have to value the work of community building and make sure that participants have access to the resources necessary to learn what they need to learn in order to

take actions and make decisions that fully engage their own knowledgeability. (p. 10)

The sociocultural perspective sees identity as developed and situated in the social practices of the settings that are most central to the individual. If we treat people as noncreative events in structures, they will resist change efforts to preserve their identities or disengage from the system and invest their creative energies in other areas of their lives. It is not in the interest of the organization to have groups organize themselves to fight change or "go-along" while they wait for the effort to pass. Coercive power can produce compliance, but it will not produce the commitment needed to make change successful (Katz & Kahn, 1978; Senge, 1996; Wallace, 2003). Doing the minimum and "laying low" is the time-honored strategy that public school teachers use to weather the waves of reform brought in by each new school superintendent. University professors are equally adept at undermining unwanted change efforts by the latest dean.

Much of the identity work carried on by academics takes place in the classroom. The vehemence with which some professors degrade teaching goes beyond behavior that reflects indifference; it is an active defense against having this part of their experience define their self-worth. For professors who have found success in teaching, the classroom is an arena for maintaining a positive identity that is anchored to their current styles of teaching. Changing the way they teach can be a direct threat to this identity. In either case, it is no small achievement to change basic elements of how professors interact with students in the classroom. One group is actively dissociated from teaching, and the other group's identity is deeply embedded in their current classroom practices. This situation makes university professors especially resistant to top–down curriculum change efforts.

An organization can be characterized as a "community of communities" (Brown & Duguid, 1991, p. 53). Communities of practice within and across organizations participate in activity structures that shape the identities of participants in relationship to that activity and as members of that community. Expertise is distributed across members of the community, increasing their interdependence. Communities of practice within organizations can be the cornerstones of vibrant learning organizations or they can organize themselves to make meaningful change almost impossible. In fact, their identities can be defined by their heroic resistance to change.

Social practice theory sees leadership as the creation of arenas for the construction of meaning. Weick (1995) emphasized the role of organizations as sense-making mechanisms. Communities of practice are defined by mutual relationships within a web of communication where information is communicated quickly (Wenger, 1998). Access to information defines membership in the community, and denial of information defines "the other." Regardless of what the administration wants to communicate to faculty, the meaning of that communication is constructed in informal conversations within communities of practice. Important arenas for meaning making, such as conversations in the halls and the coffee room, are usually hidden from administrators. Unless we establish new patterns of communication, each part of the system will lack the information required to understand the whole system.

Senge's (1990) concept of the learning organization is the most popular version of the communities of practice perspective. He has applied much of the theory that supports the combined constructivist model to the problem of organizational development and change in modern knowledge organizations. The most important variable that affects the quality of knowledge organizations is the quality of the dialogue about important problems. Vibrant learning organizations are built around these conversations. As in classrooms designed on constructivist theory, the quality of dialogue is the key ingredient for success. It is as important and at least as difficult to create constructive dialogue in academic communities as it is in classrooms.

Morgan's (1986) classic work on organizational metaphors led him to conclude that the machine metaphor that has shaped our view of organizations since the Industrial Revolution, through Fordism and Taylorism, is no longer adaptive for our times. A cornerstone of Senge's view of organizations is captured by his call to abandon the dominant classic machine metaphor we have been using to think about organizations that led to top–down control through bureaucracy:

> And the metaphor of the machine, which has given us incredible material affluence but also rigid bureaucracies, assembly-line jobs and schools, and even more frenetic, disconnected ways of living, must be superceded by the image of the living system. . . . Nature generates diversity. The industrial age has generated homogeneity, relentlessly eradicating both biological and cultural diversity. Nature focuses on means, allowing ends to emerge. The industrial age has focused on goals. Allowing them to justify whatever means were needed. (Senge, 1999, p. 74)

The change in driving metaphor from machine to living system also changes the definition of an ideal leader and the effect of diversity on the system's adaptive capacity. The classic change models characterize leaders as visionaries who inspire followers, drive change, and overcome resistance. Organizational crises bring calls for new leadership. By contrast, the leader of a living system, like a skilled gardener, nurtures growth by releasing potential energy that already exists in the system. As in nature, diversity is not seen as a threat to efficiency, but as a mechanism for generating adaptive solutions. This model sees change as bubbling up from local centers of innovation, rather than being commanded from the top. If they are adaptive, new ideas survive and thrive.

If they are nurtured by leadership (both by "top" leadership and other leaders in the system), innovations spread horizontally across communities of practice. This is the process Kuh (1996) referred to as the "rapid transformation perspective." This is why communication across boundaries within an organization is essential for the success of this type of change process. Loosely coupled systems like colleges and universities, however, are characterized by extreme fragmentation and lack of communication across boundaries. This characteristic allows enclaves to develop and prevents them from bringing wholesale change to the system. The role of leadership in this change model is to nurture promising innovations and facilitate communication across organizational barriers.

It is not enough to allow units time to develop new ideas. For change to improve the organization's productivity, the organization needs to have all its processes organized systematically to support its key transaction. If this alignment is not maintained through centralized control, new roles and mechanisms for reaching consensus will be necessary. This presents organizational leaders with a paradox: how to maintain efficiency and apply appropriate pressure and support for change without using top–down strategies.

Senge (1999) identified three roles in systems that are necessary to transform a local innovation into a systems change. First, Senge believed that local line leaders, who understand the problems of implementing change on the face-to-face, day-to-day level of the key transaction, are best equipped to develop innovations that can be successfully implemented at this level. Nonaka and Takeuchi (1995) emphasized the importance of developing shared knowledge in communities of practice. Collaborative activities are more effective because they convert tacit knowledge into shared knowledge. Although local line leaders may have a narrow view of the broader implications of an innovation on the systems level, they are in the best position to create and maintain learning communities and understand the local ecology of practice. In the university environment, local line managers are department chairs and program directors. I personally believe that departments should create programs built around the interests of students and faculty groups. Senge (1996) found that there were instances of successful change with and without effective leadership from the top of the organization, but there were no examples of successful change without leadership from local line leaders. Despite the danger that strengthening subunits can promote Balkanization rather than cooperation across the organization, it is still be the most effective change strategy. To prevent innovation from further fragmenting the system, colleges and universities need to create new roles and structures that span programs and departments.

The second essential role is the internal networker, who spans organizational boundaries by carrying information and encouraging dialogue across organizational boundaries. This is a function that is largely absent in university environments. A paradoxical characteristic of this role is that its power to facilitate change comes specifically because it has no formal power. Internal networkers cannot be effective if they are seen as having vested interests. Third, executive leaders who assume roles like mentors, supporters, and coaches can create an atmosphere where change is encouraged and change agents are nourished. In Senge's view, the most important role for top-level leaders is to function as "champions" for local line leaders. This is especially important when early attempts at change result in poorer short-term results. In my own experience, my efforts to experiment with new ways of teaching have always resulted in dips in my teaching evaluations from students. If chairs and program directors do not protect professors from negative fallout from reduced ratings, they will not be willing to experiment with new approaches to teaching. A second vital role for top-level leadership is to create what Senge (1996) called a "learning infrastructure" that supports an environment for learning and growth throughout the organization.

Although professors work in a much less oppressive environment than public school teachers, efforts to bring change to postsecondary education can be informed by research conducted on the K–12 level. Fullan's (2001) review of research in schools indicated that less than 20% had viable school-wide professional communities. Rosenholtz (1989) compared schools that were "learning enriched" with the majority of schools she categorized as "learning impoverished." In learning-enriched schools, curriculum development was seen as a collaborative effort. Teachers, staff, and administrators shared a broad consensus about values and goals. Other research on highly effective schools led to the same conclusion (Bryk, Sebring, Kerbow, Rollow, & Easton, 1998; Newman & Wehlage, 1995).

CONCLUSION

This review of theory and research on change in higher education demonstrates that the ecology of the higher education system works against efforts to establish and maintain new approaches to undergraduate teaching. Our choices of instructional strategies are limited by factors such as time, incentive systems, the time periods in which courses are offered, and the nature of the space available for teaching (Stark & Lattuca, 1997). The reward system, especially in research universities, is organized to reinforce research and individual entrepreneurial behavior.

It is clear that understanding what changes we need to make is only a small portion of the battle to improve teaching and learning in colleges and universities. The entire system is organized to resist traditional approaches to change. I was motivated to write this book because I believe the only way that teaching in higher education will change is for groups of professors to reach consensus on what types of changes need to be made on the program level and go about the business of changing the way they teach. Good courses and programs attract students. Program growth creates pressure for systems change. I understand that "street-level" change agents will need champions on the administrative level, but I really do not think administrators are the primary engines for or impediments to change. If deans and higher administrators are hearing positive feedback from students, parents, and employers, they will be happy to anoint themselves change leaders. Deans would do well to reread Tolstoy's (1869/1994) *War and Peace* and listen to General Kutuzov's insights about the relative force of leadership against the caprice of chance and the march of history. He understood that watching for small opportunities "to go with the flow" was the strongest model for leadership that could be exercised by the "driver of a skidding car."

Despite some evidence to the contrary, I think professors are predisposed to be "reflective practitioners." We want our practice to be guided by theory. Although many professors see teaching as peripheral to their core identities, I am hoping their exposure to more sophisticated theories of learning and models of teaching will stimulate interest and investment in teaching. We would not think of conducting research according to a set of "rules of thumb." We go to great lengths to understand both the phenomena we are studying and the research paradigms we are using to understand those phenomena on the deepest level possible. If we were not driven to explore a part of the world on that level, we would soon become bored and disinterested in our scholarly work. I would like to convince more professors that applying the same intensity to understanding how to teach the content in their disciplines can make them just as interested in their teaching. Although the teaching models spawned by constructivist views of learning can start us on a journey with a difficult beginning, it ultimately leads to a much more satisfying learning experience for both professors and students. Just as important, it produces learning that has much more long-term value for our students.

References

Abercrombie, M. L. (1960). *The anatomy of judgement.* Harmondsworth, England: Penguin. New York: Basic Books.

Acovelli, M., & Nowakowski, A. (1994). The business practices course: Self-study learning reengineering. *Educational Technology, 34*(9), 21–27.

Alexander, T. (2002). The aesthetics of reality: The development of Dewey's ecological theory of experience. In F. T. Burke, D. M. Hester, & R. B. Talisse (Eds.), *Dewey's logical theory: New studies and interpretations* (pp. 3–26). Nashville, TN: Vanderbilt University Press.

Anderson, J. R., Greeno, J. G., Reder, L. M., & Simon, H. A. (2000). Perspectives on learning, thinking, and activity. *Educational Researcher, 29*(4), 11–13.

Anderson, J. R., Reder, L. M., & Simon, H. A. (1996). Situated learning and education. *Educational Researcher, 25*(4), 5–11.

Anderson, J. R., Reder, L. M., & Simon, H. A. (1997). Situative versus cognitive perspectives: Form verses substance. *Educational Researcher, 26*(1), 18–21.

Apel, K.-O. (1980). *Towards a transformation of philosophy.* London: Routledge & Kegan Paul. Cited in Biesta, G. J. J., & Stams, G. J. J. M. (2001). Critical thinking and the question of crtitique: Some lessons from deconstruction. *Studies in Philosophy and Education, 20,* 57–74.

Argyris, C. (1993). *Knowledge for action.* San Francisco: Jossey-Bass.

Arievitch, I. M., & Stetsenko, A. (2002). The quality of cultural tools and cognitive development: Gal'parin's perspective and its implications. *Human Development, 43,* 69–92.

Association of American Colleges. (1985). *Integrity in the college curriculum: A report to the academic community.* Washington, DC: Association of American Colleges.

Astin, A. W. (1993). *What matters in college: Four critical years revisited.* San Francisco: Jossey-Bass.

Ausabell, D. (1963). *The psychology of meaningful verbal learning.* New York: Grune & Stratton.

Bakhtin, M. M. (1981). Forms of time and the chronotope in the novel. In M. Holquist (Ed.), *The dialogic imagination: Four essays by M. M. Bakhtin* (pp. 84–283). Austin, TX: University of Texas Press.

Barnett, R. (2001). Managing universities in a super complex age. In M. Cutright (Ed.), *Chaos theory and higher education: Leadership, planning & policy* (pp. 13–32). New York: Peter Lang.

Bascones, J., & Novak, J. D. (1985). Alternative instructional systems and the development of problem solving skills in physics. *European Journal of Science Education, 7*(3), 253–261.

Baxter-Magolda, M. B. (1999). *Creating contexts for learning and authorship.* Nashville, TN: Vanderbilt University Press.

Beach, K. (1995). Activity as a mediator of sociocultural change and individual development: The case of school-work transition in Nepal. *Mind, Culture, and Activity, 2,* 285–302.

Beer, M., & Nohria, N. (2000, May–June). Cracking the code of change. *Harvard Business Review,* pp. 133–141.

Belensky, M., Clinchy, B., Goldberg, N., & Tarule, J. (1986). *Women's ways of knowing: The development of self, voice, and mind.* New York: Basic Books.

Bennis, W. G., Benne, K. D., & Chin, R. (Eds.). (1961). *The planning of change* (2nd ed.). New York: Holt, Rinehart & Winston.

Bereiter, C. (1994). Implications of postmodernism for science, or, science as progressive discourse. *Educational Psychologist, 29*(1), 3–12.

Bereiter, C. (1997). Situated cognition and how to overcome it. In D. Kirshner & J. A. Whitson (Eds.), *Situated cognition: Social, semiotic, and psychological perspectives* (pp. 281–300). Mahwah, NJ: Lawrence Erlbaum Associates.

Berger, J. P. (2002). The influence of organizational structures of colleges and universities on student learning. *Peabody Journal of Education, 77*(3), 40–59.

Bernstein, R. J. (1966). *John Dewey.* New York: Washington Square Press.

Bernstein, R. J. (1971). *Praxis and action.* Philadelphia: University of Pennsylvania Press.

Bhabba, H. (1984). The other question: The stereotype and the colonial discourse. *Screen, 24*(6), 18–36.

Bielacszye, K., Pirolli, P., & Brown, A. L. (1995). Training in self-explanation and self regulation strategies: Investigating the effects of knowledge acquisition activities on problem solving. *Cognition and Instruction, 13,* 221–252.

Biesta, G. J. J. (1994). Education as practical intersubjectivity: Towards a critical-pragmatic understanding of education. *Educational Theory, 44*(3), 299–317.

Biesta, G. J. J., & Stams, G. J. J. M. (2001). Critical thinking and the question of critique: Some lessons from deconstruction. *Studies in Philosophy and Education, 20,* 57–74.

Blackburn, R. T., Pellino, G. R., Boberg, A., & O'Commell, C. (1980). Are instructional improvement programs off target? *Current Issues in Higher Education, 2*(1), 32–48.

Blanton, M. L. (2002). Using an undergraduate geometry course to challenge pre-service teachers' notions of discourse. *Journal of Mathematics Teacher Education, 5*(2), 117–152.

Bolman, L. G., & Deal, T. E. (2003). *Reframing organizations* (3rd ed.). San Francisco: Jossey-Bass.

Boud, D., & Walker, D. (1998). Promoting reflection in professional courses: The challenge of context. *Studies in Higher Education, 23*(2), 191–206.

Bourdieu, P. (1977). *Outline of a theory of practice.* Cambridge: Cambridge University Press.

Bourdieu, P. (1990). *The logic of practice.* Stanford, CA: Stanford University Press.

Bowen, M. (1978). *Family therapy in clinical practice.* New York: J. Aronson.

Bowlby, J. (1969). *Attachment and loss: Volume 1. Attachment.* New York: Basic Books.

Boxtel, C. van, & Roelofs, E. (2001). Investigating the quality of student discourse: What constitutes a productive student discourse? *Journal of Classroom Interaction, 36*(2), 55–62.

Boyer, E. L. (1987). *College: The undergraduate experience in America.* New York: Harper & Row.

Boyer, E. L. (1990). *Scholarship reconsidered: Priorities of the professorate.* Princeton, NJ: Carnegie Foundation for the Advancement of Teaching.

The Boyer Commission on Educating Undergraduates. (1999). *Reinventing undergraduate education: A blueprint for America's research universities.* Princeton, NJ: Carnegie Foundation for the Advancement of Teaching.

Bransford, J. D., Brophy, S., & Williams, S. (2000). When computer technologies meet the learning sciences: Issues and opportunities. *Journal of Applied Developmental Psychology, 21*(1), 59–84.

Bransford, J. D., Brown, A. L., & Cocking, R. C. (1999). *How people learn: Brain, mind, experience and school.* Washington, DC: National Academy Press.

Bransford, J. D., Franks, J. J., Vye, N. J., & Sherwood, R. D. (1989). New approaches to instruction: Why wisdom can't be told. In S. Vosniadou & A. Ortony (Eds.), *Similarity and analogical reasoning* (pp. 470–497). New York: Cambridge University Press.

Bransford, J. D., & Schwartz, D. L. (2001). Rethinking transfer: A simple proposal with multiple implications. In A. Iran-Nejad & P. D. Pearson (Eds.), *Review of research in education* (Vol. 24, pp. 61–100). Washington, DC: American Educational Research Association.

Bransford, J. D., Vye, N., & Bateman, H. (2002). Creating high-quality learning environments: Guidelines from research on how people learn. In P. A. Graham & N. G. Stacey (Eds.), *The knowledge economy and postsecondary education: Report of a workshop* (pp. 159–197). Washington, DC: The National Academy of Sciences.

Braxton, J. M., Eimers, M. T., & Bayer, A. E. (1996). The implications of teaching norms for the improvement of undergraduate education. *The Journal of Higher Education, 67*(6), 603–625.

Brickhouse, N. (2001). Embodying science: A feminist perspective on learning. *Journal of Research in Science Teaching, 38*(3), 282–295.

Brousseau, G. (1985). The crucial role of the didactic contract in the analysis and construction of situation in teaching and learning mathematics. In H. G. Steiner (Ed.), *Theory of mathematics education* (pp. 110–119). Occasional Paper 54. Bielefeld, Germany: Institute fur Didaktik der Mathematik. Cited in Cobb, P., Perlwitz, M., & Underwood, D. (1996). Constructivism and activity theory: A consideration of their similarities and differences as they relate to mathematics education. In H. Mansfield et al. (Eds.), *Mathematics for tomorrow's young children* (pp. 10–58). Dordrecht, The Netherlands: Kluwer Academic Publishers.

Brown, A. L. (1997). Transforming schools into communities of thinking and learning about serious matters. *American Psychologist, 52*(4), 399–413.

Brown, A. L., Ash, D., Rutherford, M., Nakagawa, K., Gordon, A., & Campione, J. C. (1993). Distributed expertise in the classroom. In G. Solomon (Ed.), *Distributed cognition* (pp. 188–228). New York: Cambridge University Press.

Brown, A. L., & Campione, J. C. (1994). Guided discovery in a community of learners. In K. McGilly (Ed.), *Classroom lessons: Integrating cognitive theory & classroom practice* (pp. 229–270). Cambridge, MA: MIT Press/Bradford.

Brown, A. L., & Campione, J. C. (1996). Psychological learning theory and the design of innovative environments: On procedures, principles and systems. In L. Schauble & R. Glaser (Eds.), *Contributions of instructional innovation to understanding learning* (pp. 289–325). Mahwah, NJ: Lawrence Erlbaum Associates.

Brown, J. S., Collins, A., & Duguid, P. (1989). Situated cognition and the culture of learning. *Educational Researcher, 18*(1), 32–42.

Brown, J. S., & Duguid, P. (1996). Practice at the periphery: A reply to Steven Tripp. In H. McLellan (Ed.), *Situated learning perspectives* (pp. 169–173). Englewood, NJ: Educational Technology Publications.

Brown, J. S., & Duguid, P. (2001). Knowledge and organization: A social-practice perspective. *Organizational Science, 12*(2), 198–213.

Brown, L. D. (1985). People centered development and participatory research. *Harvard Education Review, 55*(1), 69–75.

Bruffee, K. (1993). *Collaborative learning: Higher education, independence, and the authority of knowledge.* Baltimore: Johns Hopkins University Press.

Bruffee, K. A. (1999). *Collaborative learning: Higher education, interdependence, and the authority of knowledge* (2nd ed.). Baltimore: Johns Hopkins University Press.

Brunner, J. (1990). *Acts of meaning.* Cambridge: Harvard University Press.

Bryk, A., Sebring, P., Kerbow, D., Rollow, S., & Easton, J. (1998). *Charting Chicago school reform.* Boulder, CO: Westview.

Burke, F. T., Hester, D. M., & Talisse, R. B. (2002). Editor's introduction. In F. T. Burke, D. M. Hester, & R. B. Talisse (Eds.), *Dewey's logical theory: New studies and interpretations* (pp. xi–xxiv). Nashville, TN: Vanderbilt University Press.

Cahan, E. D. (1992). John Dewey and human development. *Developmental Psychology, 28*(2), 205–214.

Caravita, S. (2001). Commentary: A re-framed conceptual change theory? *Learning and Instruction, 11,* 421–429.

Centra, J. A. (1993). *Reflective faculty evaluation: Enhancing teaching and determining faculty effectiveness.* San Francisco: Jossey-Bass.

Chi, M. T. H., Slotta, J. D., & de Leeuw, N. (1994). From things to process: A theory of conceptual change for learning science concepts. *Learning and Instruction, 4,* 27–43.

Chickering, A. (1969). *Education and identity.* San Francisco: Jossey-Bass.

Chickering, A., & Gamson, Z. (1987). Seven principles for good practice in undergraduate education. *AAHE Bulletin, 39*(7), 3–7.

Cobb, P. (1994a). Constructivism in mathematics and science education. *Educational Researcher, 23*(7), 4.

Cobb, P. (1994b). Where is the mind: Constructivist and sociocultural perspectives on mathematical development. *Educational Researcher, 23*(7), 13–20.

Cobb, P., & Bowers, J. (1999). Cognitive and situated learning perspectives in theory and practice. *Educational Researcher, 28*(2), 4–15.

Cobb, P., Gravemeijer, K., Yackel, E., McClain, K., & Whitnack, J. (1997). Mathemetizing and symbolizing the emergence of chains of signification in one first-grade classroom. In D. Kirshner & J. A. Whitson (Eds.), *Situated cognition: Social, semiotic, and psychological perspectives* (pp. 151–233). Mahwah, NJ: Lawrence Erlbaum Associates.

Cobb, P., McClain, K., & Gravemeijer, K. (2003). Learning about statistical covariation. *Cognition and Instruction, 21*(1), 1–78.

Cobb, P., Perlwitz, M., & Underwood, D. (1996). Constructivism and activity theory: A consideration of their similarities and differences as they relate to mathematics education. In H. Mansfield, N. A. Pateman, & N. Bednarz (Eds.), *Mathematics for tomorrow's young children* (pp. 10–58). Dordrecht, The Netherlands: Kluwer Academic Publishers.

Cobb, P., & Yackel, E. (1996). Constructivist, emergent, and sociocultural perspectives in the context of developmental research. *Educational Psychologist, 31*(3/4), 175–190.

Cohen, D. K. (1998). School improvement and higher education. In P. M. Timpane & L. S. White (Eds.), *Higher education and school reform* (pp. 115–139). San Francisco: Jossey-Bass.

Cohen, M. D., & March, J. M. (1974). *Leadership and ambiguity: The American college president.* New York: McGraw-Hill.

Cohen, M. D., March, J. M., & Olsen, J. P. (1972). The garbage can model of organizational choice. *Administrative Science Quarterly, 17*(1), 1–25.

Collins, A., Brown, J. S., & Holum, A. (1991, Winter). Cognitive apprenticeship: Making thinking visible. *American Educator,* pp. 6–11, 38–46.

Confrey, J. (1995). How compatible are radical constructivism, sociocultural approaches, and social constructivism? In L. P. Steffe & J. Gale (Eds.), *Constructivism in education* (pp. 185–225). Hillsdale, NJ: Lawrence Erlbaum Associates.

Cunha, M. P. (2002). "The best place to be." Managing control and employee loyalty in a knowledge-intensive company. *The Journal of Applied Behavioral Science, 38*(4), 481–495.

Cushman, P. (1990). Why is the self empty. *American Psychologist, 45*(5), 599–611.

Cutright, M. (Ed.). (2001). *Chaos theory and higher education: Leadership, planning & policy.* New York: Peter Lang.

Daft, R. (2000). *Organizational theory and design* (7th ed.). Cincinnati, OH: South-Western Thompson Learning.

Davis, B., & Sumara, D. (2002). Constructivist discourses and the field of education: Problems and possibilities. *Educational Theory, 52*(4), 409–428.

Davydov, V. V. (1972/1990). *Soviet studies in mathematical education: Vol. 2. Types of generalization in instruction: Logical and psychological problems in the structuring of school curriculum.* In J. Kilpatrick (Ed.), J. Teller (Trans.). Reston, VA: National Council of Teachers of Mathematics.

Del Favero, M. (2002). Linking administrative behavior and student learning: The learning centered academic unit. *Peabody Journal of Education, 77*(3), 60–84.

Derrida, J. (1978). *Writing and difference.* Chicago: The University of Chicago Press.

Dever, J. T. (2001). Chaotic systems: Confounding or confirming the leadership role in higher education? In M. Cutright (Ed.), *Chaos theory and higher education: Leadership, planning & policy* (pp. 195–202). New York: Peter Lang.

Dewey, J. (1902/2001). The educational situation: As concerns the elementary school. *Journal of Curriculum Studies, 33*(4), 387–403. (Original publication 1902)

Dewey, J. (1903–1906). The postulate of immediate empiricism. In *Middle Works 3: Essays (1903–1906).* Carbondale, IL: Southern Illinois University Press.

Dewey, J. (1910). *How we think . . .* Mineola, NY: Dover.

Dewey, J. (1916). *Democracy and education.* New York: The Free Press, Simon & Schuster.

Dewey, J. (1917). The need for recovery in philosophy. *MW:10—Essays 1916–1917.* Carbondale, IL: Southern Illinois University Press.

Dewey, J. (1920). Changing concepts of experience and reason. MW:12—*Essays Reconstruction of philosophy.* Carbondale, IL: Southern Illinois University Press.

Dewey, J. (1922). *Human nature and conduct.* New York: Henry Holt.

Dewey, J. (1925/1958). *Experience and nature.* New York: Dover.

Dewey, J. (1927/1954). *The public and its problems.* Chicago: The Swallow Press.

Dewey, J. (1934/1980). *Art as experience.* New York: Perigee.

Dewey, J. (1938a). *Experience and education.* New York: Touchstone, Simon & Schuster.

Dewey, J. (1938b). *Logic, the theory of inquiry.* New York: Holt.

Dewey, J. (1951). *Experience and education: A reintroduction.* LW:1. Carbondale, IL: Southern Illinois University Press.

Dewey, J., & Bentley, A. F. (1949). *Knowing and the known.* Boston: Beacon.

Eckel, P., Hill, B., Green, M., & Mallon, B. (1999). *On change—Reports from the road: Insights on institutional change.* Washington, DC: American Council on Education.

Edelson, D. (1998). Learning from stories: An architecture for Socratic case based teaching. In R. Schank (Ed.), *Inside multi-media case based instruction* [electronic resource] (pp. 103–174). Mahwah, NJ: Lawrence Erlbaum Associates.

Edelson, D. (2001). Learning-for-use: A framework for the design of technology-supported inquiry activities. *Journal of Research in Science Teaching, 38*(3), 355–385.

Eldridge, M. (1998). *Transforming experience.* Nashville, TN: Vanderbilt University Press.

Engels, F. (1925). *Dialektic der natur.* Berlin, Germany: Dietz Verlag.

Engle, R. A., & Conant, F. R. (2002). Guiding principles for fostering productive disciplinary engagement: Explaining an emergent argument in a community of learners classroom. *Cognition and Instruction, 20*(4), 399–483.

Erikson, E. (1968). *Identity: Youth and crisis.* New York: Norton.

Fanon, F. (1967). *Black skins, white masks.* New York: Grove.

Fauconnier, G., & Turner, M. (1998). Conceptual integration networks. *Cognitive Science, 22,* 133–187.

Feinburg, W. (1998). Rejoinder: Meaning, pedagogy, and curriculum development: Feinburg answers Hirsch. *Educational Researcher, 27*(7), 30–36.

Fernandez, M., Wegerif, R., Mercer, N., & Rojas-Drummond, S. (2001). Re-conceptualizing "scaffolding" and the zone of proximal development in the context of symmetrical collaborative learning. *Journal of Classroom Interaction, 36*(2), 40–54.

Fishman, S. M., & McCarthy, L. (1998). *John Dewey and the challenge of classroom practice.* New York: Teachers College Press.

Flavell, J. H. (1976). Metacognitive aspects of problem solving. In L. B. Resnick (Ed.), *The nature of intelligence* (pp. 231–235). Hillsdale, NJ: Lawrence Erlbaum Associates.

Flavell, J. H. (1979). Metacognition and cognitive monitoring: A new area of cognitive-developmental inquiry. *American Psychologist, 34*(10), 906–911.

Fosnot, C. T. (1996). *Constructivism: Theory, perspectives, and practice.* New York: Teachers College Press.

Foucault, M. (1973). *The birth of the clinic: An archaeology of medical perception* (A. M. S. Smith, Trans.). New York: Pantheon.

Freud, S. (1930). *Civilization and its discontents.* New York: Norton.

Fullan, M. (2001). *The new meaning of educational change* (3rd ed.). New York: Teachers College Press.

Gaff, J. G. (1991). *New life for the college curriculum.* San Francisco: Jossey-Bass.

Gagne, R. M. (1968). Learning hierarchies. *Educational Psychologist, 6,* 1–9.

Gardiner, L. F. (1994). *Redesigning higher education: Producing dramatic gains in student learning* (Report No. 7). Washington, DC: Graduate School of Education and Human Development, The George Washington University.

Gardiner, L. F. (2000). Why we must change: The research evidence. *Thought & Action, 16*(2), 121–138.

Gardner, H. L. (1995). *Leading minds: An anatomy of leadership.* New York: Basic Books/HarperCollins.

Garrison, J. (1994a). Dewey, contexts, and texts. *Educational Researcher, 23*(1), 19–20.

Garrison, J. (1994b). Realism, Deweyan pragmatism, and educational research. *Educational Researcher, 23*(1), 5–14.

Garrison, J. (1996). A Deweyan theory of democratic listening. *Educational Theory, 46*(4), 429–451.

Garrison, J. (1997). *Dewey and Eros: Wisdom and desire in the art of teaching.* New York: Teachers College Press.

Georghiades, P. (2000). Beyond conceptual change learning in science education: Focusing on transfer, durability and metacognition. *Educational Research, 42*(2), 121–139.

Gergen, K. J. (1994a). *Realities and relationships: Soundings in social construction.* Cambridge, MA: Harvard University Press.

Gergen, K. J. (1994b). *Toward transformation in social knowledge* (2nd ed.). Thousand Oaks, CA: Sage.

Gergen, K. J. (2000). *An invitation to social construction.* London: Sage.

Gergen, K. J. (2001). *Social construction in context.* London: Sage.

Gilligan, C. (1982). *In a different voice.* Cambridge, MA: Harvard University Press.

Giroux, H. (1992). *Border crossings.* New York: Routledge.

Glaser, R. (1994, July 17–22). *Application and theory: Learning theory and the design of learning environments.* Keynote address presented at the 23rd International Congress of Applied Psychology, Madrid, Spain.

Glassman, M. (2001). Dewey and Vygotsky: Society, experience, and inquiry in educational practice. *Educational Researcher, 30*(4), 3–14.

Glassman, M. (2002). Experience and responding. *Educational Researcher, 31*(5), 24–27.

Gobbo, C., & Chi, M. (1986). How knowledge is structured and used by expert and novice children. *Cognitive Development, 1*(3), 221–237.

Gordon, T. (1970). *P.E.T., parent effectiveness training.* New York: Wyden.

Gowin, D. B. (1981). *Educating.* Ithaca, NY: Cornell University Press.

Grant, R. M. (2003). Strategic planning in a turbulent environment: Evidence from the oil majors. *Strategic Management Journal, 24,* 491–517.

Gray, P. J., Frol, R. C., & Diamond, R. M. (1992, March). *A national study of research universities: On the balance between research and undergraduate teaching.* Syracuse, NY: Syracuse University, Center for Instructional Development. Cited in Stark, J. S., & Lattuca, L. R. (1997). *Shaping academic curriculum: Academic plans in action.* Boston: Allyn & Bacon.

Greeno, J. G. (1997). On claims that answer the wrong question. *Educational Researcher, 26*(1), 5–17.

Greeno, J. G., & the Middle School Mathematics Through Applications Project Group. (1998). The situativity of knowing, learning, and research. *American Psychologist, 53*(1), 5–26.

Gregory, M. R. (2002). Constructivism, standards, and the classroom community of inquiry. *Educational Theory, 52*(4), 397–408.

Griffith, B., & Lemisko, L. S. (2001). Reshaping higher education in a post-Fordist world: Chaos and Collingwood. In M. Cutright (Ed.), *Chaos theory and higher education: Leadership, planning & policy* (pp. 175–194). New York: Peter Lang.

Grosslight, L., Unger, C., Jay, E., & Smith, C. (1991). Understanding models and their use in science: Conceptions of middle and high school students and experts. *Journal of Research in Science Teaching, 28,* 799–822.

Grotzer, T. A. (2002). Expanding our vision for educational technology: Procedural, conceptual, and structural knowledge. *Educational Technology, 42*(2), 52–59.

Habermas, J. (1971). *Knowledge and human interest.* Boston: Beacon.

Habermas, J. (1975). *Legitimation crisis* (T. McCarthy, Trans.). Boston: Beacon.

Habermas, J. (1984). *Theory of communicative action.* Boston: Beacon.

Habermas, J. (1987). *Theory of communicative action: Volume 2. Lifeworld and system: A critique of functionalist reason* (T. McCarthy, Trans.). Cambridge: Polity.

Habermas, J. (1990). Discourse ethics: Notes on a program of philosophical justification. In J. Habermas (Ed.), *Moral consciousness and communicative action* (pp. 43–115). Cambridge, MA: MIT Press.

Hall, R. (1996). Representation as shared activity: Situated cognition and Dewey's cartography of experience. *The Journal of Learning Sciences, 5*(3), 209–238.

Halpern, D., & Hakel, M. D. (2003). Applying the science of learning to the university and beyond. *Change, 35*(4), 36–41.

Hansen, D. T. (2002). Dewey's conception of an environment for teaching and learning. *Curriculum Inquiry, 32*(3), 267–280.

Harrison, A. G., & Treagust, D. F. (2001). Conceptual change using multiple interpretive perspectives: Two case studies in secondary school chemistry. *Instructional Science, 29,* 45–85.

Hawkins, M. (2000). The reassertion of traditional authority in constructivist pedagogy. *Teaching Education, 11*(3), 279–296.

Hay, K. E. (1996). The three activities of a student: A reply to Tripp. In H. McLellan (Ed.), *Situated learning perspectives* (pp. 201–212). Englewood, NJ: Educational Technology Publications.

Henry, S. E. (2001). What happens when we use Kohberg? His troubling functionalism and the potential of pragmatism in moral education. *Educational Theory, 51*(3), 259–276.

Herrington, J., & Oliver, R. (2000). An instructional design framework for authentic learning environments. *Educational Technology Research and Development, 48*(3), 23–48.

Hershkowitz, R., Schwartz, B. B., & Dreyfus, T. (2001). Abstraction in context: Epistemic actions. *Journal of Research in Mathematics Education, 32*(2), 195–222.

Hewson, P. W. (1996). Teaching for conceptual change. In D. F. Treagust, R. Duit, & B. J. Fraser (Eds.), *Improving teaching and learning is science and mathematics* (pp. 131–140). New York: Teachers College Press.

Hirsch, E. D. (1987). *Cultural literacy: What every American should know.* Boston: Houghton-Mifflin.

Hirsch, E. D. (1998). Response to Professor Feinburg. *Educational Researcher, 27*(2), 38.

Hoetker, J., & Ahlbrand, W. (1969). The persistence of recitation. *American Education Research Journal, 6*(2), 145–167.

Hogan, K., & Corey, C. (2001). Viewing classrooms as cultural contexts for fostering scientific literacy. *Anthropology and Education Quarterly, 32*(3), 214–243.

Hogan, K., & Maglienti, M. (2001). Comparing the epistemological underpinnings of students' and scientists' reasoning about conclusions. *Journal of Research in Science Teaching, 38*(6), 663–687.

Holland, D., Lachicotte, W., Skinner, D., & Cain, C. (1998). *Identity and agency in cultural worlds.* Cambridge, MA: Harvard University Press.

Honneth, A. (1995). The other justice: Habermas and the ethical challenge of postmodernism. In S. K. White (Ed.), *The Cambridge companion to Habermas* (pp. 289–323). Cambridge, England: Cambridge University Press.

House, E. R. (1992). Response to "Notes on pragmatism and scientific realism." *Educational Researcher, 21*(6), 18–19.

Jackson, P. W. (1995). If we took Dewey's aesthetics seriously, how would art be taught? In J. Garrison (Ed.), *The new scholarship on Dewey* (pp. 25–34). Boston, Dordrecht, The Netherlands: Kluwer Academic Publishers.

Jackson, P. W. (2002). *John Dewey and the philosopher's task.* New York: Teachers College Press.

Jonassen, D. H. (2002, March–April). Learning as activity. *Educational Technology,* pp. 45–51.

Jonassen, D. H., & Hernandez-Serrano, J. (2002). Case-based reasoning and instructional design: Using stories to support problem solving. *Educational Technology Research & Development, 50*(2), 65–77.

Jonassen, D. H., & Rohrer-Murphy, L. (1999). Activity theory as a framework for designing constructivist learning environments. *Educational Technology: Research and Development, 47*(1), 61–79.

Karpov, Y. V., & Haywood, H. C. (1998). Two ways to elaborate Vygotsky's concept of mediation: Implications for instruction. *American Psychologist, 53*(1), 27–36.

Katz, D., & Kahn, R. (1978). *The social psychology of organizations* (2nd ed.). New York: Wiley.

Keefer, M. W., Zeitz, C. M., & Resnick, L. B. (2000). Judging the quality of peer-led student dialogues. *Cognition and Instruction, 18*(1), 53–81.

Kegan, R. (2000). What "form" transforms? A constructive-developmental approach to transformational learning. In J. Mezirow & Associates (Eds.), *Learning as transformation: Critical perspectives on a theory in progress* (pp. 35–70). San Francisco: Jossey-Bass.

King, P., & Kitchener, K. (1994). *Developing reflective judgement: Understanding and promoting intellectual growth and critical thinking in adolescents and adults.* San Francisco: Jossey-Bass.

Kirshner, D., & Whitson, J. A. (1997). Editors introduction to situated cognition: Social, semiotic, and psychological perspectives. In D. Kirshner & J. A. Whitson (Eds.), *Situated cognition: Social, semiotic, and psychological perspectives* (pp. 1–16). Mahwah, NJ: Lawrence Erlbaum Associates.

Klein, G. A., & Calderwood, R. (1988). How do people use analogs to make decisions? In J. Kolodner (Ed.), *Proceedings: Workshop on case based reasoning (DARPA).* San Mateo, CA: Morgan Kaufmann. Cited in Jonassen, D. H., & Hernandez-Serrano, J. (2002). Case-based reasoning and instructional design: Using stories to support problem solving. *Educational Technology Research & Development, 50*(2), 65–77.

Knight, P. T., & Trowler, P. R. (2001). *Departmental leadership in higher education.* Buckingham, England: The Society for Research in Higher Education/The Open University Press.

Knorr-Cetina, K. (1999). *Epistemic cultures: How the sciences make knowledge.* Cambridge, MA: Harvard University Press.

Kohlberg, L., & Mayer, R. (1972). Development as the aim of education. *Harvard Educational Review, 42*(4), 449–496.

Krockover, G. H., Shepardson, D. P., Eichinger, D., Nakhleh, M., & Adams, P. E. (2002). Reforming and assessing undergraduate science instruction using collaborative action-based research teams. *School Science and Mathematics, 102*(6), 266–284.

Kuh, G. D. (1996). Guiding principles for creating seamless learning environments for undergraduates. *Journal of College Student Development, 37*(2), 135–148.

Lacan, J. (1977). *Ecritis: A selection.* London: Travistock.

Lantolf, J. P. (2000). Introducing sociocultural theory. In J. P. Lantolf (Ed.), *Sociocultural theory of second language learning* (pp. 1–26). Oxford, England: Oxford University Press.

Lave, J. (1988). *Cognition in practice.* Cambridge, England: Cambridge University Press.

Lave, J. (1997). The culture of acquisition and the practice of understanding. In D. Kirshner & J. A. Whitson (Eds.), *Situated cognition: Social, semiotic, and psychological perspectives* (pp. 17–35). Mahwah, NJ: Lawrence Erlbaum Associates. (Reprinted from Lave, J. 1990. *Cultural psychology: Essays on comparative and human development.* Cambridge, United Kingdom: Cambridge University Press.)

Lave, J. (1992, April). *Learning as participation in communities of practice.* Paper presented at the annual meeting of the American Educational Research Association, San Francisco, CA. Cited in Packer, J. P., & Goicochea, J. (2000). Sociocultural and constructivist theories of learning: Ontology, not just epistemology. *Educational Psychologist, 35*(4), 227–241.

Lave, J., & Wenger, E. (1991). *Situated learning: Legitimate peripheral participation.* Cambridge, England: Cambridge University Press.

Leander, K. M. (2001). "This is our freedom bus going home right now": Producing and hybridizing space-time contexts in pedagogical discourse. *Journal of Literacy Research, 33*(4), 637–679.

Lee, C. D., & Smagorinsky, P. (2000). Introduction: Constructing meaning through collaborative inquiry. In C. D. Lee & P. Smagorinsky (Eds.), *Vygotskian perspectives on literacy research* (pp. 1–18). Cambridge, England: Cambridge University Press.

Lehrer, R., & Schauble, L. (2000). Developing model-based reasoning in mathematics and science. *Journal of Applied Developmental Psychology, 21*(1), 39–48.

Lemke, J. L. (1997). Cognition, context, and learning: The social semiotic perspective. In D. Kirshner & J. A. Whitson (Eds.), *Situated cognition: Social, semiotic, and psychological perspectives* (pp. 37–55). Mahwah, NJ: Lawrence Erlbaum Associates.

Lemke, J. L. (2001). Articulating communities: Sociocultural perspectives in science education. *Journal of Research in Science Teaching, 38*(3), 296–316.

Leont'ev, A. N. (1981). *Problems of the development of mind.* Moscow: Progress Publishers.

Lin, X. D. (2001). Designing metacognitive activities. *Educational Technology Research and Development, 49*(2), 23–40.

Lin, X. D., Bransford, J., Hmelo, C., Kantor, R., Hickey, T. S., Secules, T., et al. (1995, September/October). Instructional design and development of learning communities: An invitation to dialogue. *Educational Technology,* pp. 53–63.

Lin, X. D., Hmelo, C., Kinzer, C. K., & Secules, T. J. (1999). Designing technology to support reflection. *Educational Technology Research and Development, 47*(3), 43–62.

Lin, X. D., & Lehman, J. D. (1999). Supporting learning of variable control in a computer-based biology environment: Effects of prompting college students to reflect on their own thinking. *Journal of Research in Science Teaching, 36*(7), 837–858.

Lothstein, A. (1978). Salving from the dross: John Dewey's anarco-communalism. *The Philosophical Forum, 10*(1), 55–103.

Lucas, A. F. (1989). Motivating faculty to improve the quality of teaching. In A. F. Lucas (Ed.), *The department chairperson's role in enhancing college teaching* (pp. 5–15). San Francisco: Jossey-Bass.

Manyak, P. C. (2001). Participation, hybridity, and carnival: A situated analysis of a dynamic literacy practice in a primary-grade English immersion class. *Journal of Literacy Research, 33*(3), 423–465.

Marchese, T. J. (1997). The new conversations about learning: Insights from neuroscience and anthropology, cognitive science and workplace studies. In AAHE Staff (Ed.), *Assessing impact: Evidence and action* (pp. 79–95). Presentations from the AAHE Conference on Assessment and Quality (Miami Beach, FL, June 11–15, 1997). Washington, DC: American Association for Higher Education.

Marx, C. (1890/1981). *Das Kapital.* Berlin, Germany: Dietz Verlag.

McCarthy, C. L., & Sears, E. (2000). Deweyan pragmatism and the quest for true belief. *Educational Theory, 50*(2), 213–227.

McCarty, L. P., & Schwandt, T. A. (2000). Seductive illusions: von Glasersfeld and Gergen on epistemology and education. In D. C. Phillips (Ed.), *Constructivism in education: Opinions and second opinions on controversial issues. Ninety Ninth Yearbook of the University of Chicago Press* (pp. 41–85). Chicago: University of Chicago Press.

McKeatchie, W. J., Pintrich, R. R., Lin, Y. G., & Smith, D. (1986). *Teaching and learning in the college classroom: A review of research literature.* Ann Arbor, MI: National Center to Improve Teaching and Learning, University of Michigan.

McLaren, P., & Farahmandpur, R. (2000). Reconsidering Marx in post-Marxist times: A requiem for postmodernism. *Educational Researcher, 29*(3), 25–33.

McLellen, H. (1996). Situated learning: Multiple perspectives. In H. McLellen (Ed.), *Situated learning perspectives* (pp. 5–17). Englewood, NJ: Educational Technology Publications.

McTighe, J., & Wiggins, G. (1999). *The understanding by design handbook.* Alexandria, VA: ASCD.

Mead, G. H. (1934). *Mind, self and society from the standpoint of a social behaviorist.* Chicago: University of Chicago Press.

Mezirow, J. (2000). Learning to think like an adult: Core concepts of transformational theory. In J. Mezirow & Associates (Eds.), *Learning as transformation: Critical perspectives on a theory in progress* (pp. 3–34). San Francisco: Jossey-Bass.

Mintzberg, H., & Rose, J. (1992). *Strategic management upside down: A study of McGill University from 1829 to 1980.* Montreal: McGill University. Cited in Mintzberg, H., & Westley, F. (1992). Cycles of organizational change. *Strategic Management Journal, 13,* 39–59.

Mintzberg, H., & Westley, F. (1992). Cycles of organizational change. *Strategic Management Journal, 13,* 39–59.

Moll, L. (1992). Funds of knowledge for teaching: Using a qualitative approach to connect homes and classrooms. *Theory into Practice, 31*(2), 132–141.

Moore, J. L., Lin, X., Schwartz, D., Petrosino, A., Hickey, D. T., Campbell, O., & the Cognition and Technology Group. (1996). In H. McLellan (Ed.), *Situated learning perspectives* (pp. 213–215). Englewood, NJ: Educational Technology Publications.

Morgan, G. (1986). *Images of organization.* Newbury Park, CA: Sage.

Morrison, K. (1998). *Management theories for educational change.* London: Paul Chapman.

Mossberg, B. (2001). Leadership's natural ally: Applying chaos and complexity theories to academe. In M. Cutright (Ed.), *Chaos theory and higher education: Leadership, planning & policy* (pp. 205–248). New York: Peter Lang.

National Center for Postsecondary Improvement. (2002). *Beyond dead reckoning: Research priorities for redirecting American higher education.* Stanford, CA: National Center for Postsecondary Improvement.

National Institute of Education. (1984). *Involvement in learning: Realizing the potential of American higher education.* Washington, DC: Author.

Newman, D., Griffin, P., & Coleman, M. (1989). *The construction zone.* Cambridge, United Kingdom: Cambridge University Press.

Newmann, F., & Wehlage, G. (1995). *Successful school restructuring.* Madison, WI: Center on Organization and Restructuring of Schools.

Nonaka, I., & Takeuchi, H. (1995). *The knowledge creating company.* Oxford, England: Oxford University Press.

Novak, G. (1975). *Pragmatism versus Marxism.* New York: Pathfinder.

Novak, J. D. (2002). Meaningful learning: The essential factor for conceptual change in limited or inappropriate propositional hierarchies leading to empowerment of learners. *Science Education, 86*(4), 548–571.

Oakeshott, M. (1962). *Rationalism in politics.* London: Methuen & Co. Cited in Tripp, S. D. (1996). Theories, traditions, and situated learning. In H. McLellan (Ed.), *Situated learning perspectives* (pp. 155–166). Englewood, NJ: Educational Technology Publications.

Ogbanna, E., & Harris, L. C. (1998). Managing organizational culture: Compliance or genuine change? *British Journal of Management, 9,* 273–288.

Oliver, K. M. (2000, November–December). Methods of developing constructivist learning on the web. *Educational Technology,* pp. 5–18.

Packer, J. P., & Goicochea, J. (2000). Sociocultural and constructivist theories of learning: Ontology, not just epistemology. *Educational Psychologist, 35*(4), 227–241.

Pang, P. M. N., & Hung, D. W. L. (2001, July–August). Activity theory as a framework for analyzing CBT and e-learning environments. *Educational Technology,* pp. 36–42.

Parenger, W. A. (1990). *John Dewey and the paradox of liberal reform.* Albany, NY: State University of New York Press.

Pascarella, E. T., & Terenzini, P. T. (1991). *How college affects students.* San Francisco: Jossey-Bass.

Pea, R. (1993). Practices of distributed intelligence and designs for education. In G. Solomon (Ed.), *Distributed cognitions: Psychological and educational considerations* (pp. 47–87). New York: Cambridge University Press.

Pendley, B., Bretz, R. L., & Novak, J. D. (1994). Concept maps as a tool to assess instruction in chemistry. *Journal of Chemical Education, 70*(1), 9–15.

Perry, W. G. (1970). *Forms of intellectual and ethical development in the college years: A scheme.* Troy, MO: Holt, Rinehart & Winston.

Peters, T. J., & Waterman, R. H. (1982). *In search of excellence.* New York: HarperCollins.

Petraglia, J. (1998). *Reality by design: The rhetoric and technology of authenticity in education.* Mahwah, NJ: Lawrence Erlbaum Associates.

Phillips, D. C. (1995). The good, the bad, and the ugly: The many faces of constructivism. *Educational Researcher, 24*(7), 5–12.

Piaget, J. (1937/1971). *The construction of reality in the child* (M. Cook, Trans.). New York: Basic Books.

Piaget, J. (1952). *The origins of intelligence in children* (M. Cook, Trans.). New York: International Universities Press.

Piaget, J. (1967). *Six psychological studies* (A. Tenzor & D. Elkind, Trans.). New York: Random House.

Piaget, J. (1970). *Genetic epistemology* (E. Duckworth, Trans.). New York: Columbia University Press.

Pierce, J. W., & Kalkman, D. L. (2003). Applying learner-centered principles in teacher education. *Theory Into Practice, 42*(2), 127–132.

Polkinghorne, D. (1988). *Narrative knowing and the human sciences.* Albany: State University of New York.

Popkewitz, T. S. (1998). Dewey, Vygotsky, and the social administration of the individual: Constructivist pedagogy as systems of ideas in historical spaces. *American Educational Research Journal, 35*(4), 535–579.

Posner, G. J., Strike, K. A., Hewson, P. W., & Gertzog, W. A. (1982). Accommodation of a scientific conception: Toward a theory of conceptual change. *Science Education, 66,* 211–227.

Prawat, R. S. (1995). Misreading Dewey: Reform, projects, and the language game. *Educational Researcher, 24*(7), 13–22.

Prawat, R. S. (2002). Dewey and Vygotsky viewed through the rearview mirror—and dimly at that. *Educational Researcher, 31*(5), 16–20.

The Private Universe Project. (M. Schnepps, Director). (1989). Cambridge, MA: Harvard Smith-sonian Institution for Astrophysics.

Putnam, R. T., & Borko, H. (2000). What do new views of knowledge and thinking have to say about research on teacher learning? *Educational Researcher, 29*(1), 4–15.

Rasmussen, J. (2001). The importance of communication in teaching: A systems-theory approach to the scaffolding metaphor. *Journal of Curriculum Studies, 33*(5), 569–582.

Ravich, D. (2000). *Left back: A century of failed school reforms.* New York: Simon & Schuster.

Ravich, D., & Finn, C. E. (1987). *What do our 17-year-olds know?* New York: Harper & Row.

Resnick, L. (1987). Learning in school and out. *Educational Researcher, 16*(9), 13–20.

Reynolds, R. E., Sinatra, G. M., & Jetton, T. L. (1996). Views of knowledge acquisition and representation: A continuum from experience centered to mind centered. *Educational Psychologist, 31*(2), 93–104.

Rittle-Johnson, B., Siegler, R. S., & Alibali, M. W. (2001). Developing conceptual understanding and procedural skill in mathematics: An iterative process. *Journal of Educational Psychology, 93*(2), 346–362.

Rodgers, C. (2002). Defining reflection: Another look at John Dewey and reflective thinking. *Teachers College Record, 104*(4), 842–866.

Rogers, C. R. (1961). *On becoming a person.* Boston: Houghton-Mifflin.

Ronald, K., & Roskelly, H. (2001). Untested feasibility: Imagining the pragmatic possibility of Paulo Freire. *College English, 63*(5), 612–632.

Rosenholtz, S. (1989). *Teachers' workplace: The social organization of schools.* New York: Longman.

Rosenthal, S. B. (2002). The logical reconstruction of experience: Dewey and Lewis. In F. T. Burke, D. M. Hester, & R. B. Talisse (Eds.), *Dewey's logical theory: New studies and interpretations* (pp. 72–92). Nashville, TN: Vanderbilt University Press.

Roskos, K., Vukelich, C., & Risko, V. (2001). Reflection and learning to teach reading: A critical review of literacy and general teacher education studies. *Journal of Literacy Research, 33*(4), 595–635.

Sacks, P. (1996). *Generation X goes to college.* Chicago and LaSalle, IL: Open Court.

Schank, R. (1992). *Goal based scenarios* (Tech. Rep. No. 36). Evanston, IL: The Institute for Learning Sciences, Northwestern University.

Schank, R. (1999). *Dynamic memory revisited.* Cambridge, England: Cambridge University Press.

Schein, E. (1969). The mechanisms of change. In W. G. Bennis, K. D. Benne, & R. Chin (Eds.), *The planning of change* (pp. 98–107). New York: Holt, Rinehart & Winston.

Schon, D. (1983). *The reflective practitioner: How professionals think in action.* New York: Basic Books.

Schutz, A. (2001). John Dewey's conundrum: Can democratic schools empower? *Teachers College Record, 103*(2), 267–302.

Schwartz, D. L., & Bransford, J. D. (1998). A time for telling. *Cognition and Instruction, 16*(4), 475–522.

Scribner, S. (1997). Mind and social practice: Selected writings of Sylvia Scribner. In E. Toback, R. Joffe-Falmagne, M. Parlee, L. Marting, & A. Scribner-Kapelman (Eds.). New York: Cambridge University Press.

Senge, P. (1990). *The fifth discipline.* New York: Doubleday.

Senge, P. (1996). Leading learning organizations: The bold, the powerful, and the invisible. In M. Goldsmith & F. Hesselbein (Eds.), *The leader of the future* (pp. 41–57). San Francisco: Jossey-Bass.

Senge, P. (1999). Leadership in living organizations. In F. Hesselback, M. Goldsmith, & I. Somerville (Eds.), *Leading beyond the walls* (pp. 73–90). San Francisco: Jossey-Bass.

Seo, M., & Creed, W. E. D. (2002). Institutional contradictions, praxis, and institutional change: A dialectical perspective. *Academy of Management Review, 27*(2), 222–247.

Shook, J. R. (2000a). *Dewey's empirical theory of knowledge and reality.* Nashville, TN: Vanderbilt University Press.

Shook, J. R. (2000b). Prospects for mathematizing Dewey's logical theory. In F. T. Burke, D. M. Hester, & R. B. Talisse (Eds.), *Dewey's logical theory: New studies and interpretations* (pp. 121–159). Nashville, TN: Vanderbilt University Press.

Shulman, L. (1993, November/December). Teaching as community property. *Change,* pp. 6–7.

Simpson, D. J. (2001). John Dewey's concept of the student. *Canadian Journal of Education, 2,* 183–200.

Simpson, T. L. (2002). Dare I oppose constructivist theory? *The Educational Forum, 66,* 347–354.

Smagorinsky, P. (2001). If meaning is constructed, what is it made form? Toward a cultural theory of reading. *Review of Educational Research, 71*(1), 133–169.

Smith, L., & Geoffrey, W. (1968). *The complexities of an urban classroom.* New York: Holt, Rinehart & Winston.

Sproul, L., & Kieslers, S. (1991). A two-level perspective on electronic mail organizers. *Journal of Organizational Computing, 1*(2), 125–134.

Stanic, G. M. A., & Russell, D. (2002). Continuity in *How We Think. Teachers College Record, 104*(6), 1229–1263.

Stark, J. S., & Lattuca, L. R. (1997). *Shaping academic curriculum: Academic plans in action.* Boston: Allyn & Bacon.

Stevens, R. (1912). *The question as a measure of efficiency in instruction.* New York: Teachers College.

Stevens, W. (1990). *The collected poems of Wallace Stevens.* New York: Vintage Books.

St. Julian, J. (1997). Explaining learning: The research trajectory of situated cognition and the implications of connectionism. In D. Kirshner & J. A. Whitson (Eds.), *Situated cognition: Social, semiotic, and psychological perspectives* (pp. 71–82). Mahwah, NJ: Lawrence Erlbaum Associates.

Strauss, A. (1984). Social worlds and their segmentation processes. *Studies in Symbolic Interactionism, 2,* 123–139.

Tabor, K. (2001). The mismatch between assumed prior knowledge and the learner's conceptions: A topology of learning impediments. *Educational Studies, 27*(2), 159–171.

Taconis, R., Ferguson-Hessler, M. G. M., & Broekkamp, H. (2001). Teaching science problem solving: An overview of experimental work. *Journal of Research in Science Teaching, 38*(4), 442–468.

Terhart, E. (2003). Constructivism and teaching: A new paradigm in general didactics? *Journal of Curriculum Studies, 35*(1), 25–44.

Thompson, J., Licklider, B., & Jungst, S. (2003). Learner-centered teaching: Postsecondary strategies that promote "Thinking like a professional." *Theory Into Practice, 42*(2), 133–141.

Tien, L. T., Roth, V., & Kampmeier, J. A. (2002). Implementation of a peer-led team learning instructional approach in an undergraduate organic chemistry course. *Journal of Research in Science Teaching, 39*(7), 606–632.

Tolstoy, L. (1869/1994). *War and peace* (C. Garnett, Trans.). New York: The Modern Library.

Tripp, S. D. (1996). Theories, traditions, and situated learning. In H. McLellan (Ed.), *Situated learning perspectives* (pp. 155–166). Englewood, NJ: Educational Technology Publications.

Trowler, R. R. (1998). *Academics responding to change: New higher education frameworks and academic cultures.* Buckingham: SRHE/Open University Press.

van Merrienboer, J. G., Seel, N. M., & Kirschner, P. A. (2002). Mental models as a new foundation for instructional design. *Instructional Design, 42*(2), 60–66.

van Oers, B. (1996). Learning mathematics as meaningful activity. In P. Nesher, L. Steffe, P. Cobb, G. Goldin, & B. Greer (Eds.), *Theories of mathematical learning* (pp. 91–113). Mahwah, NJ: Lawrence Erlbaum Associates.

von Glasersfeld, E. (1995). *Radical constructivism: A way of knowing and learning.* London: Falmer.

Vosniadou, S., Ionnides, C., Dimitrakopoulou, A., & Papademetriou, E. (2001). Designing learning environments to promote conceptual change in science. *Learning and Instruction, 11*, 381–419.

Vygotsky, L. S. (1978). *Mind in society: The development of higher psychological processes.* In M. Cole, V. John-Steiner, S. Scribner, & E. Souberman (Eds.). Cambridge, MA: Harvard University Press.

Vygotsky, L. S. (1981). The genesis of higher mental functions. In J. V. Wertsch (Ed.), *The concept of activity in Soviet psychology* (pp. 144–188). Armonk, NY: Sharpe.

Walkerdine, V. (1997). Redefining the subject in situated cognition theory. In D. Kirshner & J. A. Whitson (Eds.), *Situated cognition: Social, semiotic, and psychological perspectives* (pp. 57–70). Mahwah, NJ: Lawrence Erlbaum Associates.

Walkerdine, V. (1988). *The mastery of reason.* London: Routledge.

Wallace, M. (2003). Managing the unmanagable? Coping with complex educational change. *Educational Management and Administration, 31*(1), 9–29.

Watson, L. W., & Stage, F. K. (1999). *Enhancing student learning: Setting the campus context.* Washington, DC: American College Personnel Association.

Weick, K. E. (1976). Educational organizations as loosely coupled systems. *Administrative Science Quarterly, 21*, 1–19.

Weick, K. E. (1995). *Sensemaking in organizations.* Thousand Oaks, CA: Sage.

Wells, G. (2000). Dialogic inquiry in education. In C. D. Lee & P. Smagorinsky (Eds.), *Vygotskian perspectives on literacy research* (pp. 51–85). Cambridge, England: Cambridge University Press.

Wenger, E. (1998). *Communities of practice: Learning, meaning, and identity.* Cambridge, England: Cambridge University Press.

Wertsch, J. V. (2000). Vygotsky's two minds on the nature of meaning. In C. D. Lee & P. Smagorinsky (Eds.), *Vygotskian perspectives on literacy research* (pp. 19–30). Cambridge, England: Cambridge University Press.

Wertsch, J. V., & Toma, C. (1995). Discourse and learning in the classroom: A structural approach. In L. P. Steffe & J. Gale (Eds.), *Constructivism in education* (pp. 159–174). Hillsdale, NJ: Lawrence Erlbaum Associates.

Wiggins, G., & McTighe, J. (1997). *Understanding by design.* Alexandria, VA: ASCD.

Williams, W. C. (1955). From Asphonel, that greenery flower in *Journey to love.* New York: Random House.

Wingspread Group on Higher Education. (1993). *An American imperative: Higher expectations for higher education.* Racine, WI: Johnson Foundation.

Wong, D., Pugh, K., & the Dewey Ideas Group at Michigan State. (2001). Learning science: A Deweyan perspective. *Journal of Research in Science Teaching, 38*(3), 317–336.

Wood, D., Brunner, J., & Ross, G. (1976). The role of tutoring in problem-solving. *Journal of Child Psychology and Child Psychiatry, 17*, 89–100.

Young, M. F. (1993). Instructional design for situated cognition. *Educational Technology Research and Development, 41*(1), 43–58.

Young, R. E. (1990). Habermas' ontology of learning: Reconstructing Dewey. *Educational Theory, 40*(4), 471–482.

Young, R. E. (1992). *Critical theory and classroom talk* (The Language and Education Library Series 2, Editor D. Corson). Cleveland, OH: Multilingual Matters, Ltd.

Zeichner, K., & Liston, D. (1985). Varieties of discourse in supervisory conferences. *Teaching and Teacher Education, 1*, 155–174.

APPENDIX A
Scoring Guide for Application of Theory for Cases in HOD 1200

1—Inadequate—F to D+

- Fails to identify specific organizational characteristics, events, and behaviors that fit into the domain of the frame.
- Fails to cite theories from the reading.

2—Minimal—C– to B–

- Identifies and generally describes organizational characteristics, events, and behaviors that represent reasonable examples of the frames.
- Recognizes situations that can be explained by a theory that fits within the frame.

3—Adequate—B/B+

- Describes the characteristics of the organization that represent examples of the frame **and** *provides details* (e.g., in the structural frame: includes job descriptions of key people, an organizational chart, the mission of the organization and its primary objectives, and is specific about things that do not exist, such as "the organization has no technostructure").
- Connects specific examples of organizational characteristics, events, and behaviors that fit into the domain of the frame with theories that connect to the examples.
- Provides page references from the reading.
- Uses systems-level explanations for behavior rather than the psychological characteristics of individuals.
- Uses the theories to identify possible problems and identify solutions.

4—Good—A–

- Connects specific examples of organizational characteristics, events, and behaviors that fit into the domain of the frame with theories that connect to the examples **and** explains **why** these theories enrich your understanding of the organization, and systematically connects the theory to the case.

- Demonstrates an ability to explain the same organizational characteristics from more than one perspective (using different frames, different theories for the same incident).

- Uses the theories to identify possible problems and identify solutions, says what you would suggest changing **and** why you think the theory points to your solutions.

5—Excellent—A/A+

- Uses the theories to identify possible problems and identify solutions, suggests what should be changed, why the theory points to this suggestion **and** connects the analysis to the big ideas and deep principles in the course.

- Critiques the theories' strengths and weaknesses for explaining the success or failure of the organization. Explains **why** the theories and the deep principles behind them offer a **good explanation** for what happened in the organization **or why** a theory fails to increase your understanding of the organization. (For example, Theory X would predict that employees would be unproductive in this situation, when in fact the employees were satisfied and highly motivated. Then go on to say why you think the theory did not fit this situation.)

- Challenges theories you disagree with and explains why you reject the theory.

- Systematically links theory, research, and personal experience to your personal developing model of organizations.

APPENDIX B
HOD 1200—Understanding Organizations

BIG IDEAS AND DEEP PRINCIPLES

The following points list the big ideas and deep principles for the HOD 1200 course. They are a set of organizational perspectives and theories that you should understand by the end of the course. You should be able to compare these theories to your own mental models and everyday theories about how organizations work. These points are not truths about organizations. They represent my own theories in areas where there are competing theories about organizations and organizational change. Although all of these points can be supported with theory and research on human and organizational development, there are other valid theories of organizations. Each of these points represents theoretical biases that shape the way the course is taught and the professor's way of seeing organizational life. They are the personal theories of organizations (my own mental models) that shape my responses to critical incidents in organizations.

1. Organizations and events within organizations can be profitably viewed from a number of different perspectives (e.g., leadership and the four frames we will use in this course: Structural, Human Resource, Political, & Symbolic).

2. The course has a bias toward the theory that, under most conditions, open communication leads to more positive results than closed communication. In the course, we will use a model developed by Argyris (Model II

communication) that will serve as an organizational version of the sensitive responsive dialogue we studied in previous courses.

3. The course is biased toward the position that people are generally motivated toward personal growth and self-actualization. This means that we assume people's need for competence, usefulness, belongingness, and intimacy can be satisfied within an organization in ways that benefit both the person and the organization. This is an assumption of the Human Resources frame. Further, we assume that organizations can be organized to both further the goal of increasing its members' ability to become effective reflective-generative practitioners and achieve a level of excellence as measured by its ability to achieve its organizational goals. However, we recognize that effective organizational skills include the ability to know when this faith in people is misplaced and when circumstances call for the use of power and politics.

4. The course is biased toward the position that narratives (e.g., stories, scripts, and myths) are powerful organizers of meaning for human beings—both on the organizational level and on the level of personal identity. An important quality of leadership is the ability to communicate an organizational vision that is meaningful to members of the organization on various levels of sophistication.

5. The course presents an "ecological systems" perspective of organizations:

(a) Systems are characterized by interdependent, transactional relationships between subsystems and a nested relationship among subsystems, systems, and supersystems. An "ecological systems" perspective includes seeing an organization and its external (e.g., competitors, government regulations, global economy) and internal contexts as a dynamic ecology.

(b) A systems perspective assumes that each component has a tendency to structure itself as a semipermeable system with structural coupling to other systems on the same and other levels. Students should understand how this creates resistance to change and points to the importance of attending to boundary issues and communication across boundaries.

(c) A system is best understood by examining its dynamic processes rather than its individual parts, including inputs and outputs from and to other systems and between subsystems.

(d) An organization is not one system, but a number of overlapping, interacting systems with different and often antagonistic objectives.

(e) Individuals are seen as partially embedded in systems. The way we see and think about an organization that we belong to is heavily influenced by the patterns of communication and accepted practices within that organization, but we are capable of breaking away from that perspective.

6. Organizations, like all systems, are powerful shapers of individual behavior. Even the behaviors of disturbed and disturbing people are best thought of as indicators of problems in the system rather than causes (until all else fails, avoid the fundamental attribution error).

7. There are many structural forces on many levels that shape organizational behavior, including our communicative behavior. Cultural artifacts such as language and organizations mediate our transactions with the world and create structures that shape our behaviors and patterns of communication.

(a) Some of the structures that shape our behaviors in organizations come from our genetic "primate" heritage (e.g., dominance structure, attention structure, and leadership structure).

(b) Some of the structures that shape our behaviors in organizations come from the mental models and social practices (especially patterns of communication) we have acquired through our participation in our family systems and other social institutions such as schools.

(c) Some of the structures that shape our behaviors in organizations come from our cultural heritage (especially language and hierarchical systems of inclusion and exclusion).

(d) Some of the structures that shape our behaviors in organizations come from the structure of the organization, especially the barriers (both physical and social) and affordances (opportunities for growth) offered by the organization.

8. My personal theory of organizational change assumes that organizations are structured as systems and subsystems that have a tendency to organize themselves as separate units, suboptimize, and resist change. I believe involving people in decision making and maximizing communication across boundaries (structural, cultural, communities of practice, and coalitions of self-interest and shared values) facilitates change. It is more effective to reduce resistance to change than to increase pressure for change. Because members are only partially embedded in organizational and cultural life, they are capable of recognizing contradictions and organizing change efforts.

Structural Frame

1. An organization needs to be structured to facilitate achieving the goals and objectives that have been established to meet the needs of its stakeholders.

   (a) Rationality is *one* of the essential perspectives for achieving organizational success.
   (b) Structures must be designed to fit organizational circumstances.
   (c) Tasks must be organized to allow members to handle complexity and achieve the efficiency required for success.
   (d) It is important to organize organizational structure and processes to focus on enhancing the organization's key transactions.
   (e) Systems must be structured to deal effectively and efficiently with their supersystems and subsystems.
   (f) A rational analysis of key processes within an organizational system and at the key points of input and output at structural couplings is important for organizational survival.

Human Resource Frame

1. Identity and the structure of the self are important constructs that affect the way people shape and are shaped by their participation in organizational life.
2. People and organizations are mutually dependent: Organizations need employees who are motivated, creative, and talented, and people need careers, income, and opportunities for meaningful work.
3. Organizations will not be successful over the long term if they exploit people and fail to meet their needs (people need belongingness, usefulness, and competence).
4. A poor fit between organizations and people damages both and a good fit benefits both.

Political Frame

1. Scarce resources create conflict.
2. Fundamental value differences and enduring differences between subgroups and individuals generate the use of power to achieve goals.
3. The power relationships that exist in the dominant culture tend to be reproduced in the structure of the organization and the patterns of communication within the organization.

Symbolic Frame

1. It is often more important what an event means than what "really happened."
2. The same event has different meanings for different people.
3. High levels of ambiguity and uncertainty undercut rational analysis, problem solving, and decision making. In this situation, symbols, stories, myths, and metaphors resolve confusion.

Author Index

Subject Index